The Antique Gift Shop

vol.4

Lee Eun

D0886127

About the Creator

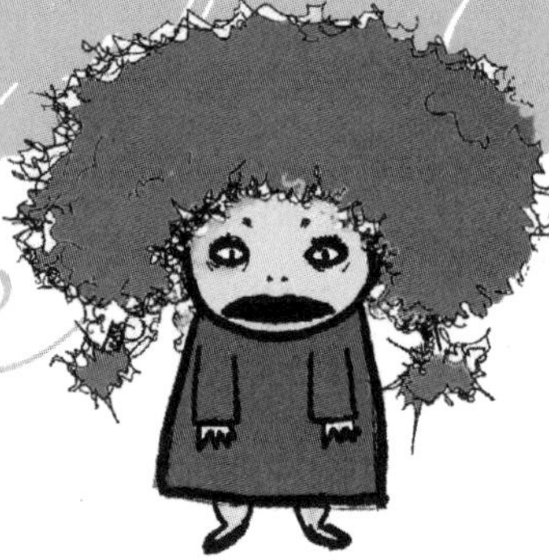

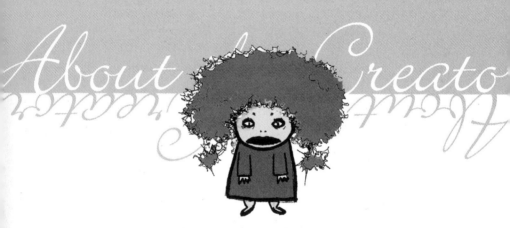

Eun Lee

Birthday
February 29th, Aries.

Blood type
AB

Her debut comic
<Beholder> from magazine <NINE>

Her other works
<Monica>, <The Eye of the Dragon>, <The Rebellion of the 36° Cs>.

Words from the Creator

The Antique Gift Shop is going to be made into a movie. I always wanted to write a movie scenario and this book has made my dreams come true. It's happening faster than I thought but I'm so happy and thankful. Please pray that the Antique Gift Shop will be a good movie!

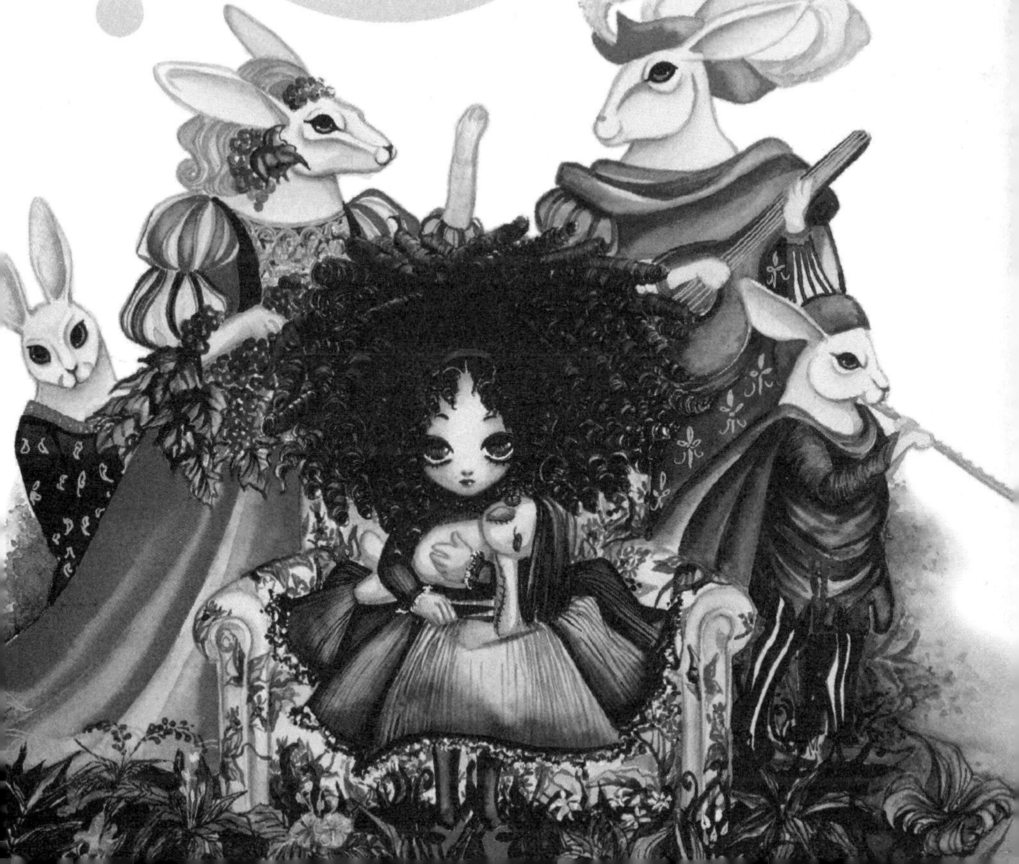

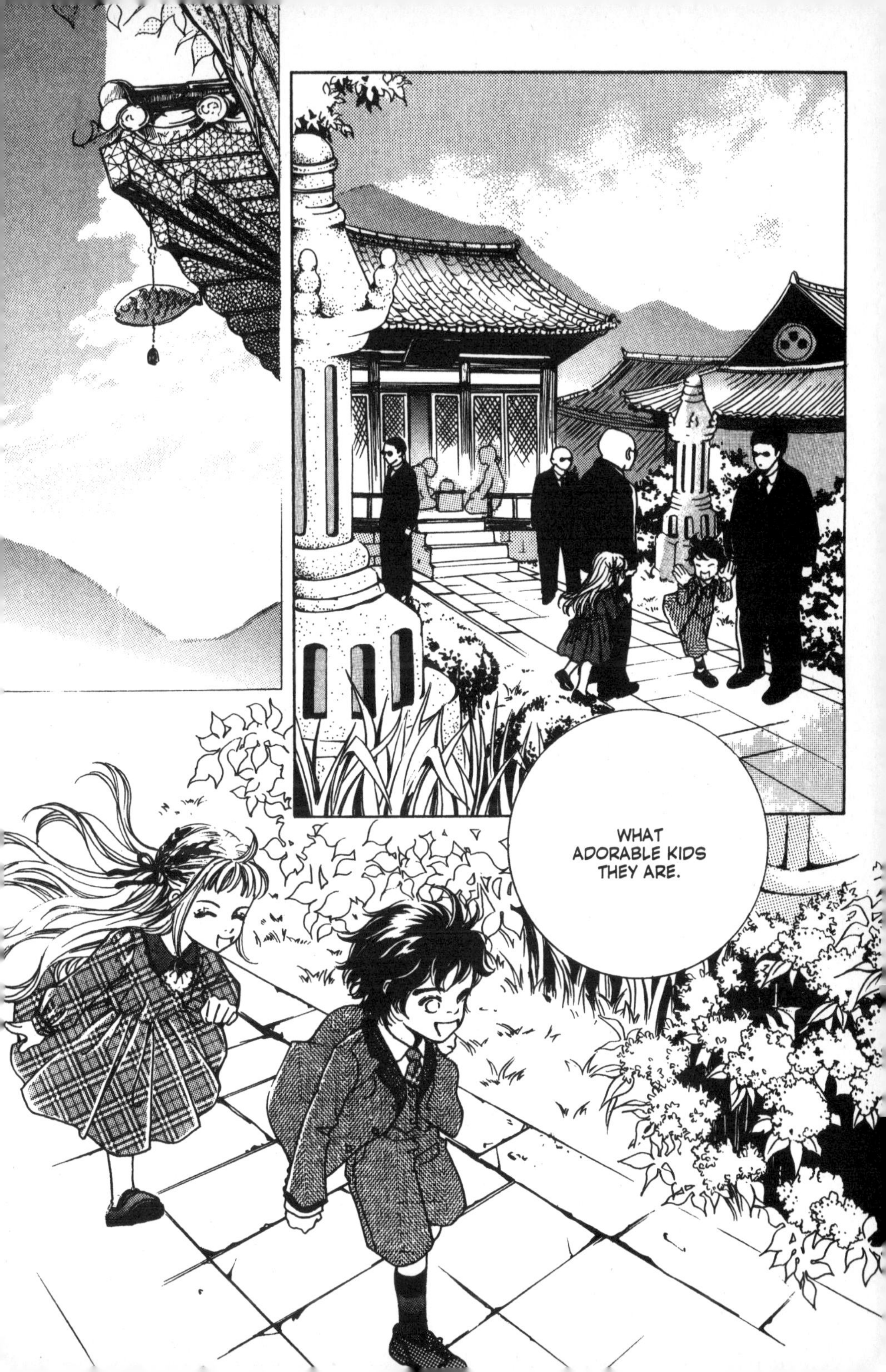
WHAT ADORABLE KIDS THEY ARE.

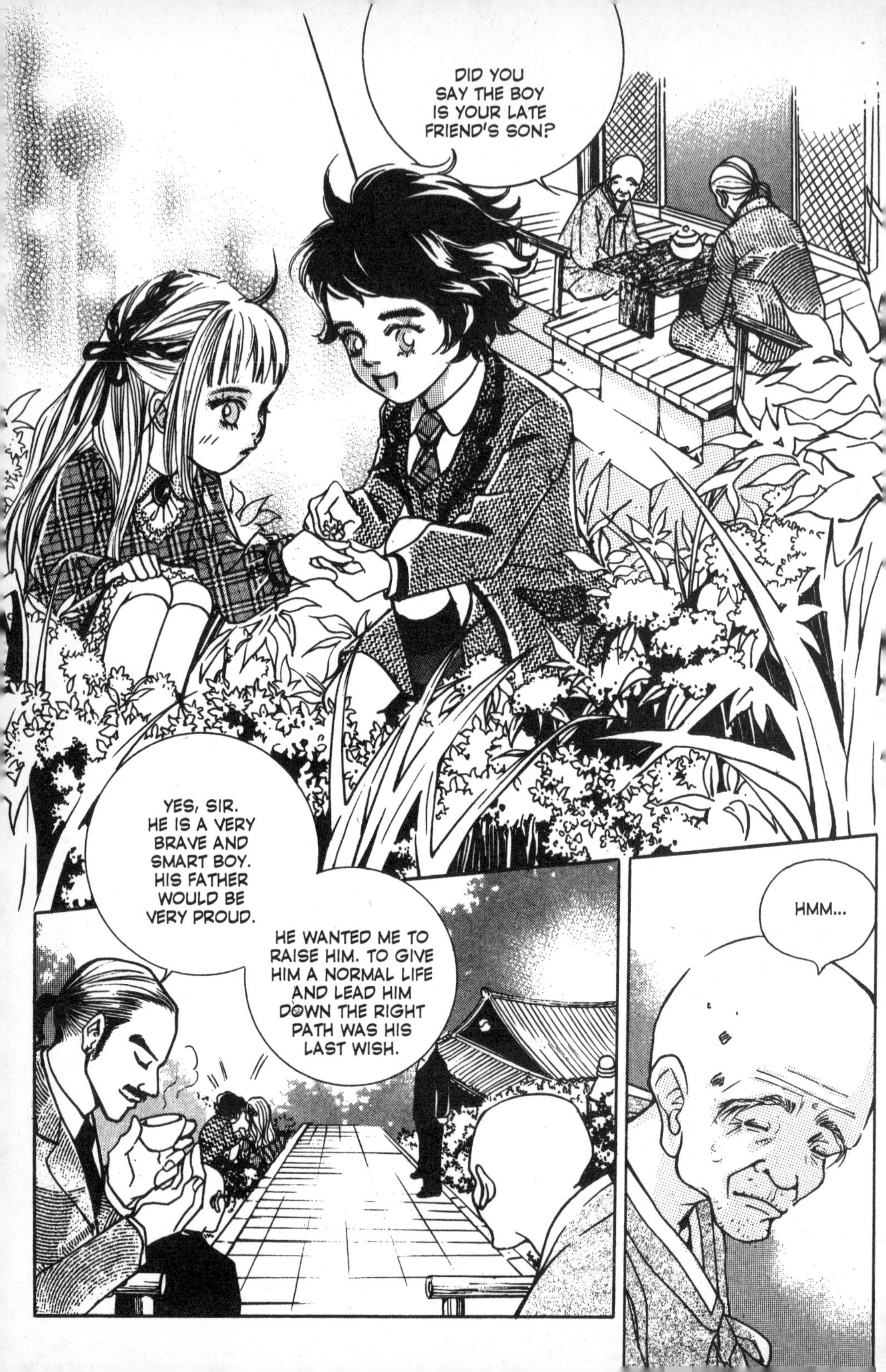
DID YOU SAY THE BOY IS YOUR LATE FRIEND'S SON?
YES, SIR. HE IS A VERY BRAVE AND SMART BOY. HIS FATHER WOULD BE VERY PROUD.
HE WANTED ME TO RAISE HIM. TO GIVE HIM A NORMAL LIFE AND LEAD HIM DOWN THE RIGHT PATH WAS HIS LAST WISH.
HMM...

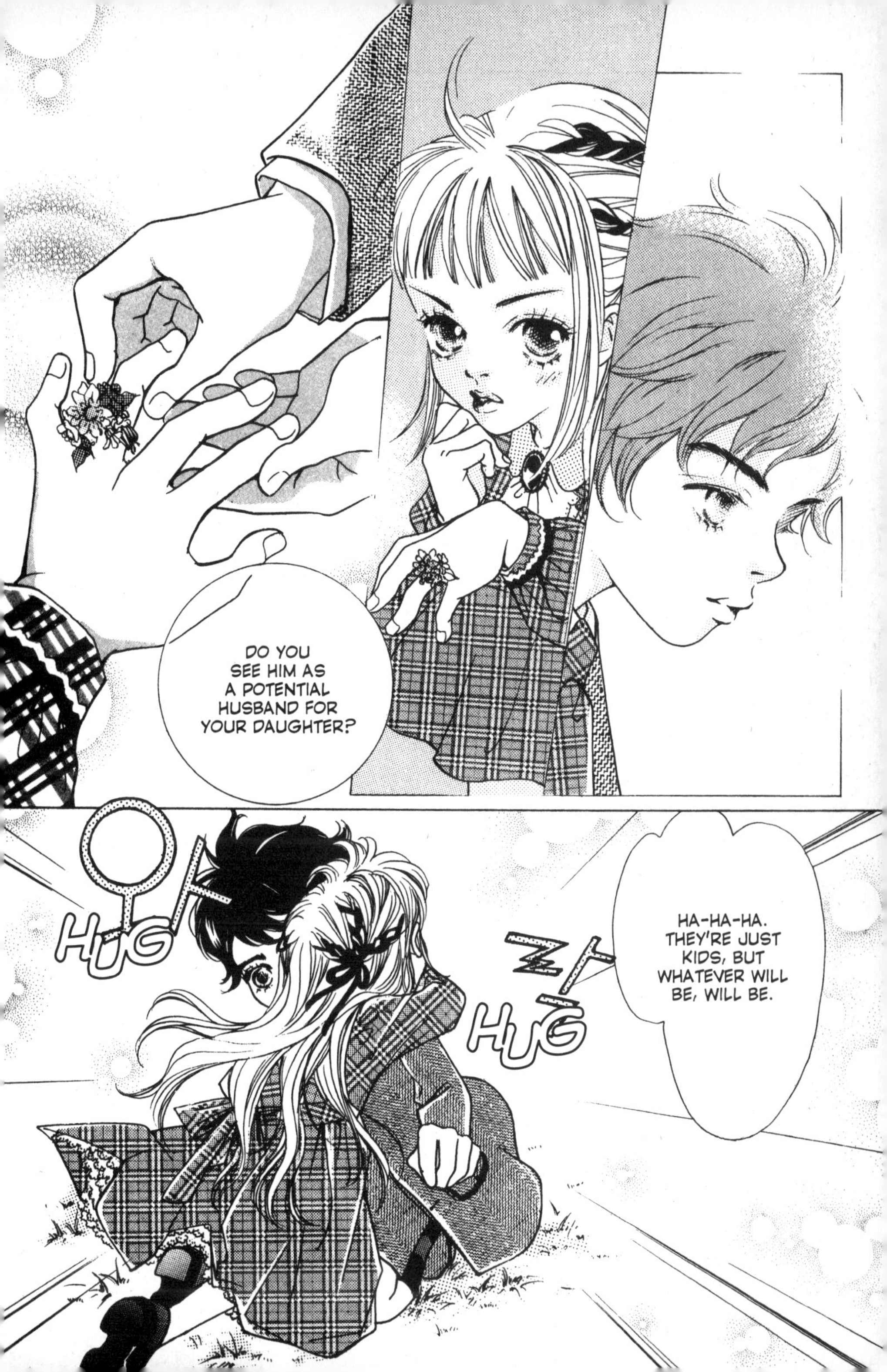
DO YOU SEE HIM AS A POTENTIAL HUSBAND FOR YOUR DAUGHTER?
HUG
HUG
HA-HA-HA. THEY'RE JUST KIDS, BUT WHATEVER WILL BE, WILL BE.

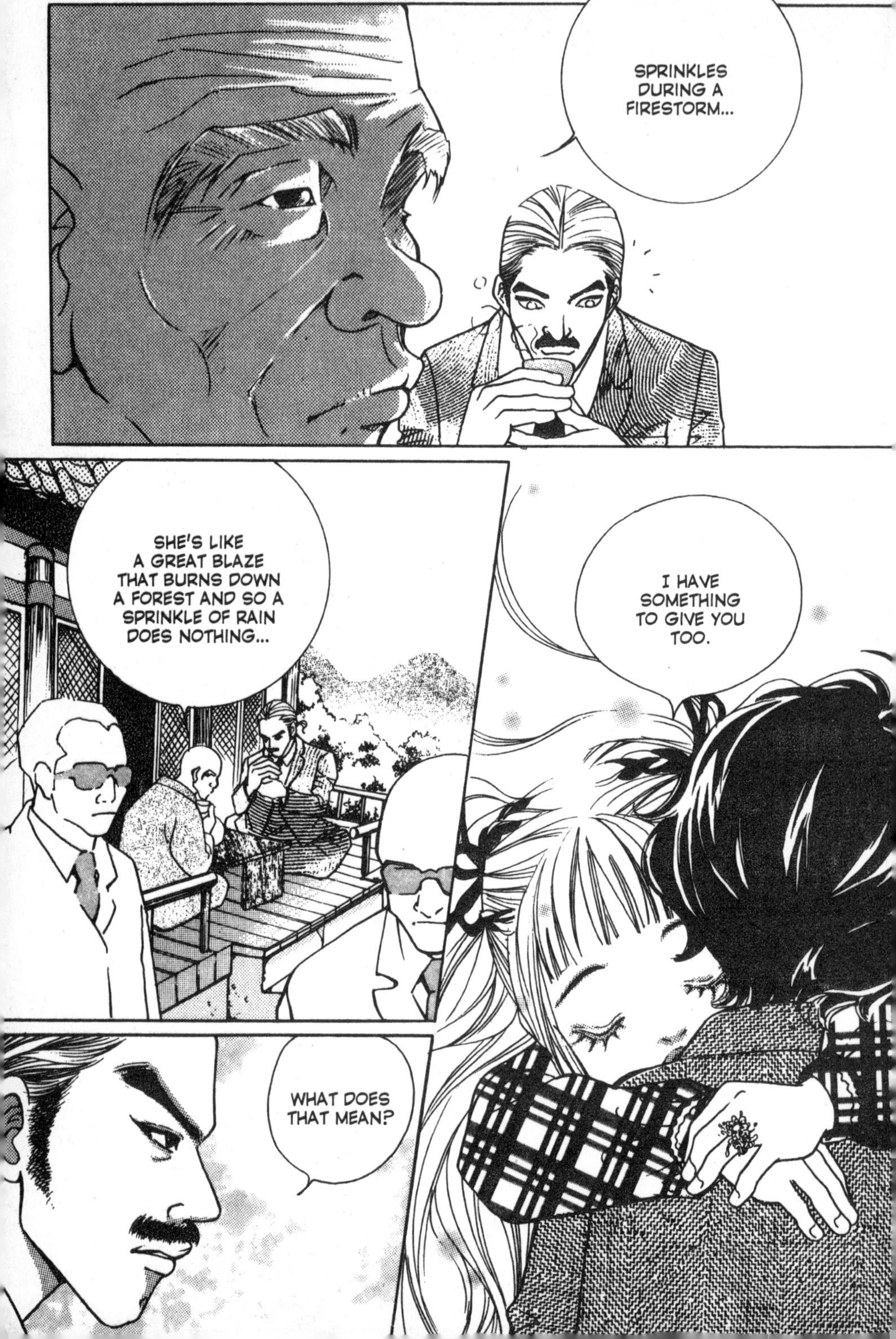
SPRINKLES DURING A FIRESTORM...
SHE'S LIKE A GREAT BLAZE THAT BURNS DOWN A FOREST AND SO A SPRINKLE OF RAIN DOES NOTHING...
WHAT DOES THAT MEAN?
I HAVE SOMETHING TO GIVE YOU TOO.

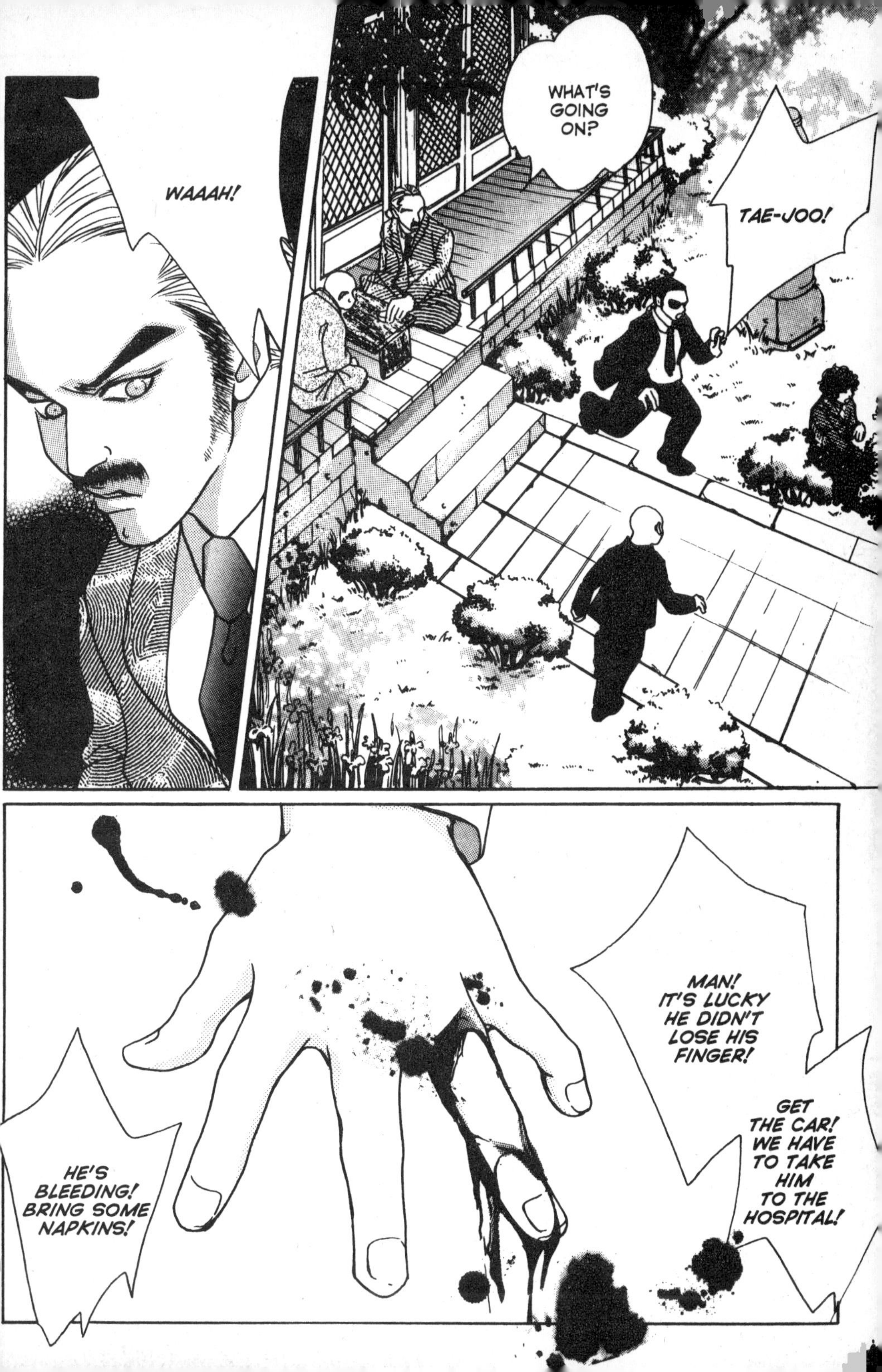
WAAAH!
WHAT'S GOING ON?
TAE-JOO!
HE'S BLEEDING! BRING SOME NAPKINS!
MAN! IT'S LUCKY HE DIDN'T LOSE HIS FINGER!
GET THE CAR! WE HAVE TO TAKE HIM TO THE HOSPITAL!

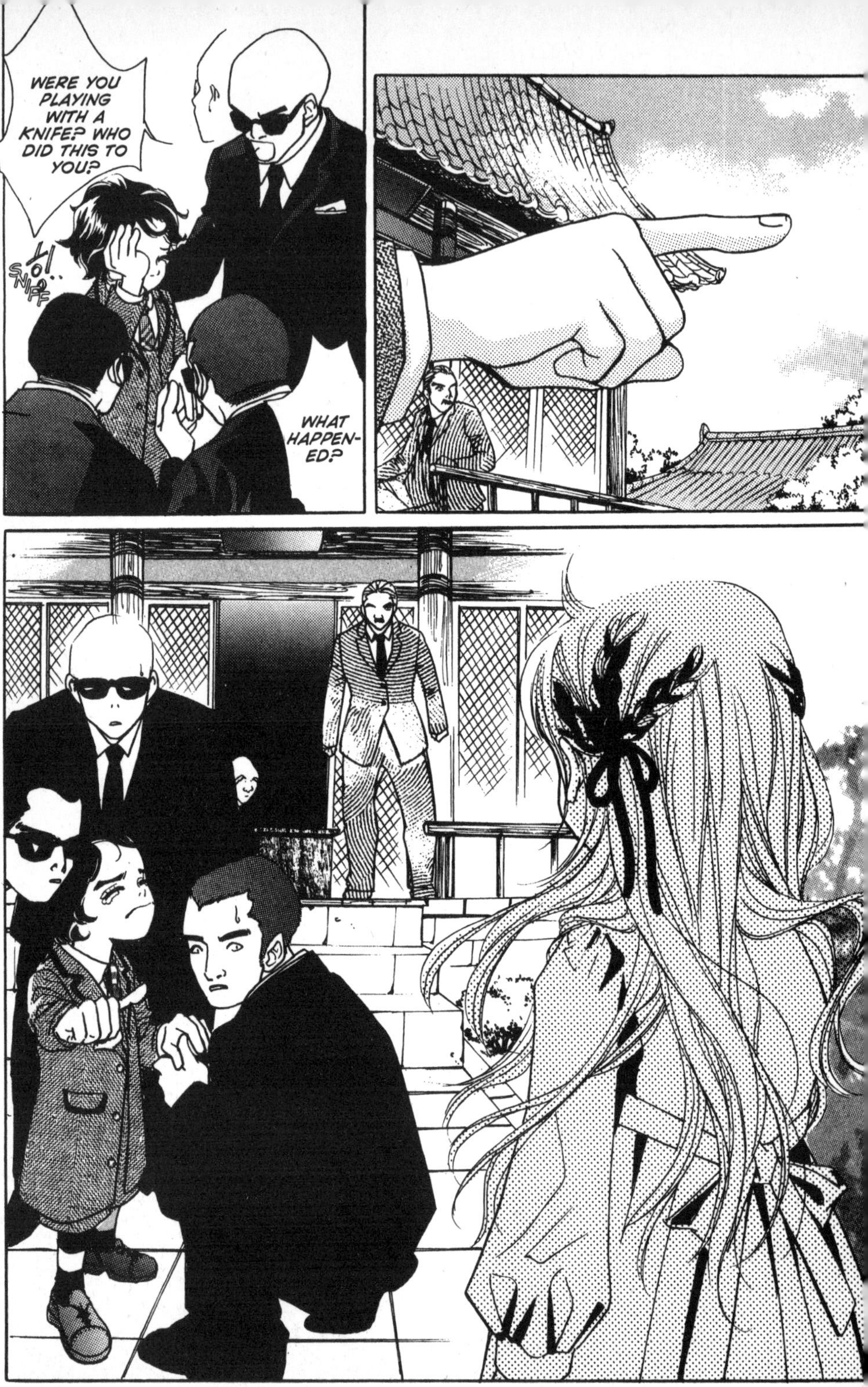
WERE YOU PLAYING WITH A KNIFE? WHO DID THIS TO YOU?
SNIFF
WHAT HAPPEN-ED?

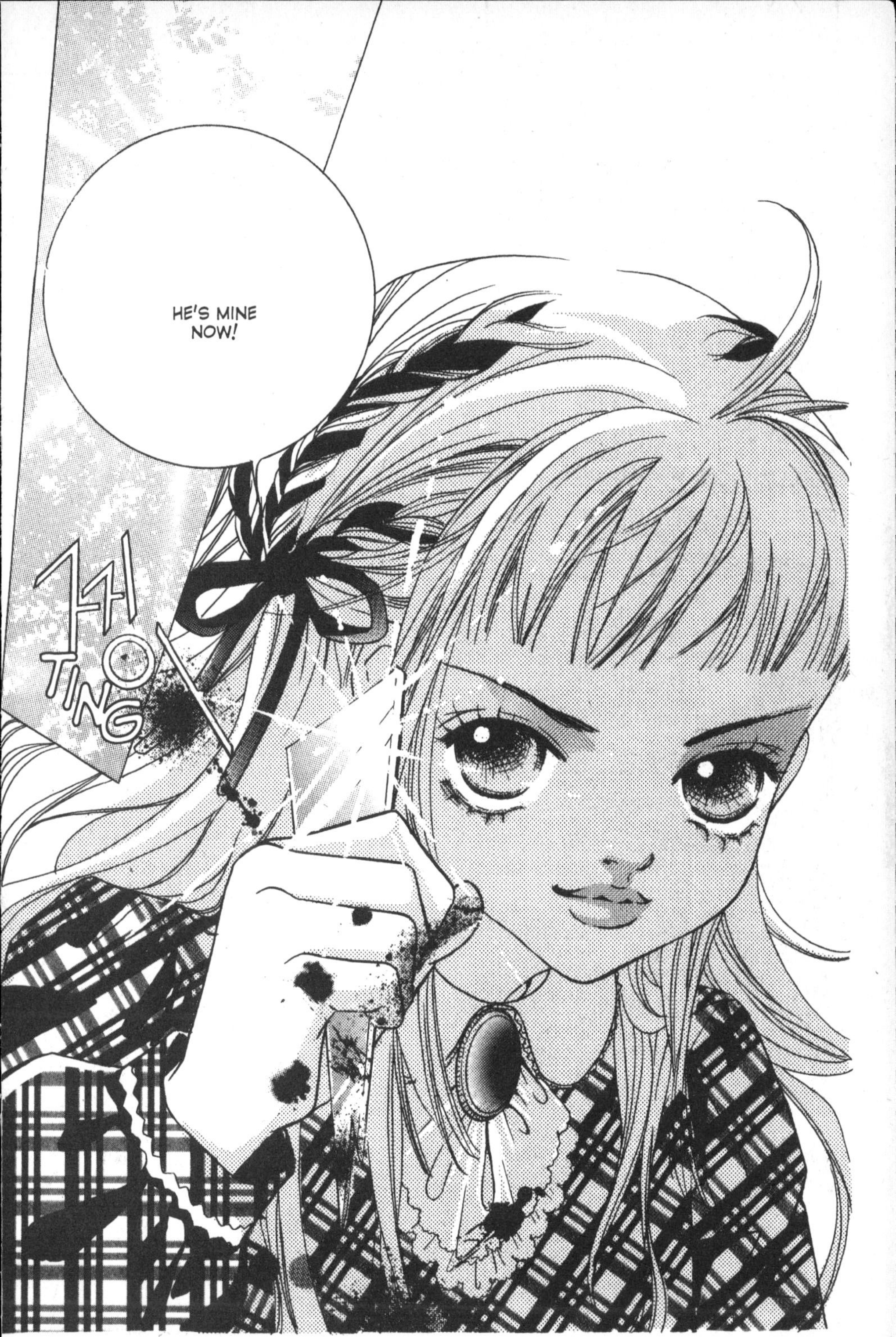
HE'S MINE NOW!
TING

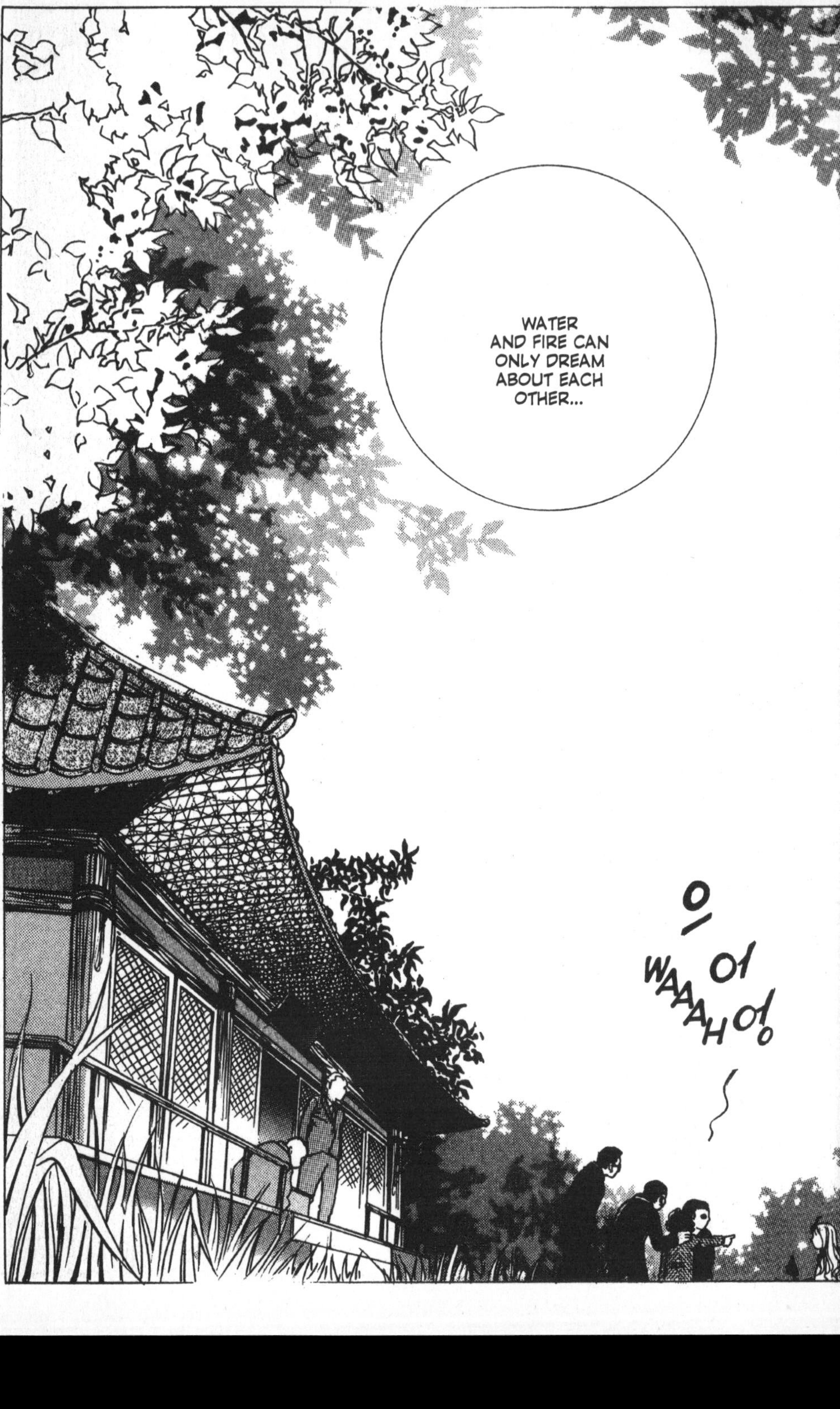
WATER AND FIRE CAN ONLY DREAM ABOUT EACH OTHER...
WAAAAH

Chapter 6
Four Posts Of Fate

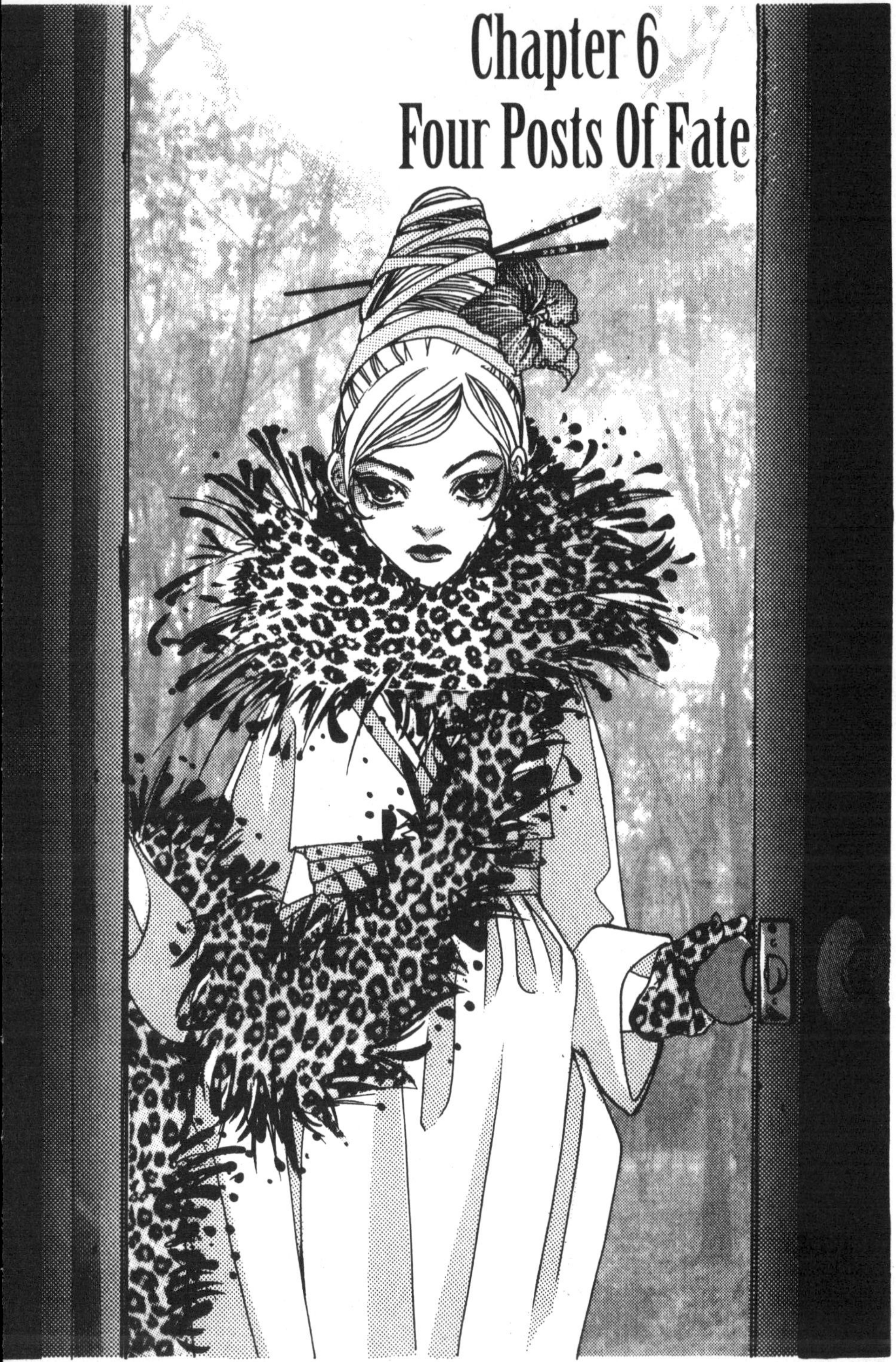

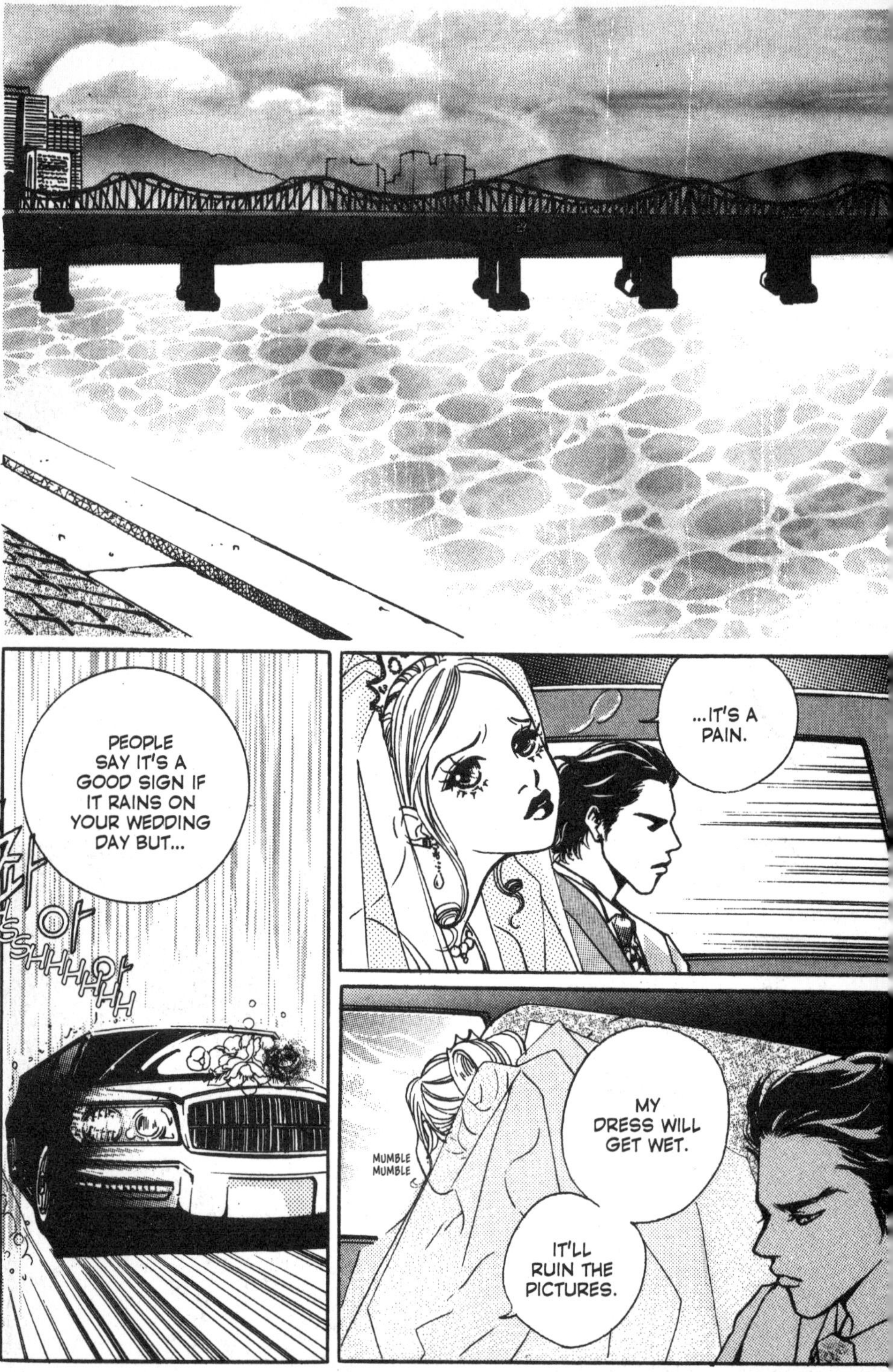
PEOPLE SAY IT'S A GOOD SIGN IF IT RAINS ON YOUR WEDDING DAY BUT...
쏴아아
HSSHHHHHH
...IT'S A PAIN.
MUMBLE MUMBLE
MY DRESS WILL GET WET.
IT'LL RUIN THE PICTURES.

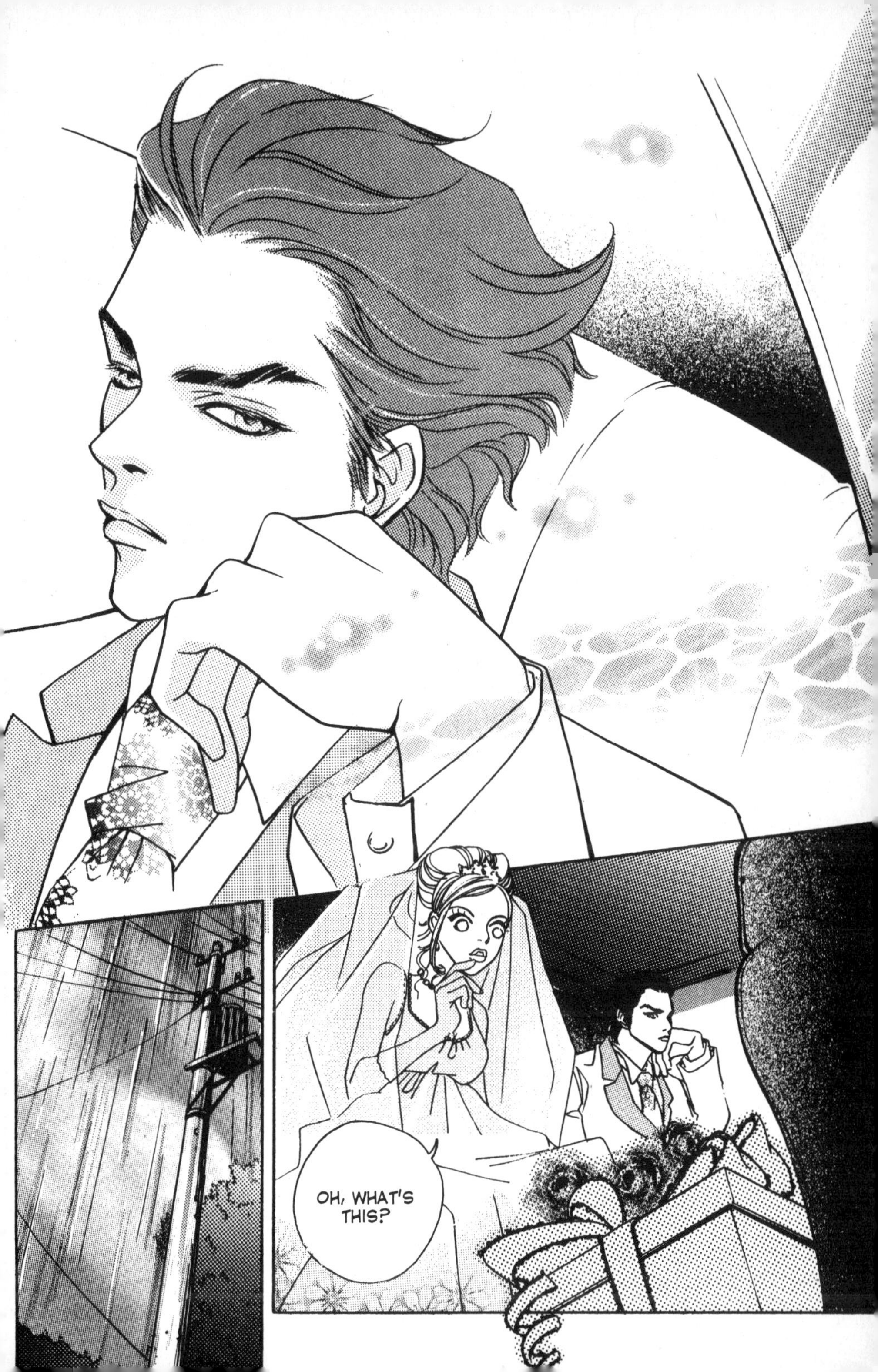
OH, WHAT'S THIS?

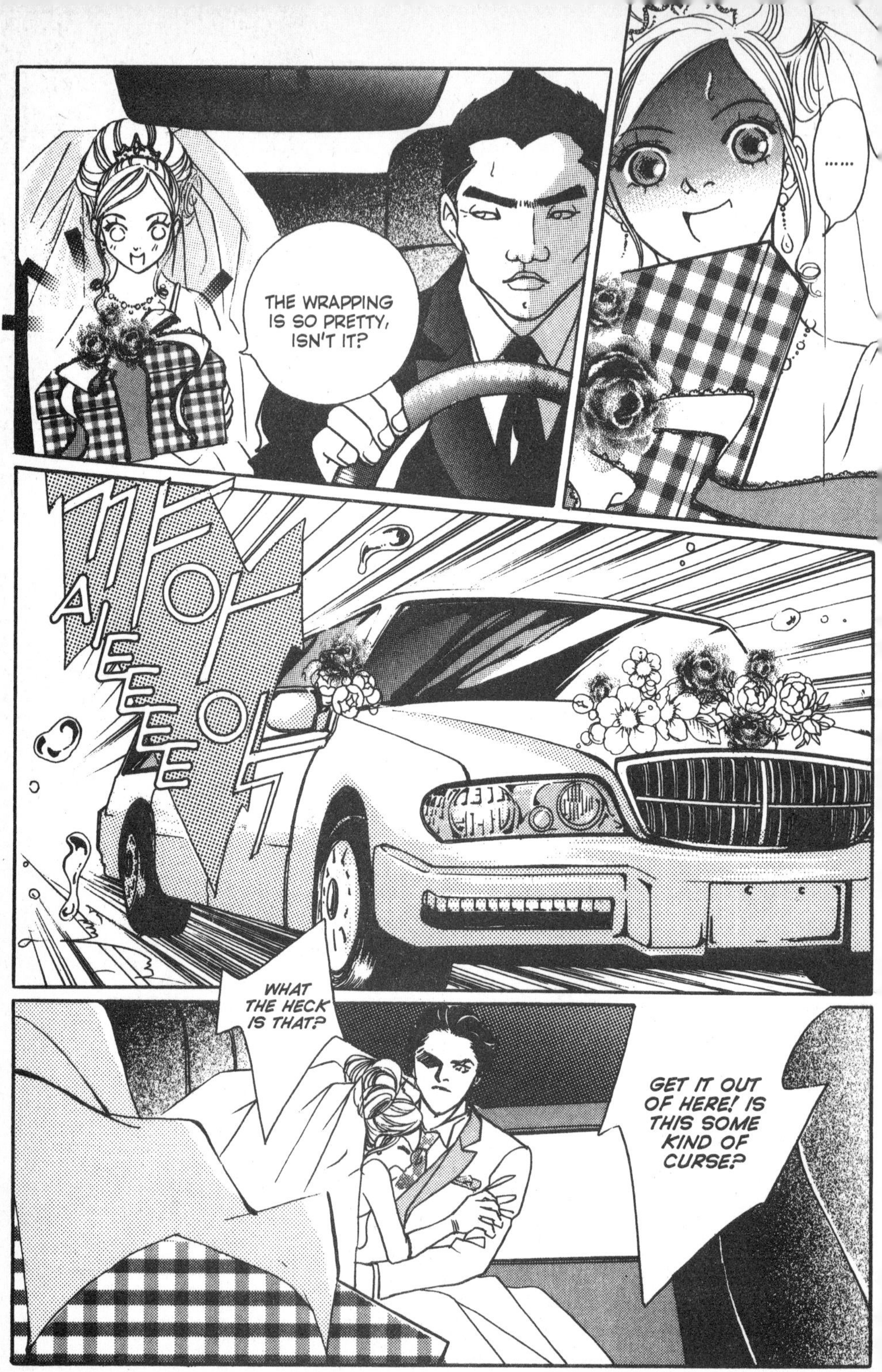
THE WRAPPING IS SO PRETTY, ISN'T IT?
......
AIEEEEE
WHAT THE HECK IS THAT?
GET IT OUT OF HERE! IS THIS SOME KIND OF CURSE?

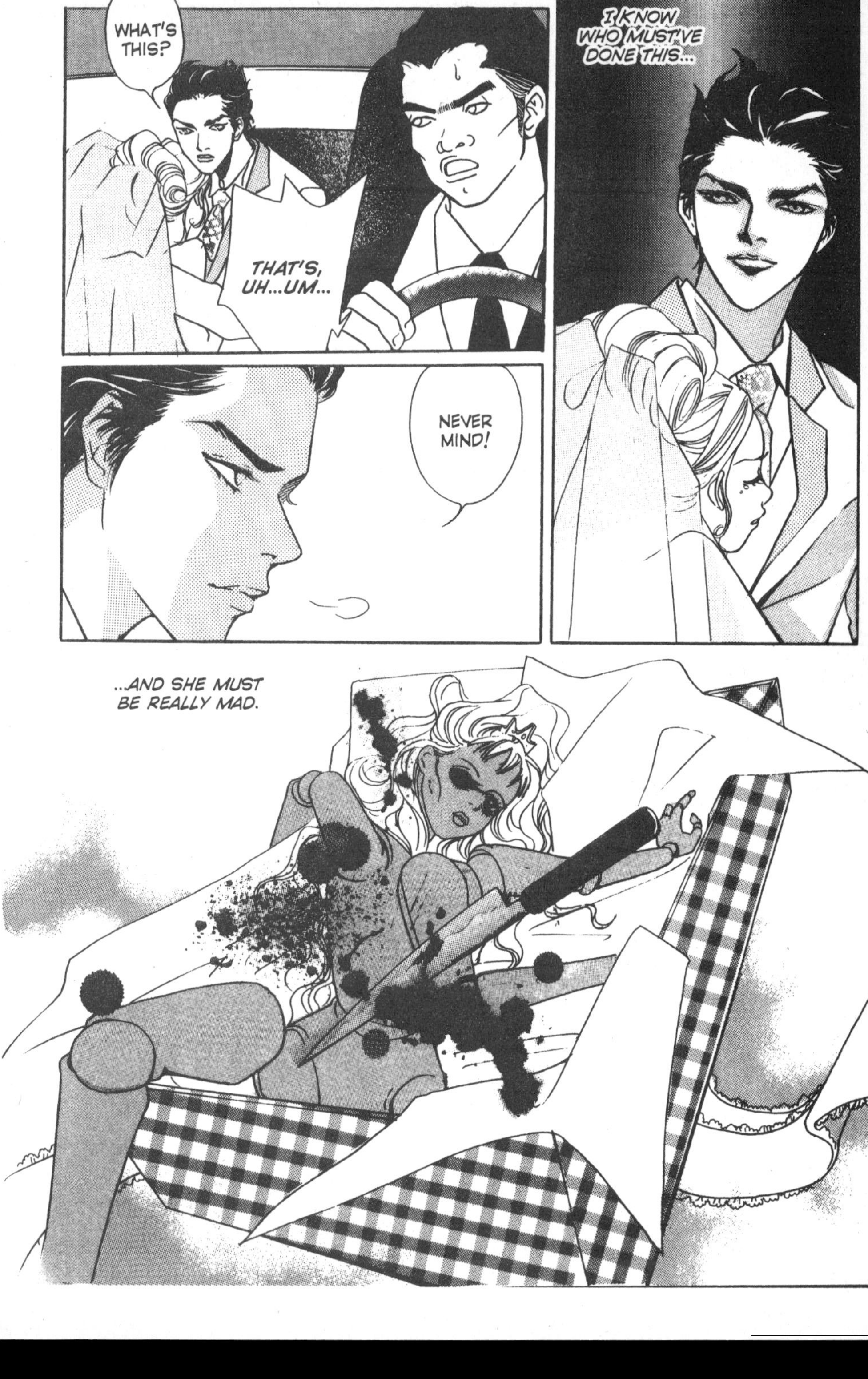
WHAT'S THIS?
THAT'S, UH...UM...
NEVER MIND!
I KNOW WHO MUST'VE DONE THIS...
...AND SHE MUST BE REALLY MAD.

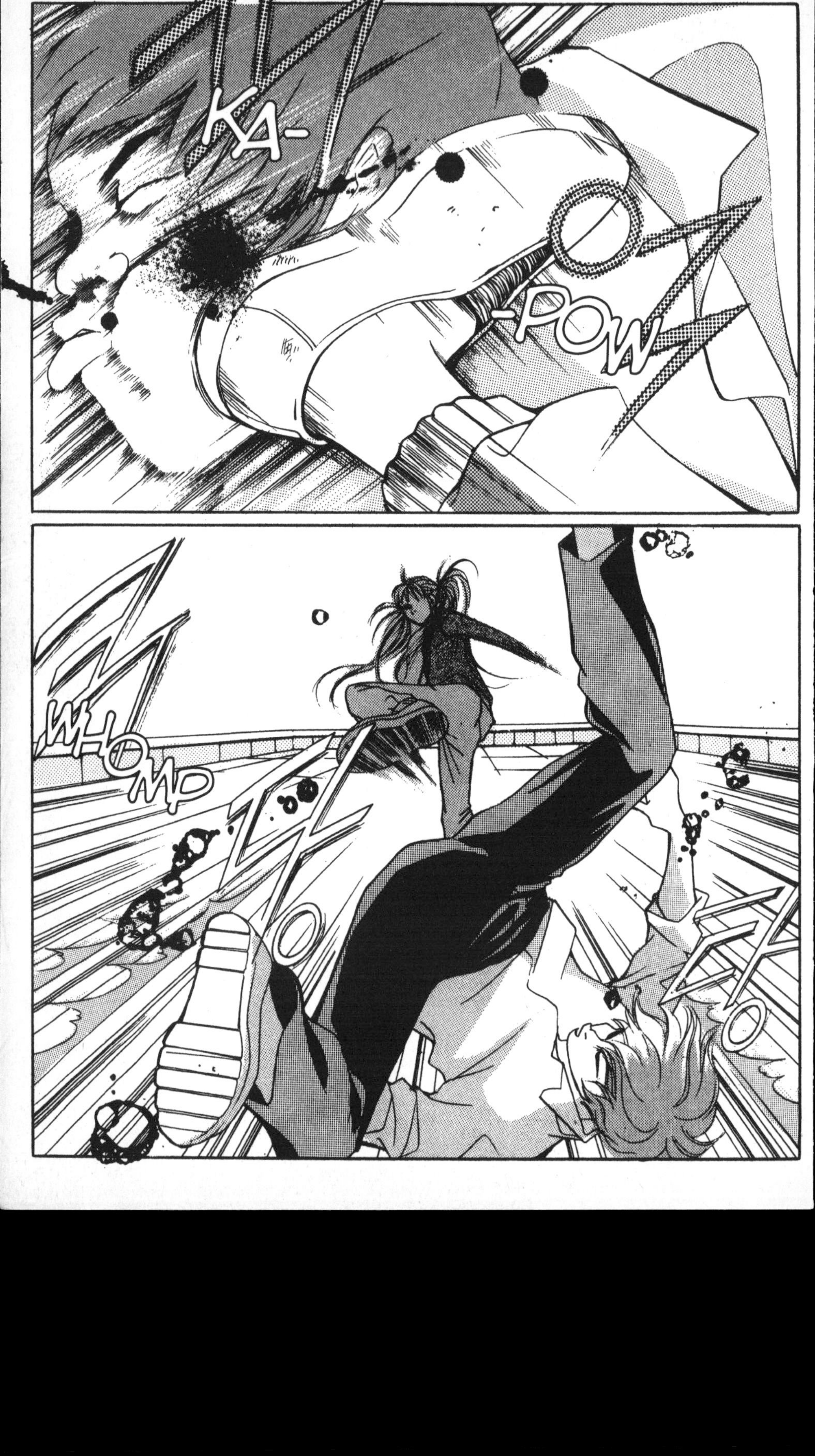
KA-
-POW
WHOMP

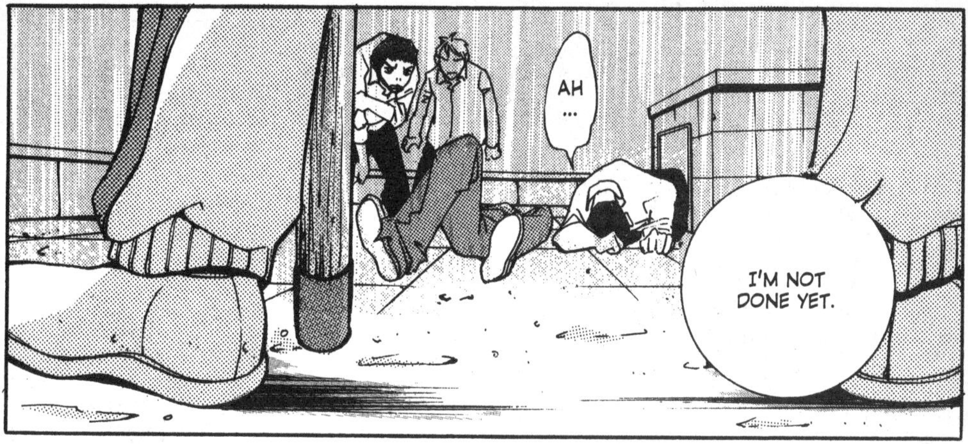
AH ...
I'M NOT DONE YET.
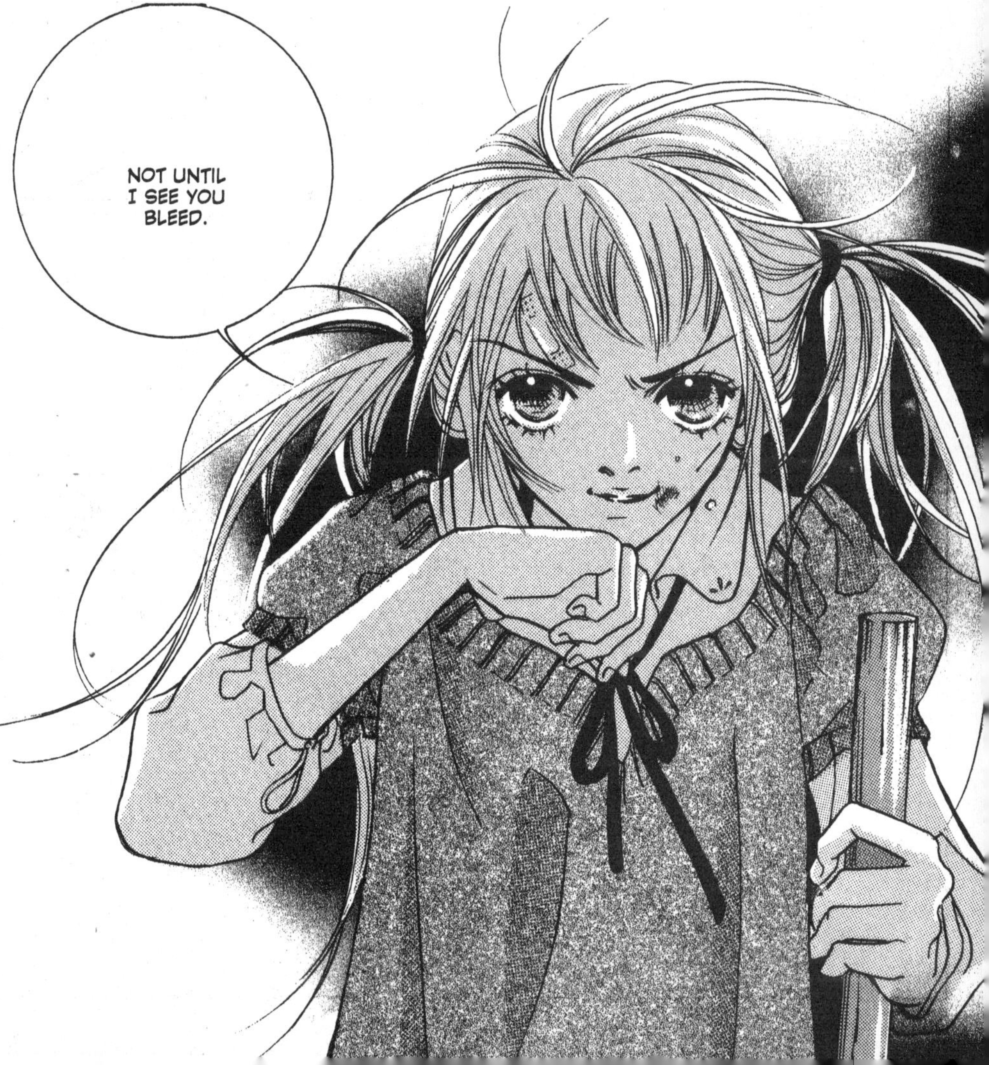
NOT UNTIL I SEE YOU BLEED.

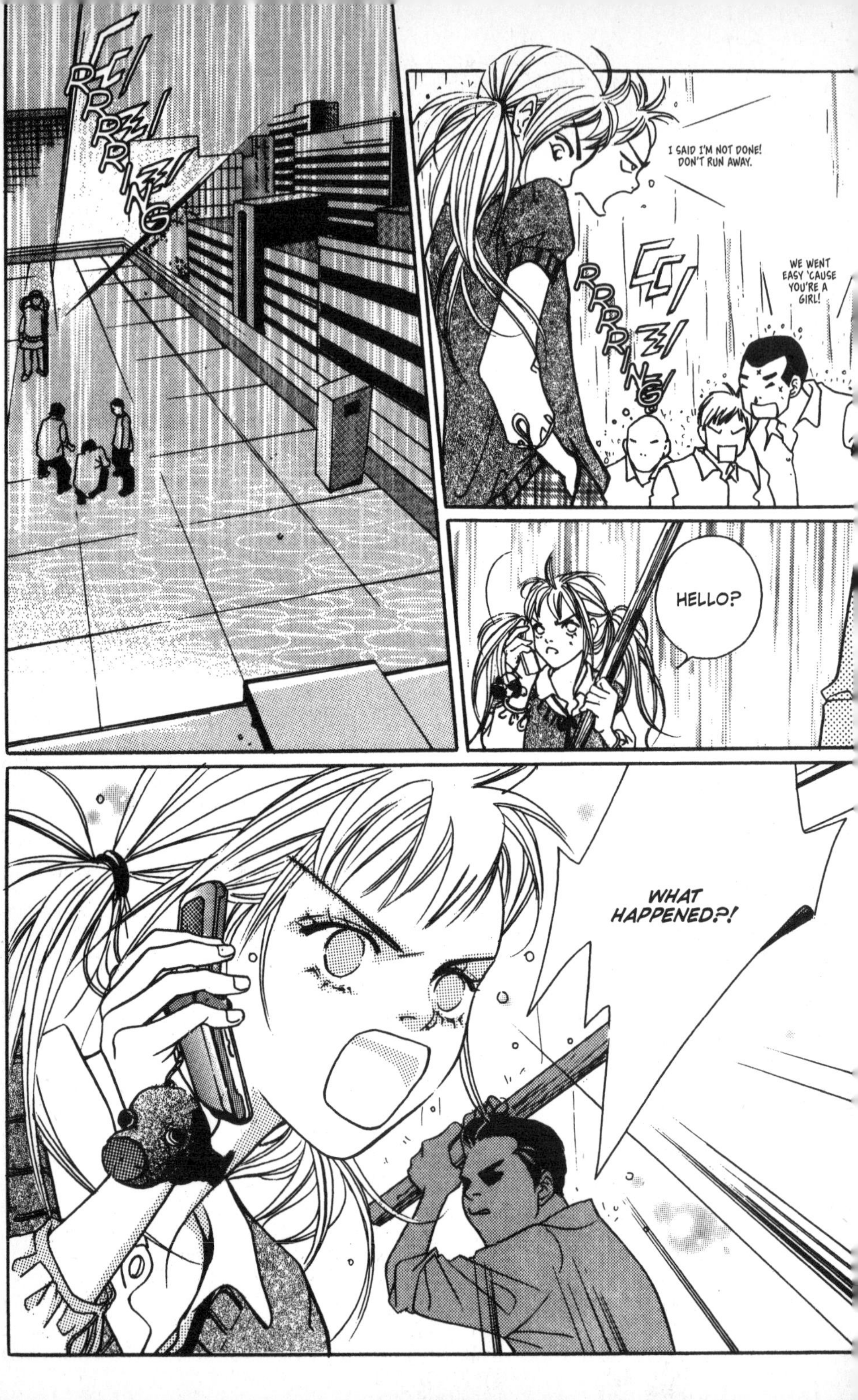
RRRRING
I SAID I'M NOT DONE! DON'T RUN AWAY.
RRRRING
WE WENT EASY 'CAUSE YOU'RE A GIRL!
HELLO?
WHAT HAPPENED?!

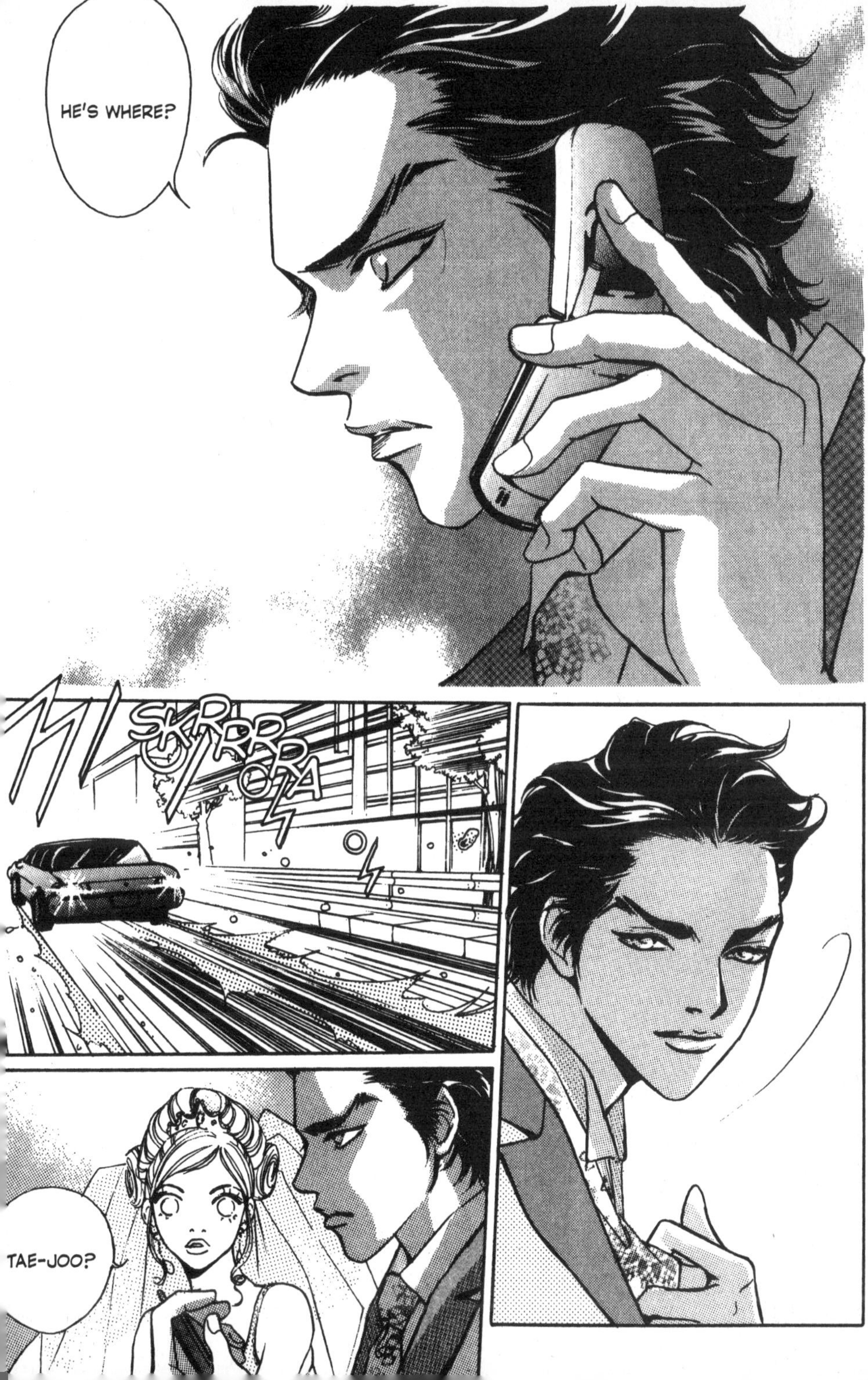
HE'S WHERE?
SKRRRRA
TAE-JOO?

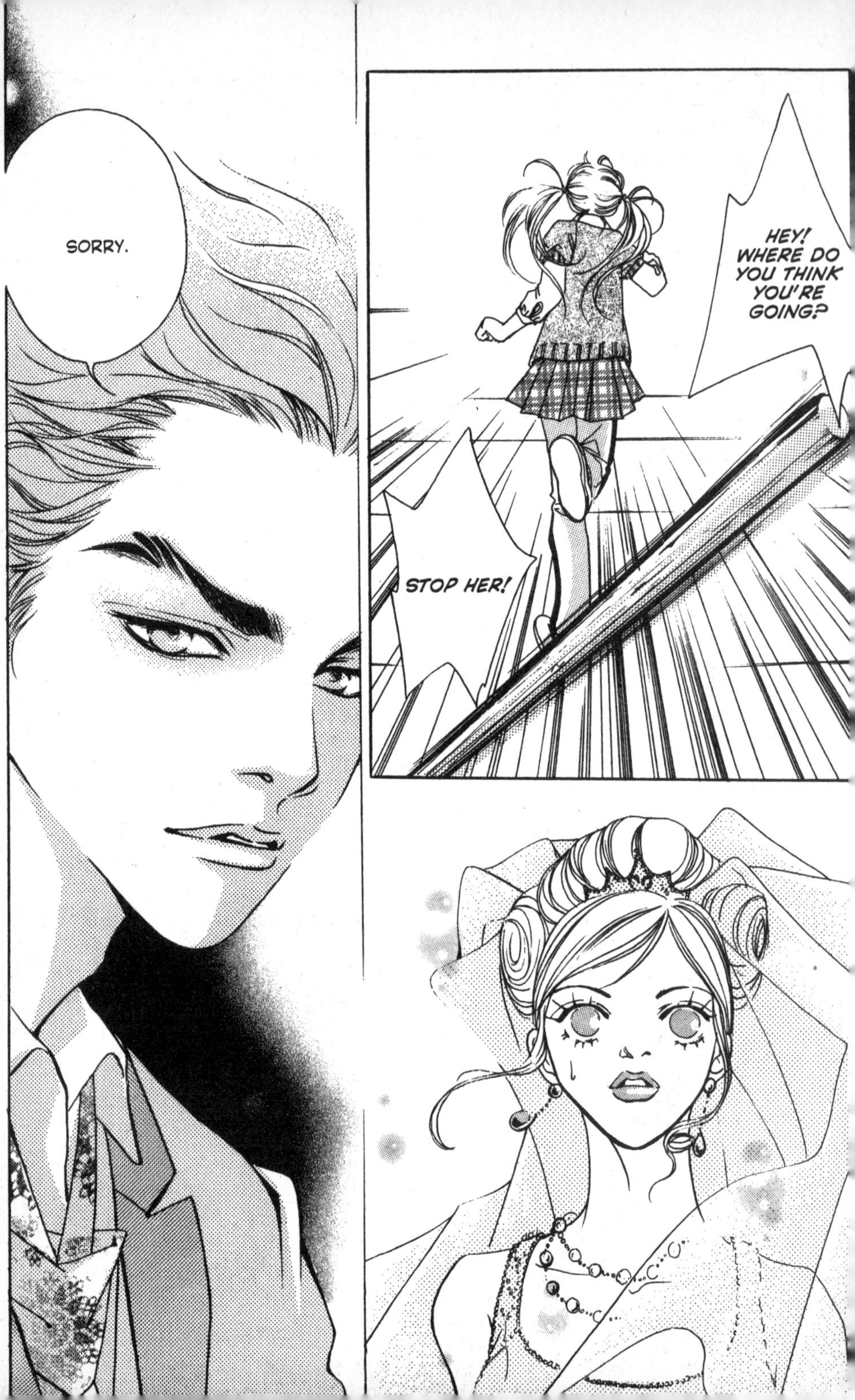
SORRY.
HEY! WHERE DO YOU THINK YOU'RE GOING?
STOP HER!

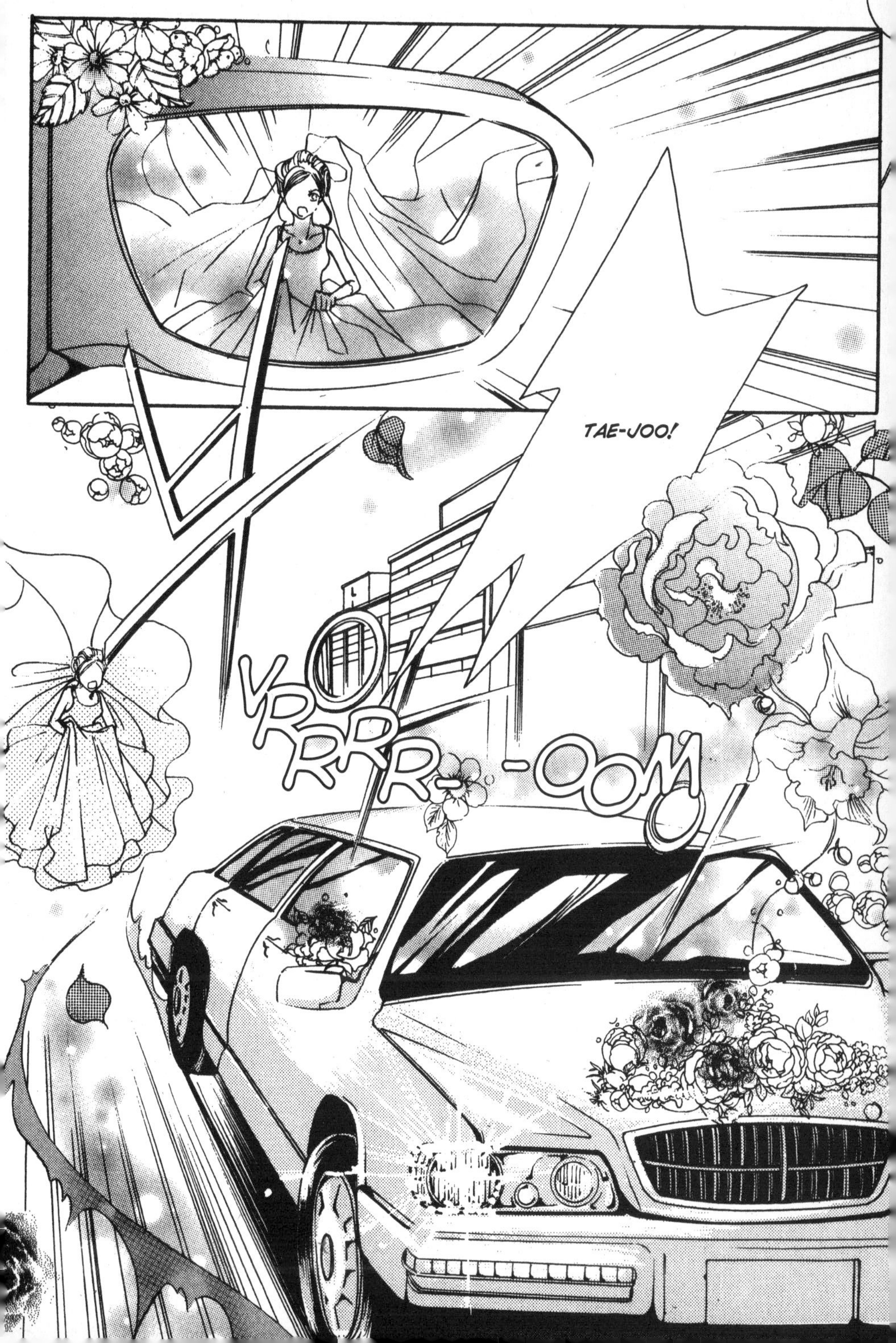
TAE-JOO!
VROOO
RRRR- -OOM

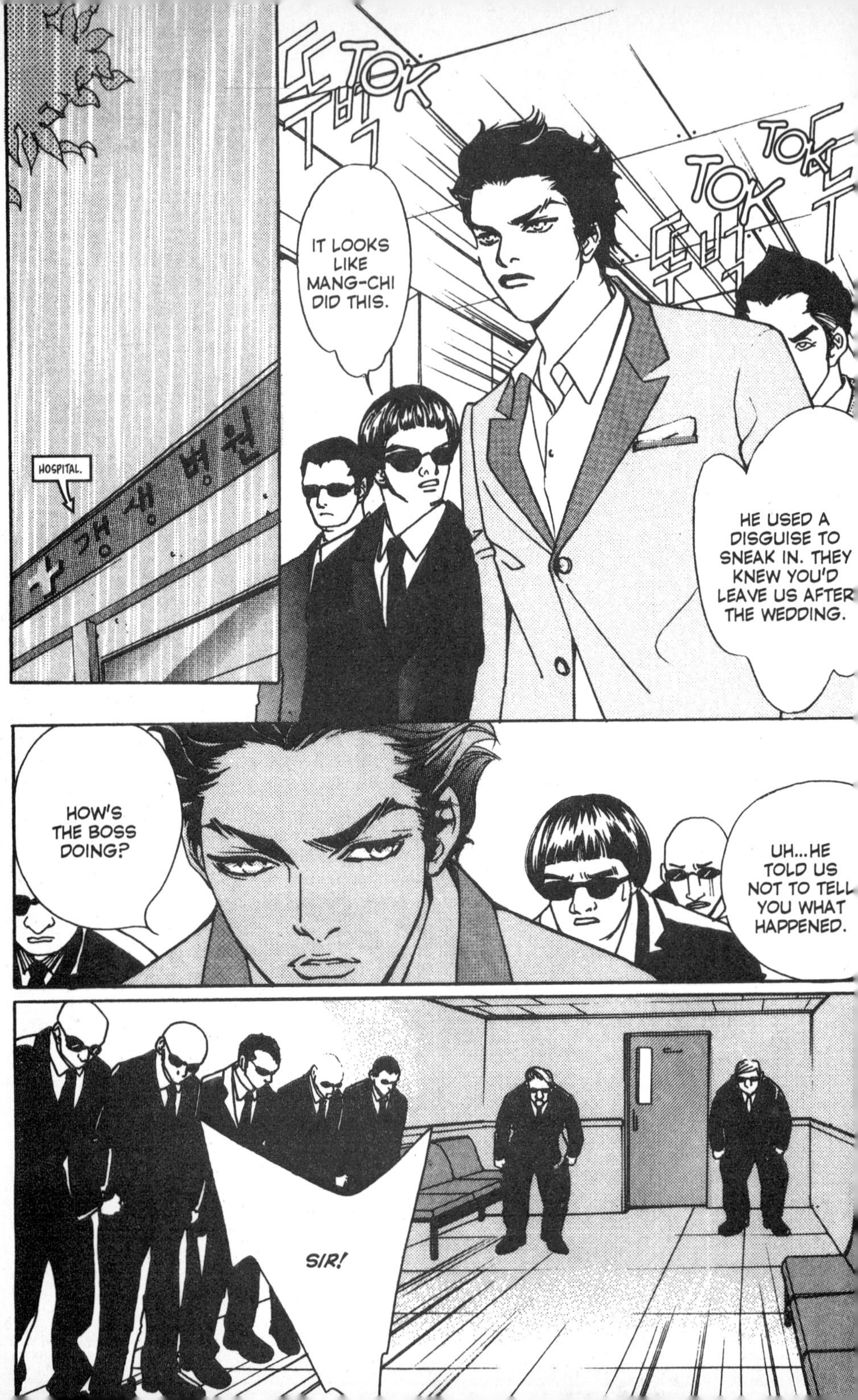
HOSPITAL.
TOK
IT LOOKS LIKE MANG-CHI DID THIS.
TOK TOK
HE USED A DISGUISE TO SNEAK IN. THEY KNEW YOU'D LEAVE US AFTER THE WEDDING.
HOW'S THE BOSS DOING?
UH...HE TOLD US NOT TO TELL YOU WHAT HAPPENED.
SIR!

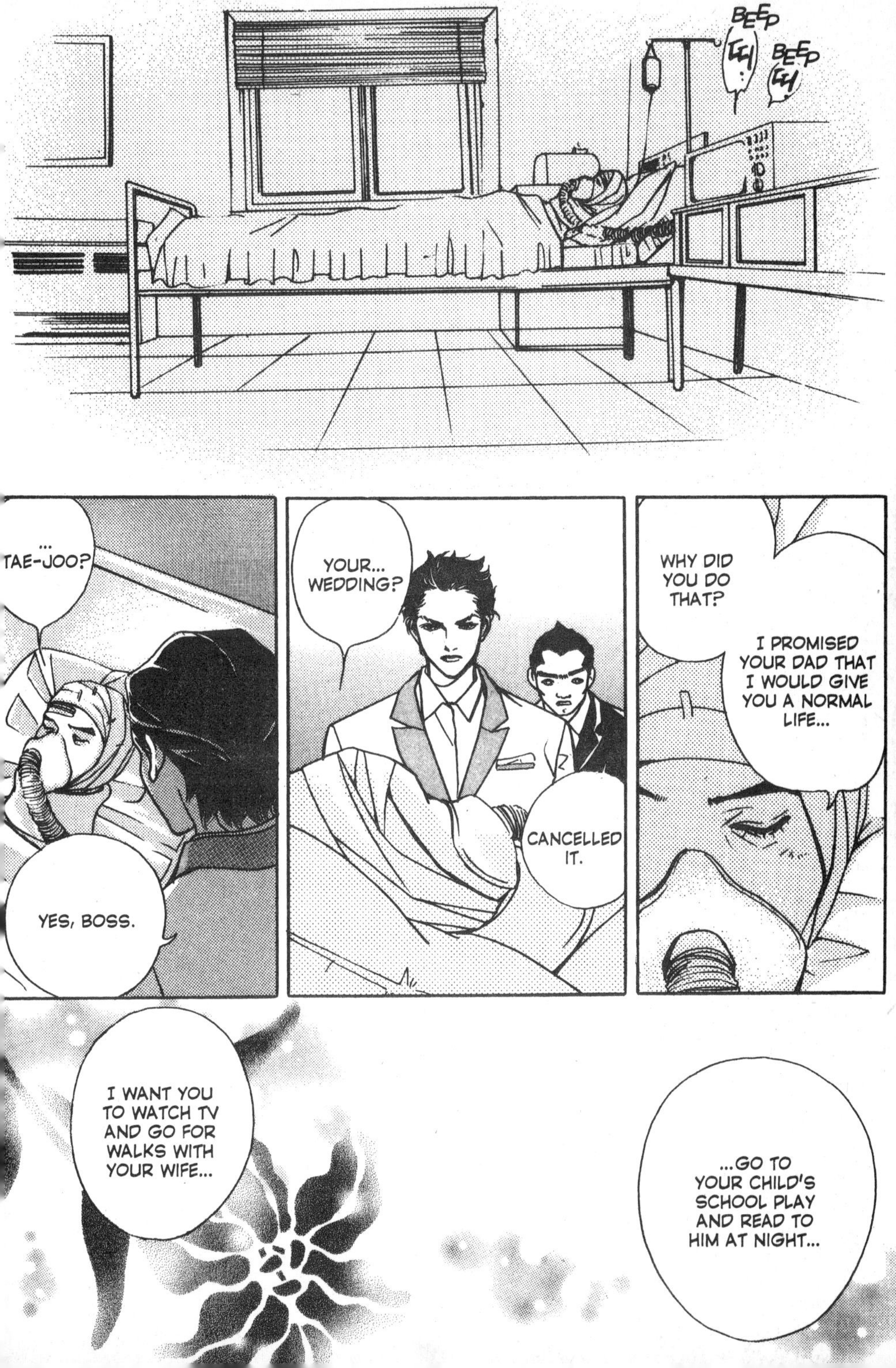
BEEP
BEEP
... TAE-JOO?
YES, BOSS.
YOUR... WEDDING?
CANCELLED IT.
WHY DID YOU DO THAT?
I PROMISED YOUR DAD THAT I WOULD GIVE YOU A NORMAL LIFE...
I WANT YOU TO WATCH TV AND GO FOR WALKS WITH YOUR WIFE...
...GO TO YOUR CHILD'S SCHOOL PLAY AND READ TO HIM AT NIGHT...

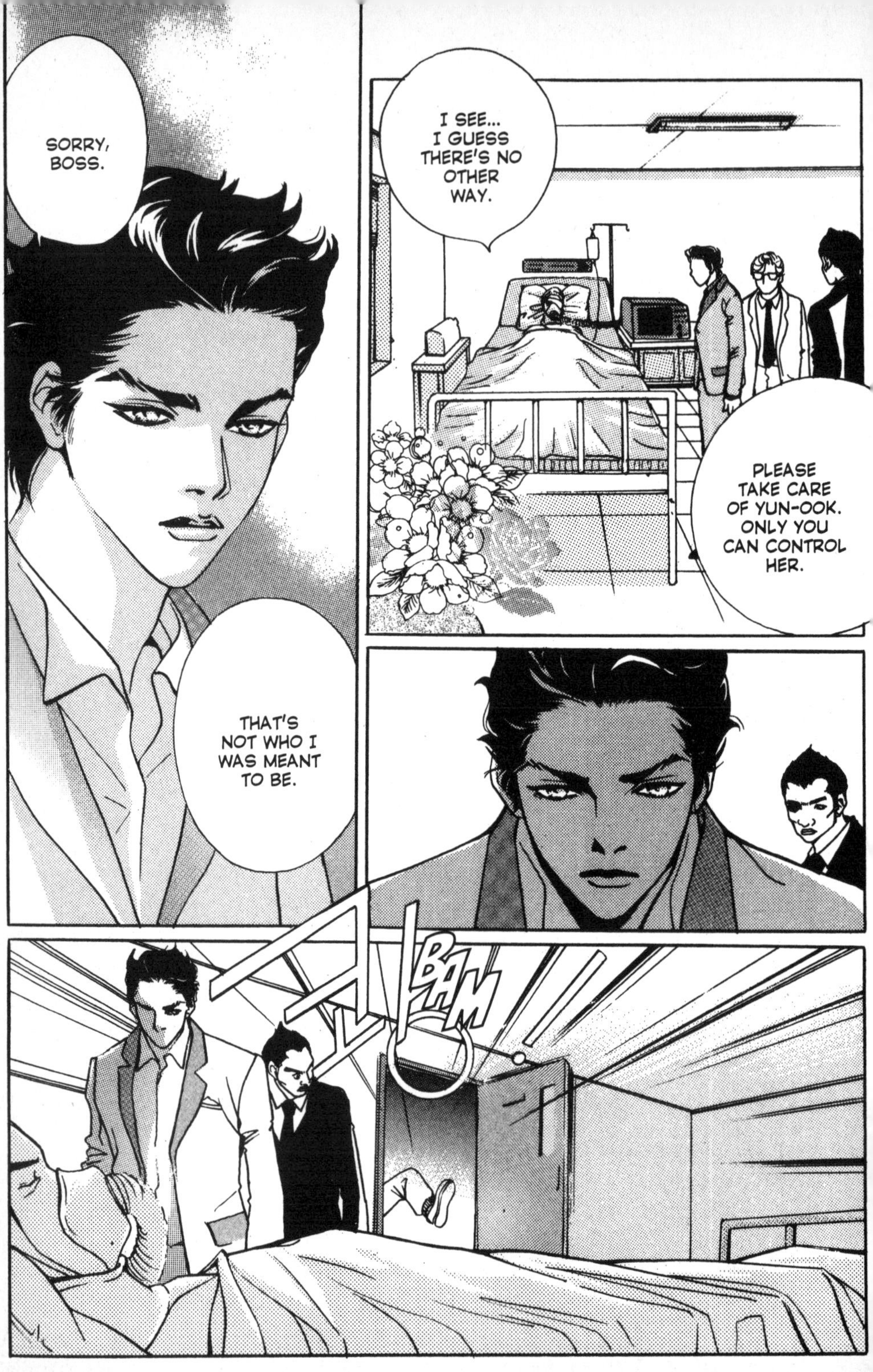
SORRY, BOSS.
THAT'S NOT WHO I WAS MEANT TO BE.
I SEE... I GUESS THERE'S NO OTHER WAY.
PLEASE TAKE CARE OF YUN-OOK. ONLY YOU CAN CONTROL HER.
BAM
BAM

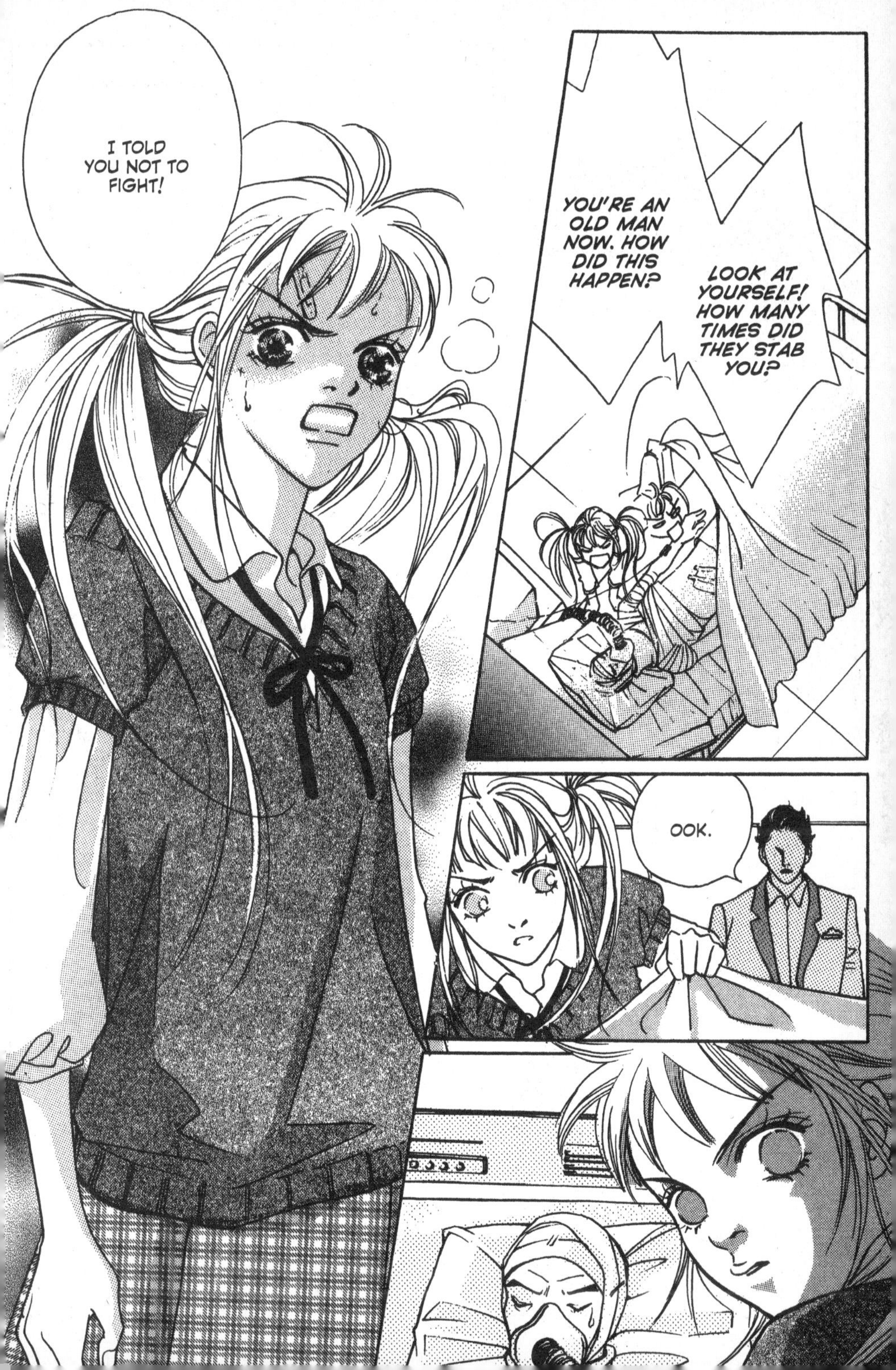
I TOLD YOU NOT TO FIGHT!
YOU'RE AN OLD MAN NOW. HOW DID THIS HAPPEN?
LOOK AT YOURSELF! HOW MANY TIMES DID THEY STAB YOU?
OOK.

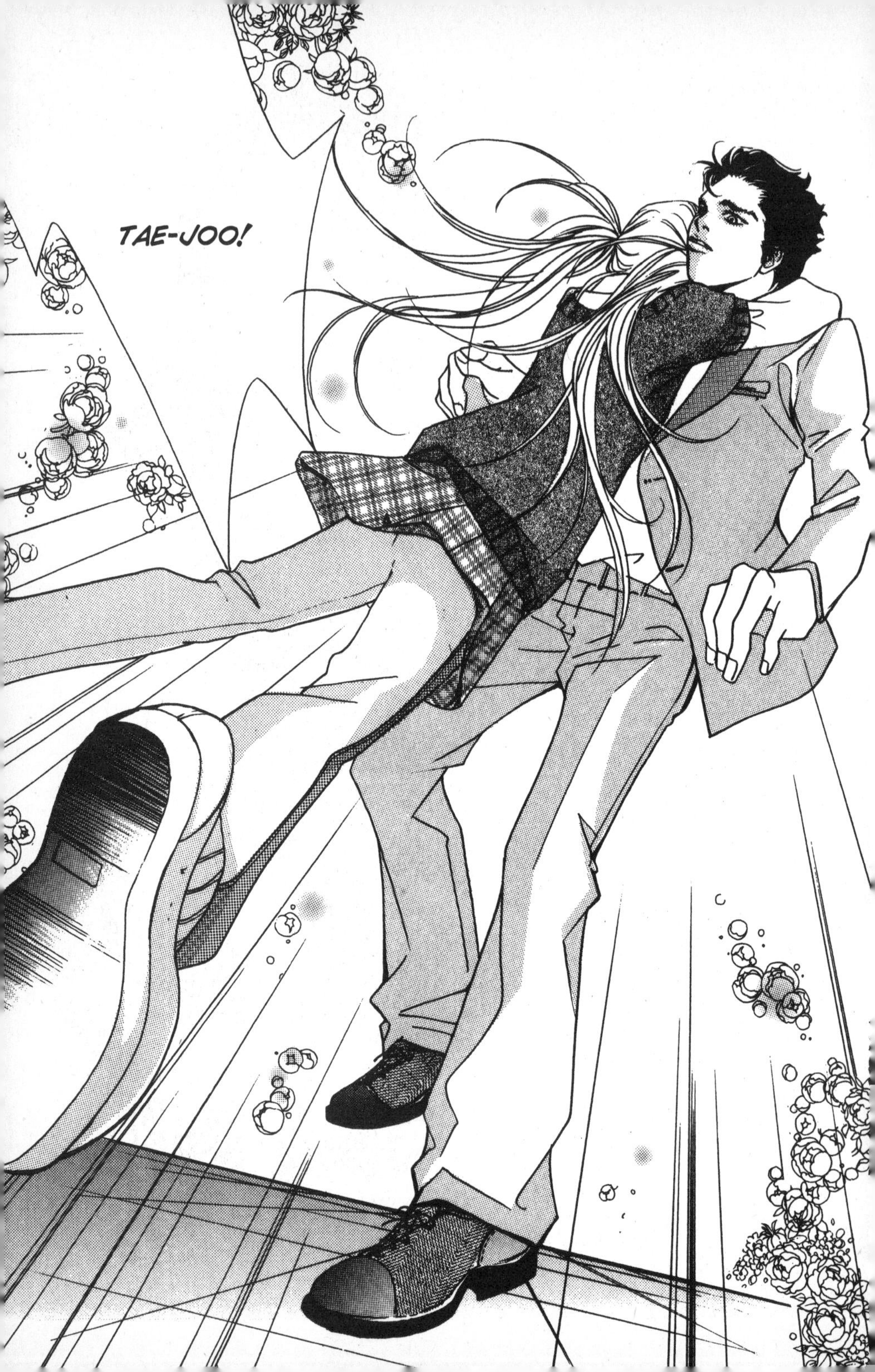
TAE-JOO!

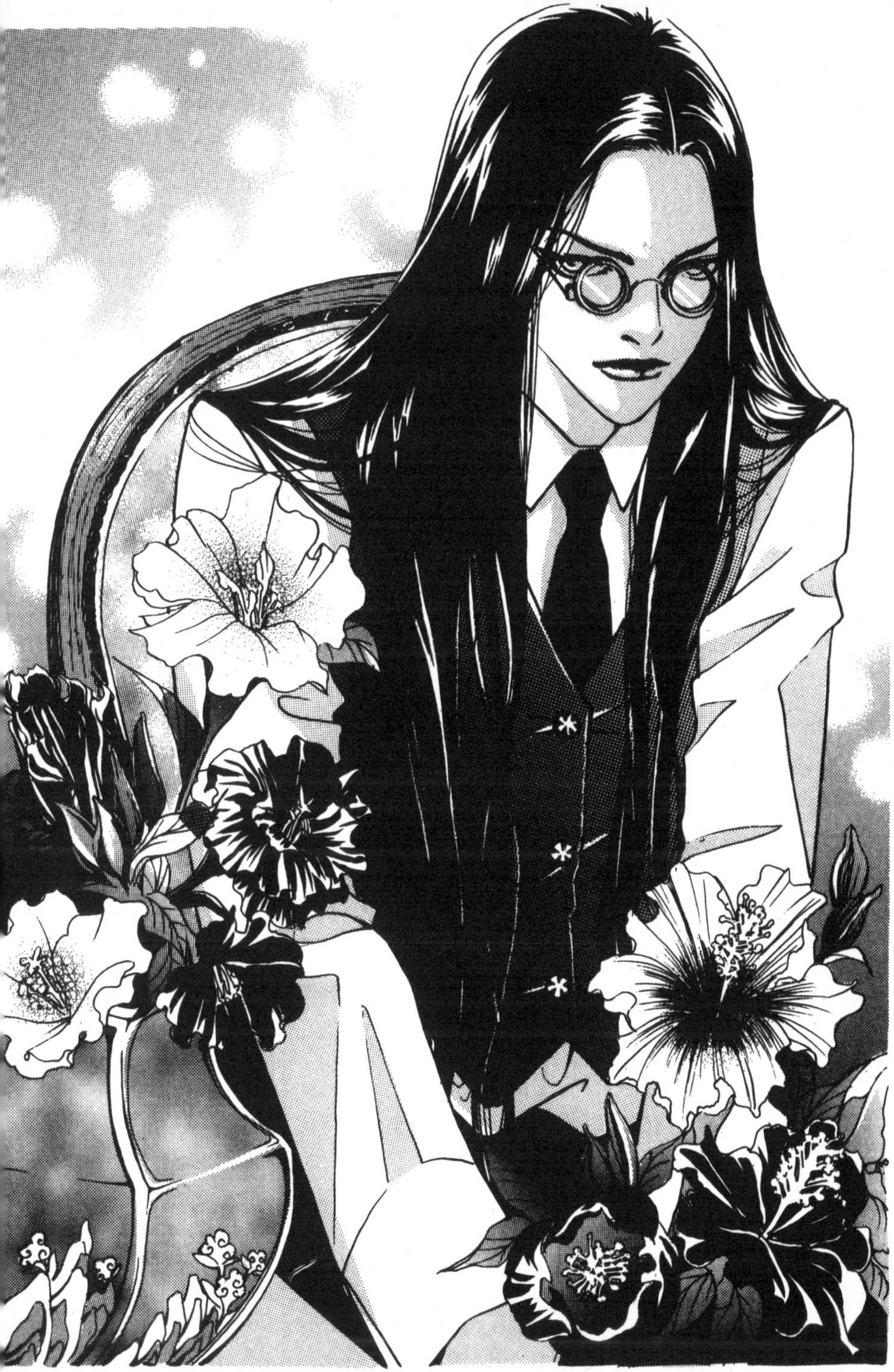

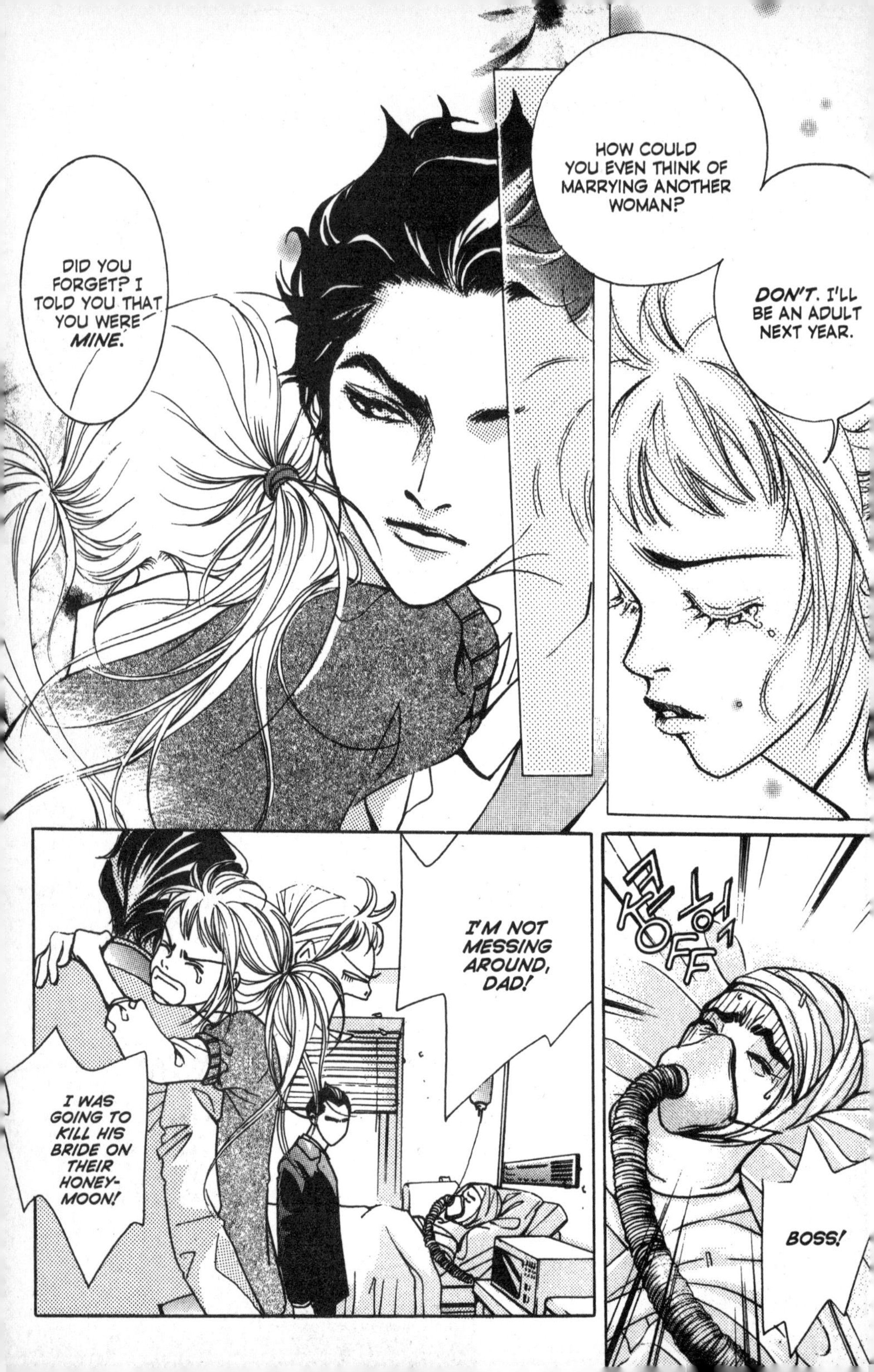
DID YOU FORGET? I TOLD YOU THAT YOU WERE *MINE*.
HOW COULD YOU EVEN THINK OF MARRYING ANOTHER WOMAN?
DON'T. I'LL BE AN ADULT NEXT YEAR.
I'M NOT MESSING AROUND, DAD!
I WAS GOING TO KILL HIS BRIDE ON THEIR HONEY-MOON!
KOFF
BOSS!

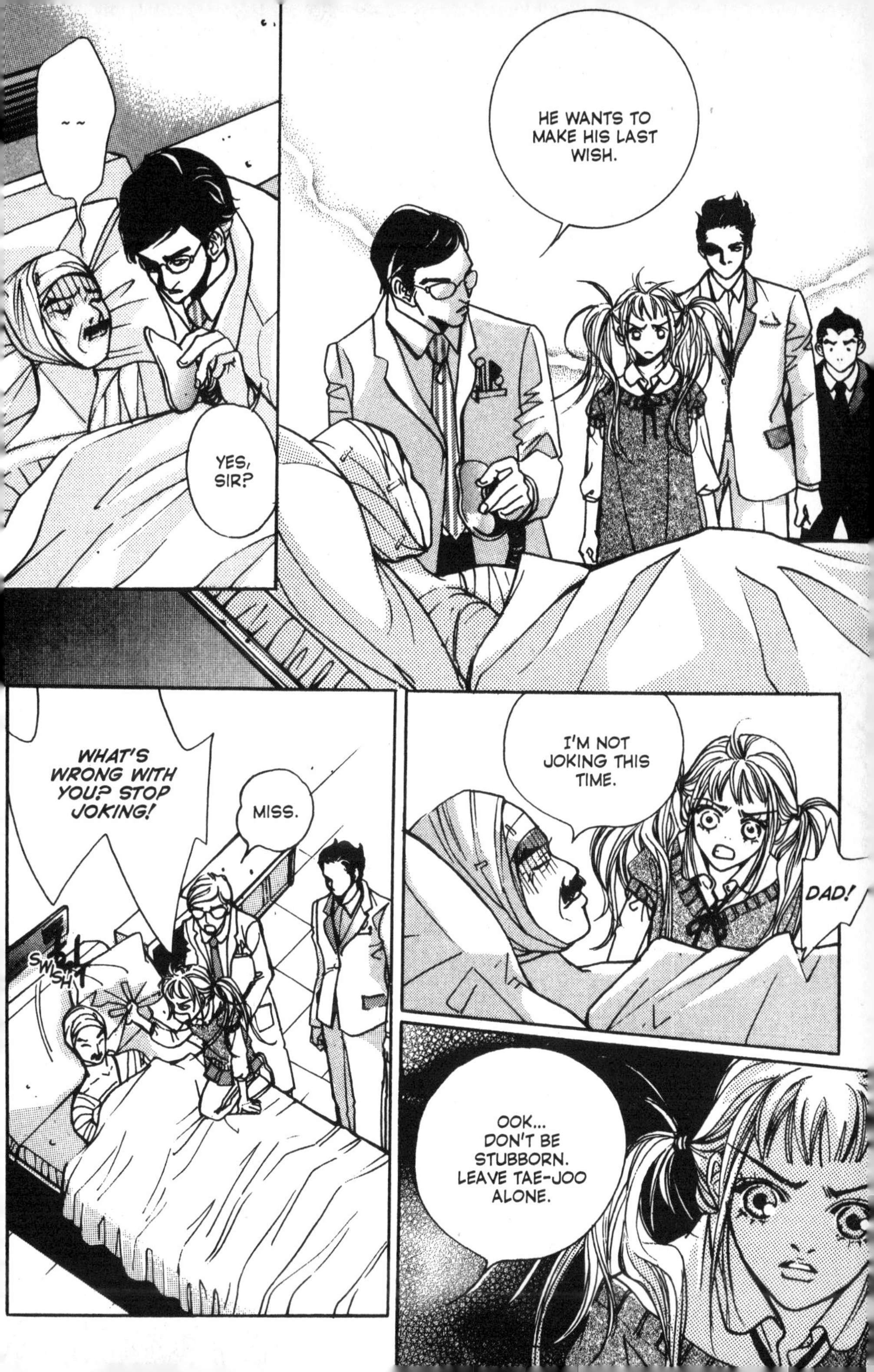
~ ~
YES, SIR?
HE WANTS TO MAKE HIS LAST WISH.
WHAT'S WRONG WITH YOU? STOP JOKING!
MISS.
SWISH
I'M NOT JOKING THIS TIME.
DAD!
OOK... DON'T BE STUBBORN. LEAVE TAE-JOO ALONE.

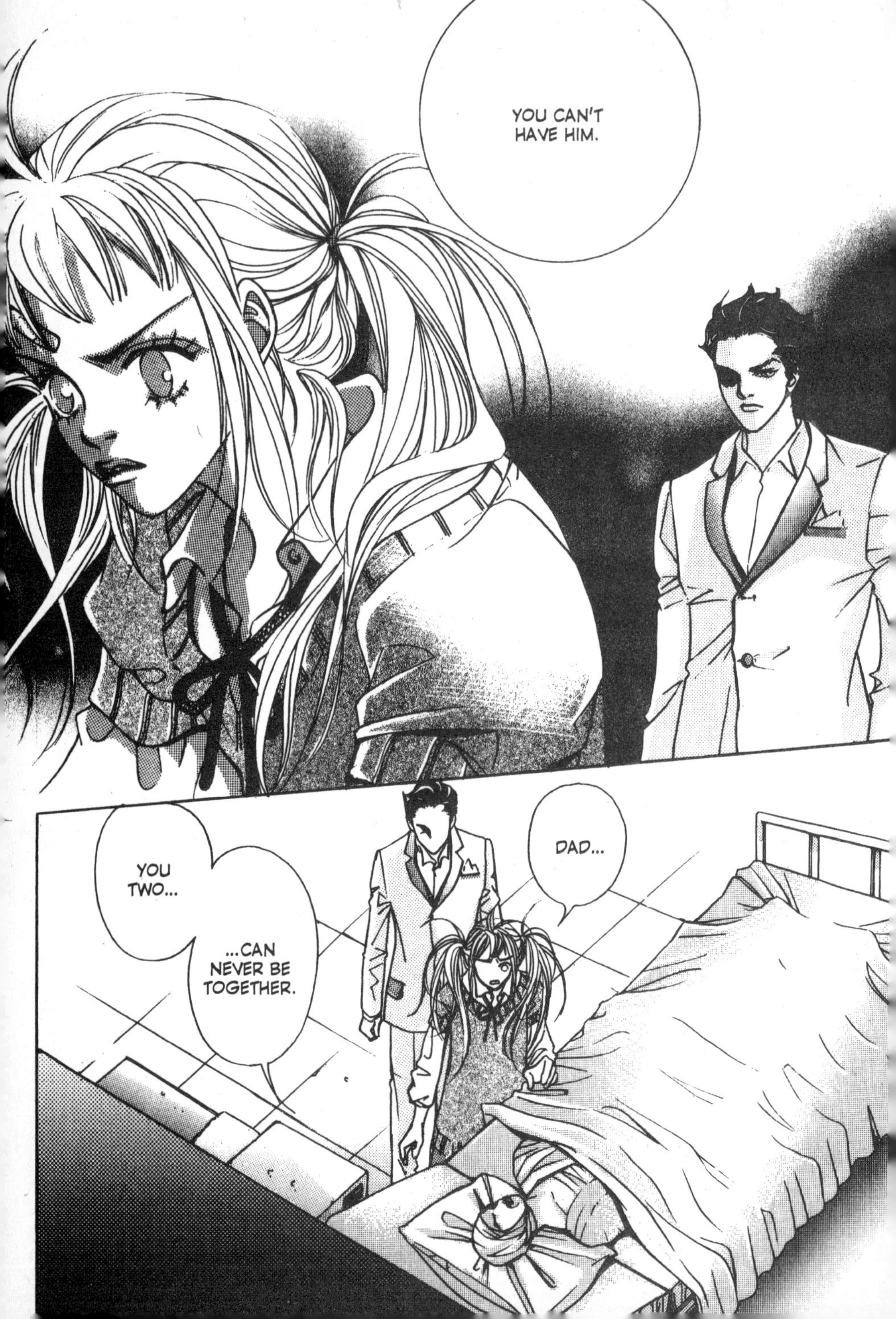
YOU CAN'T HAVE HIM.
YOU TWO...
...CAN NEVER BE TOGETHER.
DAD...

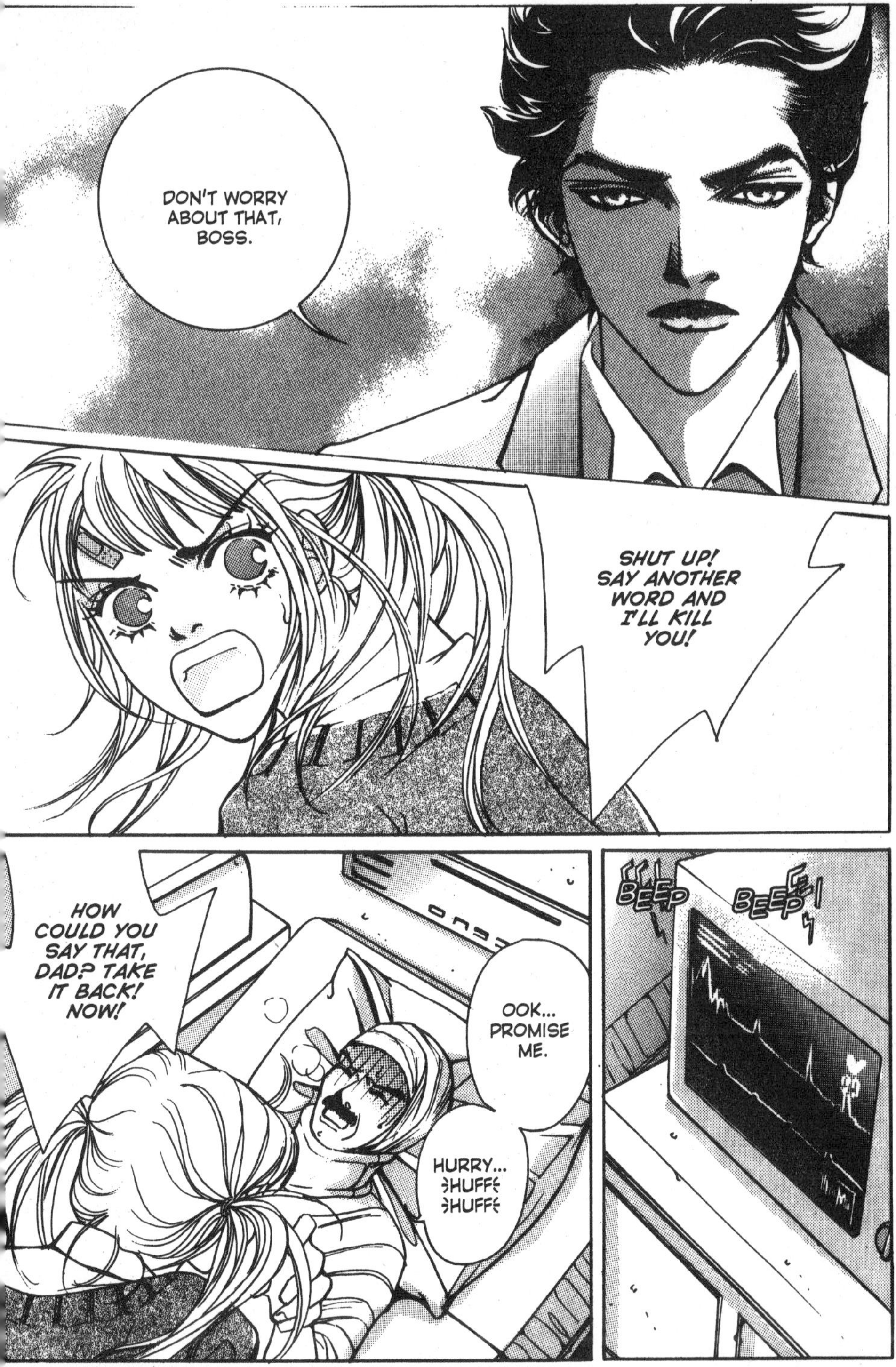
DON'T WORRY ABOUT THAT, BOSS.
SHUT UP! SAY ANOTHER WORD AND I'LL KILL YOU!
HOW COULD YOU SAY THAT, DAD? TAKE IT BACK! NOW!
OOK... PROMISE ME.
HURRY... HUFF HUFF
BEEP
BEEP

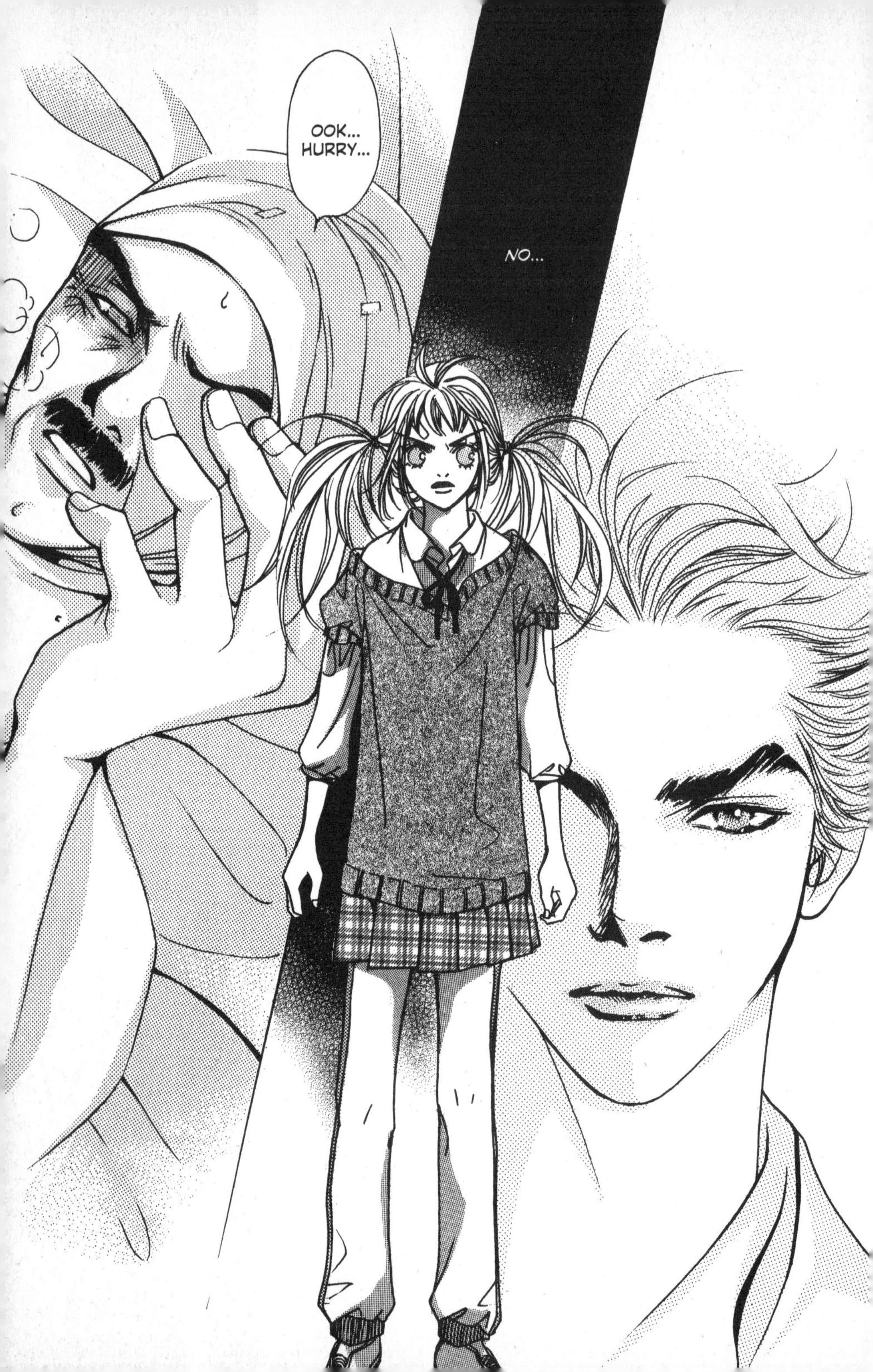
OOK... HURRY...
NO...

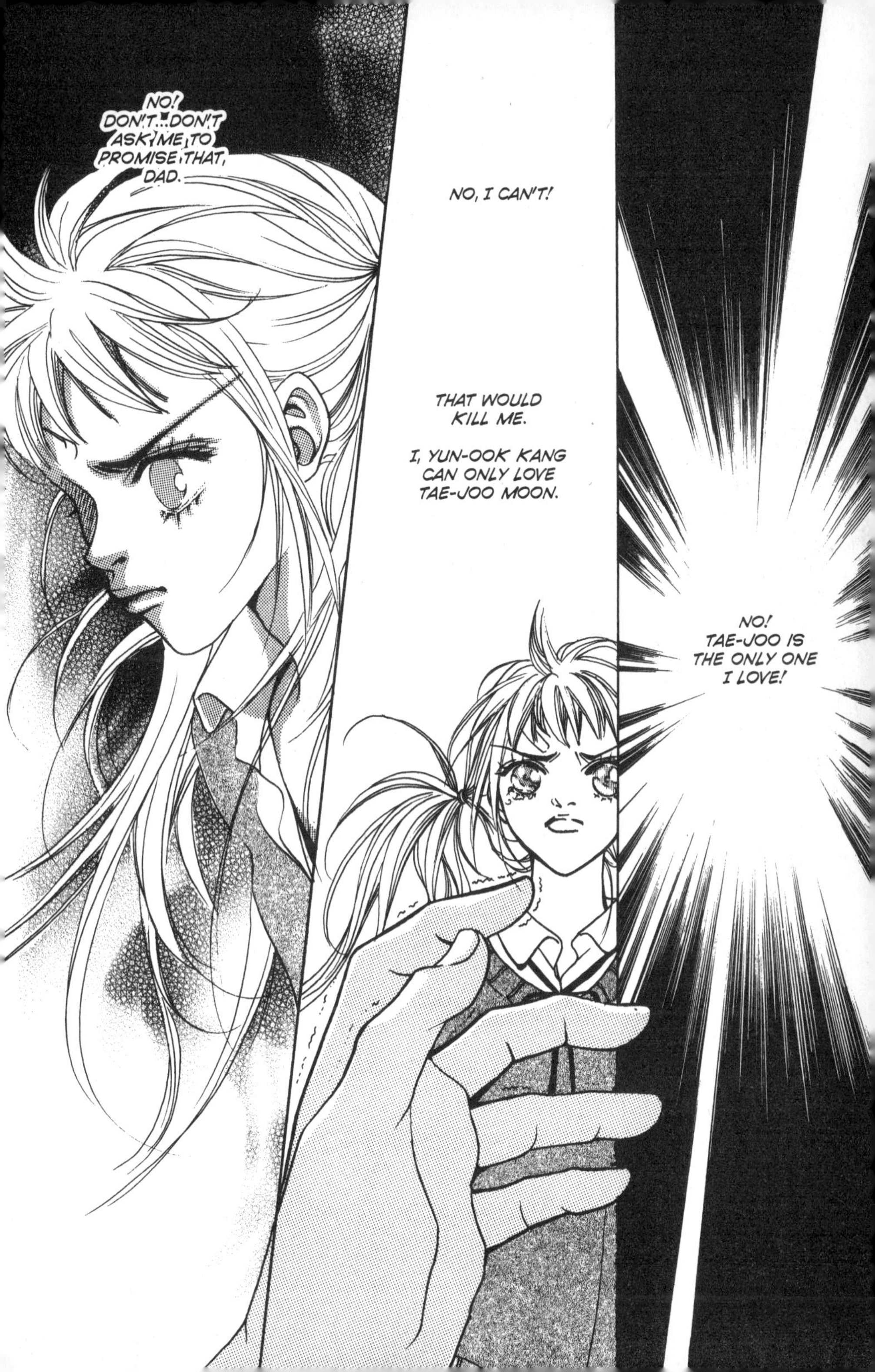
NO! DON'T...DON'T ASK ME TO PROMISE THAT, DAD.
NO, I CAN'T!
THAT WOULD KILL ME.
I, YUN-OOK KANG CAN ONLY LOVE TAE-JOO MOON.
NO! TAE-JOO IS THE ONLY ONE I LOVE!

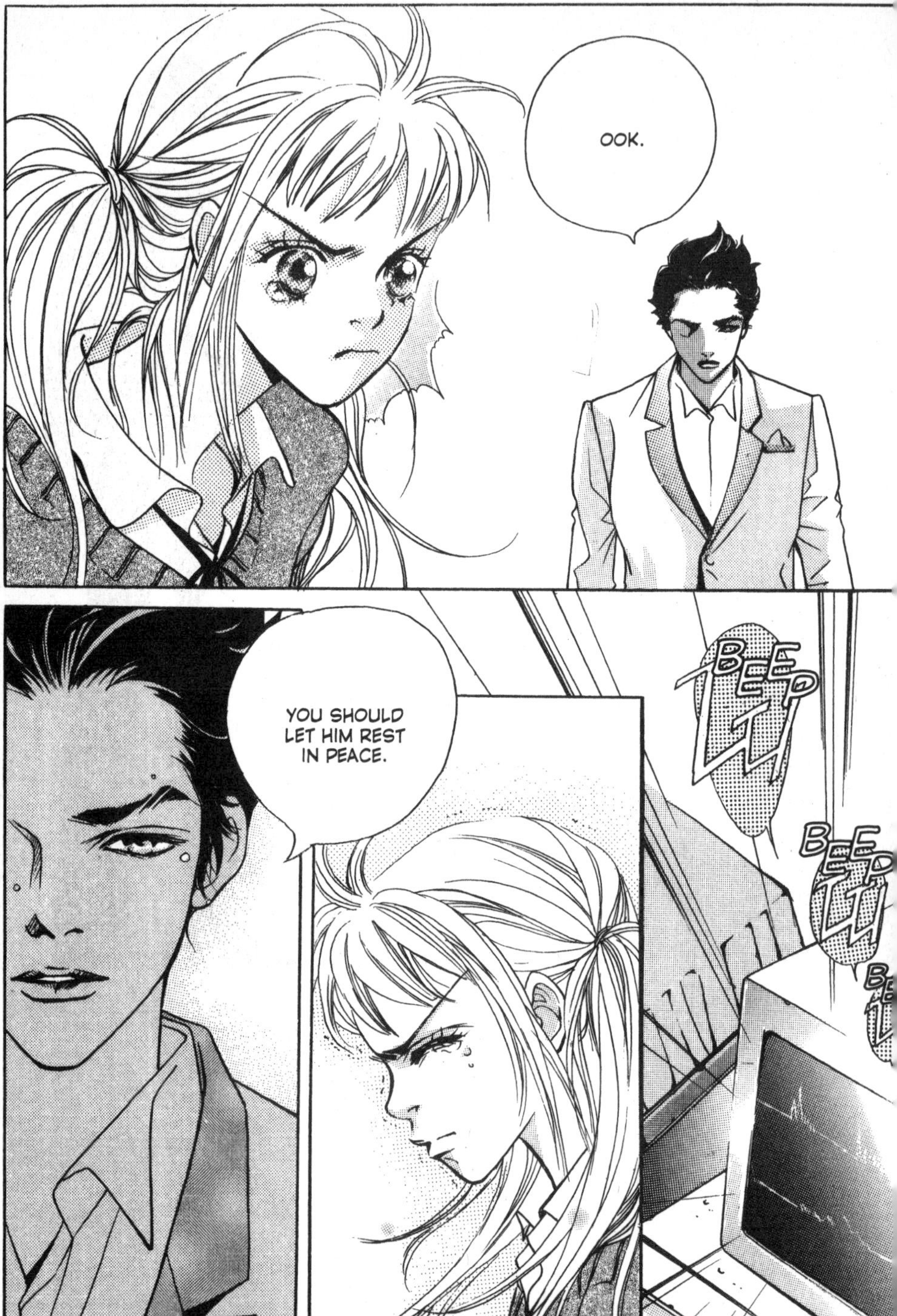
OOK.
YOU SHOULD LET HIM REST IN PEACE.
BEEP
BEEP

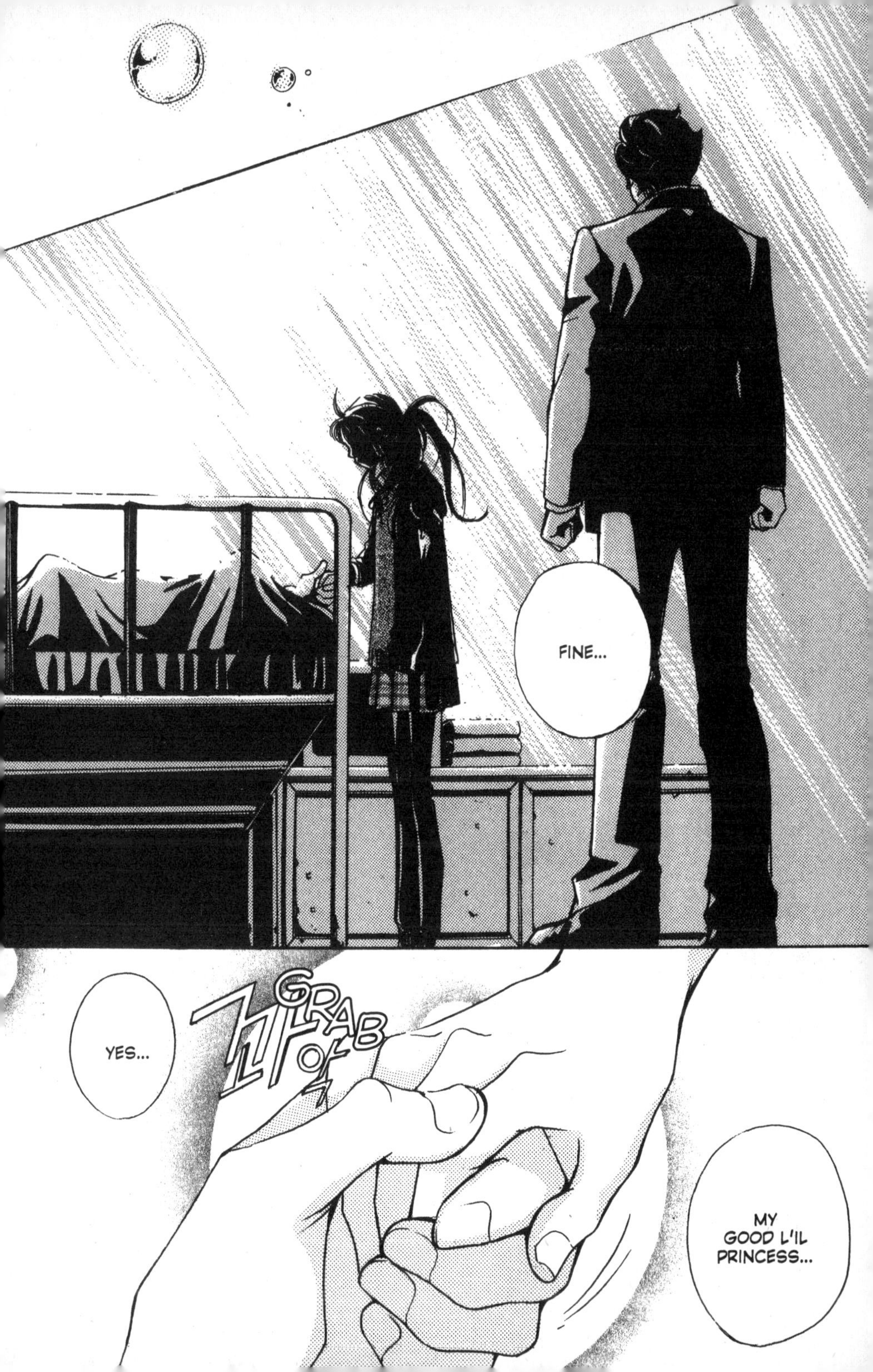
FINE...
YES...
GRAB
MY GOOD L'IL PRINCESS...

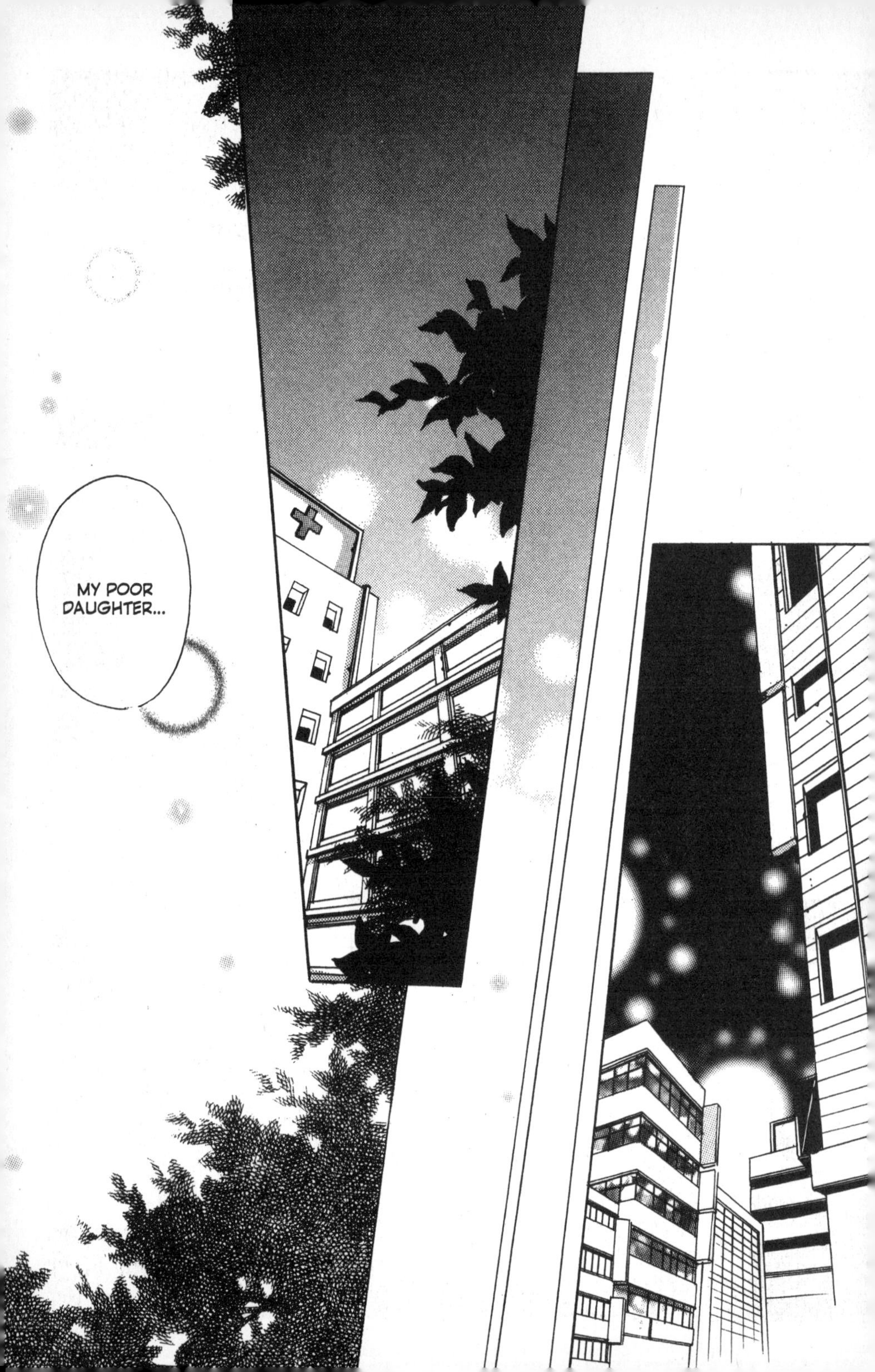
MY POOR DAUGHTER...

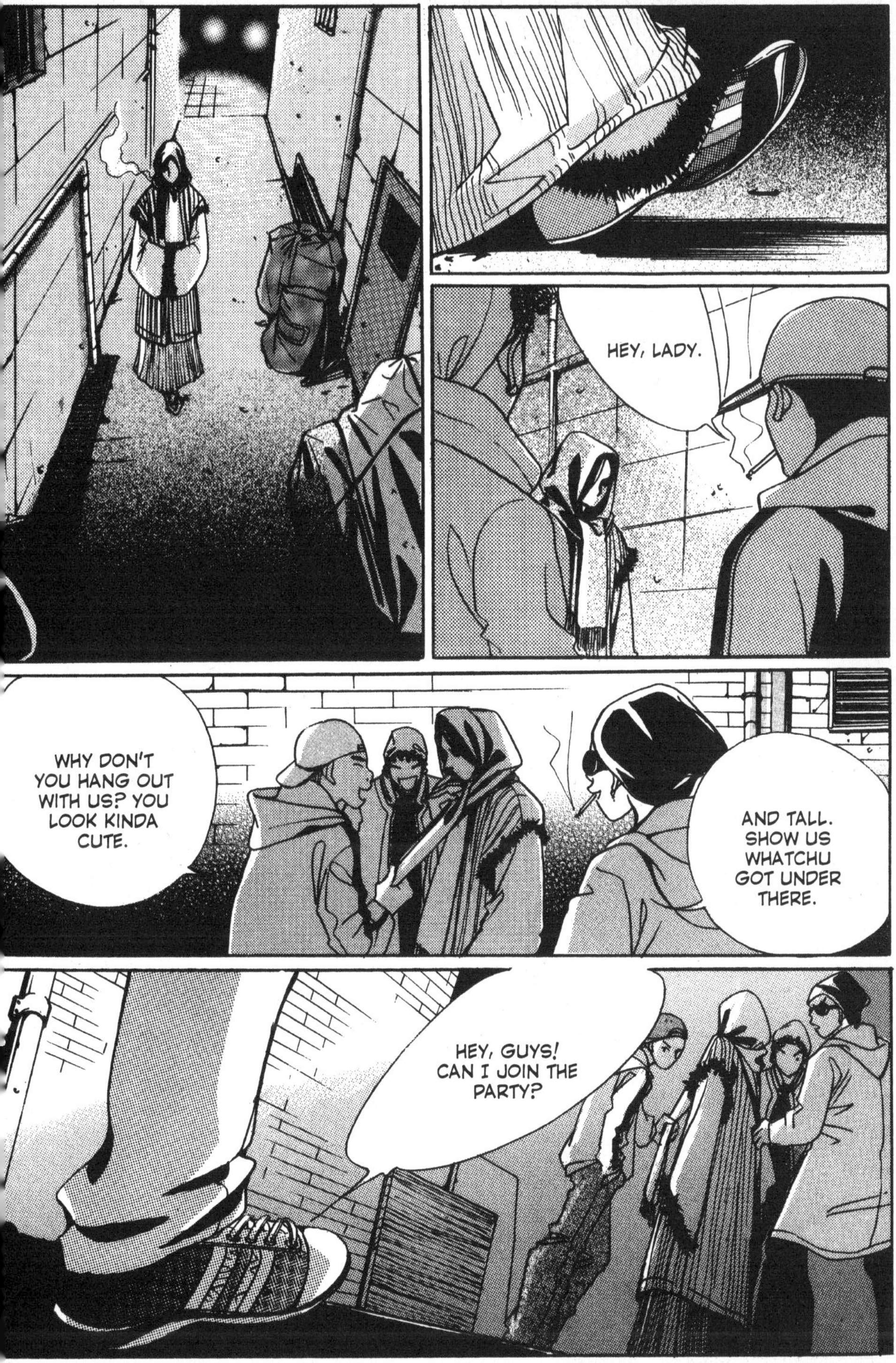
HEY, LADY.
WHY DON'T YOU HANG OUT WITH US? YOU LOOK KINDA CUTE.
AND TALL. SHOW US WHATCHU GOT UNDER THERE.
HEY, GUYS! CAN I JOIN THE PARTY?

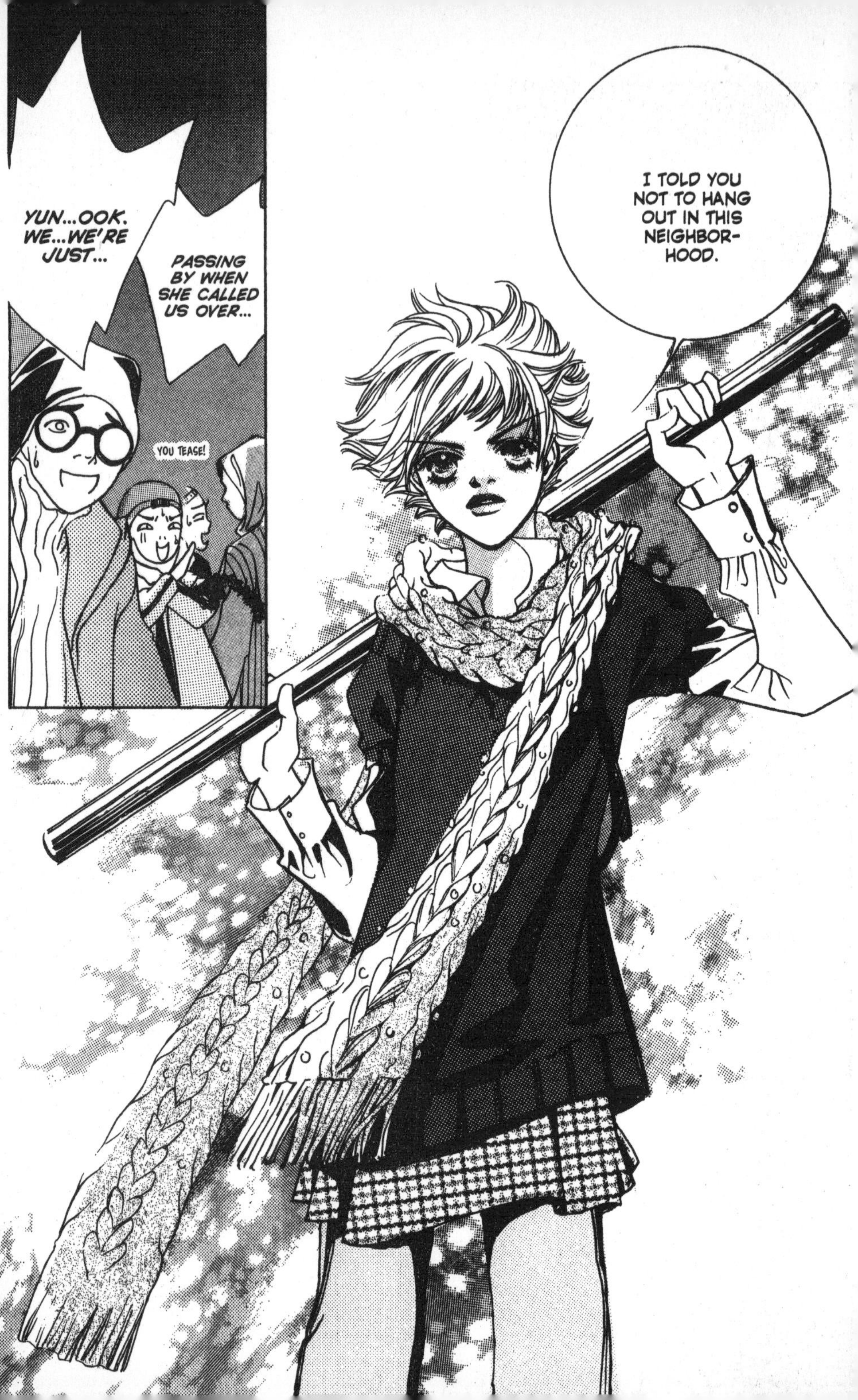
YUN...OOK. WE...WE'RE JUST...
PASSING BY WHEN SHE CALLED US OVER...
YOU TEASE!
I TOLD YOU NOT TO HANG OUT IN THIS NEIGHBOR-HOOD.

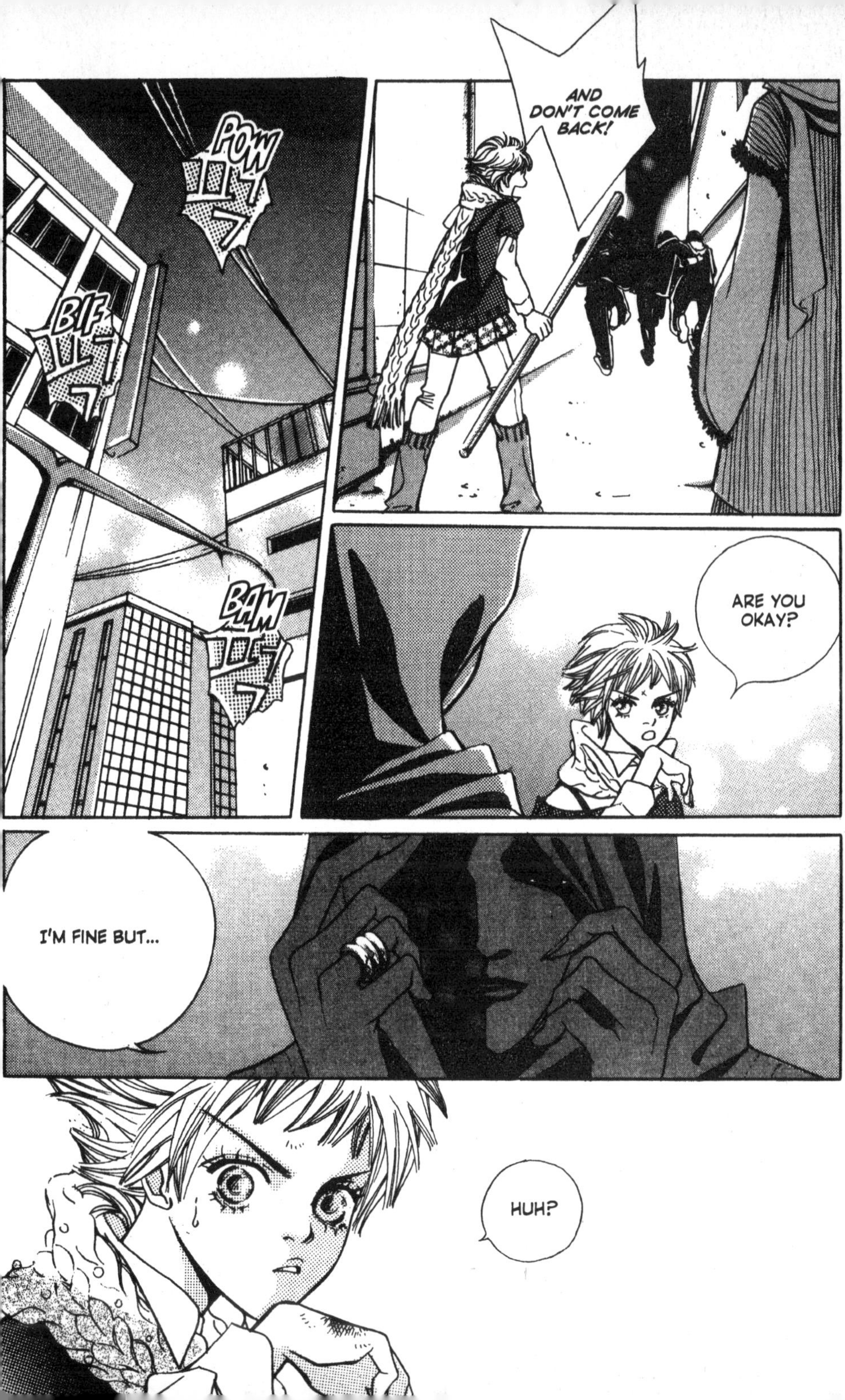
POW
BIF
BAM
AND DON'T COME BACK!
ARE YOU OKAY?
I'M FINE BUT...
HUH?

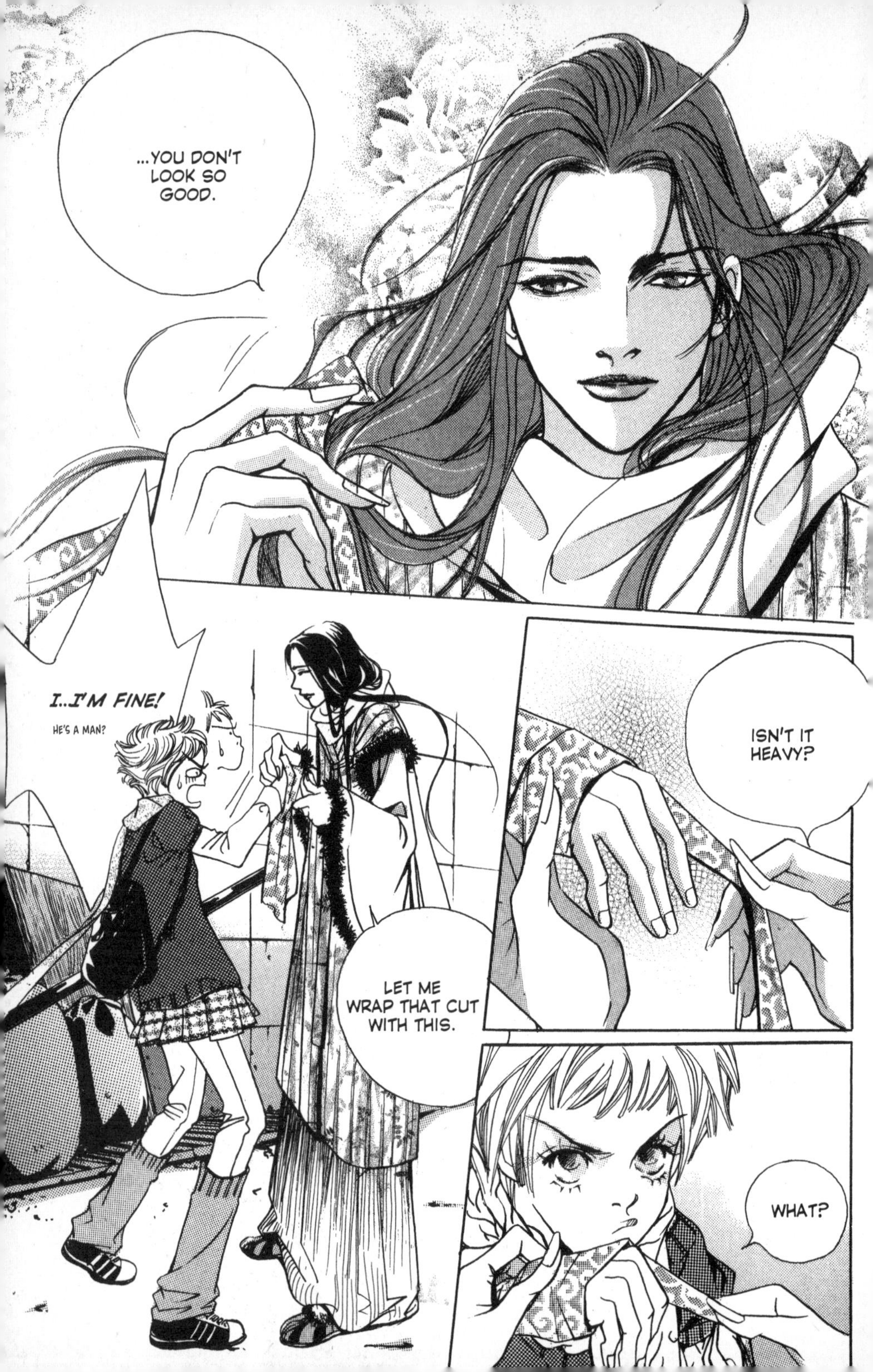
...YOU DON'T LOOK SO GOOD.
I..I'M FINE!
HE'S A MAN?
LET ME WRAP THAT CUT WITH THIS.
ISN'T IT HEAVY?
WHAT?

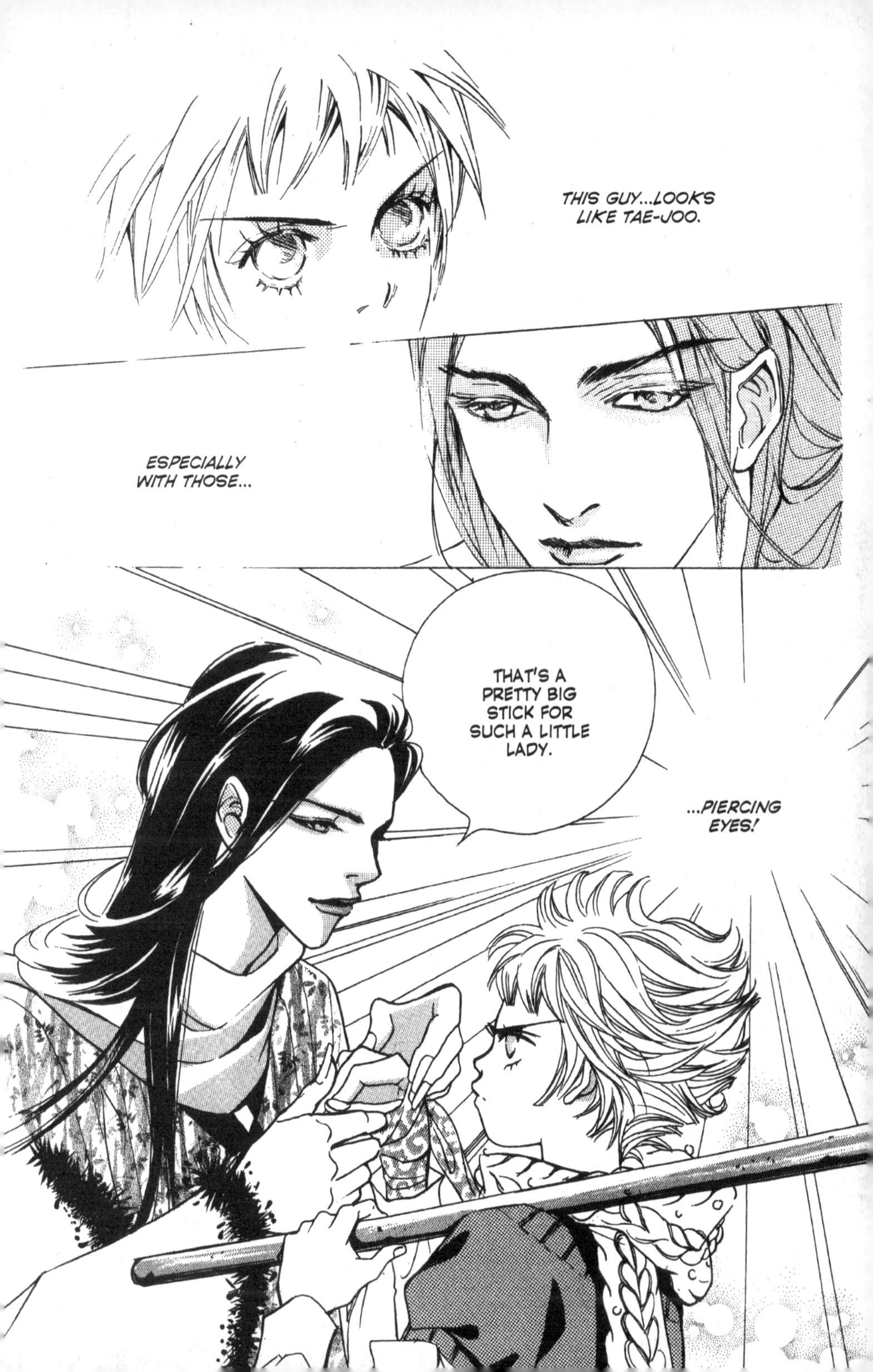
THIS GUY...LOOKS LIKE TAE-JOO.
ESPECIALLY WITH THOSE...
THAT'S A PRETTY BIG STICK FOR SUCH A LITTLE LADY.
...PIERCING EYES!

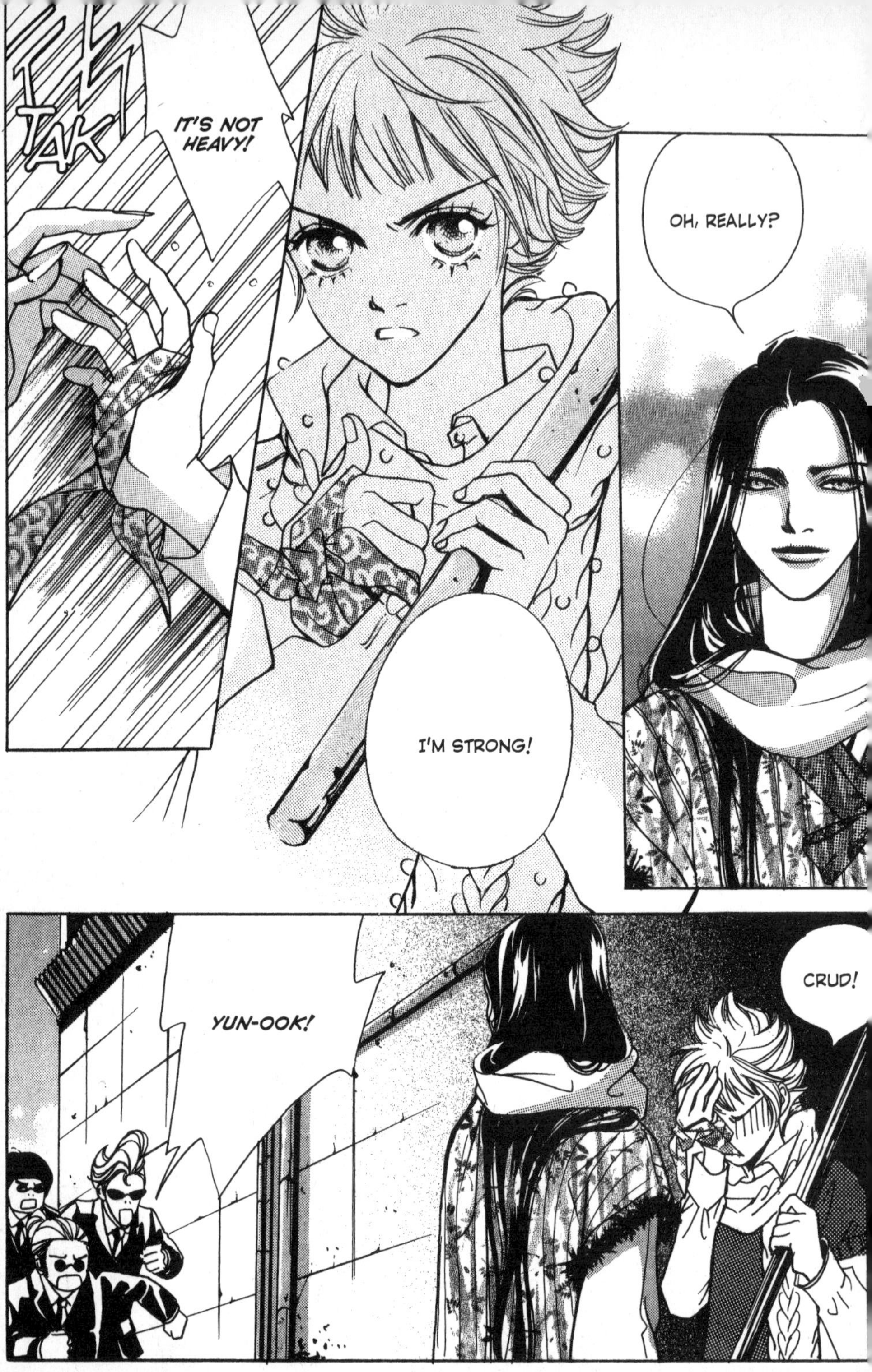
TAK
IT'S NOT HEAVY!
I'M STRONG!
OH, REALLY?
YUN-OOK!
CRUD!

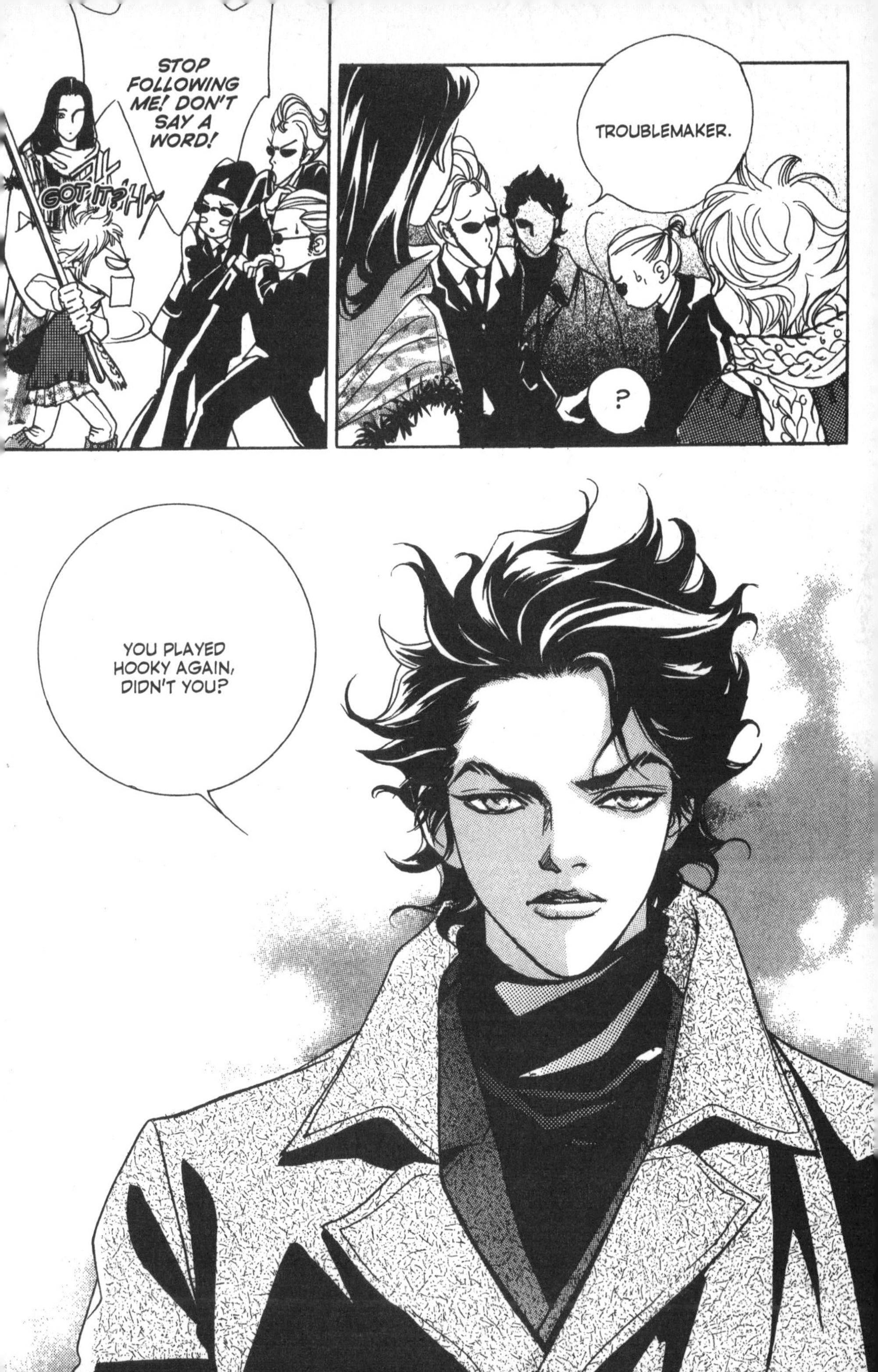

STOP FOLLOWING ME! DON'T SAY A WORD!
GOT IT?
TROUBLEMAKER.
?
YOU PLAYED HOOKY AGAIN, DIDN'T YOU?

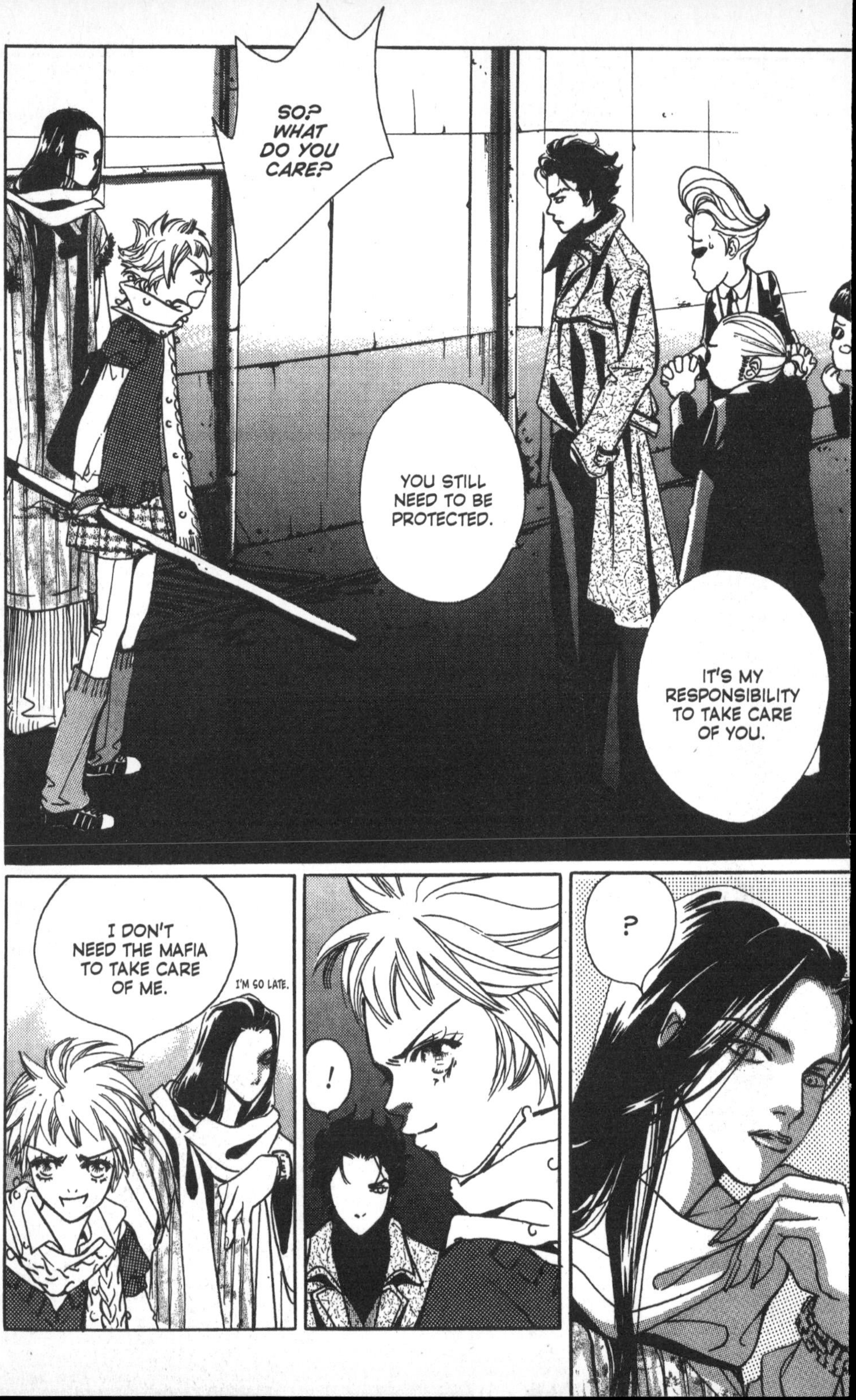
SO? WHAT DO YOU CARE?
YOU STILL NEED TO BE PROTECTED.
IT'S MY RESPONSIBILITY TO TAKE CARE OF YOU.
I DON'T NEED THE MAFIA TO TAKE CARE OF ME.
I'M SO LATE.
!
?

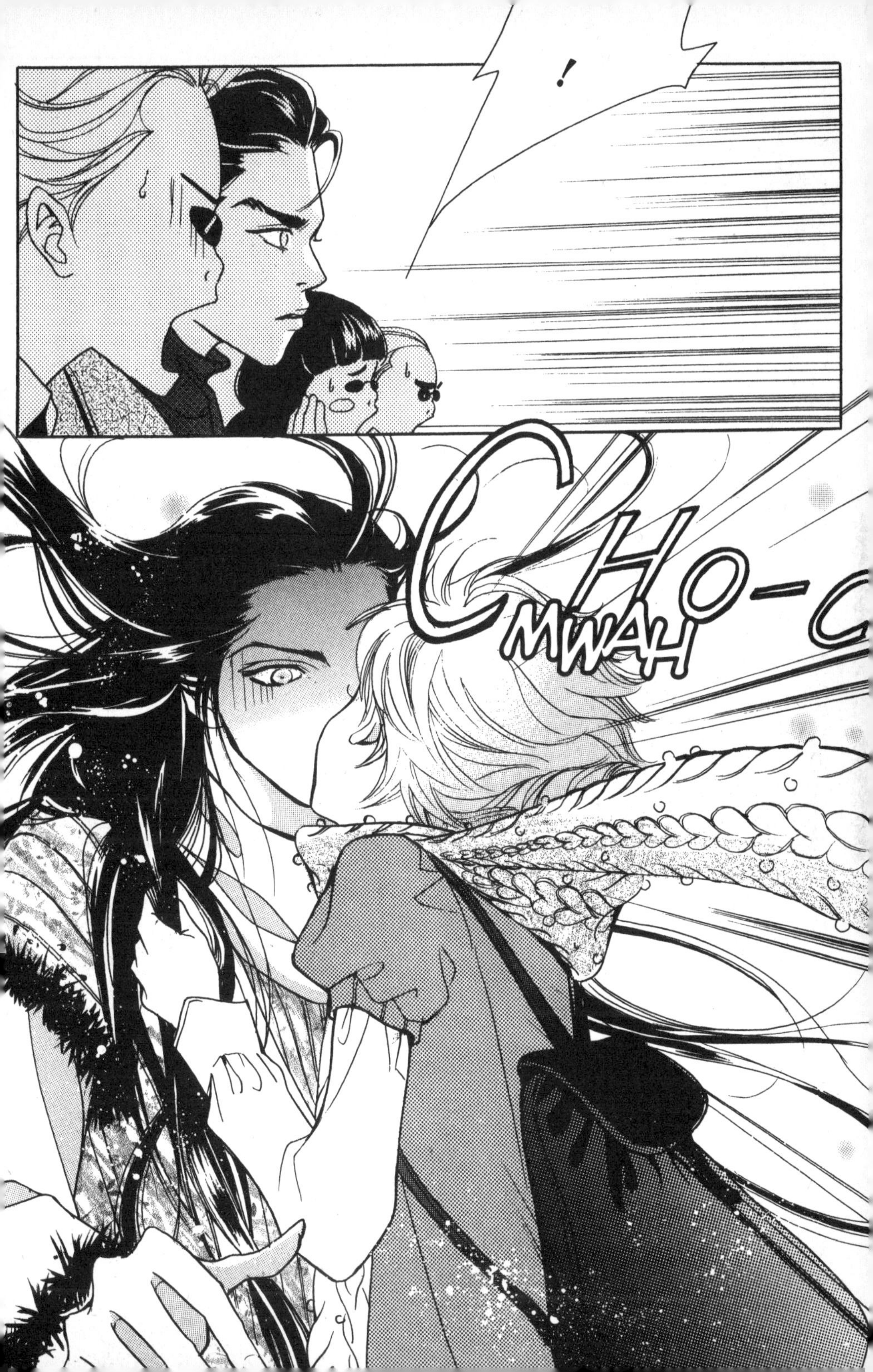
!
CHO-
MWAH

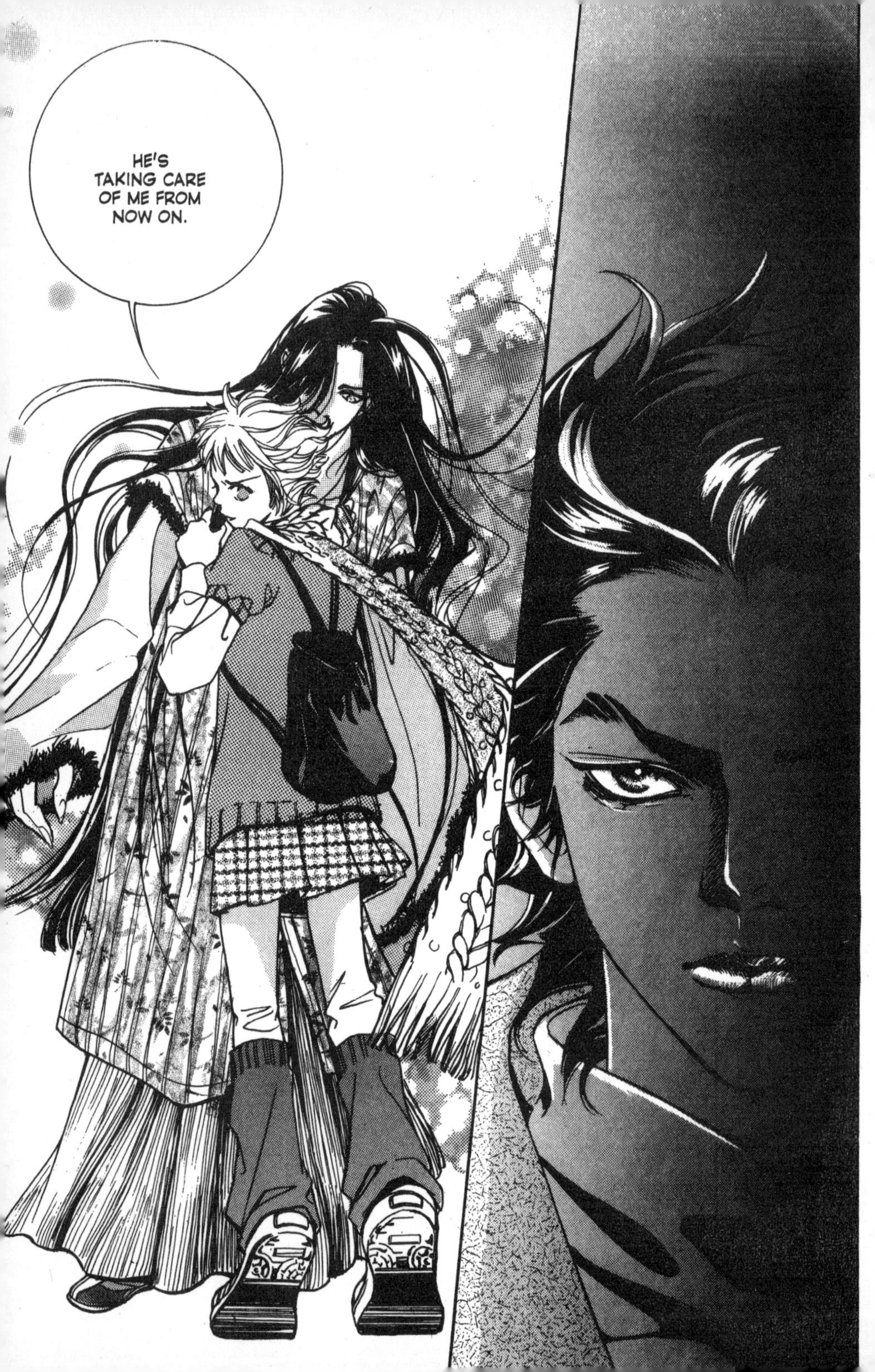
HE'S TAKING CARE OF ME FROM NOW ON.

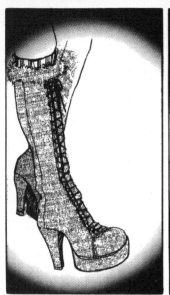

?!

WHAT THE--.

두리번 SWISH

SWISH 두리번

WHY DO I GET THE FEELING THAT SOMEONE'S PEEKING ON ME?

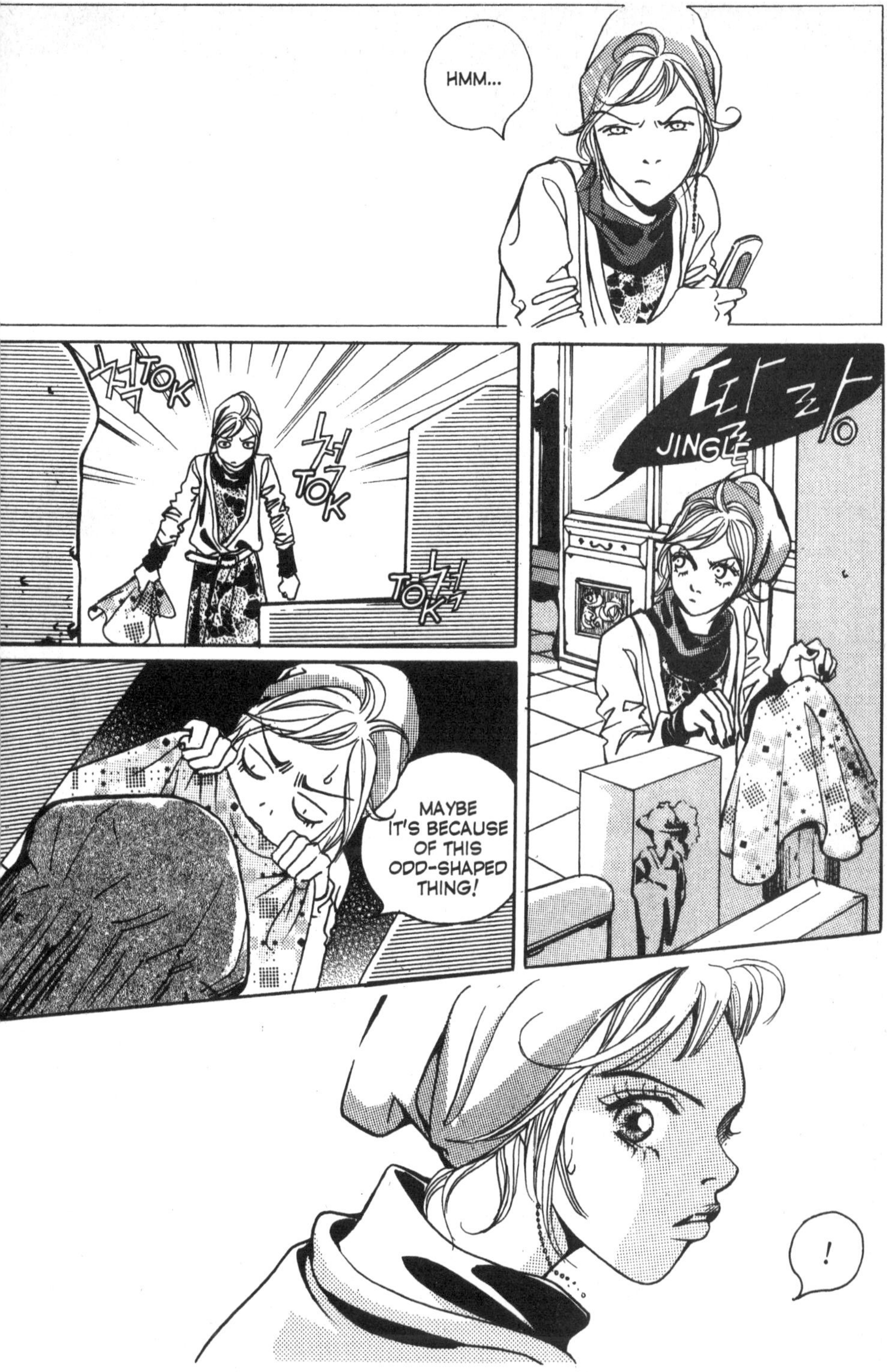
HMM...
TOK
TOK
TOK
MAYBE IT'S BECAUSE OF THIS ODD-SHAPED THING!
JINGLE
!

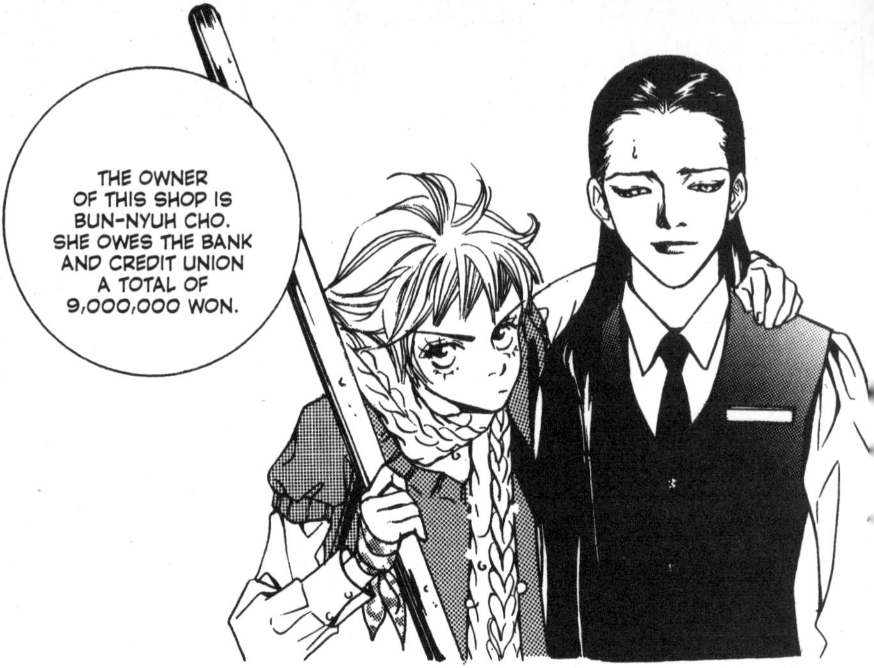
THE OWNER OF THIS SHOP IS BUN-NYUH CHO. SHE OWES THE BANK AND CREDIT UNION A TOTAL OF 9,000,000 WON.

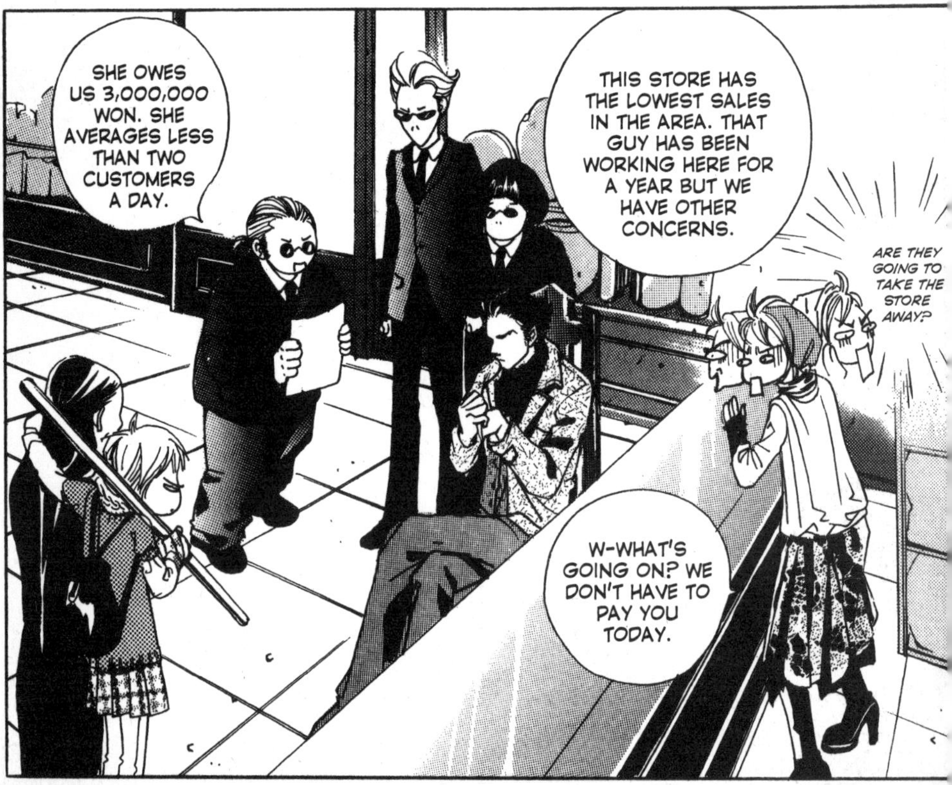
SHE OWES US 3,000,000 WON. SHE AVERAGES LESS THAN TWO CUSTOMERS A DAY.
THIS STORE HAS THE LOWEST SALES IN THE AREA. THAT GUY HAS BEEN WORKING HERE FOR A YEAR BUT WE HAVE OTHER CONCERNS.
ARE THEY GOING TO TAKE THE STORE AWAY?
W-WHAT'S GOING ON? WE DON'T HAVE TO PAY YOU TODAY.

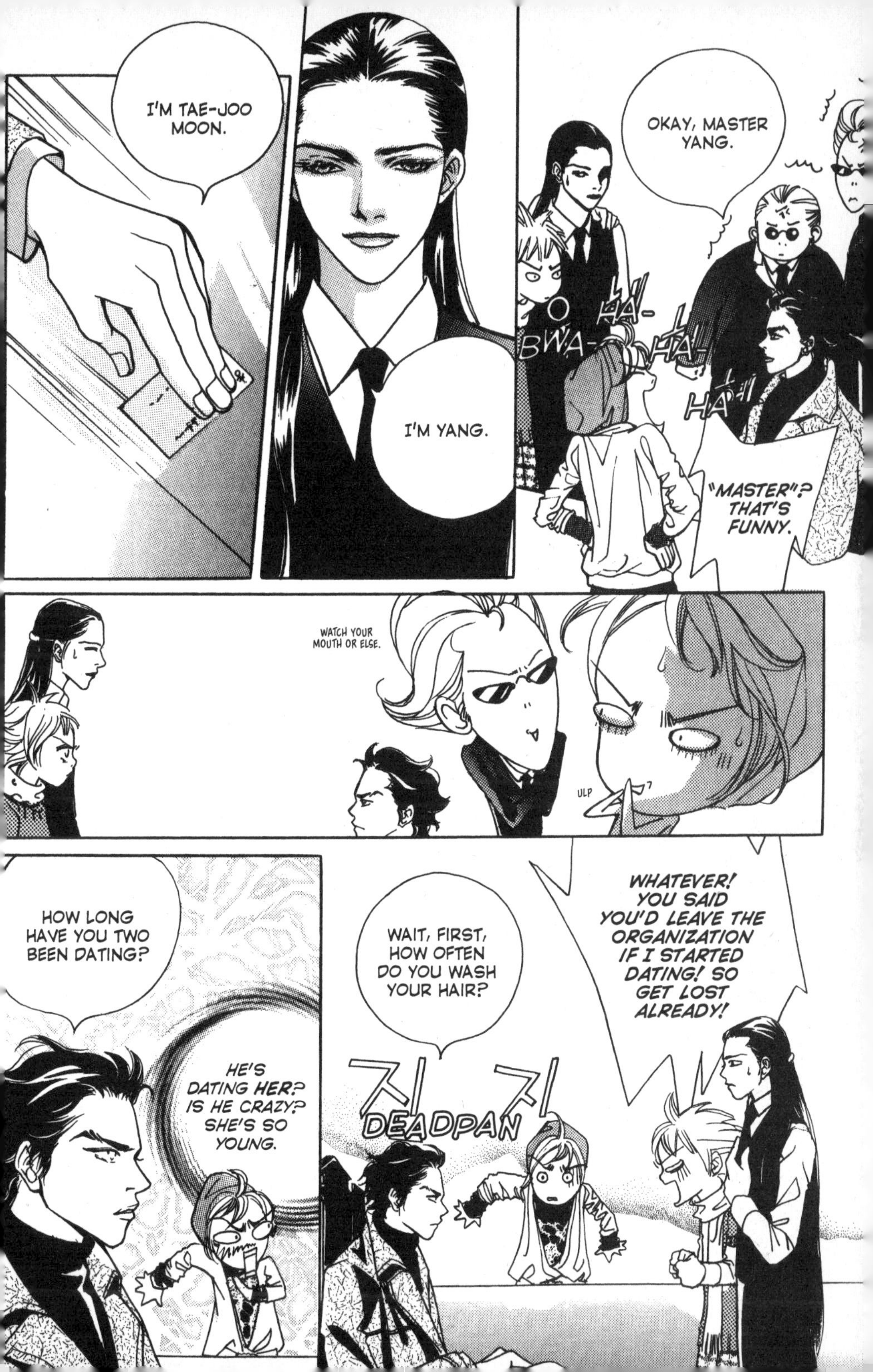
I'M TAE-JOO MOON.
I'M YANG.
OKAY, MASTER YANG.
BWA-HA-
HA-
HA-
HA
"MASTER"? THAT'S FUNNY.
WATCH YOUR MOUTH OR ELSE.
ULP
HOW LONG HAVE YOU TWO BEEN DATING?
HE'S DATING HER? IS HE CRAZY? SHE'S SO YOUNG.
WAIT, FIRST, HOW OFTEN DO YOU WASH YOUR HAIR?
지 지
DEADPAN
WHATEVER! YOU SAID YOU'D LEAVE THE ORGANIZATION IF I STARTED DATING! SO GET LOST ALREADY!

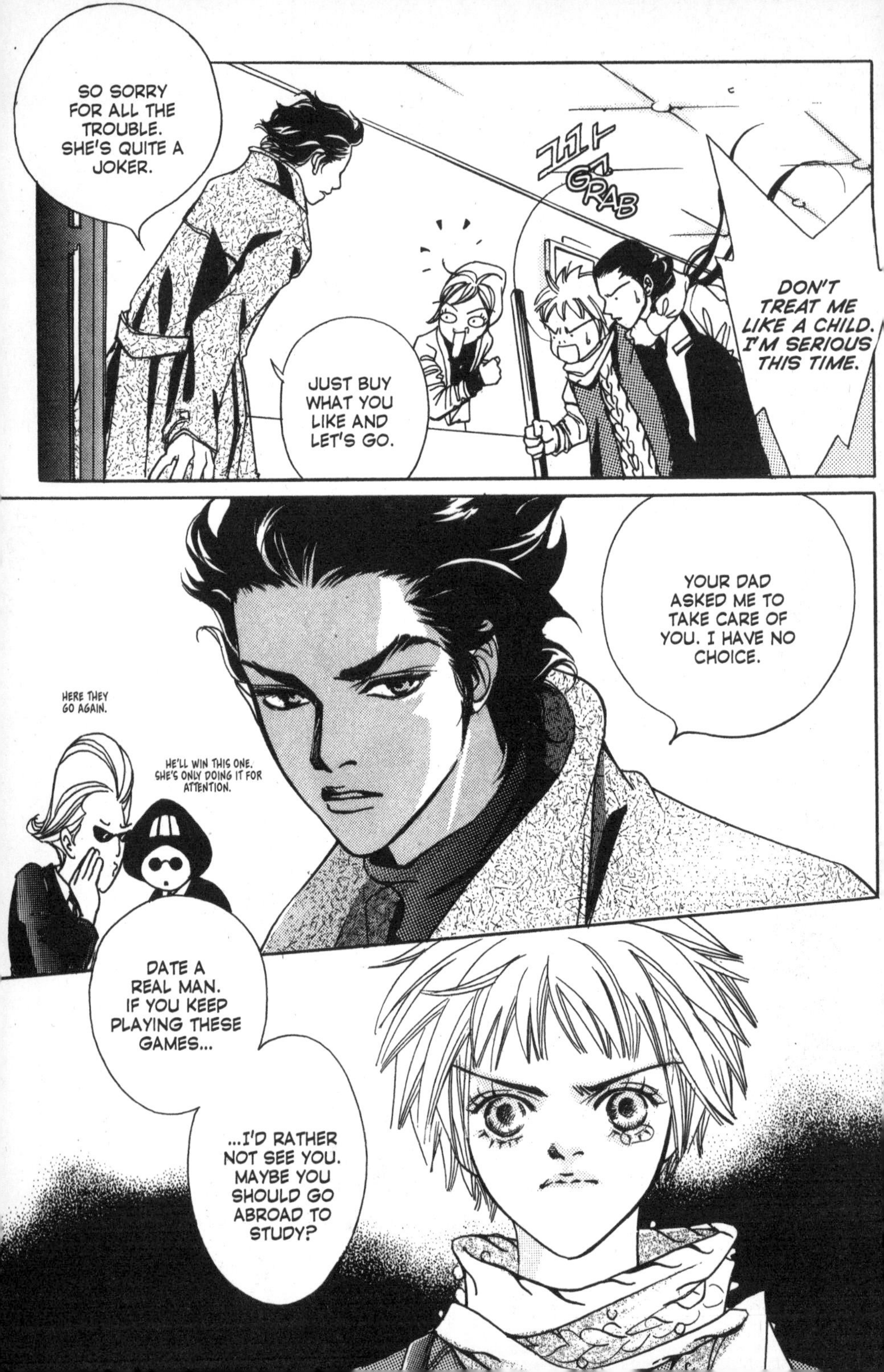
SO SORRY FOR ALL THE TROUBLE. SHE'S QUITE A JOKER.
GRAB
JUST BUY WHAT YOU LIKE AND LET'S GO.
DON'T TREAT ME LIKE A CHILD. I'M SERIOUS THIS TIME.
YOUR DAD ASKED ME TO TAKE CARE OF YOU. I HAVE NO CHOICE.
HERE THEY GO AGAIN.
HE'LL WIN THIS ONE. SHE'S ONLY DOING IT FOR ATTENTION.
DATE A REAL MAN. IF YOU KEEP PLAYING THESE GAMES...
...I'D RATHER NOT SEE YOU. MAYBE YOU SHOULD GO ABROAD TO STUDY?

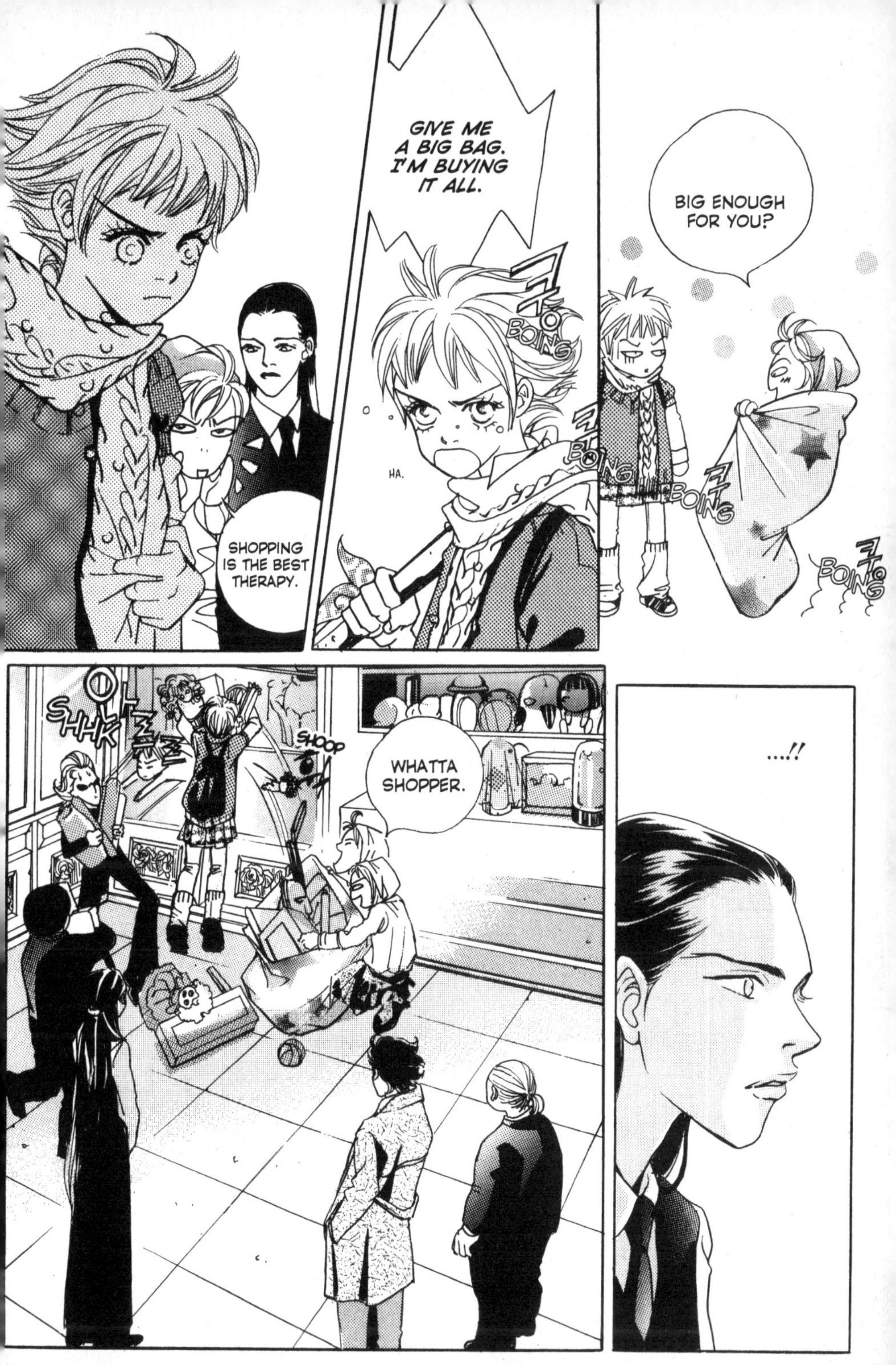
SHOPPING IS THE BEST THERAPY.
GIVE ME A BIG BAG. I'M BUYING IT ALL.
BOING
HA.
BOING
BIG ENOUGH FOR YOU?
BOING
BOING
SHHK
SHOOP
WHATTA SHOPPER.
...!!

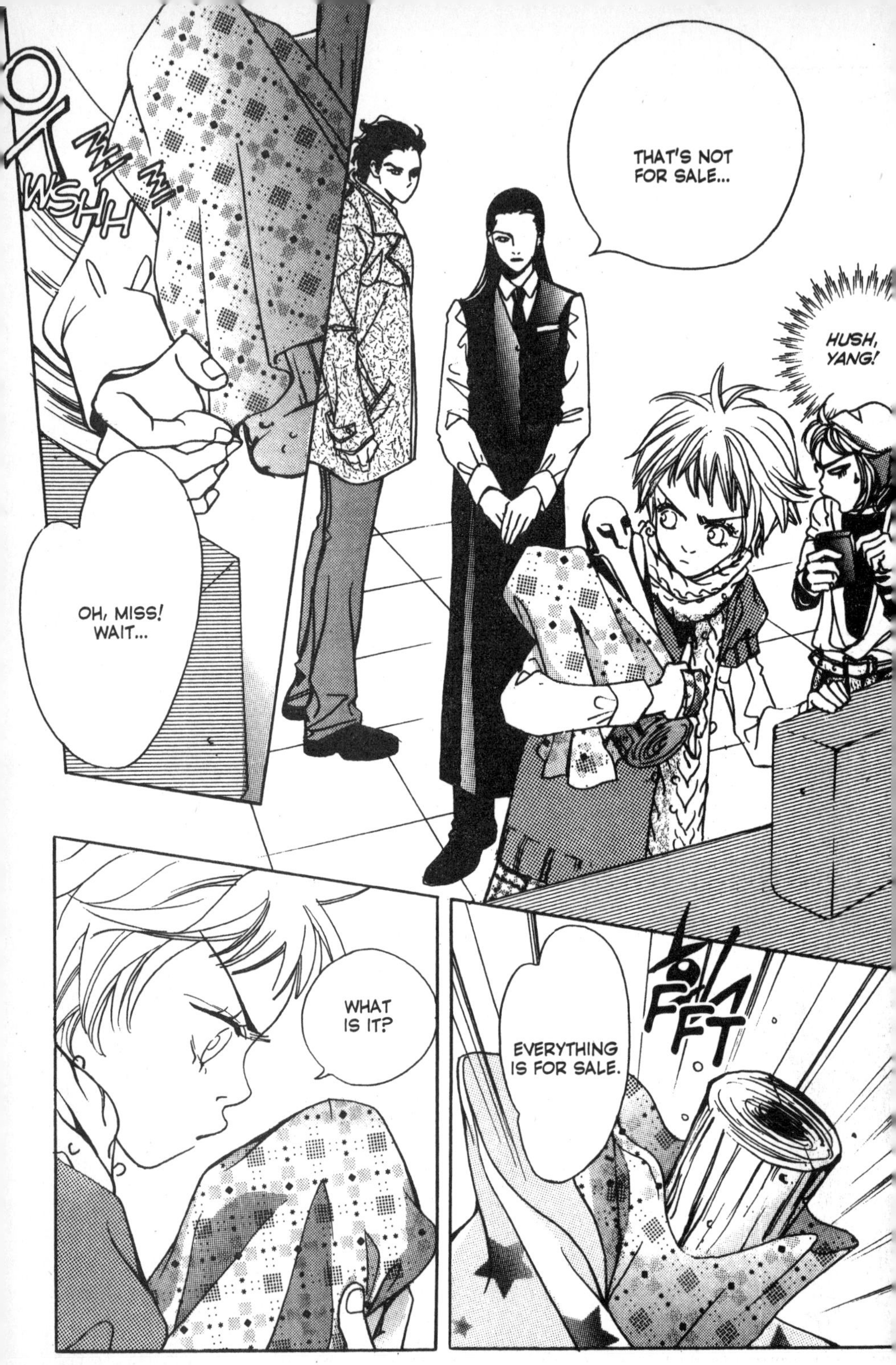
WSHH
THAT'S NOT FOR SALE...
HUSH, YANG!
OH, MISS! WAIT...
WHAT IS IT?
FFT
EVERYTHING IS FOR SALE.

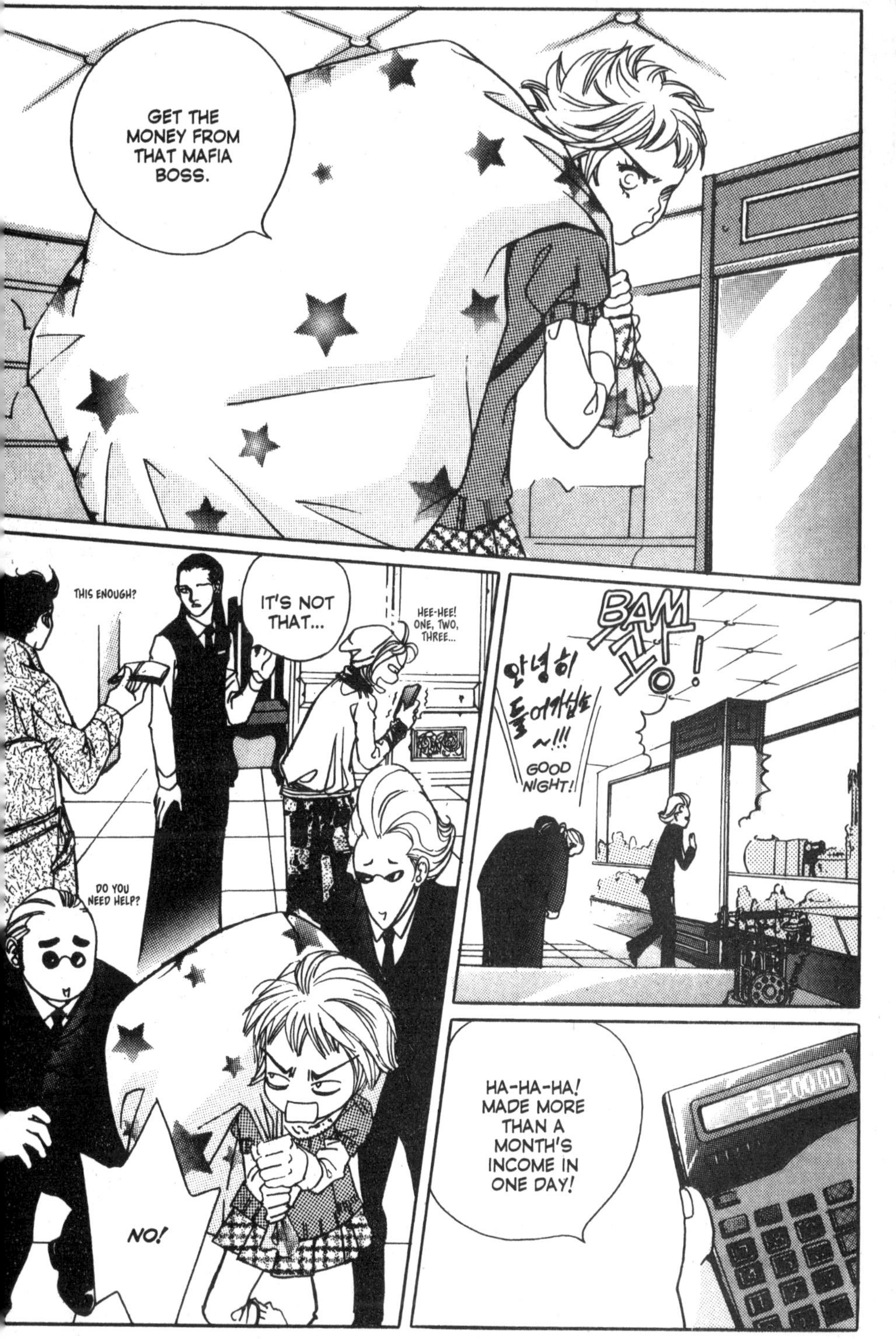
GET THE MONEY FROM THAT MAFIA BOSS.
THIS ENOUGH?
IT'S NOT THAT...
HEE-HEE! ONE, TWO, THREE...
DO YOU NEED HELP?
NO!
BAM
안녕히 들어가십쇼~!!!
GOOD NIGHT!
HA-HA-HA! MADE MORE THAN A MONTH'S INCOME IN ONE DAY!

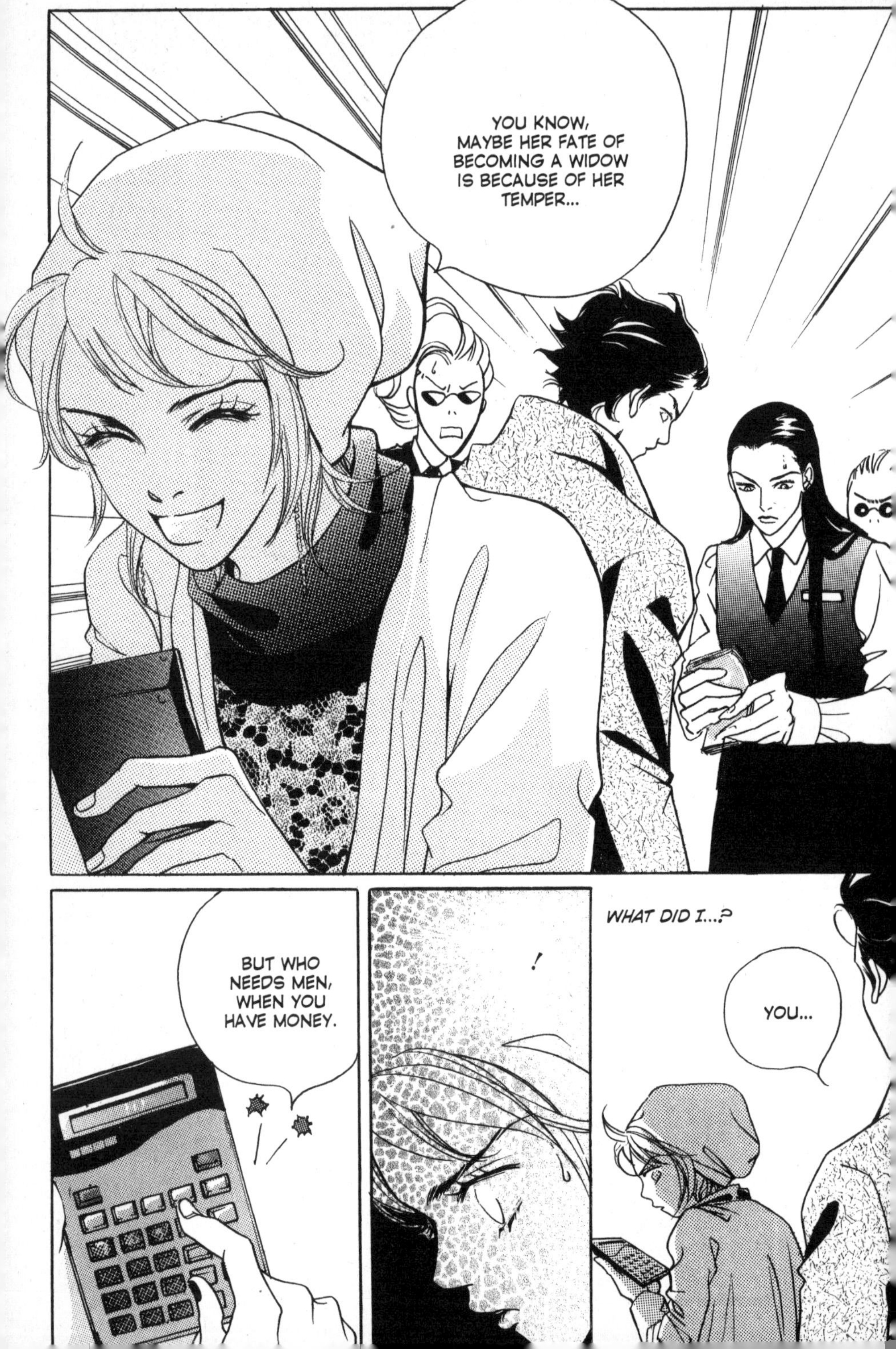
YOU KNOW, MAYBE HER FATE OF BECOMING A WIDOW IS BECAUSE OF HER TEMPER...
BUT WHO NEEDS MEN, WHEN YOU HAVE MONEY.
!
WHAT DID I...?
YOU...

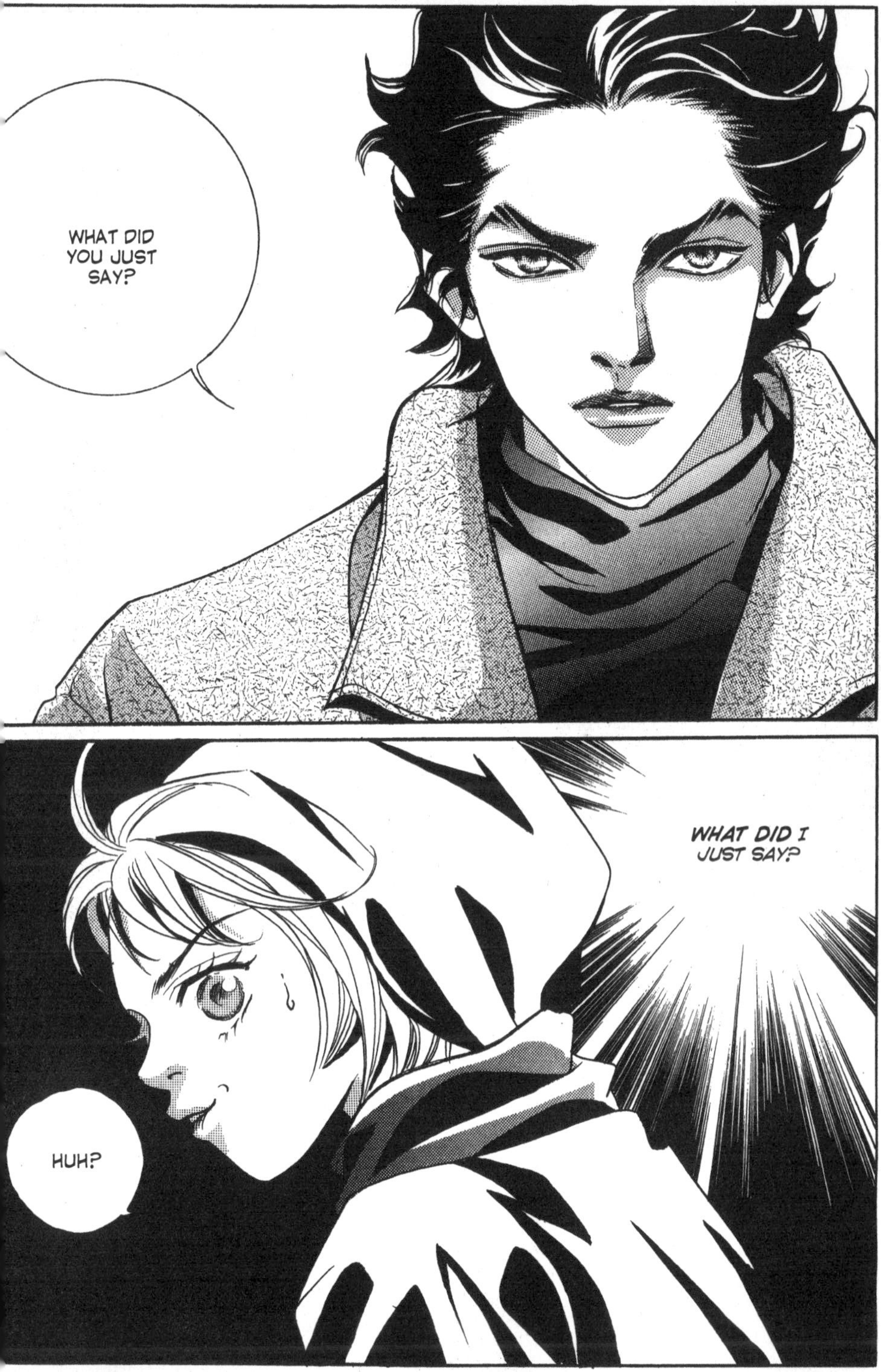
WHAT DID YOU JUST SAY?
WHAT DID I JUST SAY?
HUH?

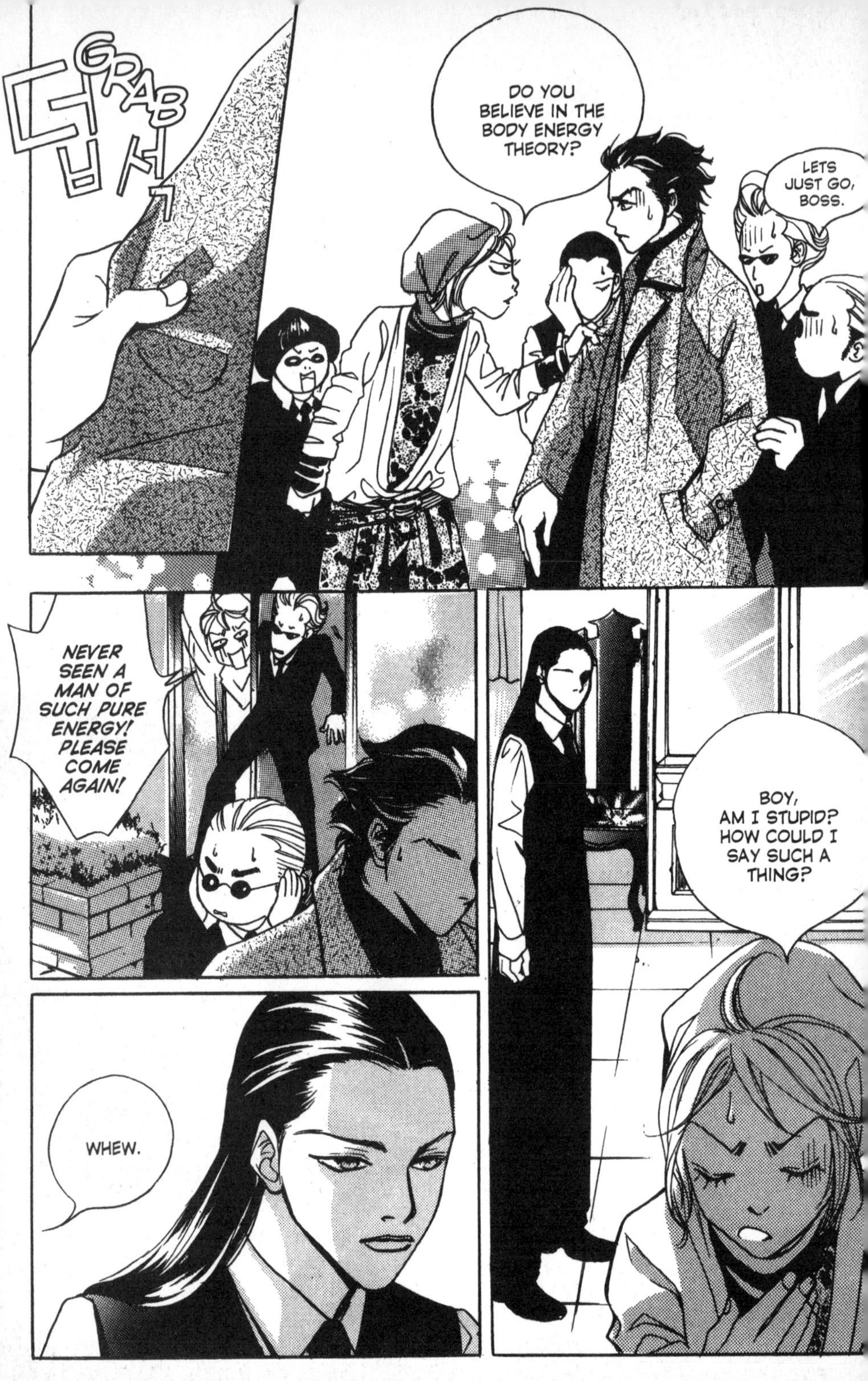

GRAB
덥석
DO YOU BELIEVE IN THE BODY ENERGY THEORY?
LETS JUST GO, BOSS.
NEVER SEEN A MAN OF SUCH PURE ENERGY! PLEASE COME AGAIN!
BOY, AM I STUPID? HOW COULD I SAY SUCH A THING?
WHEW.

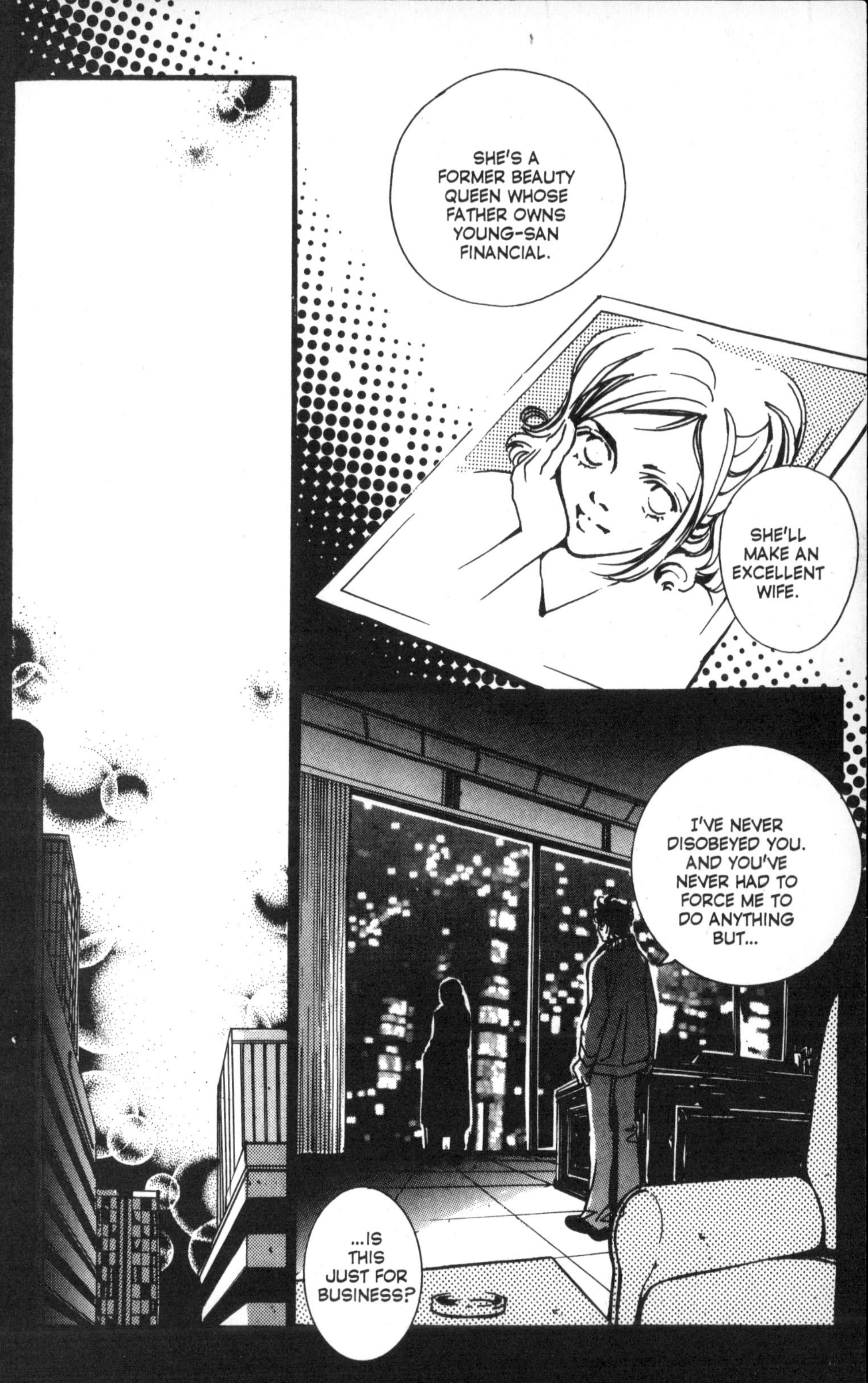
SHE'S A FORMER BEAUTY QUEEN WHOSE FATHER OWNS YOUNG-SAN FINANCIAL.
SHE'LL MAKE AN EXCELLENT WIFE.
I'VE NEVER DISOBEYED YOU. AND YOU'VE NEVER HAD TO FORCE ME TO DO ANYTHING BUT...
...IS THIS JUST FOR BUSINESS?

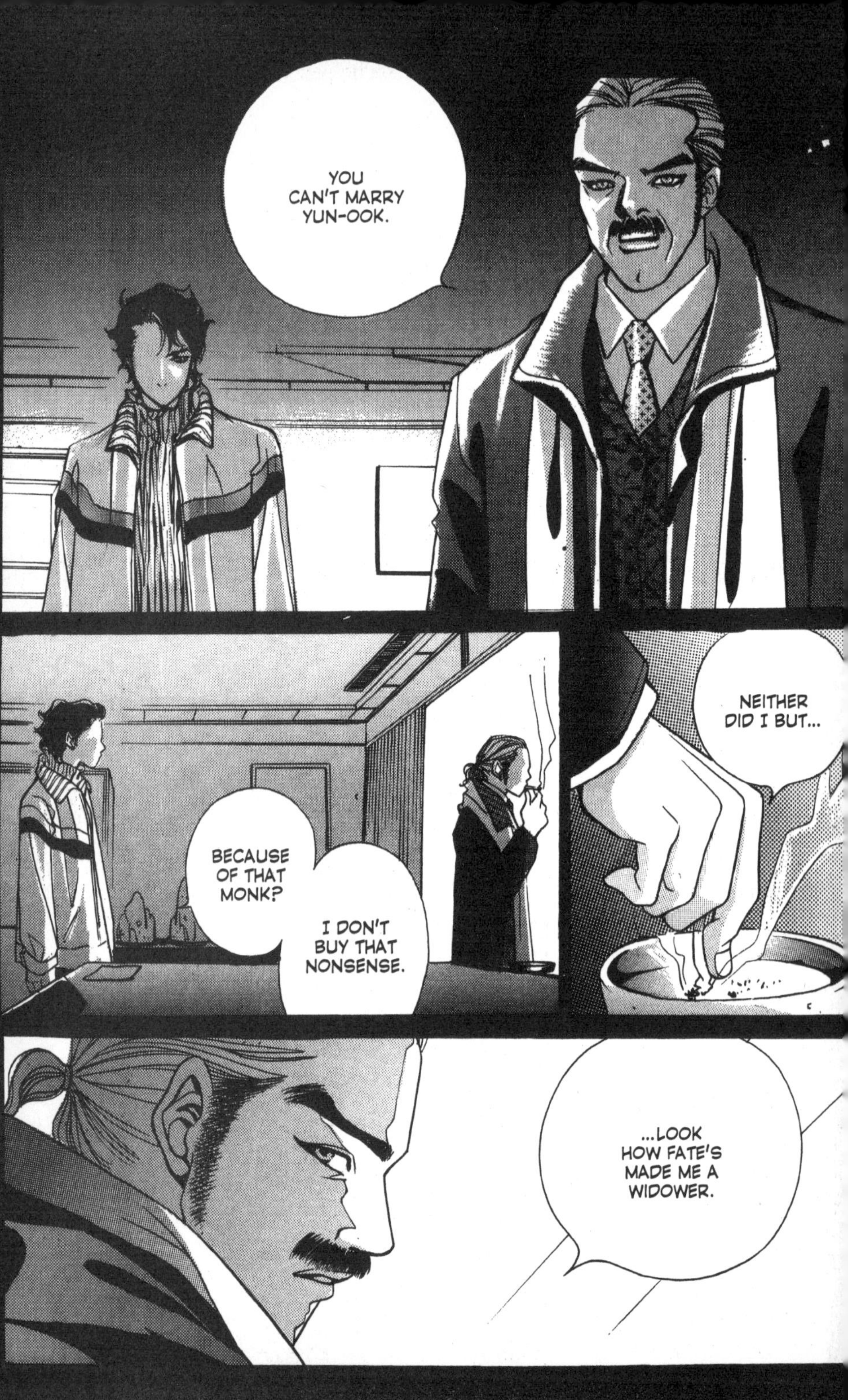
YOU CAN'T MARRY YUN-OOK.
BECAUSE OF THAT MONK?
I DON'T BUY THAT NONSENSE.
NEITHER DID I BUT...
...LOOK HOW FATE'S MADE ME A WIDOWER.

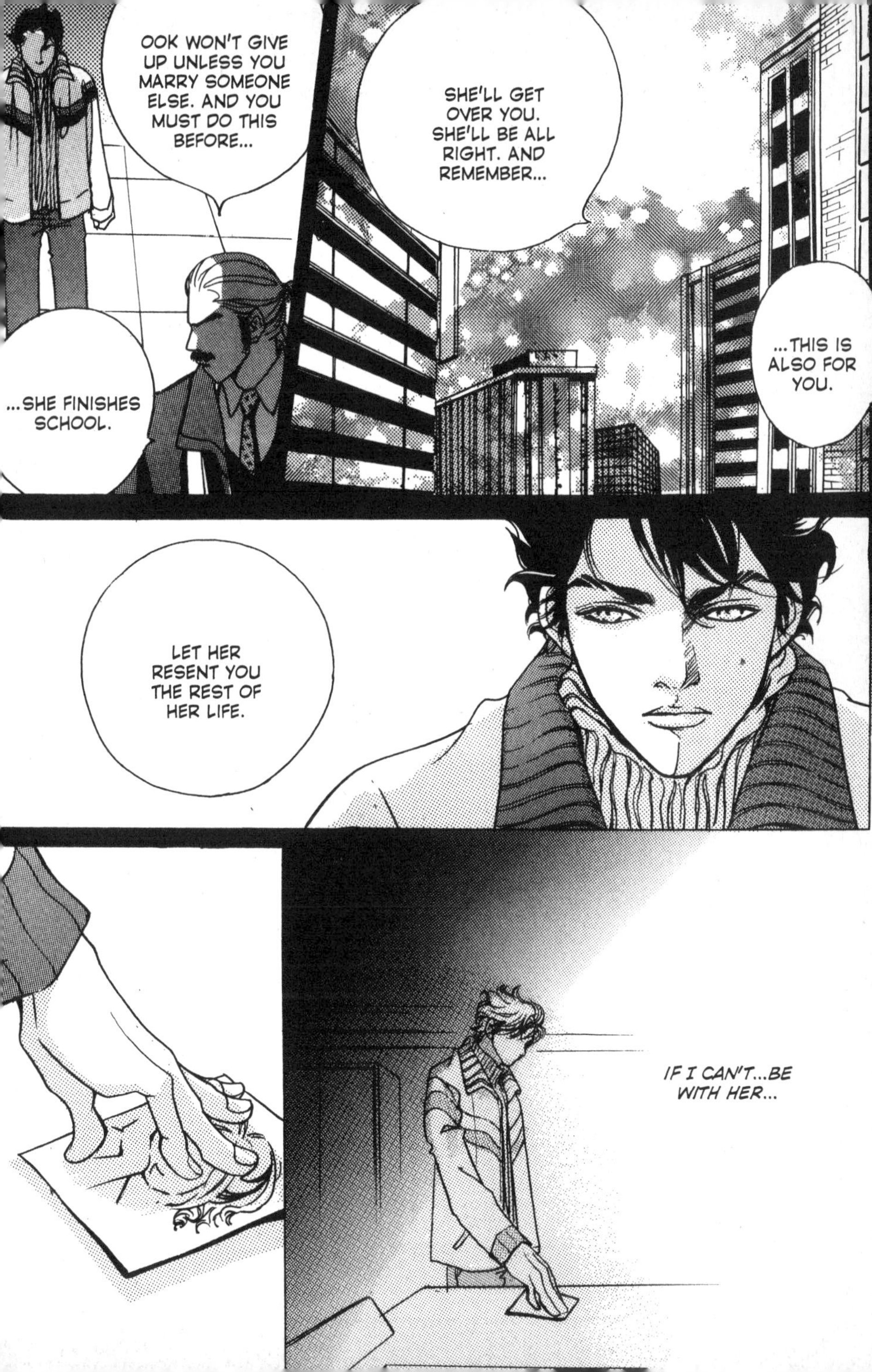
OOK WON'T GIVE UP UNLESS YOU MARRY SOMEONE ELSE. AND YOU MUST DO THIS BEFORE...
...SHE FINISHES SCHOOL.
SHE'LL GET OVER YOU. SHE'LL BE ALL RIGHT. AND REMEMBER...
...THIS IS ALSO FOR YOU.
LET HER RESENT YOU THE REST OF HER LIFE.
IF I CAN'T...BE WITH HER...

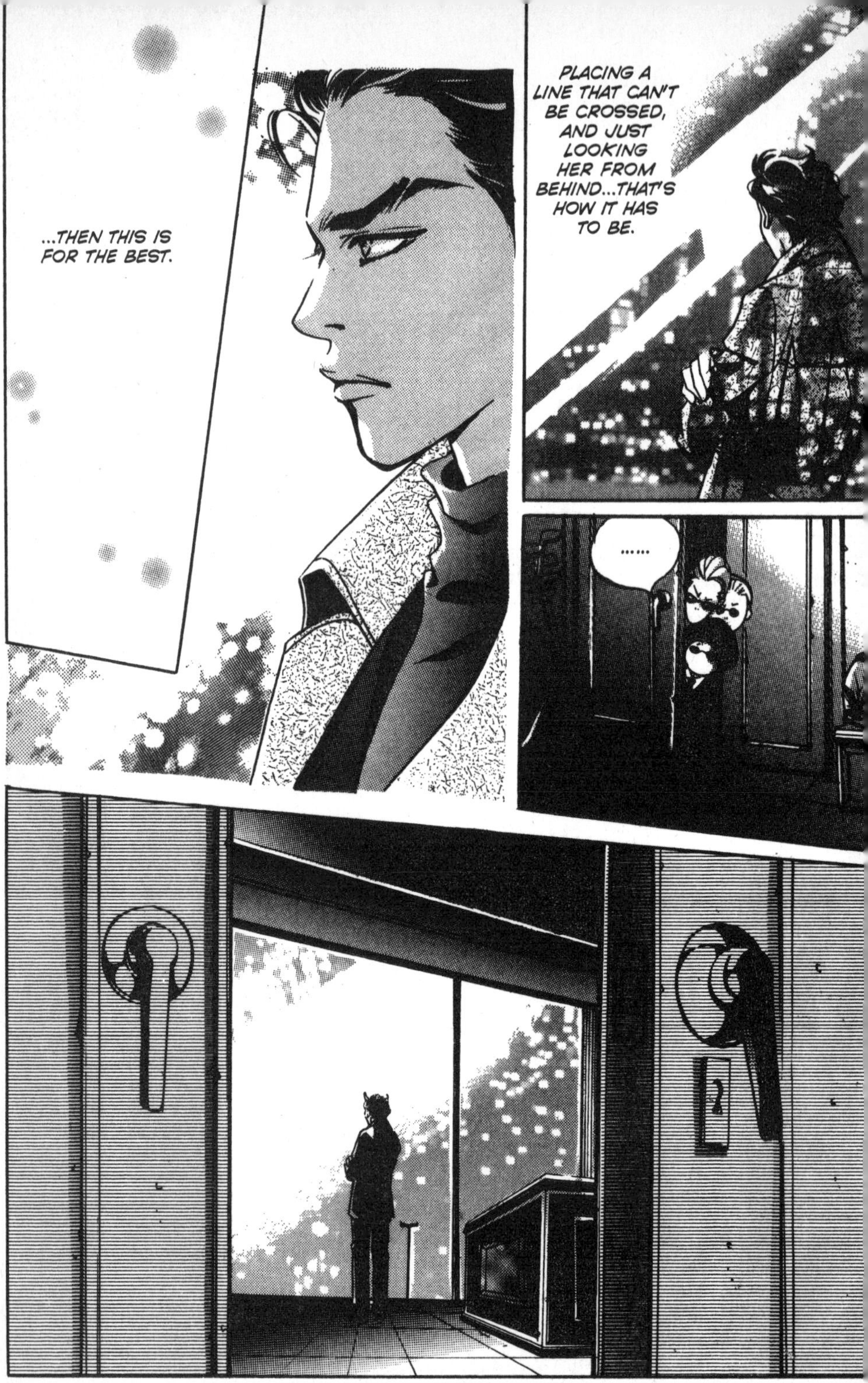
...THEN THIS IS FOR THE BEST.
PLACING A LINE THAT CAN'T BE CROSSED, AND JUST LOOKING HER FROM BEHIND...THAT'S HOW IT HAS TO BE.
......

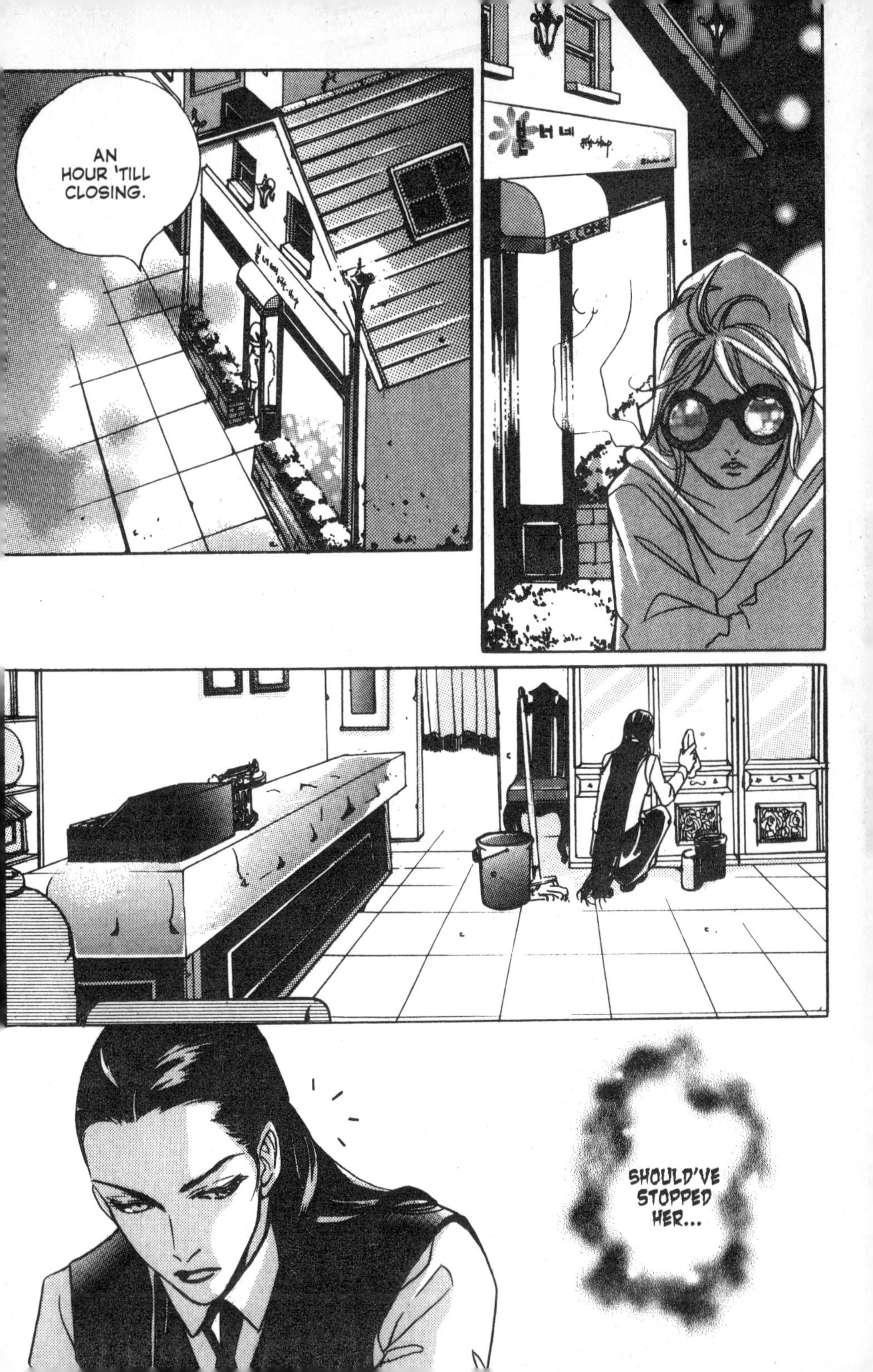
AN HOUR 'TILL CLOSING.
SHOULD'VE STOPPED HER...

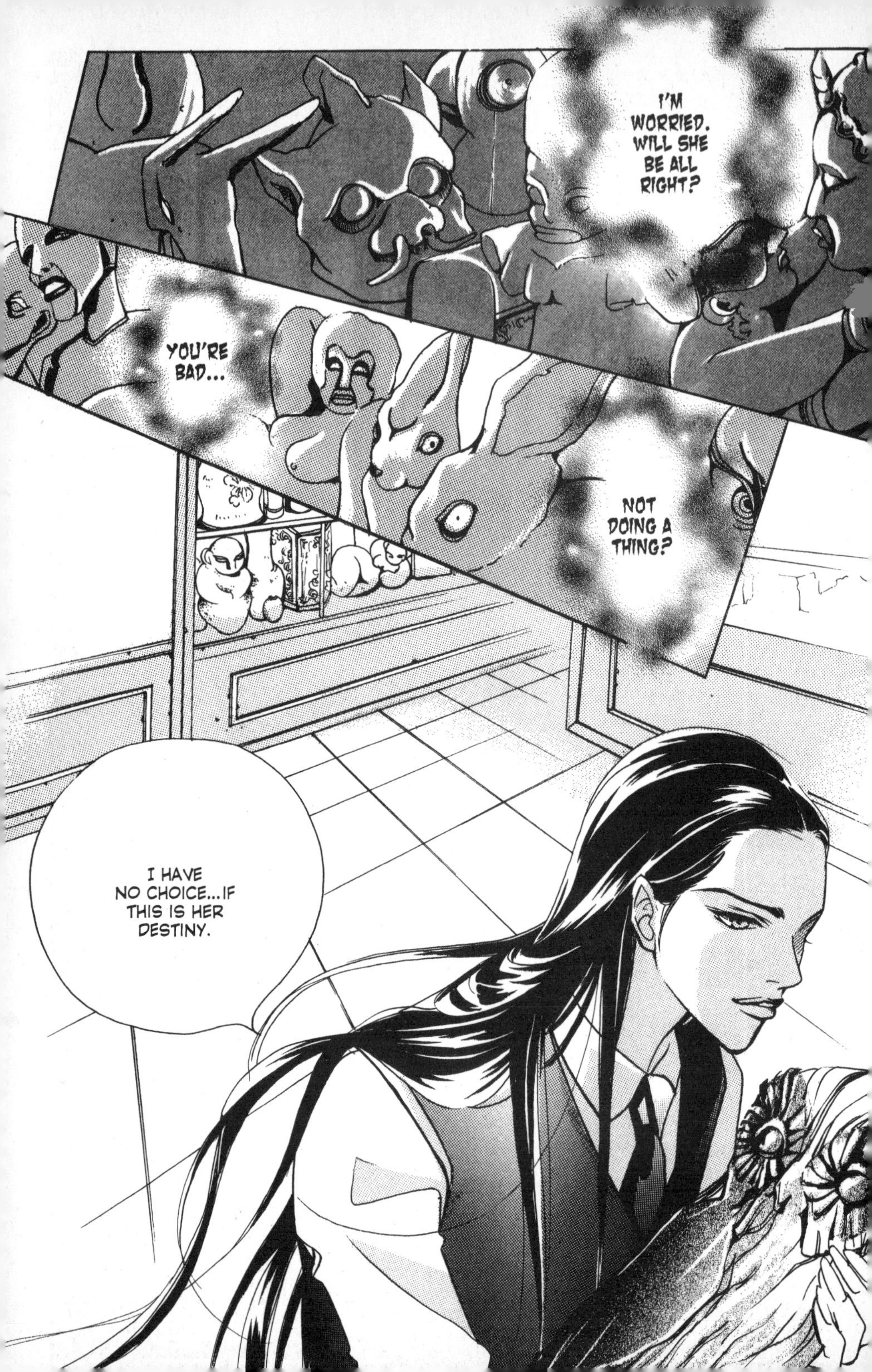
I'M WORRIED. WILL SHE BE ALL RIGHT?
YOU'RE BAD...
NOT DOING A THING?
I HAVE NO CHOICE...IF THIS IS HER DESTINY.

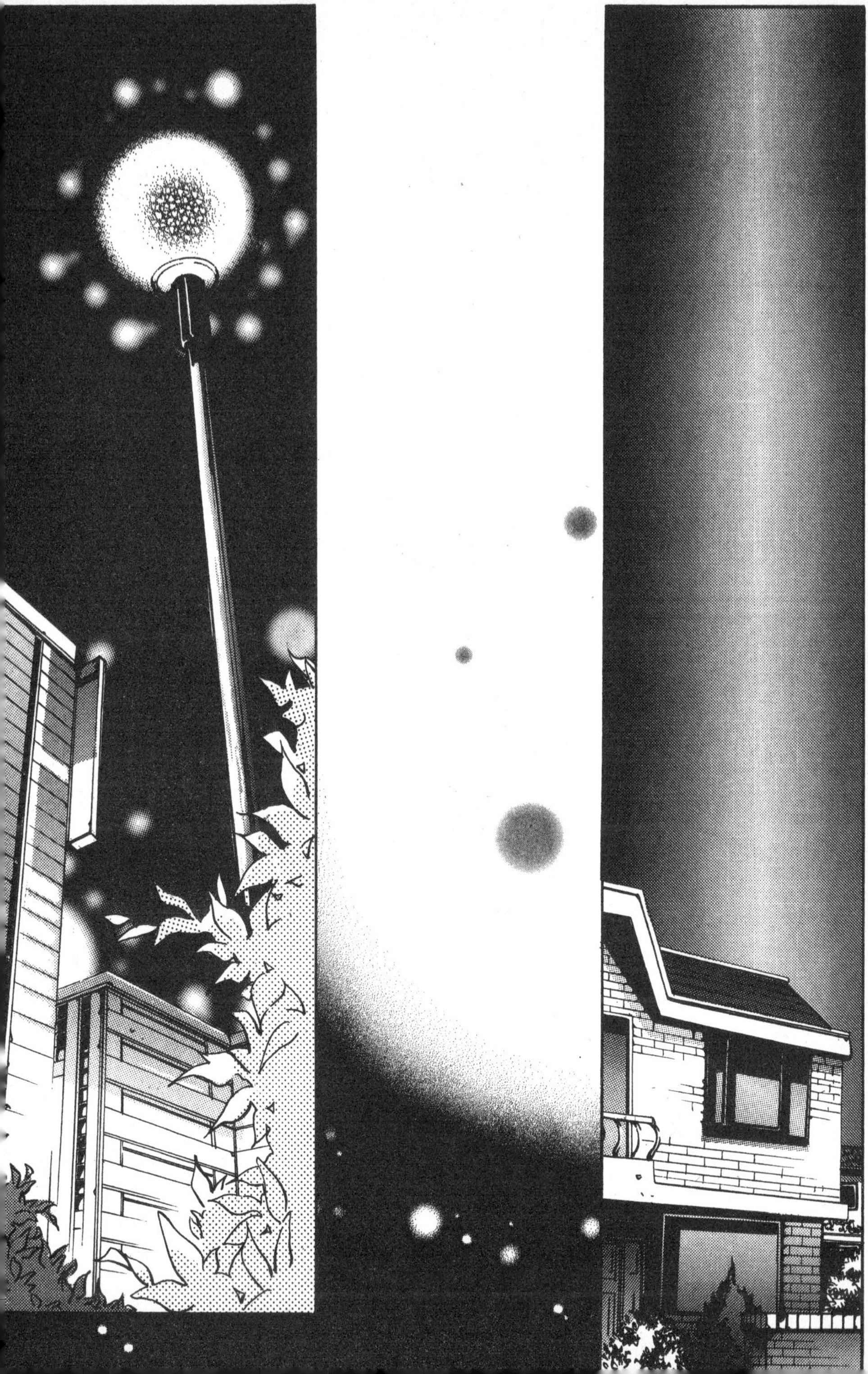

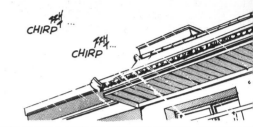

CHIRP ...

CHIRP ...

WOOZY ~

OHH...
WHAT'S...

...WRONG
WITH ME?

OHH...

SO TIRED.

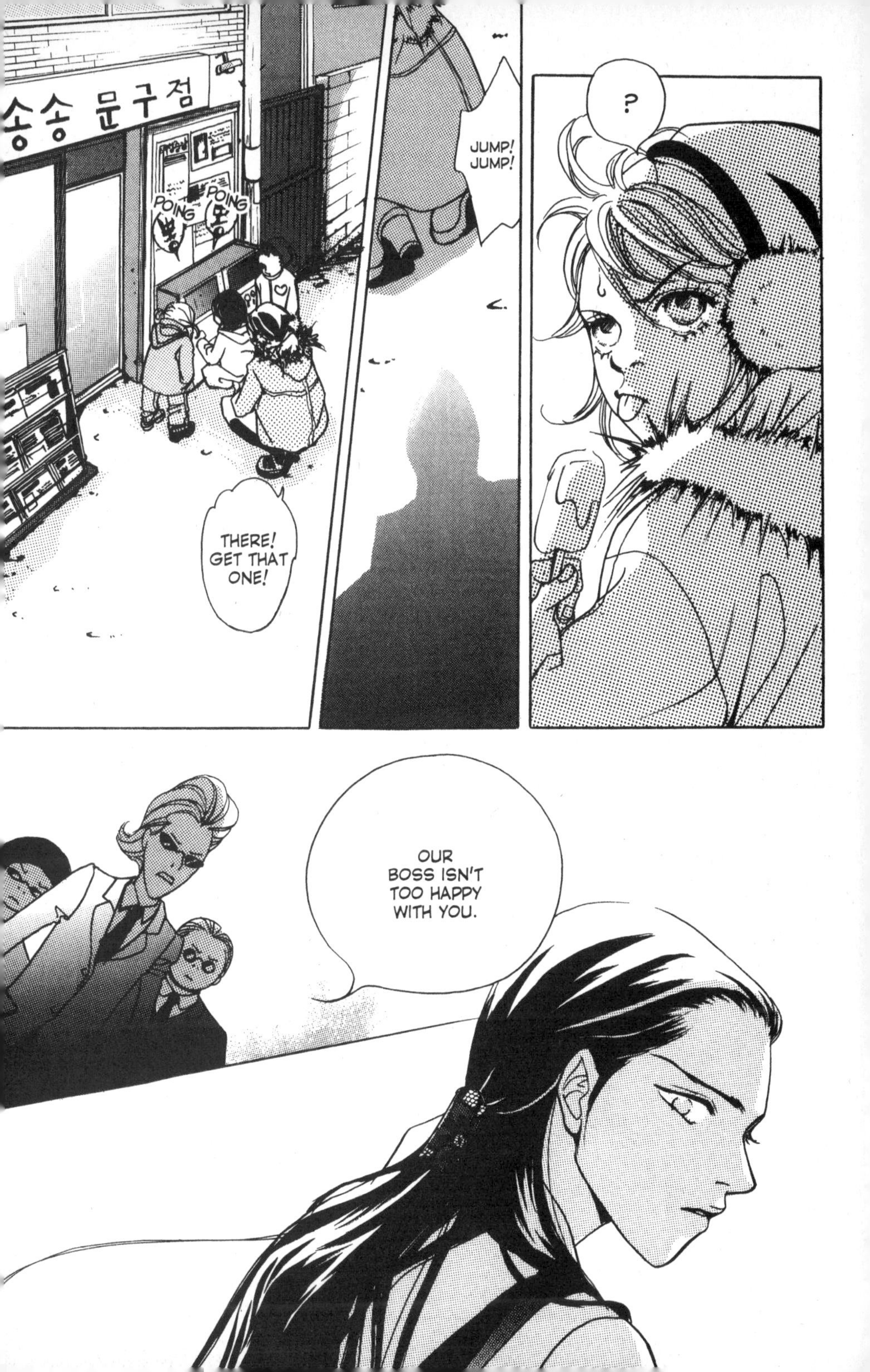
송송 문구점
POING 뽕
POING 뽕
THERE! GET THAT ONE!
JUMP! JUMP!
?
OUR BOSS ISN'T TOO HAPPY WITH YOU.

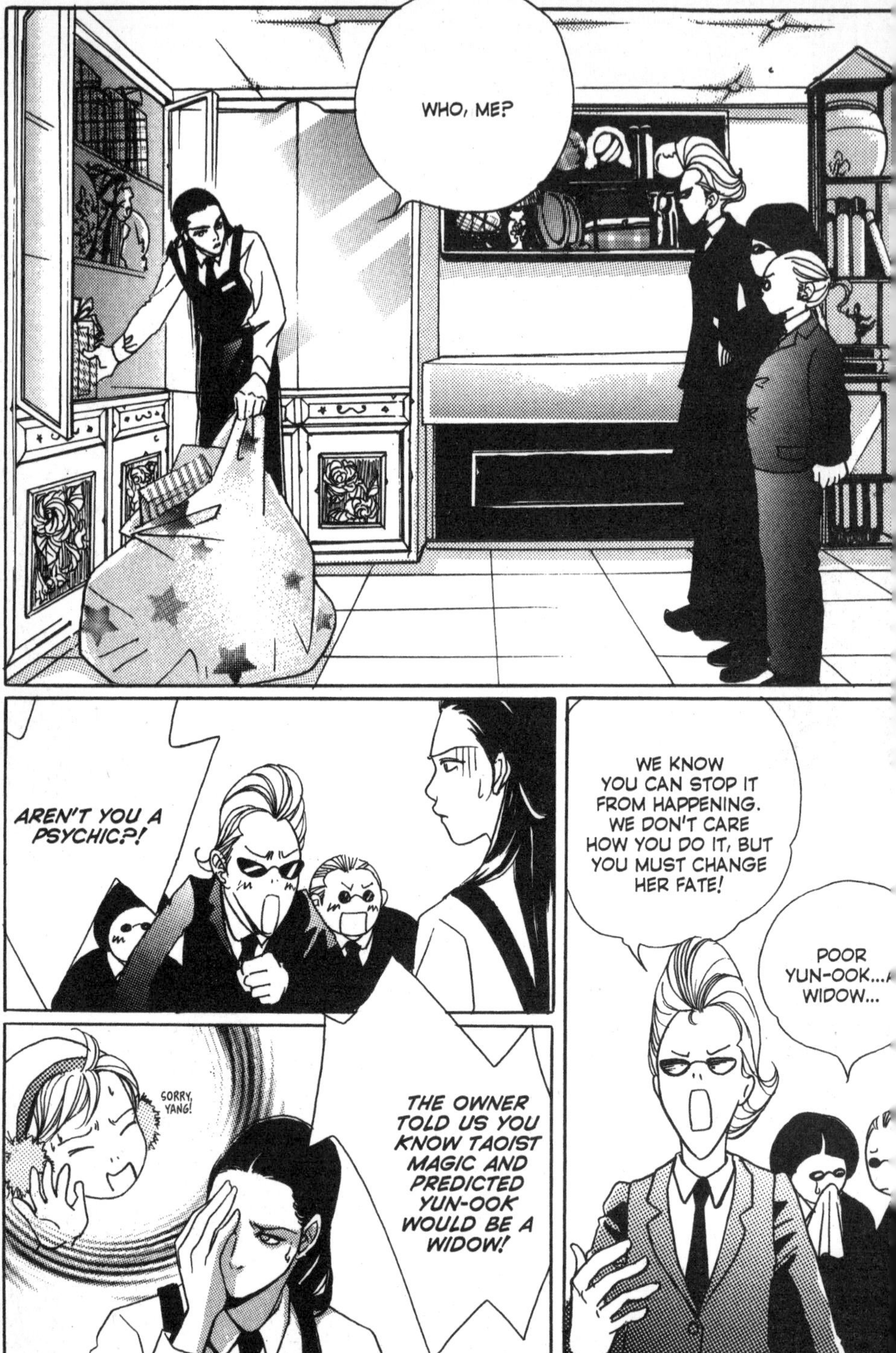
WHO, ME?
AREN'T YOU A PSYCHIC?!
SORRY, YANG!
THE OWNER TOLD US YOU KNOW TAOIST MAGIC AND PREDICTED YUN-OOK WOULD BE A WIDOW!
WE KNOW YOU CAN STOP IT FROM HAPPENING. WE DON'T CARE HOW YOU DO IT, BUT YOU MUST CHANGE HER FATE!
POOR YUN-OOK... WIDOW...

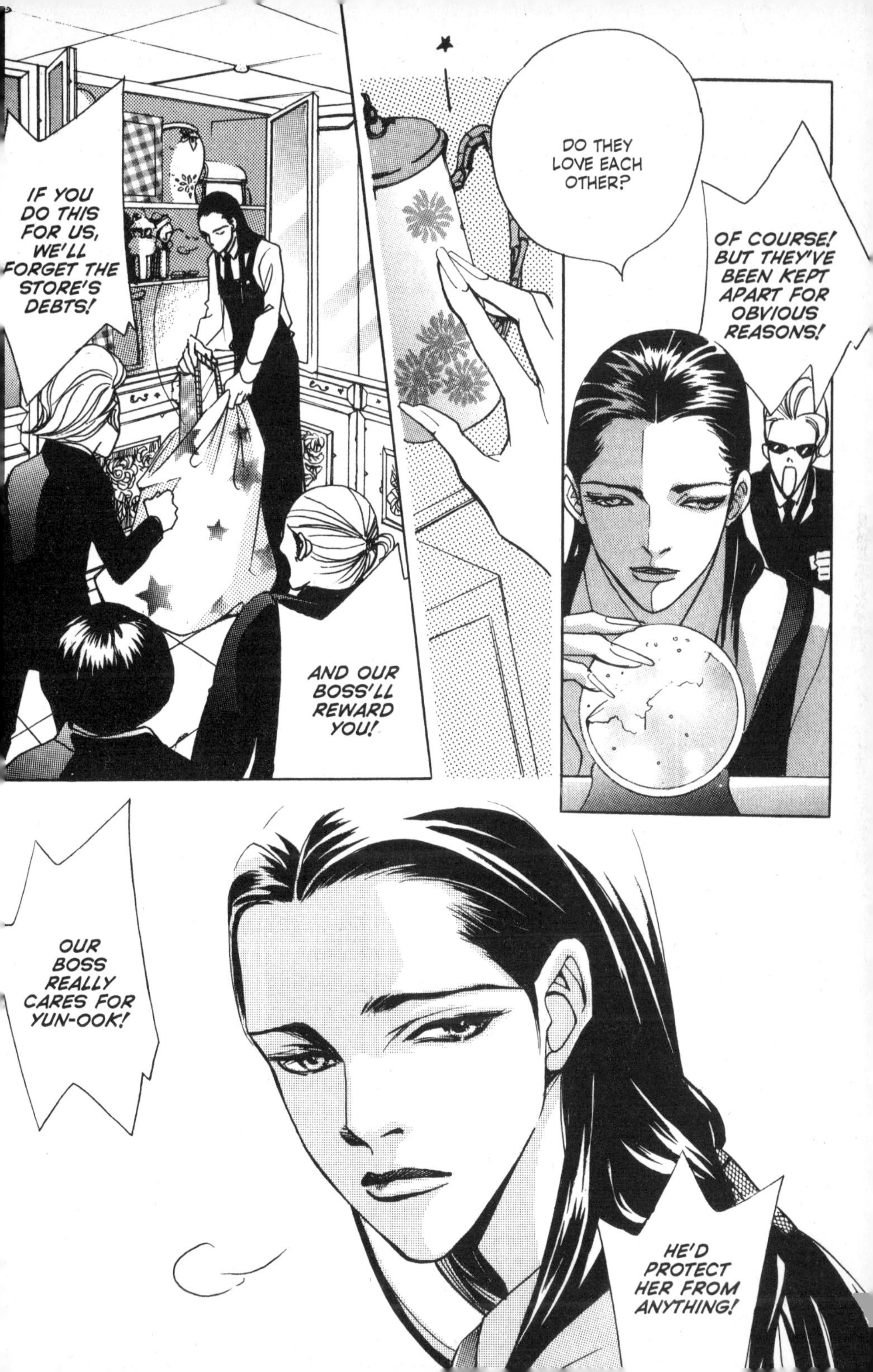
IF YOU DO THIS FOR US, WE'LL FORGET THE STORE'S DEBTS!
AND OUR BOSS'LL REWARD YOU!
DO THEY LOVE EACH OTHER?
OF COURSE! BUT THEY'VE BEEN KEPT APART FOR OBVIOUS REASONS!
OUR BOSS REALLY CARES FOR YUN-OOK!
HE'D PROTECT HER FROM ANYTHING!

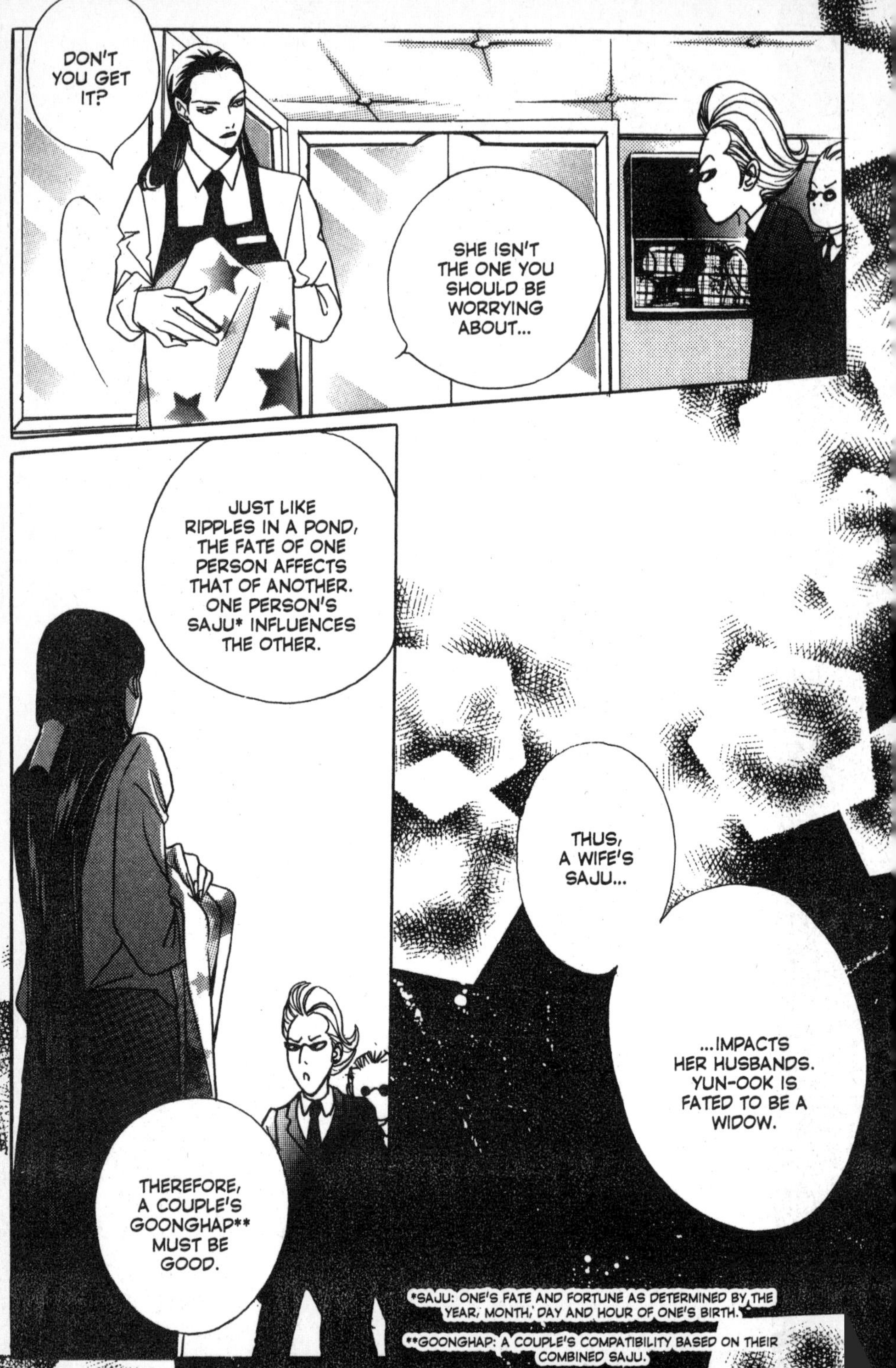
DON'T YOU GET IT?
SHE ISN'T THE ONE YOU SHOULD BE WORRYING ABOUT...
JUST LIKE RIPPLES IN A POND, THE FATE OF ONE PERSON AFFECTS THAT OF ANOTHER. ONE PERSON'S SAJU* INFLUENCES THE OTHER.
THEREFORE, A COUPLE'S GOONGHAP** MUST BE GOOD.
THUS, A WIFE'S SAJU...
...IMPACTS HER HUSBANDS. YUN-OOK IS FATED TO BE A WIDOW.
*SAJU: ONE'S FATE AND FORTUNE AS DETERMINED BY THE YEAR, MONTH, DAY AND HOUR OF ONE'S BIRTH.
**GOONGHAP: A COUPLE'S COMPATIBILITY BASED ON THEIR COMBINED SAJU.

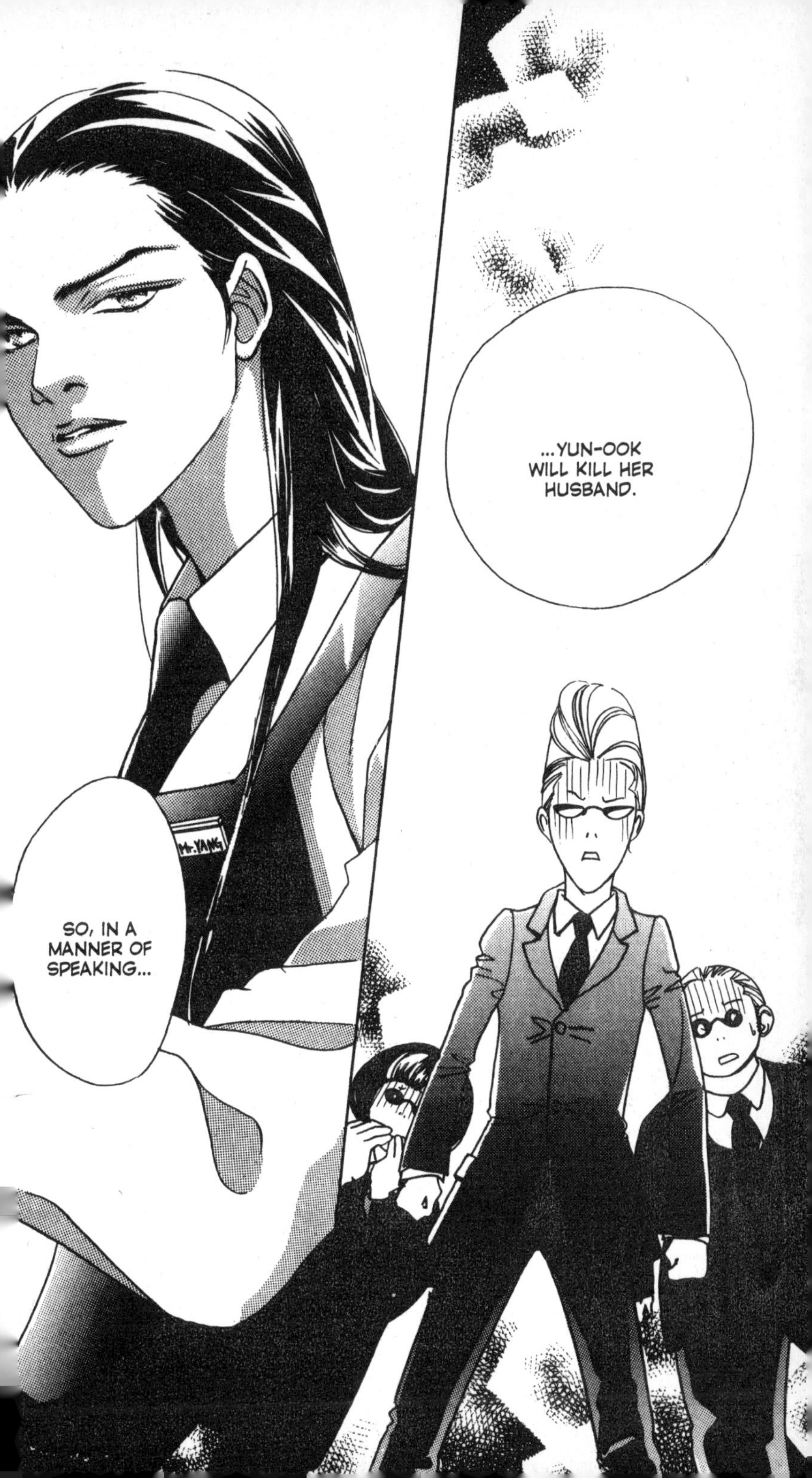
Mr.YANG
SO, IN A MANNER OF SPEAKING...
...YUN-OOK WILL KILL HER HUSBAND.

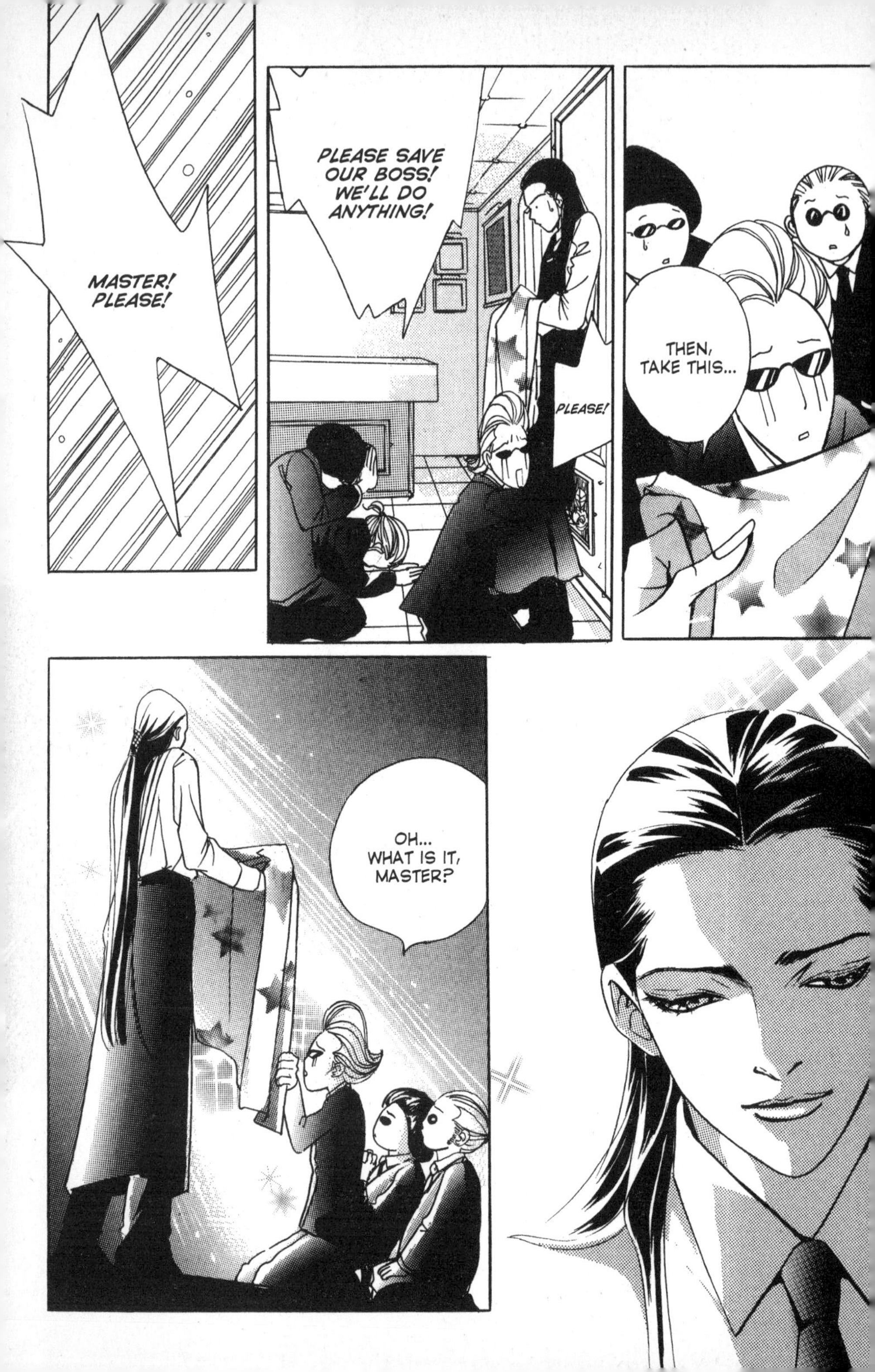
MASTER! PLEASE!
PLEASE SAVE OUR BOSS! WE'LL DO ANYTHING!
PLEASE!
THEN, TAKE THIS...
OH... WHAT IS IT, MASTER?

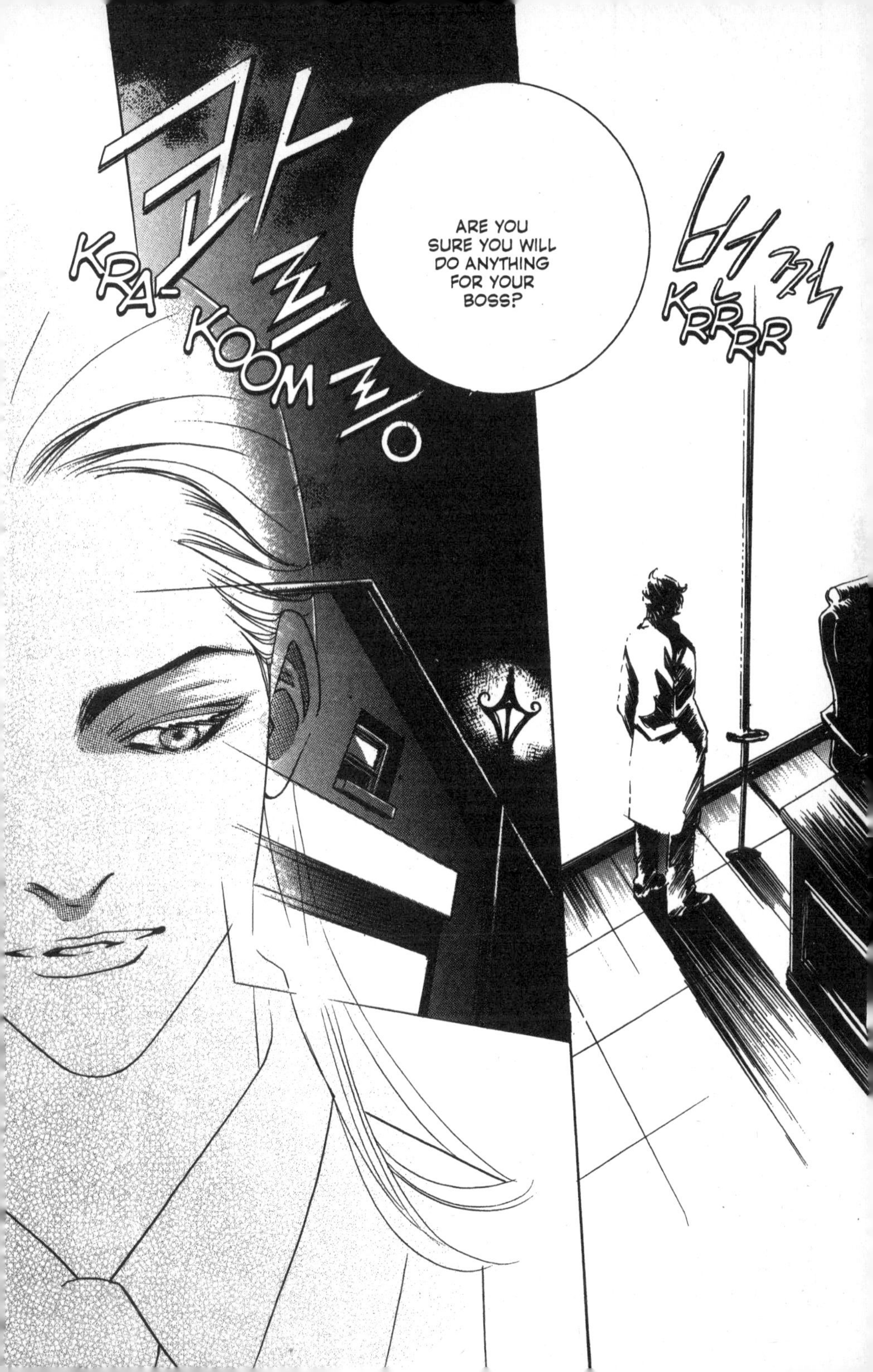
KRA-KOOM
ARE YOU SURE YOU WILL DO ANYTHING FOR YOUR BOSS?
KRRRR

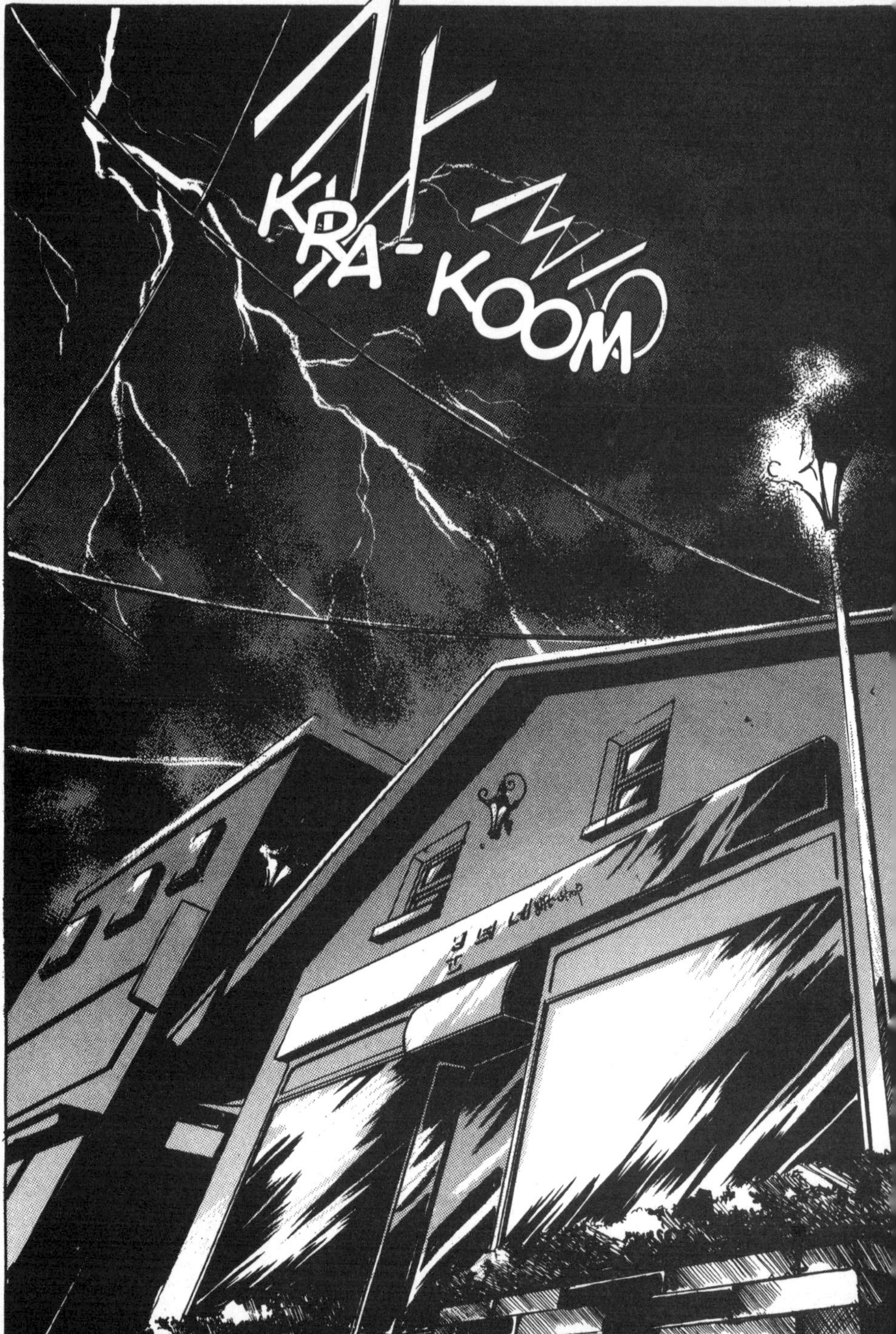
KRA-KOOM

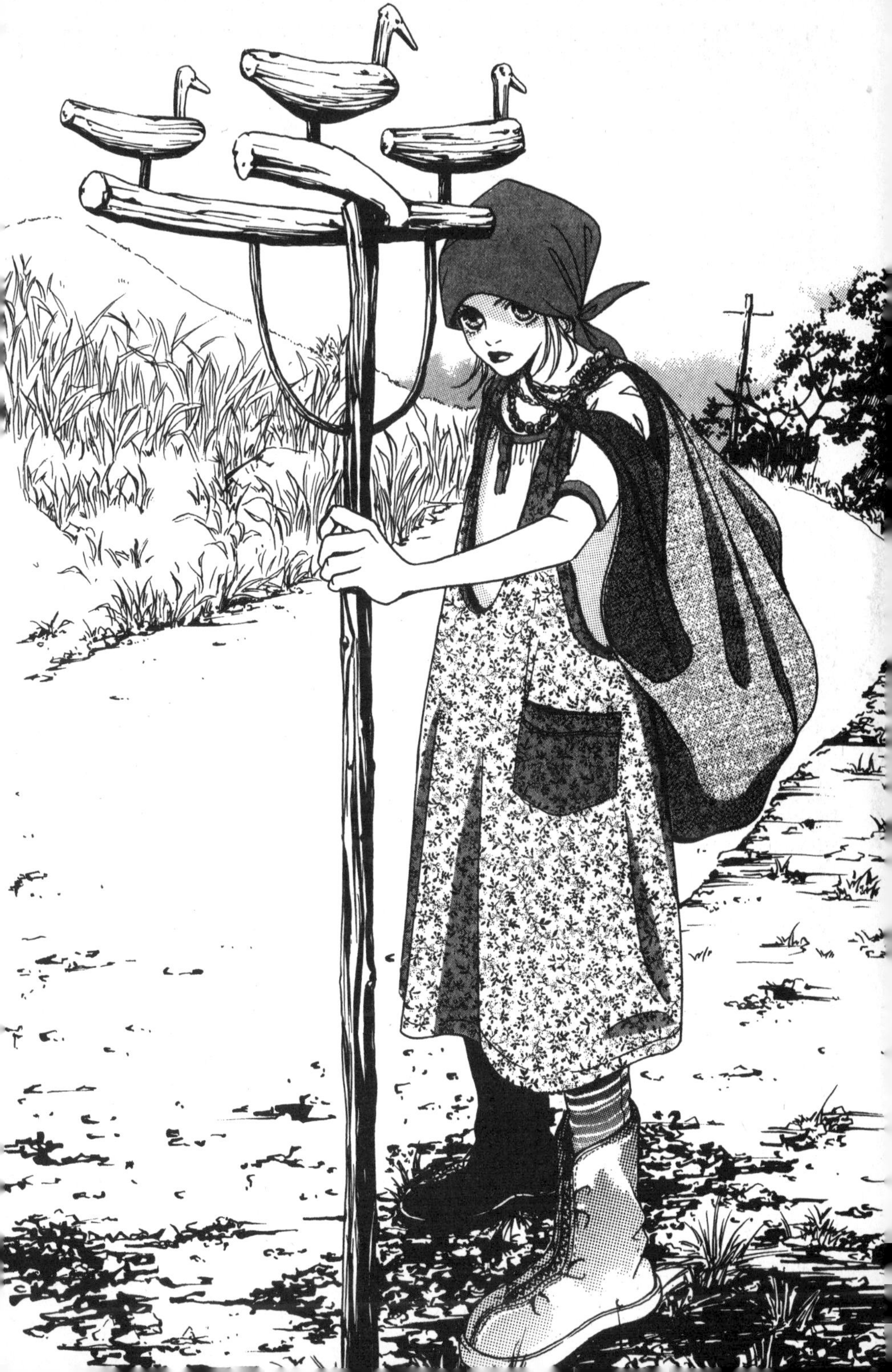

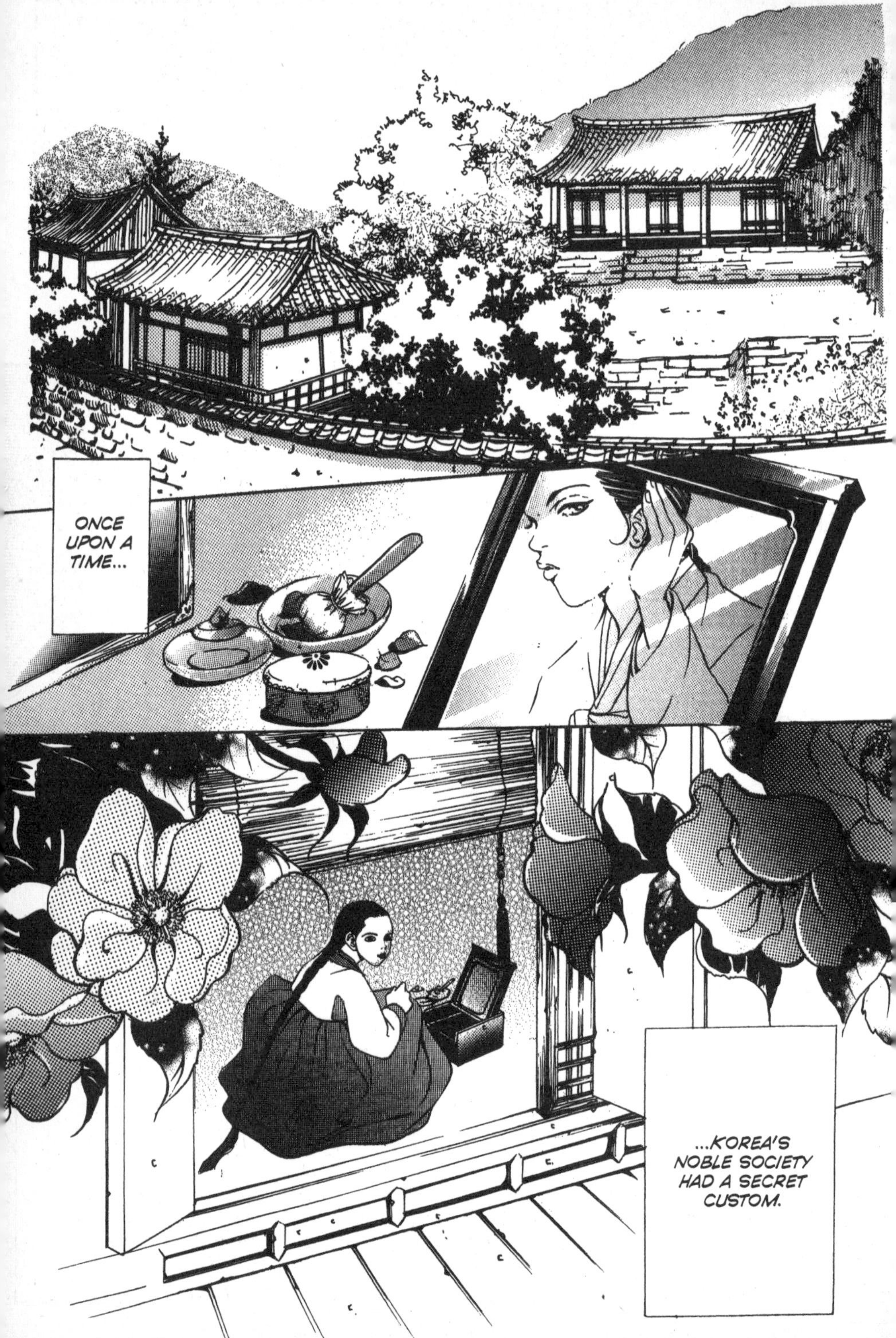
ONCE UPON A TIME...
...KOREA'S NOBLE SOCIETY HAD A SECRET CUSTOM.

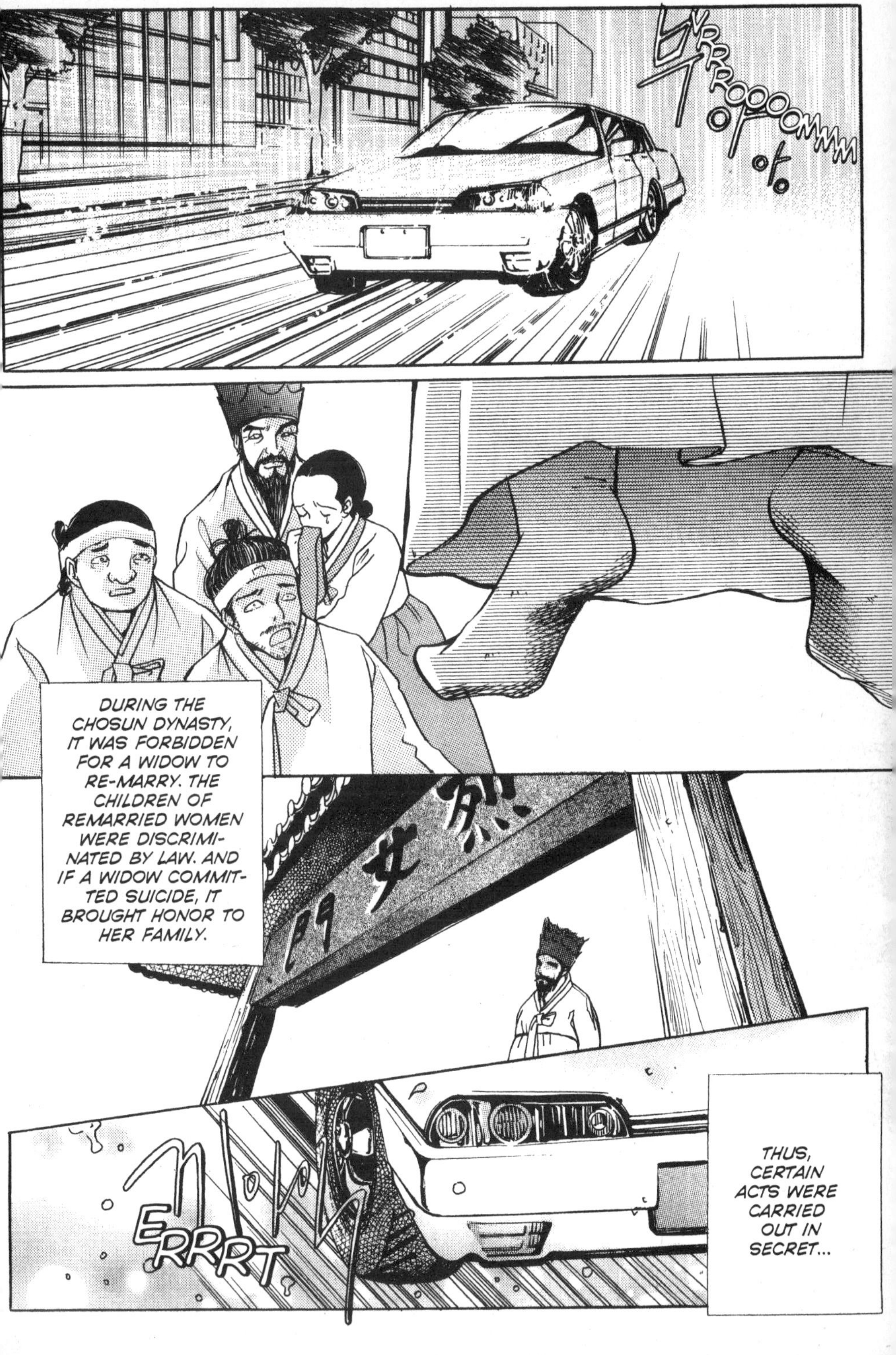
VRRROOOOOMMMM
DURING THE CHOSUN DYNASTY, IT WAS FORBIDDEN FOR A WIDOW TO RE-MARRY. THE CHILDREN OF REMARRIED WOMEN WERE DISCRIMI-NATED BY LAW. AND IF A WIDOW COMMIT-TED SUICIDE, IT BROUGHT HONOR TO HER FAMILY.
ERRRT
THUS, CERTAIN ACTS WERE CARRIED OUT IN SECRET...

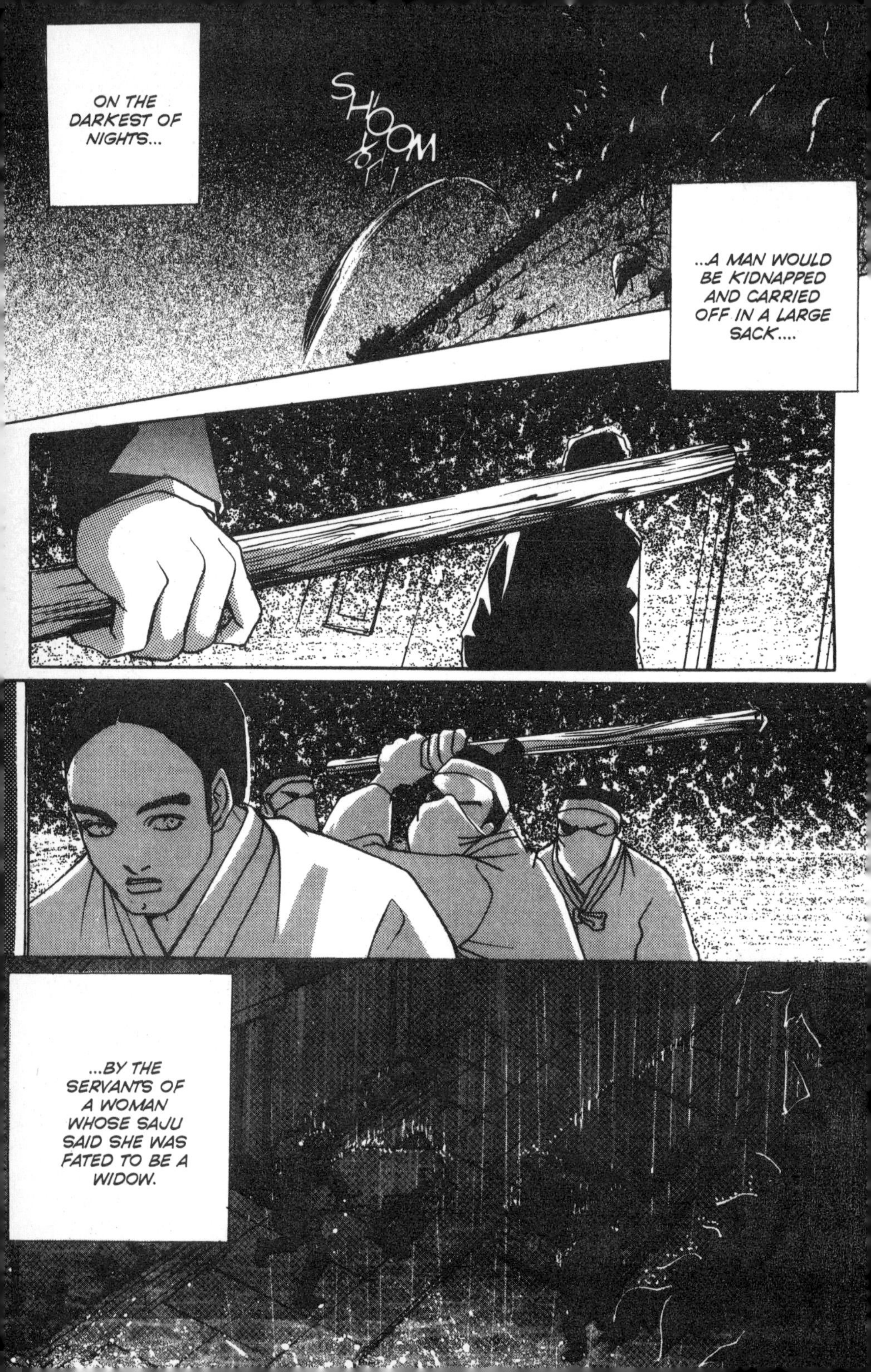
ON THE DARKEST OF NIGHTS...
SHOOM
...A MAN WOULD BE KIDNAPPED AND CARRIED OFF IN A LARGE SACK....
...BY THE SERVANTS OF A WOMAN WHOSE SAJU SAID SHE WAS FATED TO BE A WIDOW.

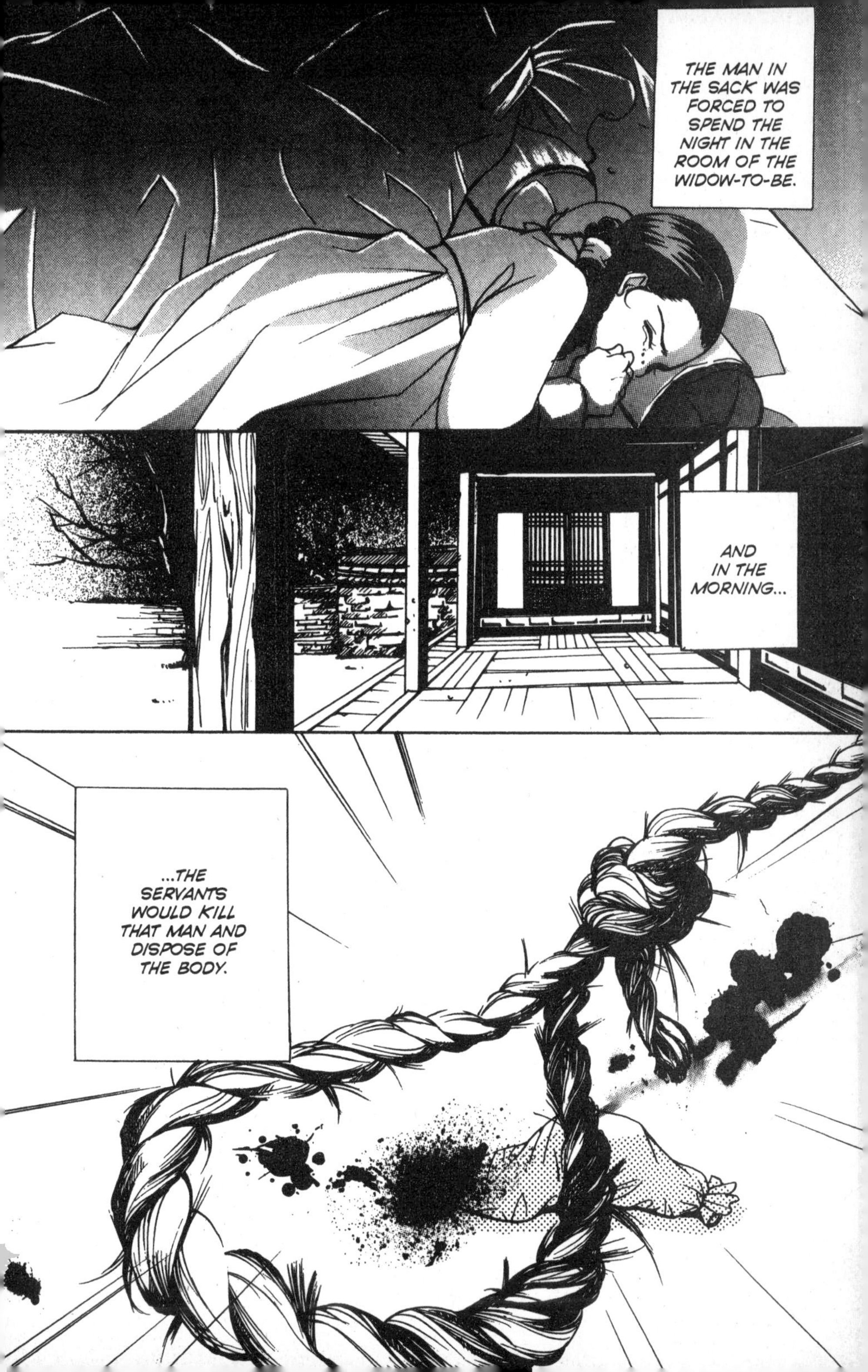
THE MAN IN THE SACK WAS FORCED TO SPEND THE NIGHT IN THE ROOM OF THE WIDOW-TO-BE.
AND IN THE MORNING...
...THE SERVANTS WOULD KILL THAT MAN AND DISPOSE OF THE BODY.

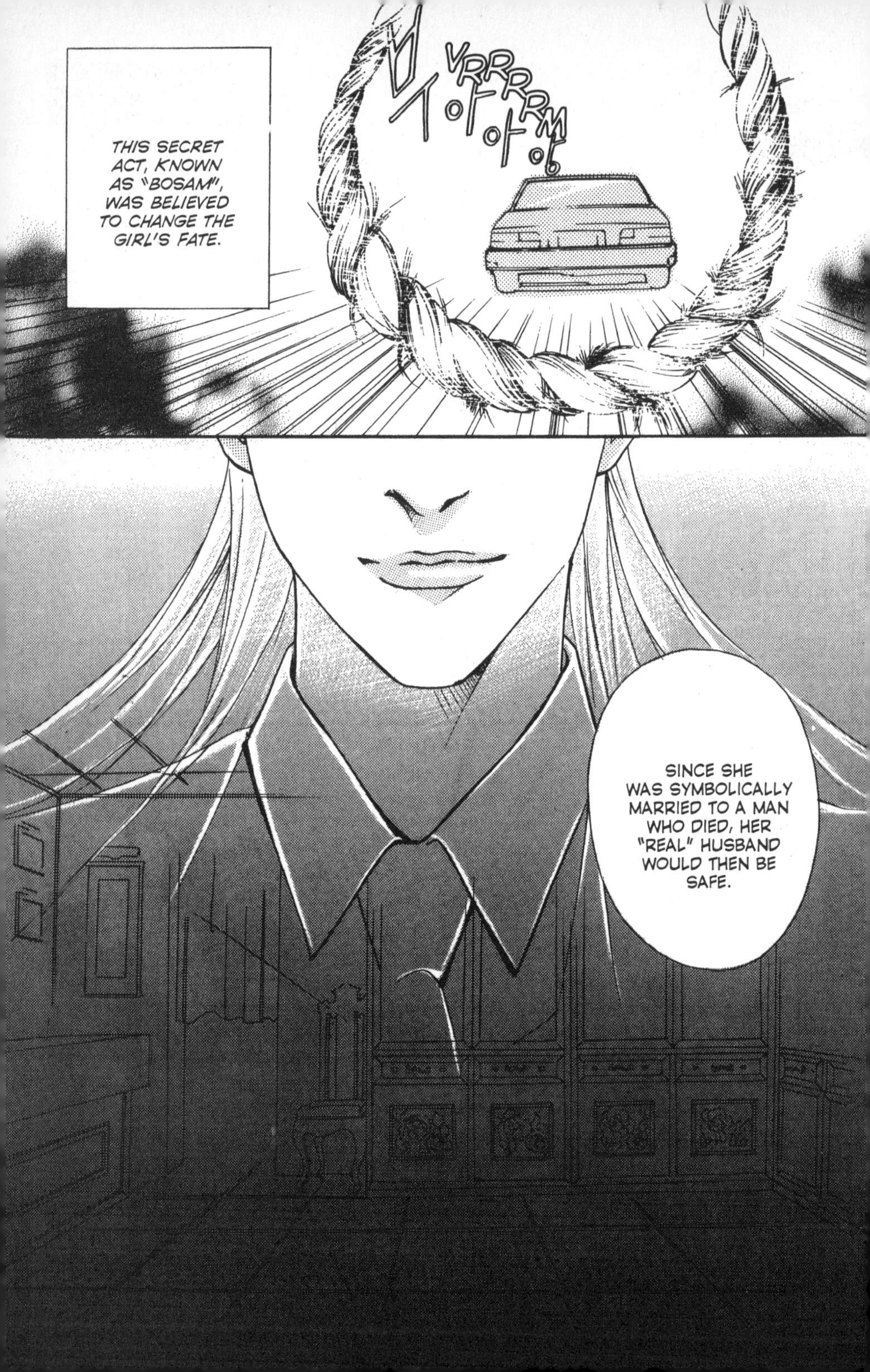
THIS SECRET ACT, KNOWN AS "BOSAM", WAS BELIEVED TO CHANGE THE GIRL'S FATE.
부아아앙
VRRRRM
SINCE SHE WAS SYMBOLICALLY MARRIED TO A MAN WHO DIED, HER "REAL" HUSBAND WOULD THEN BE SAFE.

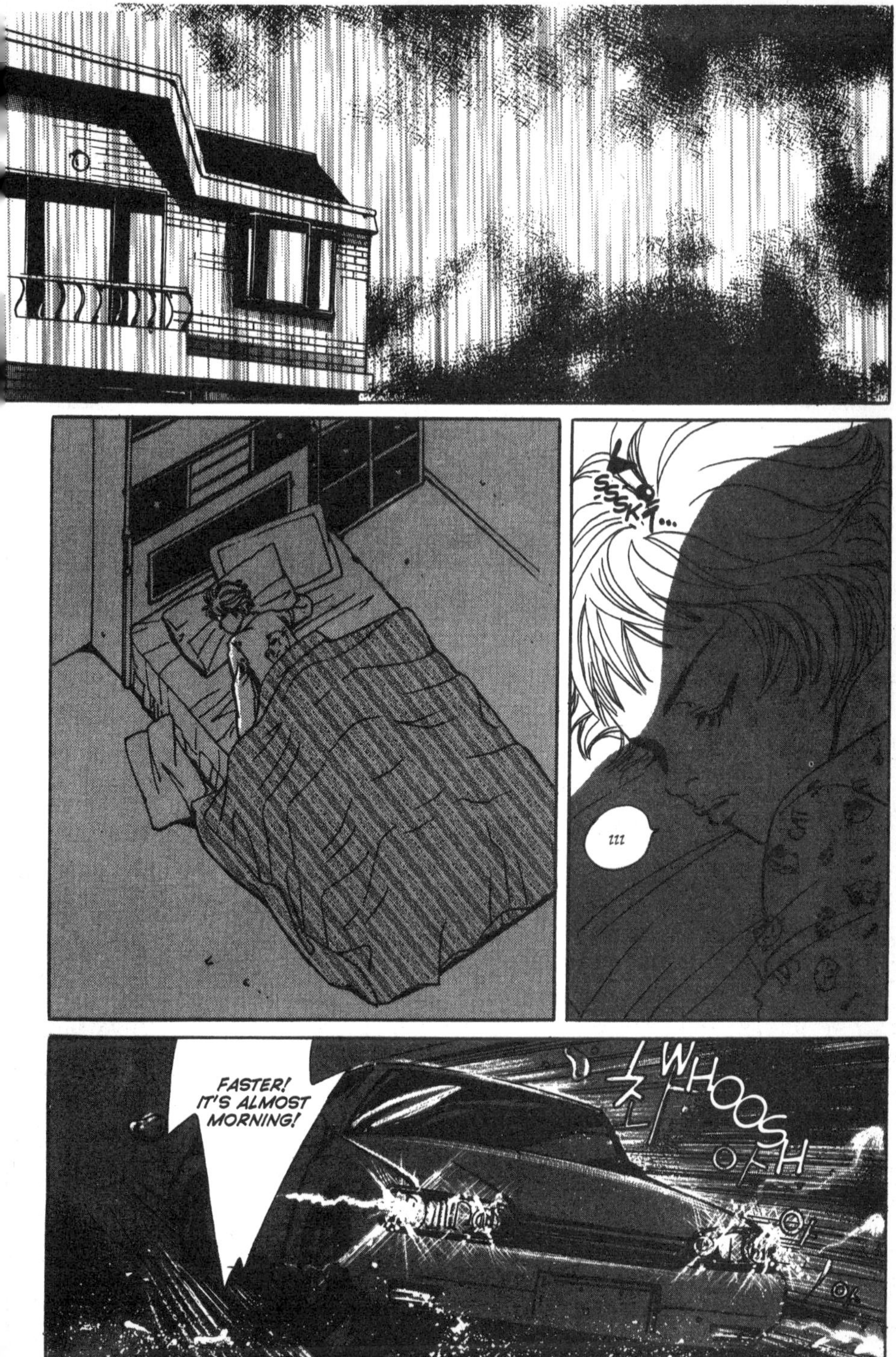
SSSKA...
zzz
FASTER! IT'S ALMOST MORNING!
WHOOSH

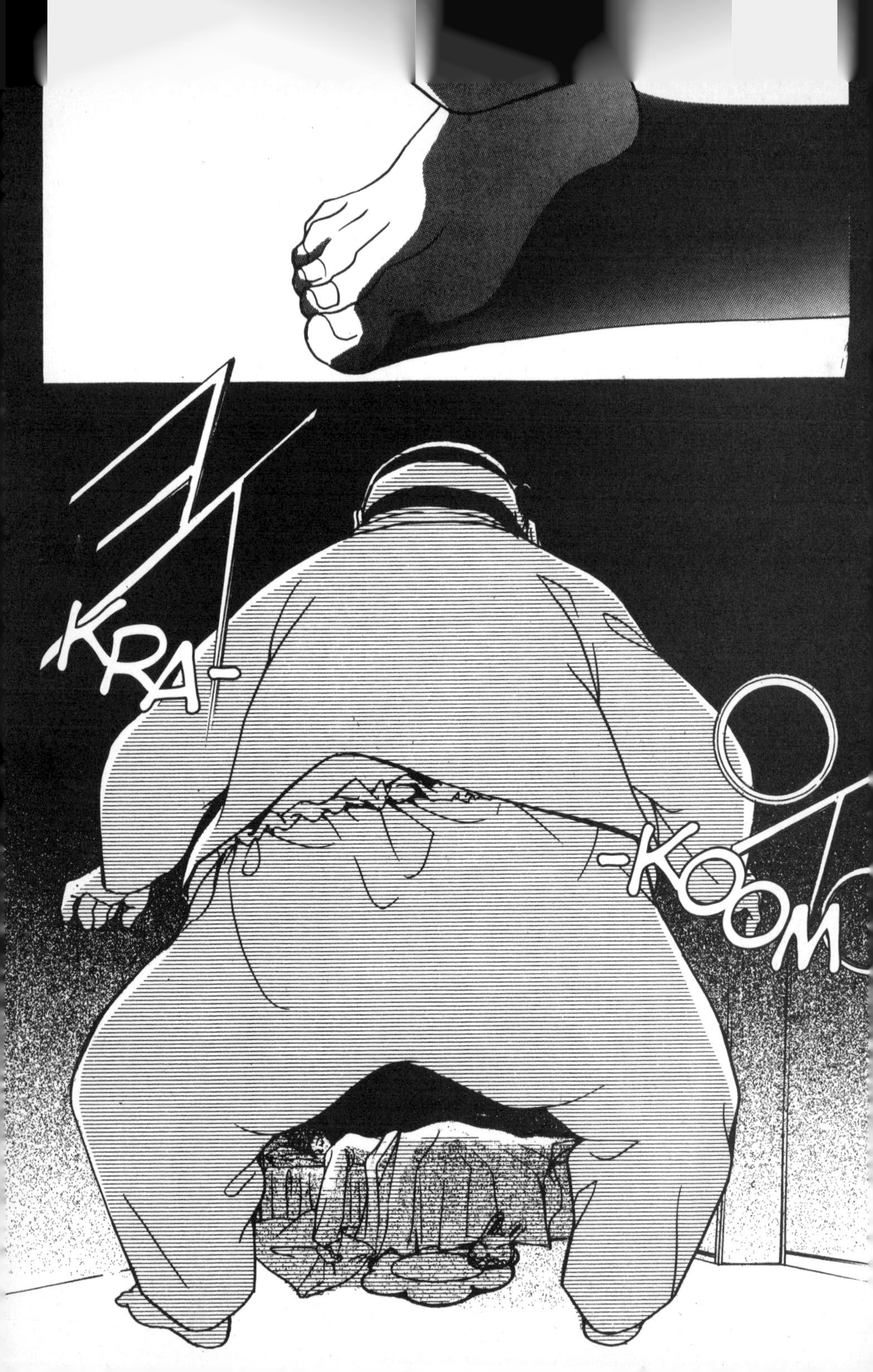
KRA-
-KOOM

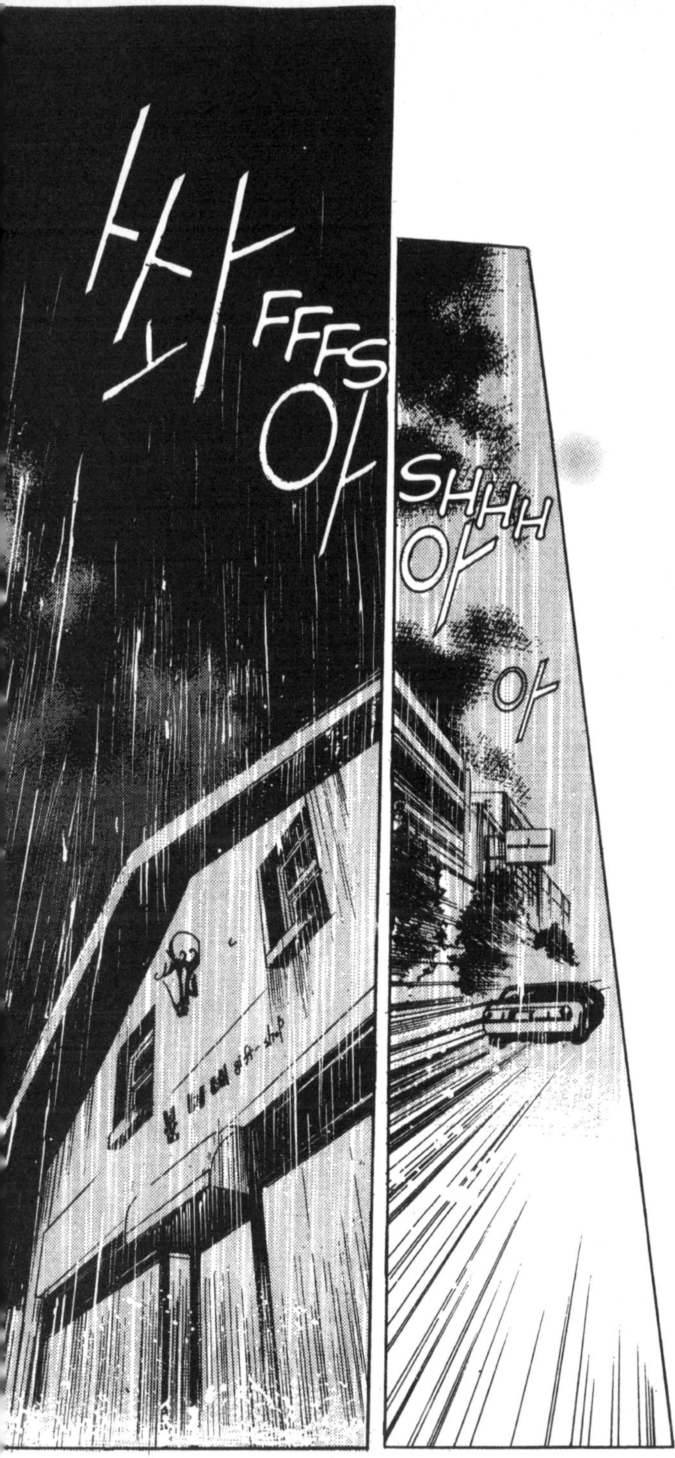
쏴
FFFFS
아
SHHHH
아
아

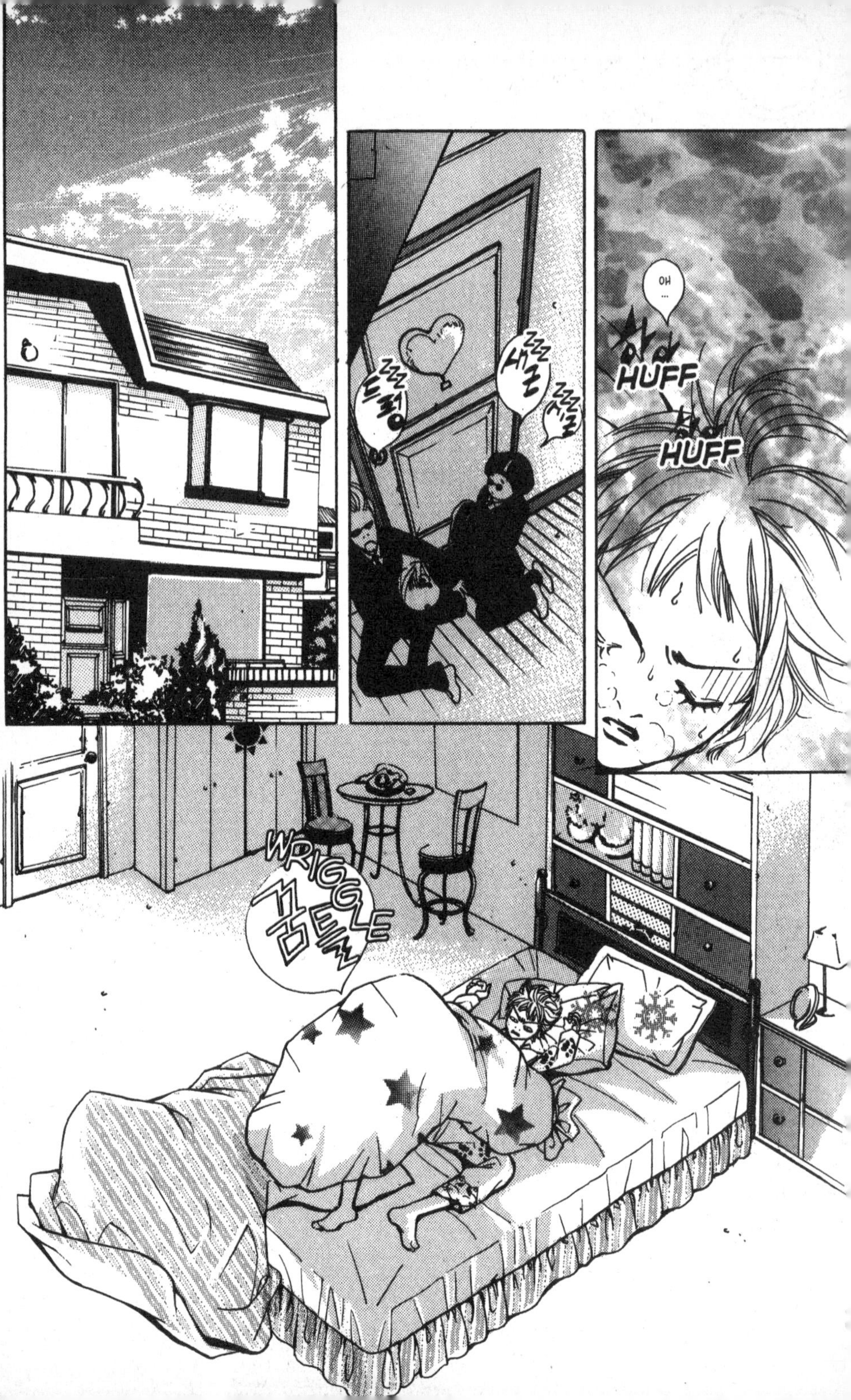

드르렁 ZZZ
새근 ZZZ
새근 ZZZ
OH ...
HUFF
HUFF
WRIGGLE

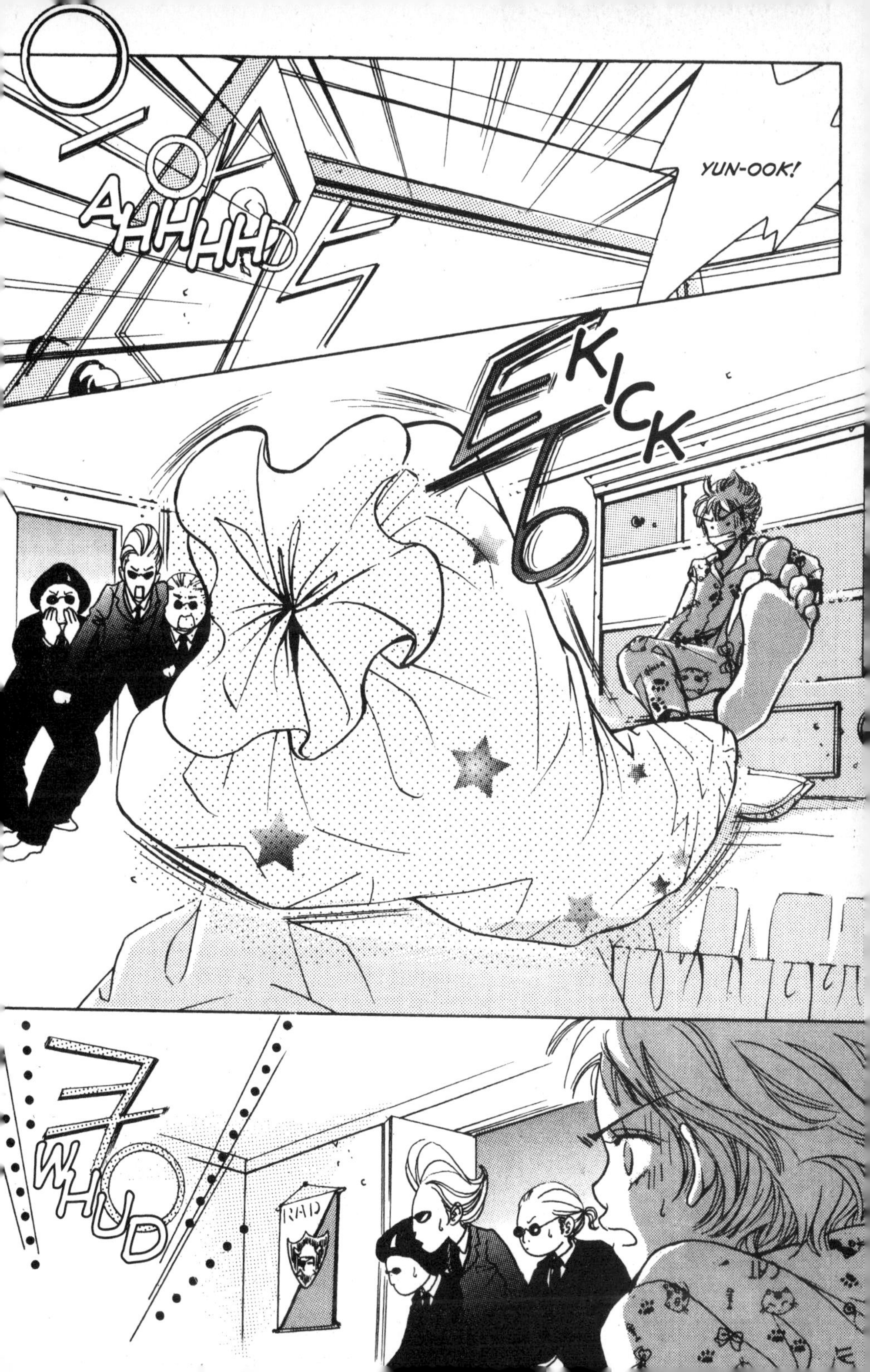
OOAHHHH
YUN-OOK!
KICK
WHUD

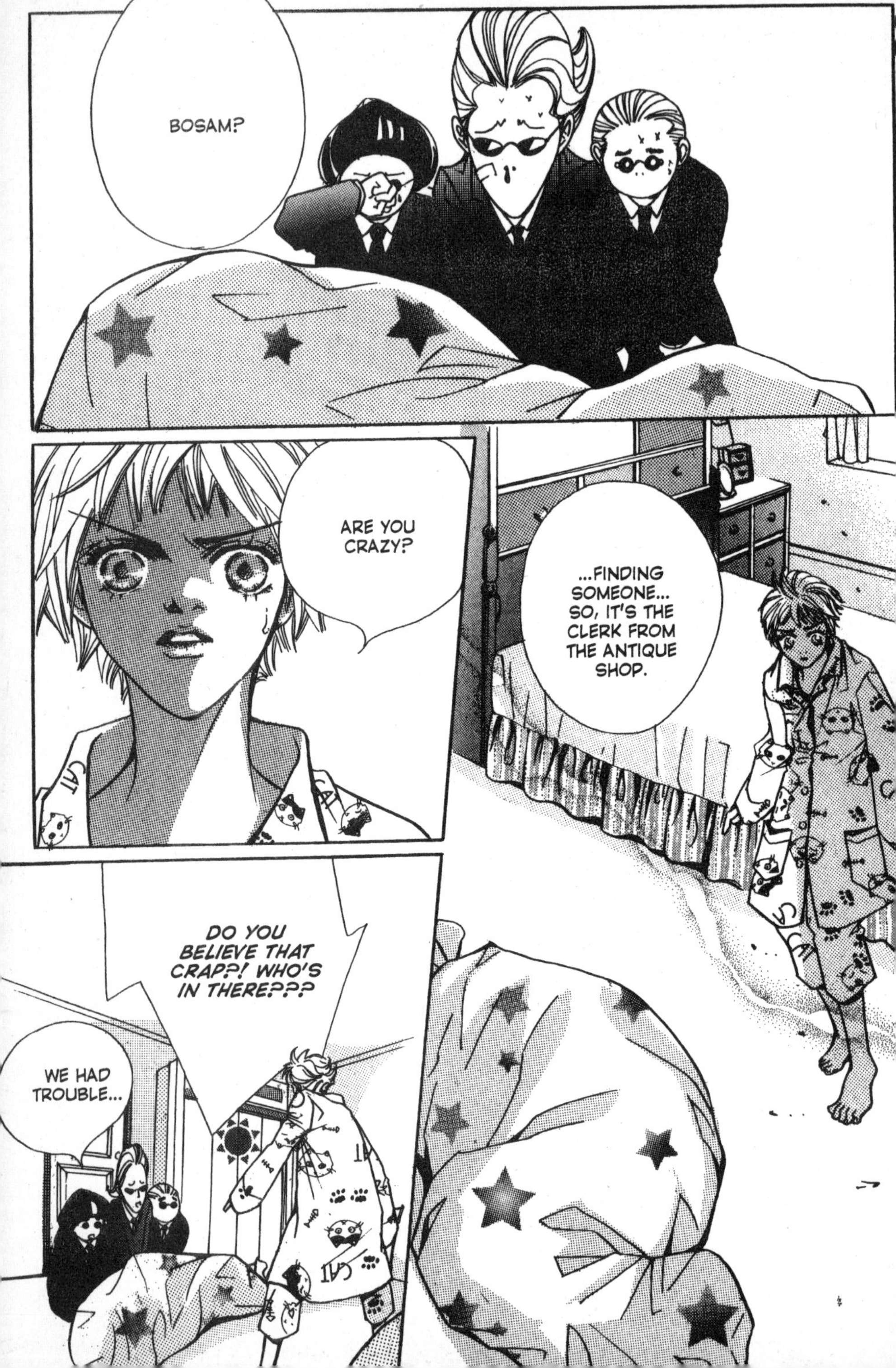
BOSAM?
ARE YOU CRAZY?
...FINDING SOMEONE... SO, IT'S THE CLERK FROM THE ANTIQUE SHOP.
DO YOU BELIEVE THAT CRAP?! WHO'S IN THERE???
WE HAD TROUBLE...

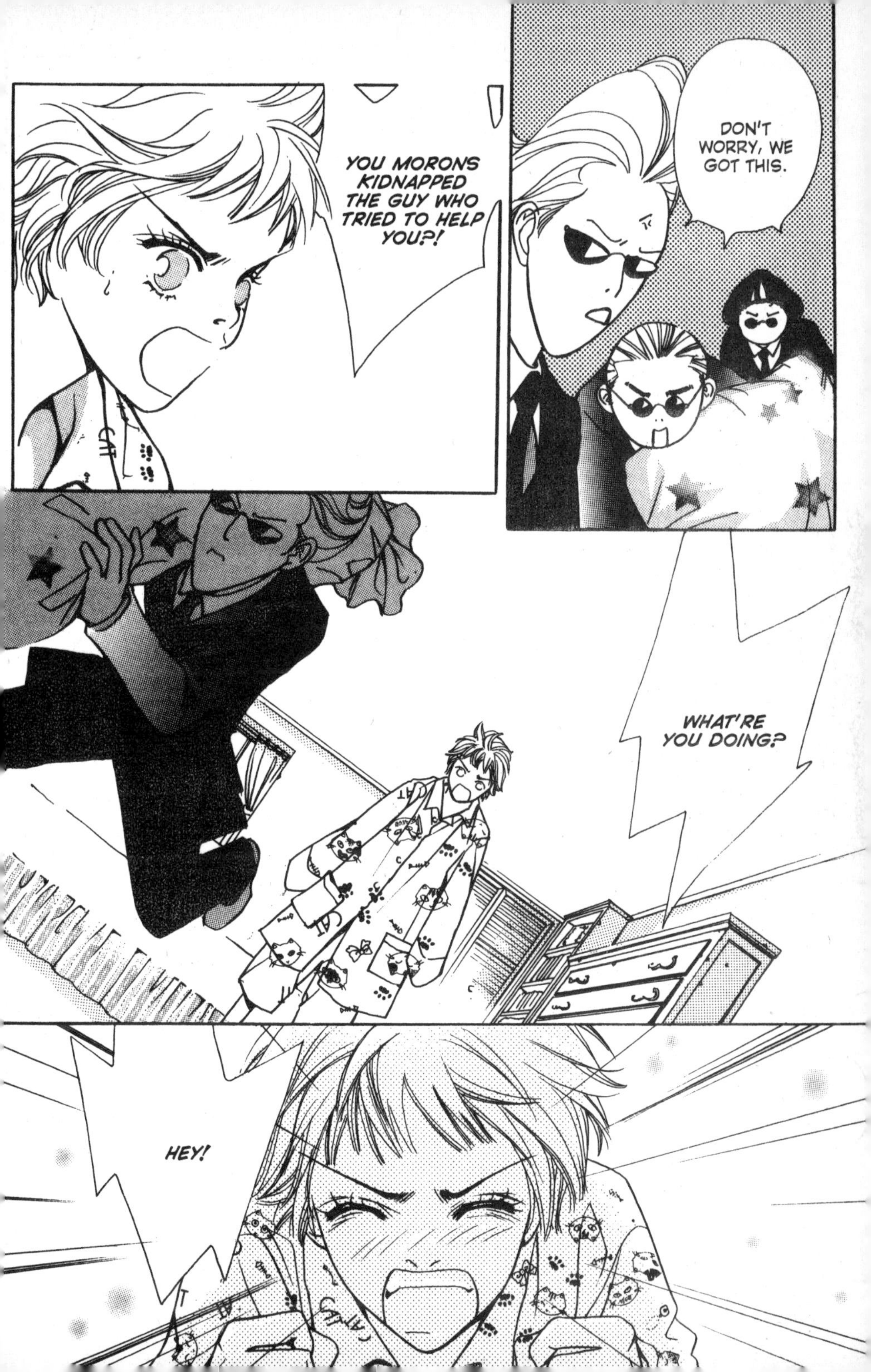
YOU MORONS KIDNAPPED THE GUY WHO TRIED TO HELP YOU?!
DON'T WORRY, WE GOT THIS.
WHAT'RE YOU DOING?
HEY!

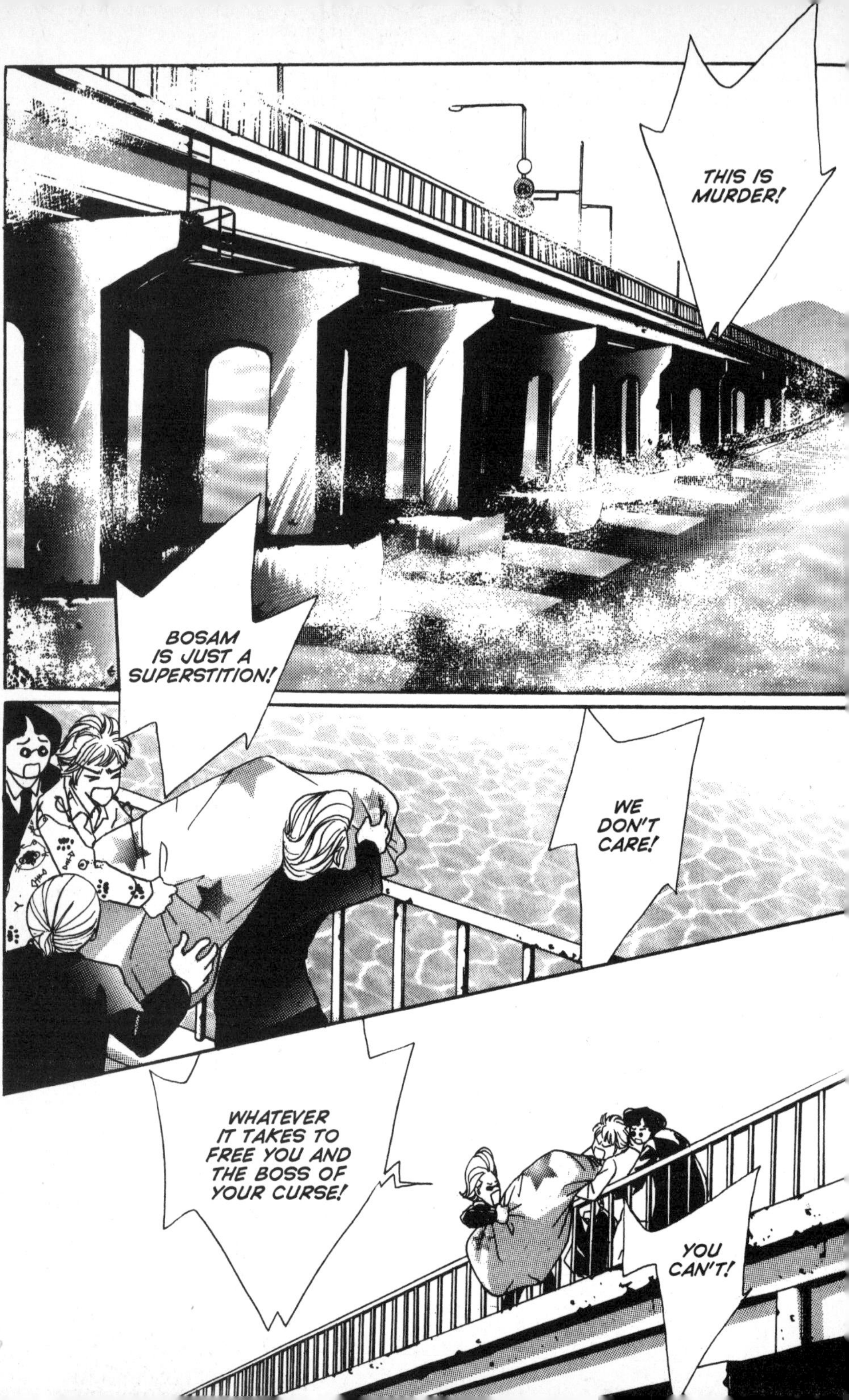
THIS IS MURDER!
BOSAM IS JUST A SUPERSTITION!
WE DON'T CARE!
WHATEVER IT TAKES TO FREE YOU AND THE BOSS OF YOUR CURSE!
YOU CAN'T!

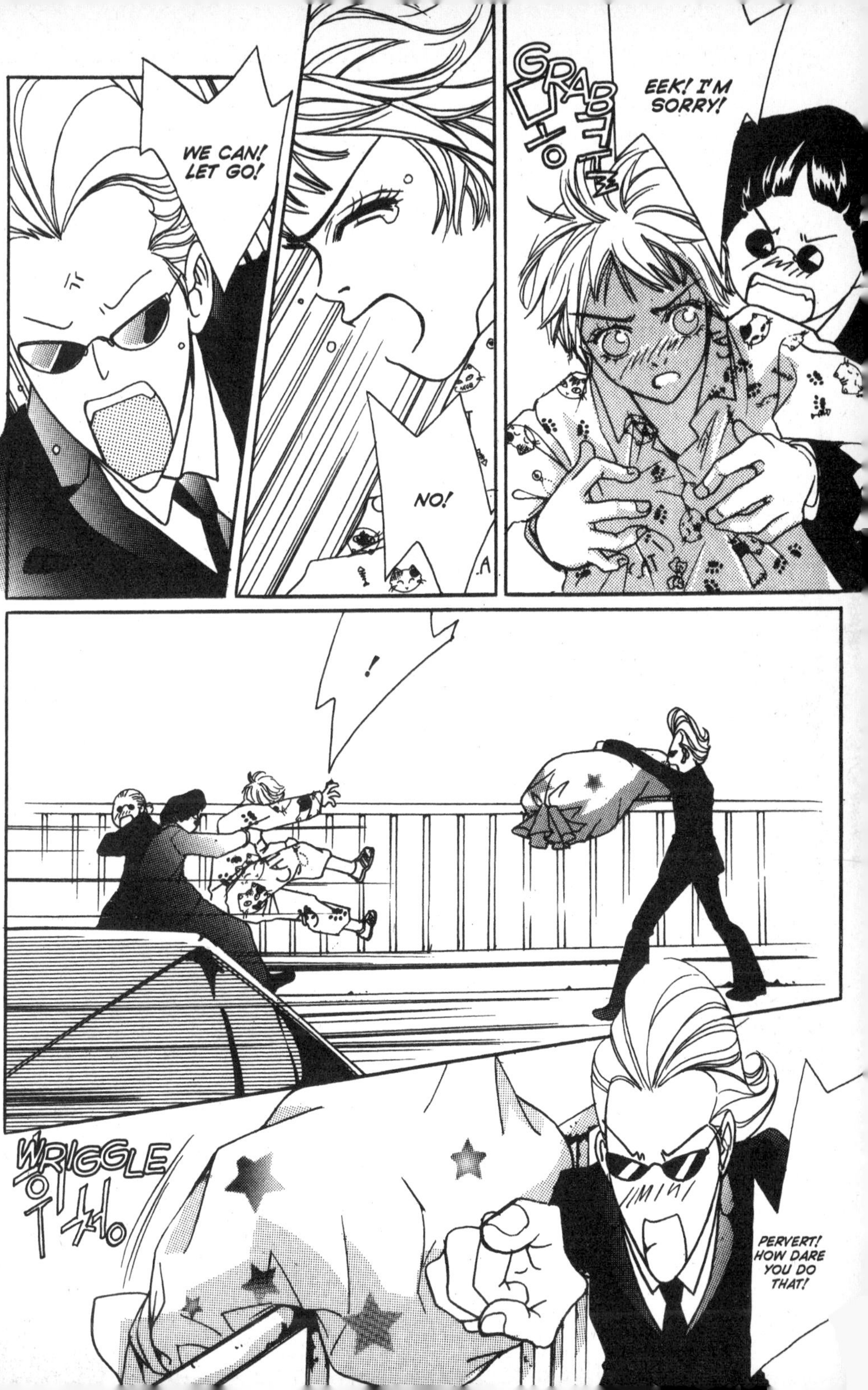
WE CAN! LET GO!
NO!
GRAB
EEK! I'M SORRY!
!
WRIGGLE
PERVERT! HOW DARE YOU DO THAT!

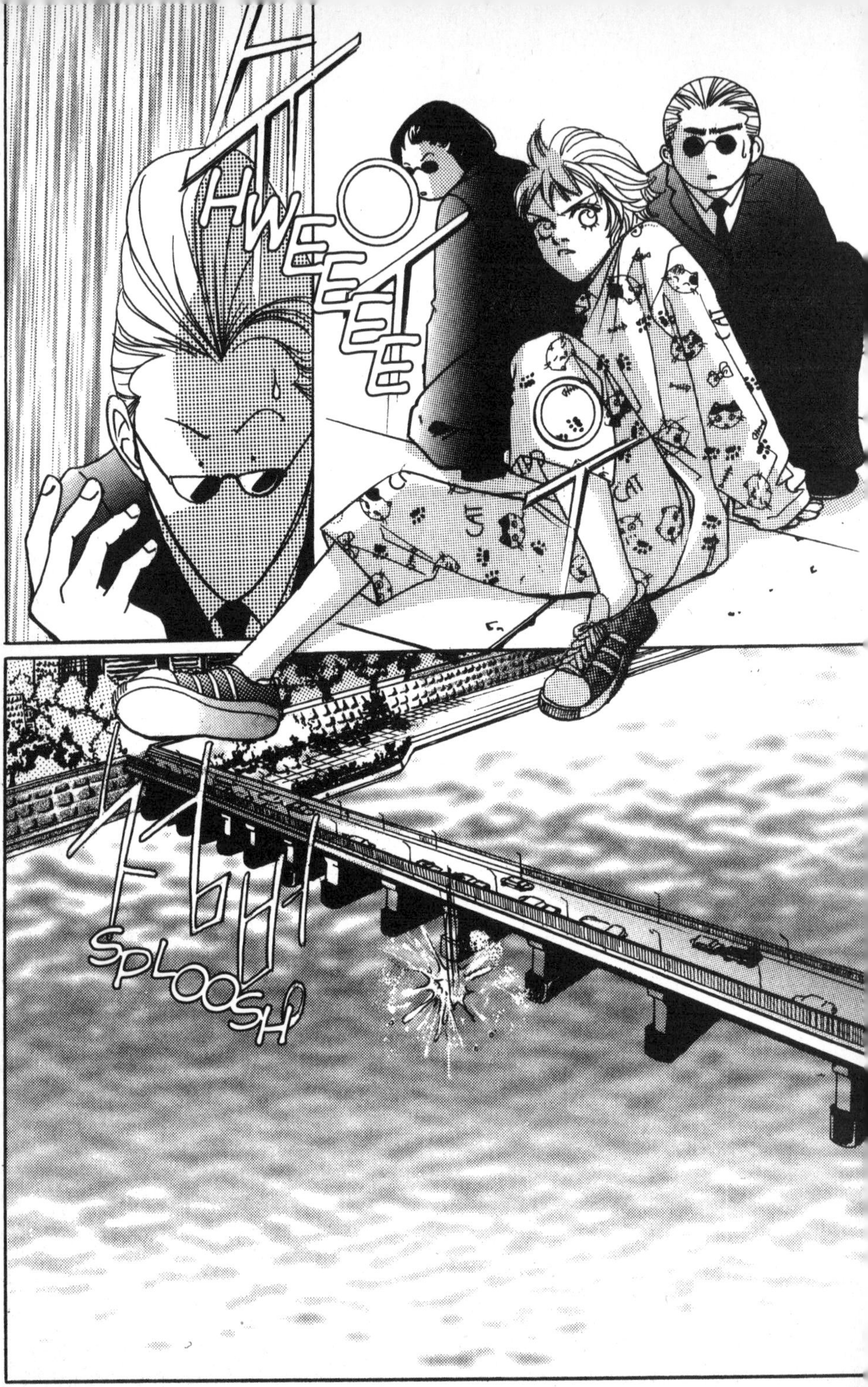
HWEEEEE
SPLOOSH

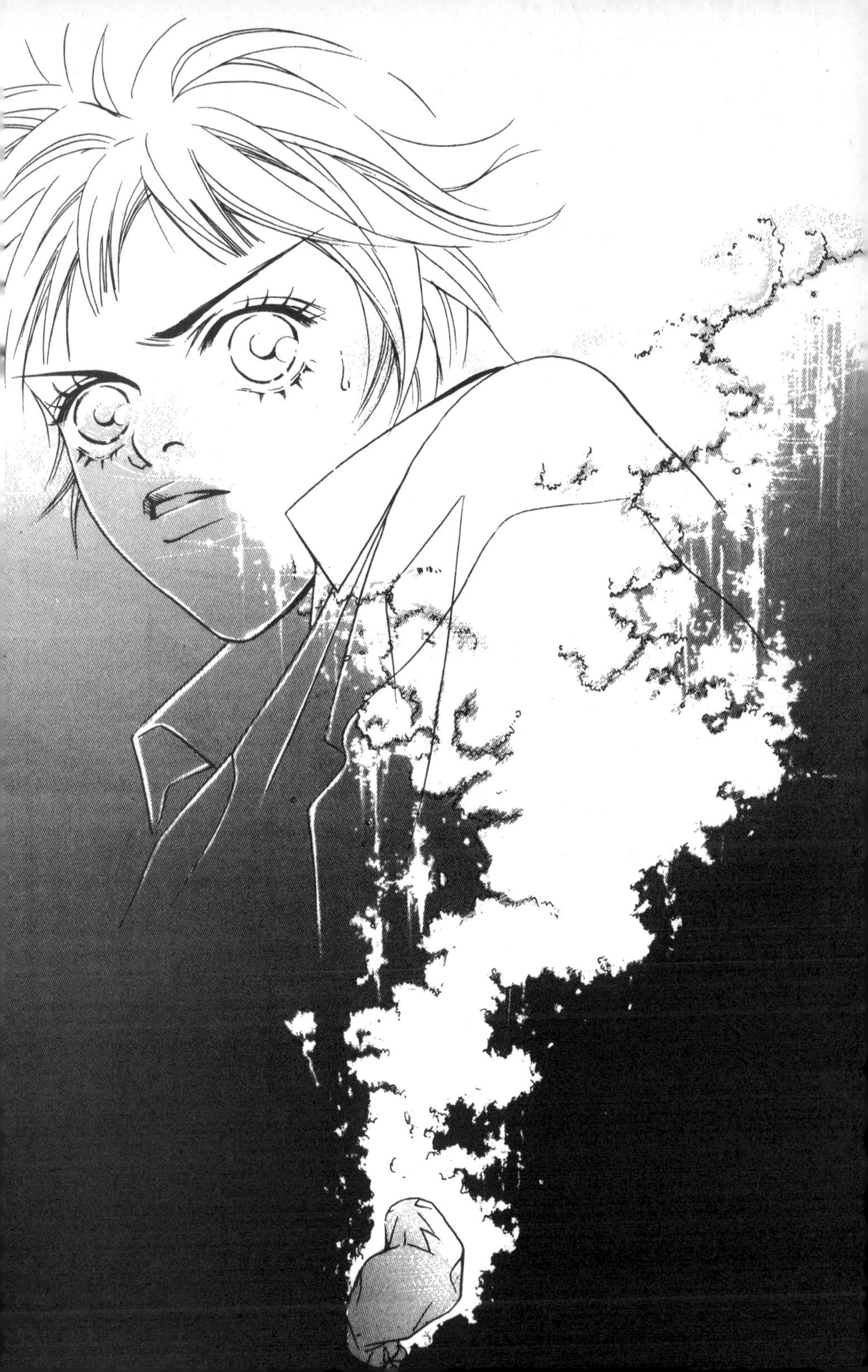

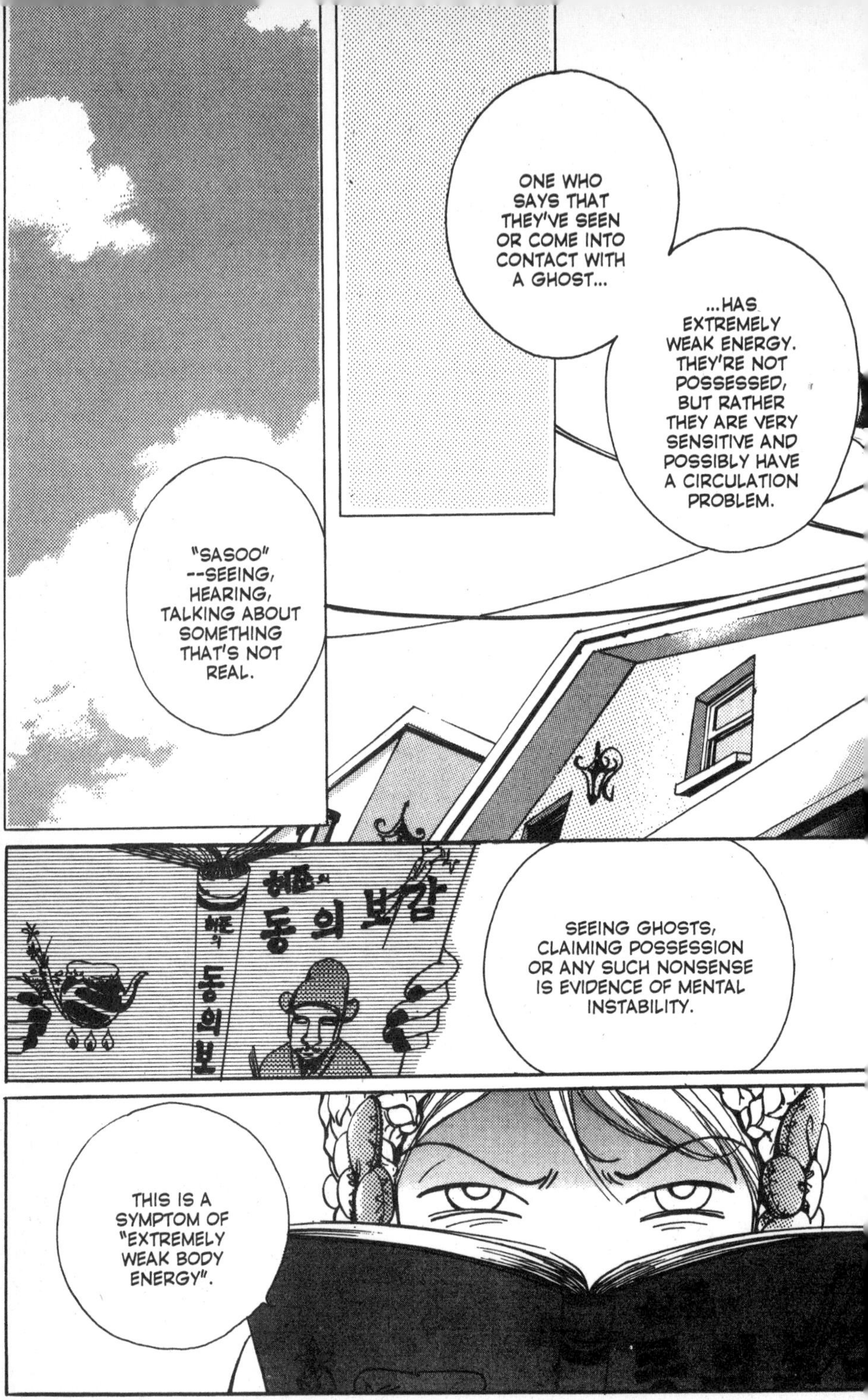
ONE WHO SAYS THAT THEY'VE SEEN OR COME INTO CONTACT WITH A GHOST...
...HAS EXTREMELY WEAK ENERGY. THEY'RE NOT POSSESSED, BUT RATHER THEY ARE VERY SENSITIVE AND POSSIBLY HAVE A CIRCULATION PROBLEM.
"SASOO" --SEEING, HEARING, TALKING ABOUT SOMETHING THAT'S NOT REAL.
동의보감
SEEING GHOSTS, CLAIMING POSSESSION OR ANY SUCH NONSENSE IS EVIDENCE OF MENTAL INSTABILITY.
THIS IS A SYMPTOM OF "EXTREMELY WEAK BODY ENERGY".

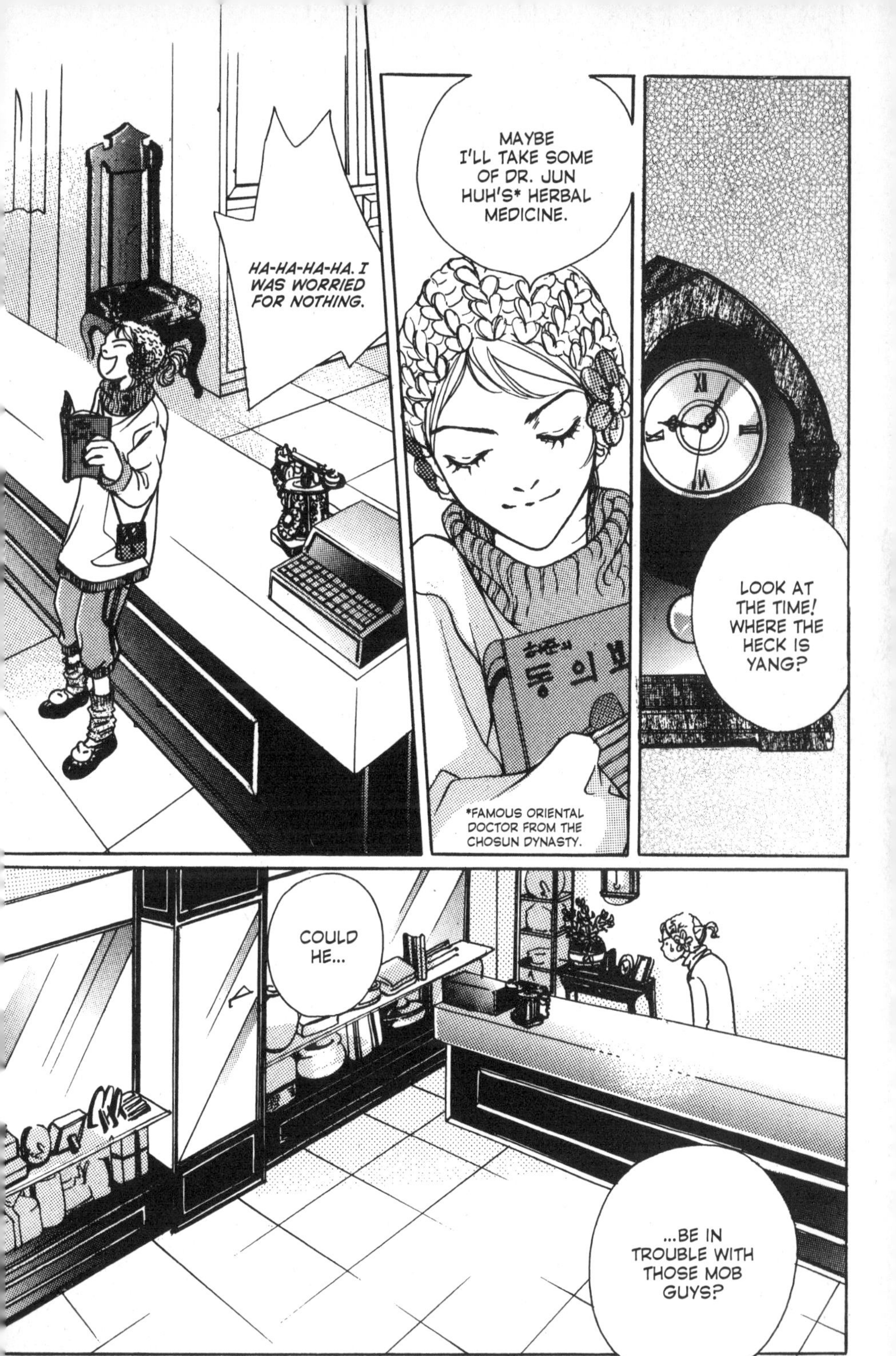
HA-HA-HA-HA. I WAS WORRIED FOR NOTHING.
MAYBE I'LL TAKE SOME OF DR. JUN HUH'S* HERBAL MEDICINE.
*FAMOUS ORIENTAL DOCTOR FROM THE CHOSUN DYNASTY.
LOOK AT THE TIME! WHERE THE HECK IS YANG?
COULD HE...
...BE IN TROUBLE WITH THOSE MOB GUYS?

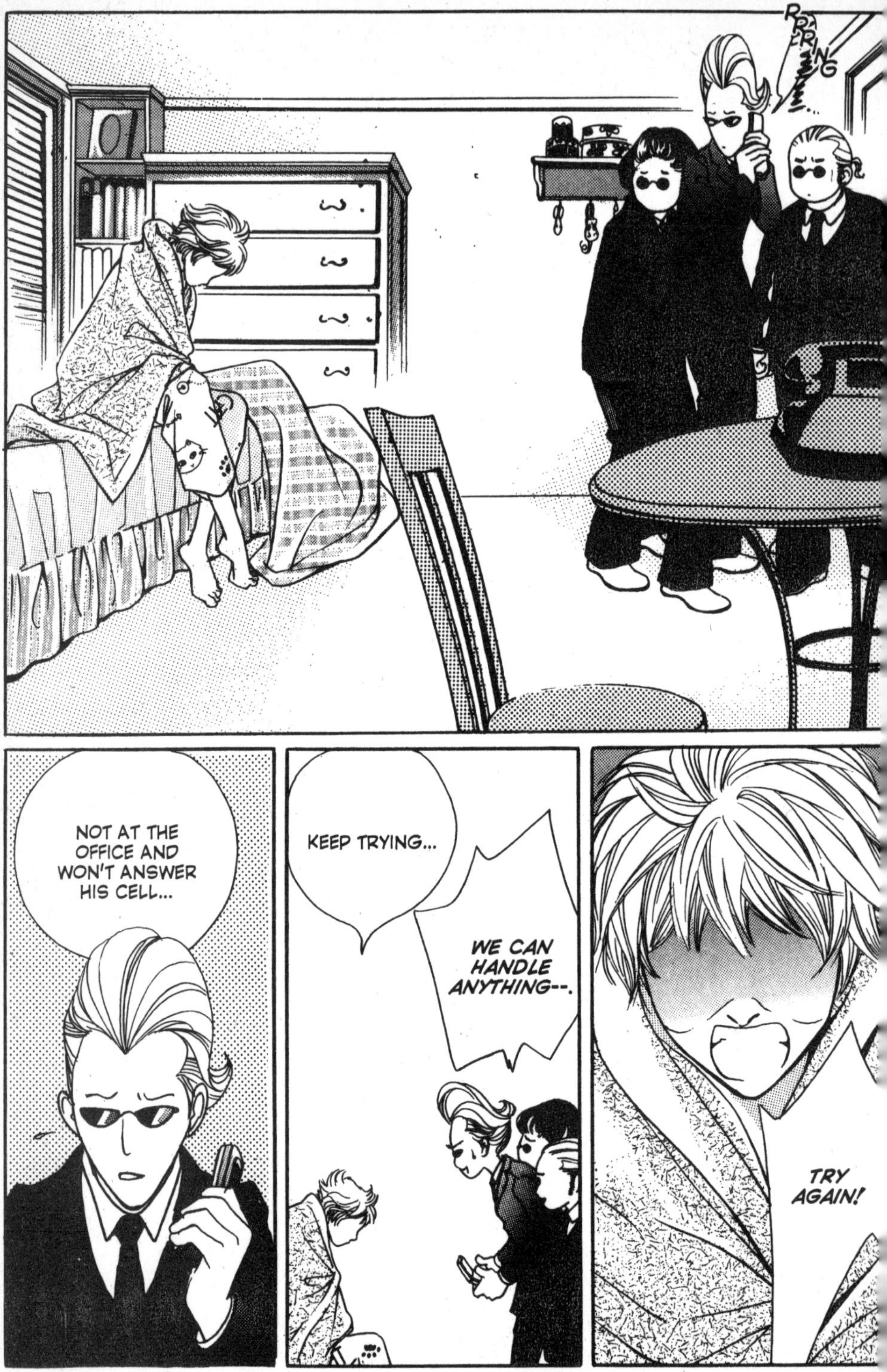
RRRING...
NOT AT THE OFFICE AND WON'T ANSWER HIS CELL...
KEEP TRYING...
WE CAN HANDLE ANYTHING--.
TRY AGAIN!

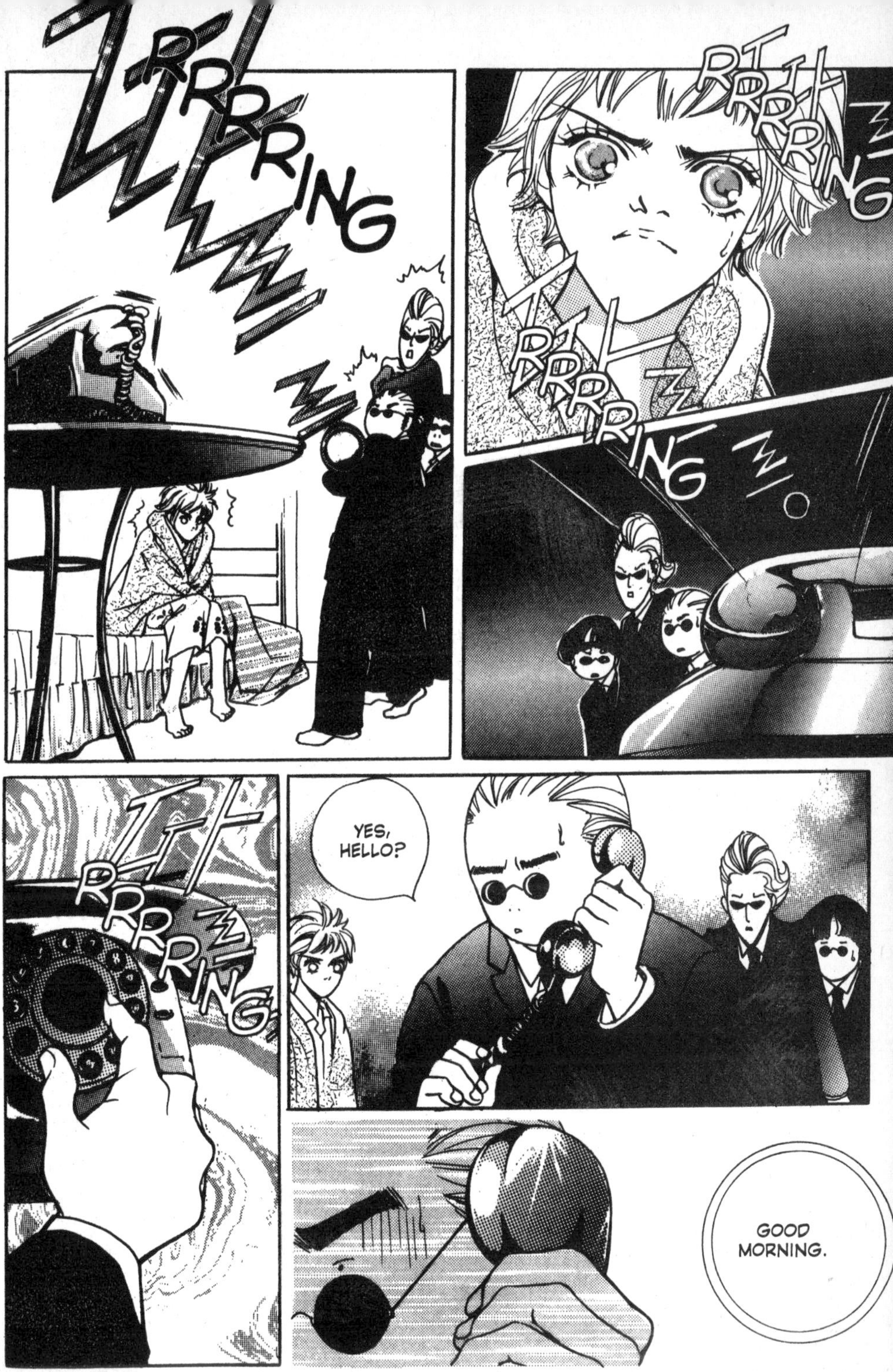
RRRRRING
RRRRRING
RRRRRING
RRRRRING
YES, HELLO?
GOOD MORNING.

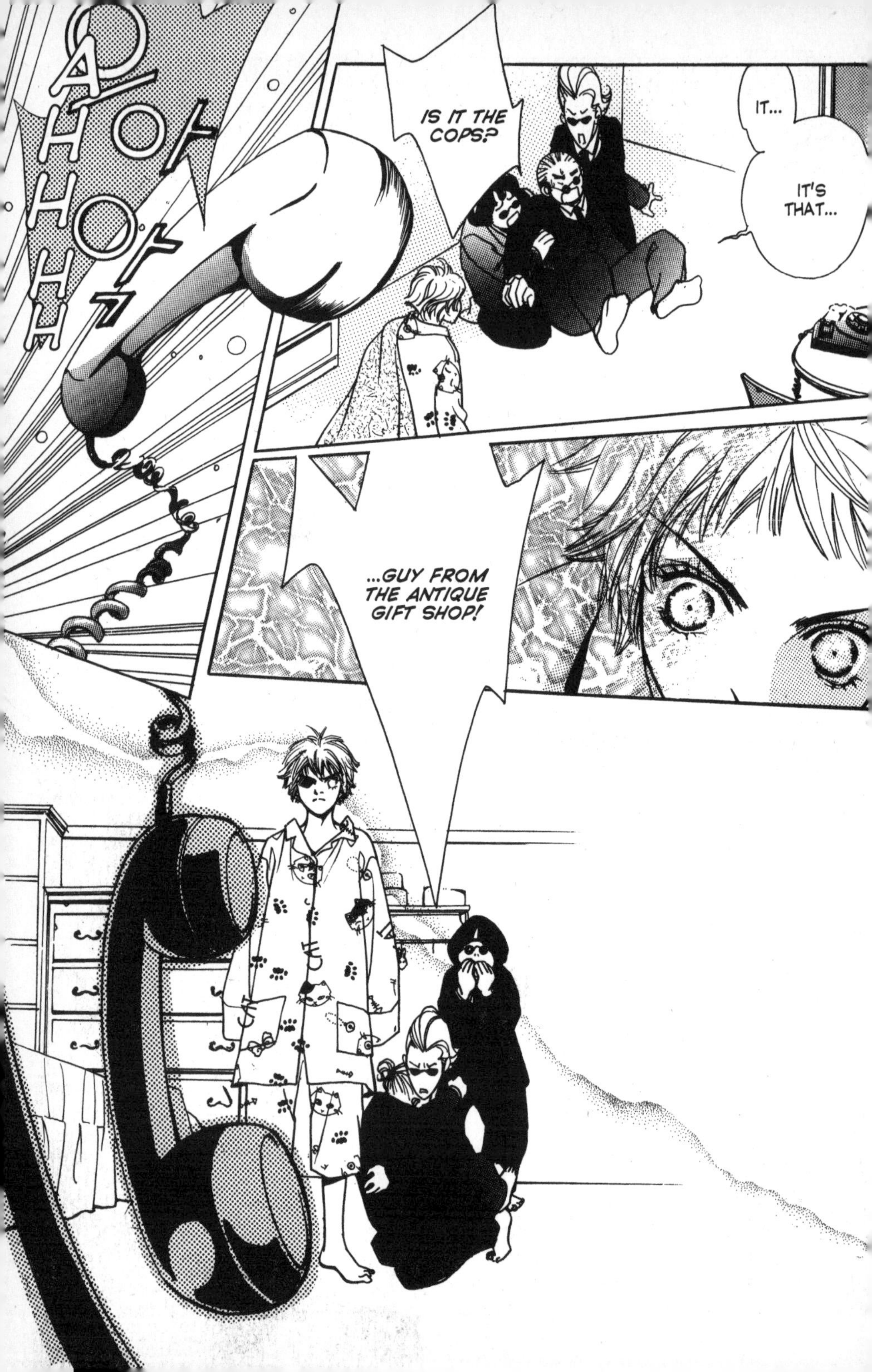
AHOHOHOHH
IS IT THE COPS?
IT...
IT'S THAT...
...GUY FROM THE ANTIQUE GIFT SHOP!

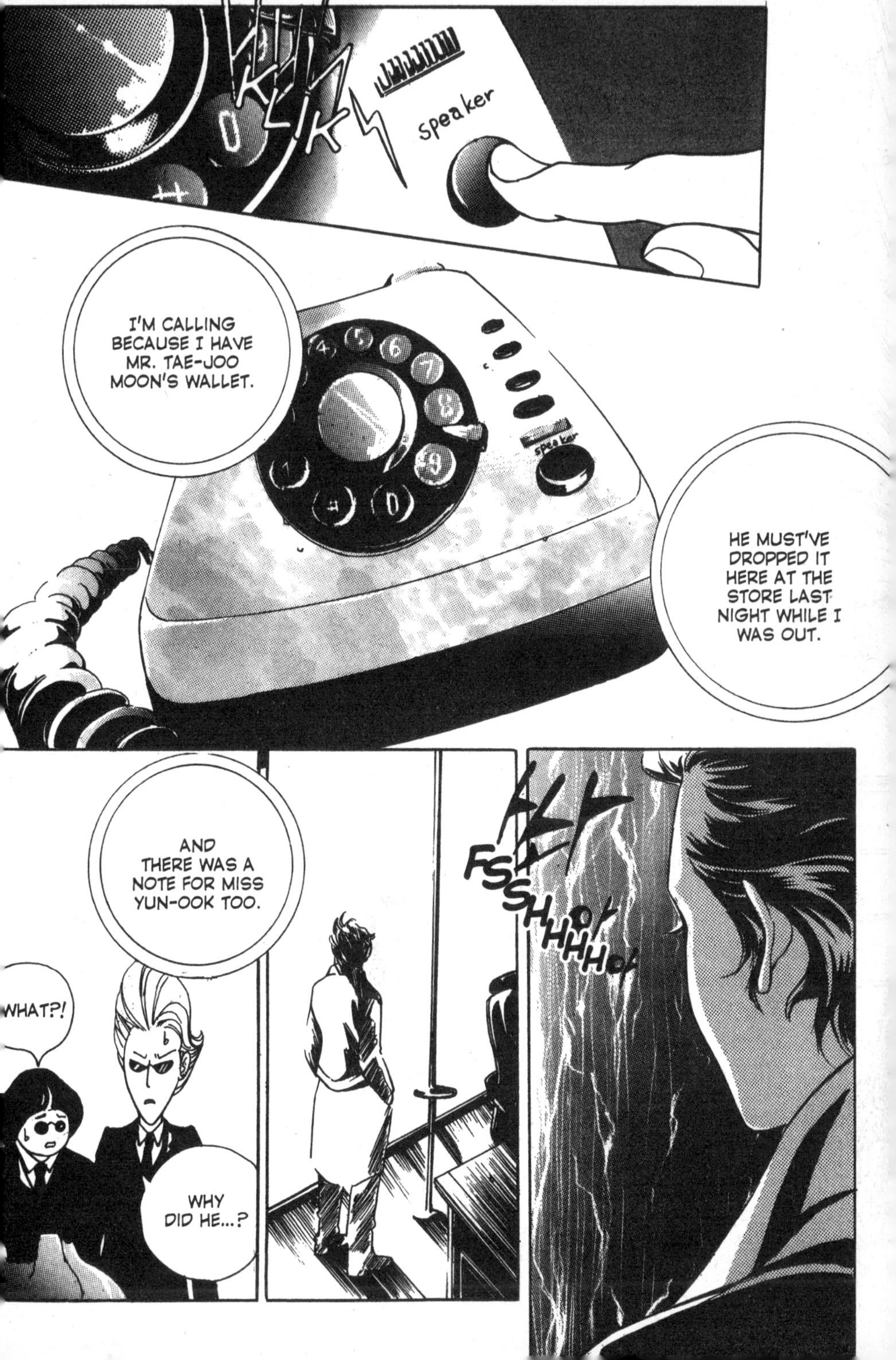
KLIK
speaker
I'M CALLING BECAUSE I HAVE MR. TAE-JOO MOON'S WALLET.
speaker
HE MUST'VE DROPPED IT HERE AT THE STORE LAST NIGHT WHILE I WAS OUT.
AND THERE WAS A NOTE FOR MISS YUN-OOK TOO.
WHAT?!
WHY DID HE...?
FSSHHH

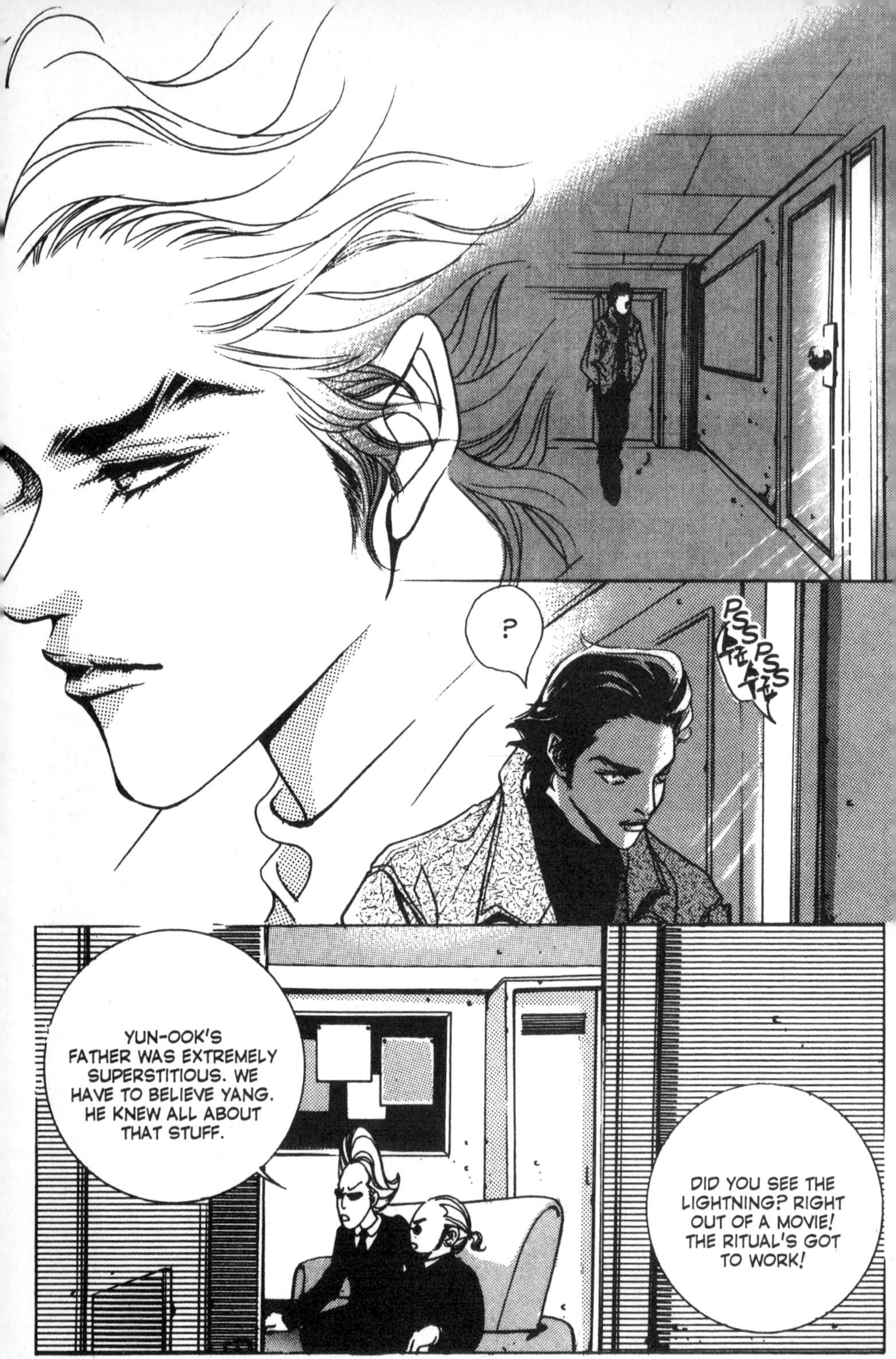
?
PSS PSS
YUN-OOK'S FATHER WAS EXTREMELY SUPERSTITIOUS. WE HAVE TO BELIEVE YANG. HE KNEW ALL ABOUT THAT STUFF.
DID YOU SEE THE LIGHTNING? RIGHT OUT OF A MOVIE! THE RITUAL'S GOT TO WORK!

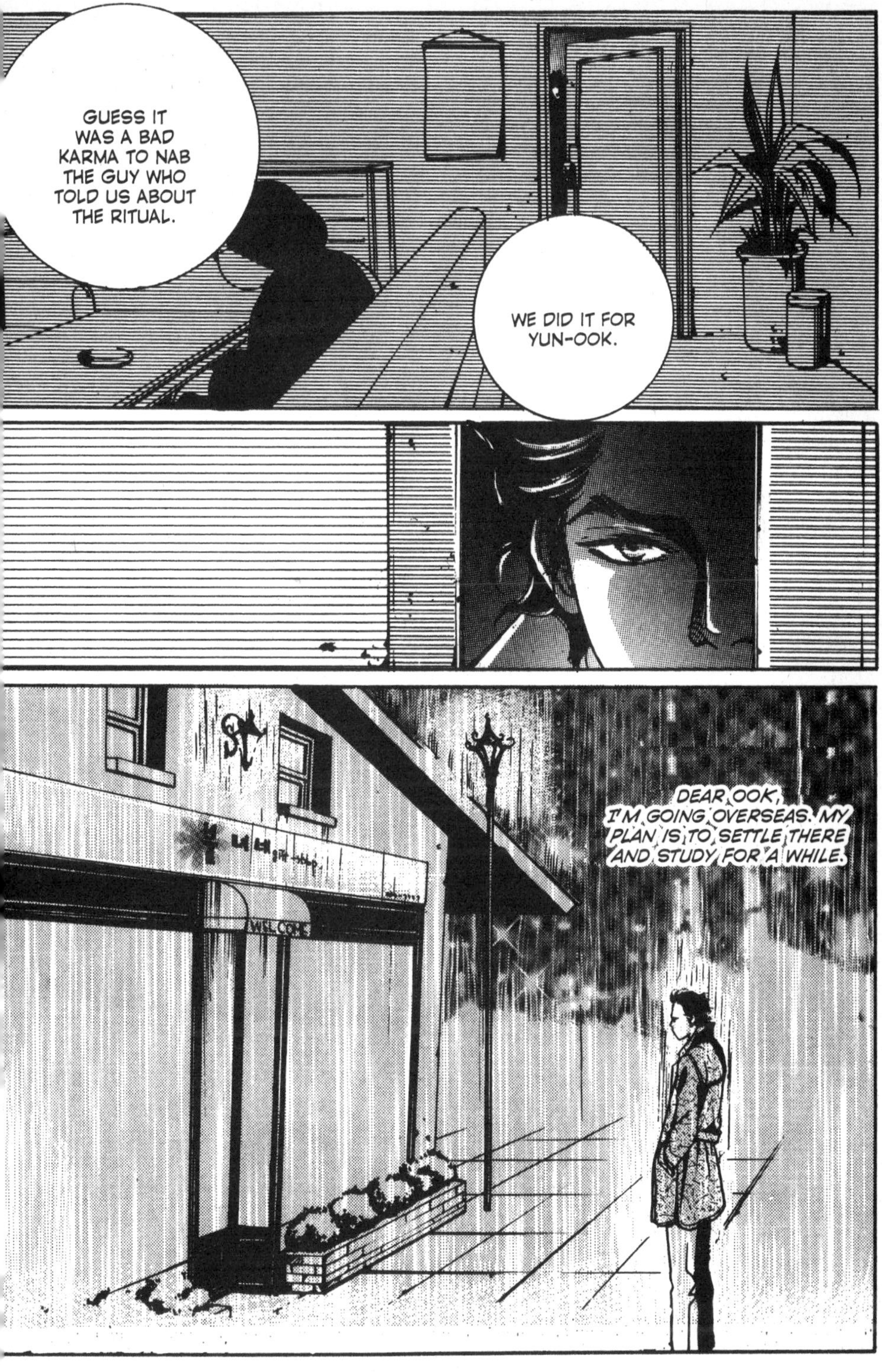
GUESS IT WAS A BAD KARMA TO NAB THE GUY WHO TOLD US ABOUT THE RITUAL.
WE DID IT FOR YUN-OOK.
DEAR OOK, I'M GOING OVERSEAS. MY PLAN IS TO SETTLE THERE AND STUDY FOR A WHILE.

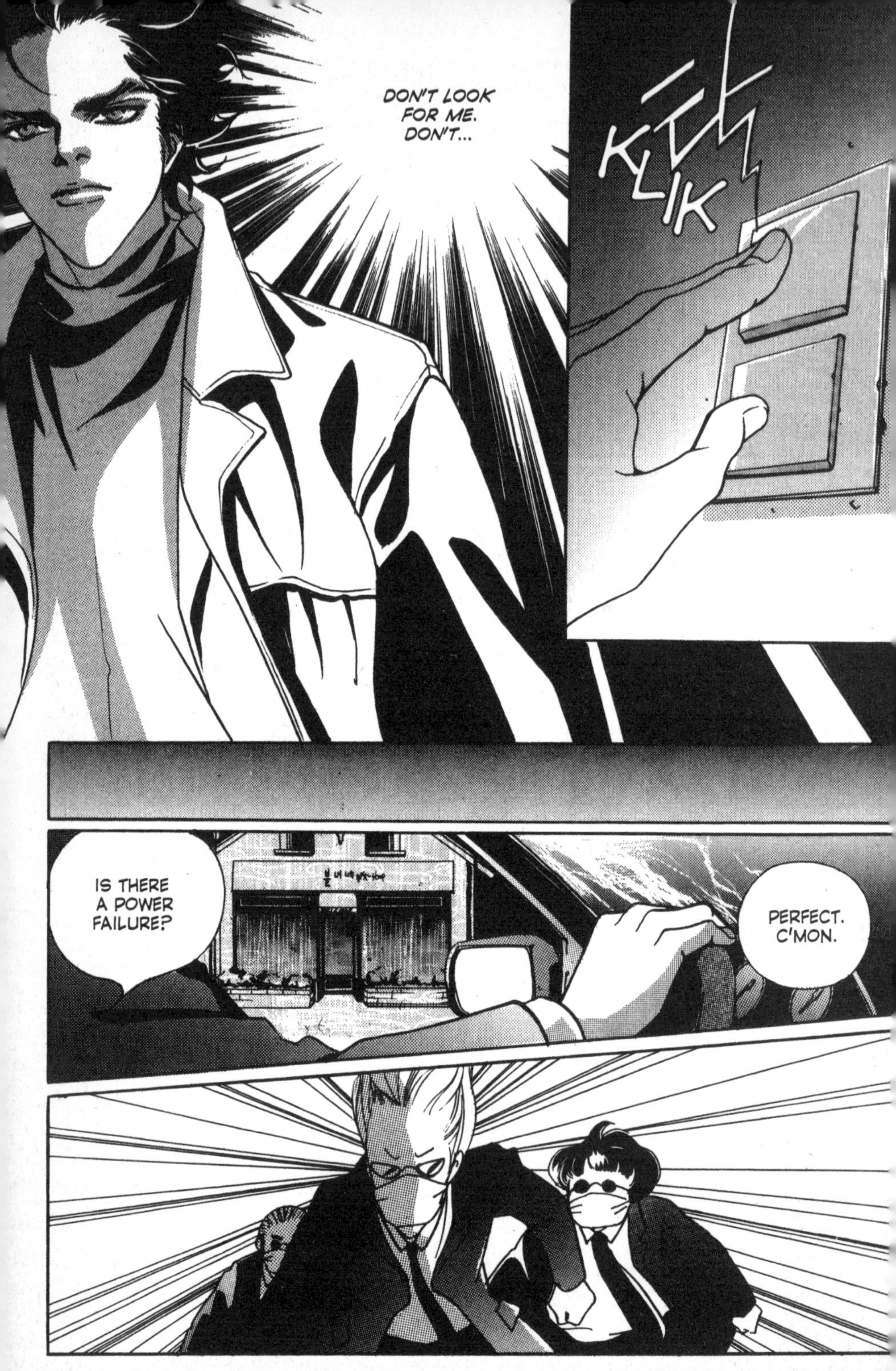
DON'T LOOK FOR ME. DON'T...
KLIK
IS THERE A POWER FAILURE?
PERFECT. C'MON.

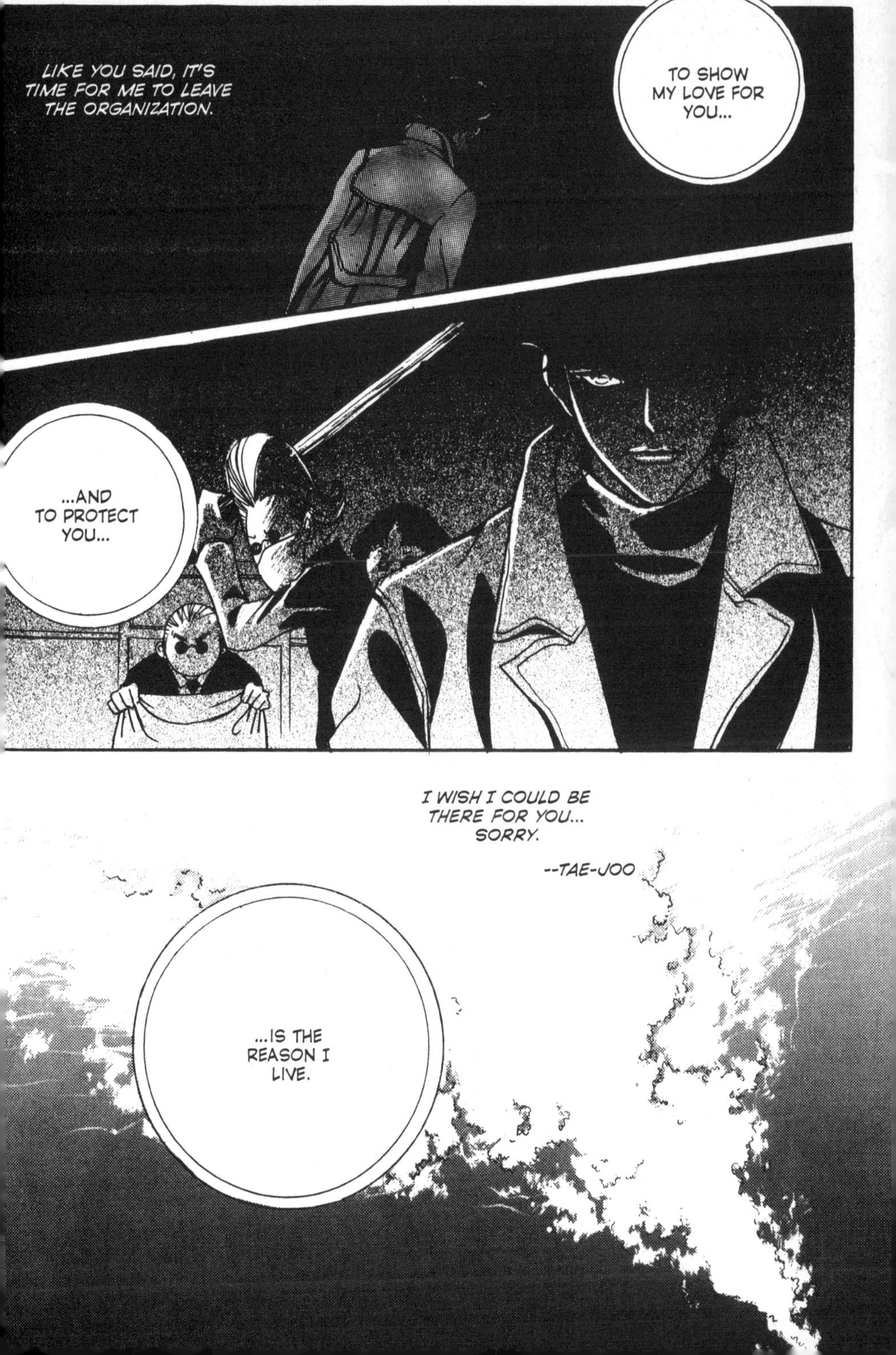
LIKE YOU SAID, IT'S TIME FOR ME TO LEAVE THE ORGANIZATION.
TO SHOW MY LOVE FOR YOU...
...AND TO PROTECT YOU...
I WISH I COULD BE THERE FOR YOU... SORRY.
--TAE-JOO
...IS THE REASON I LIVE.

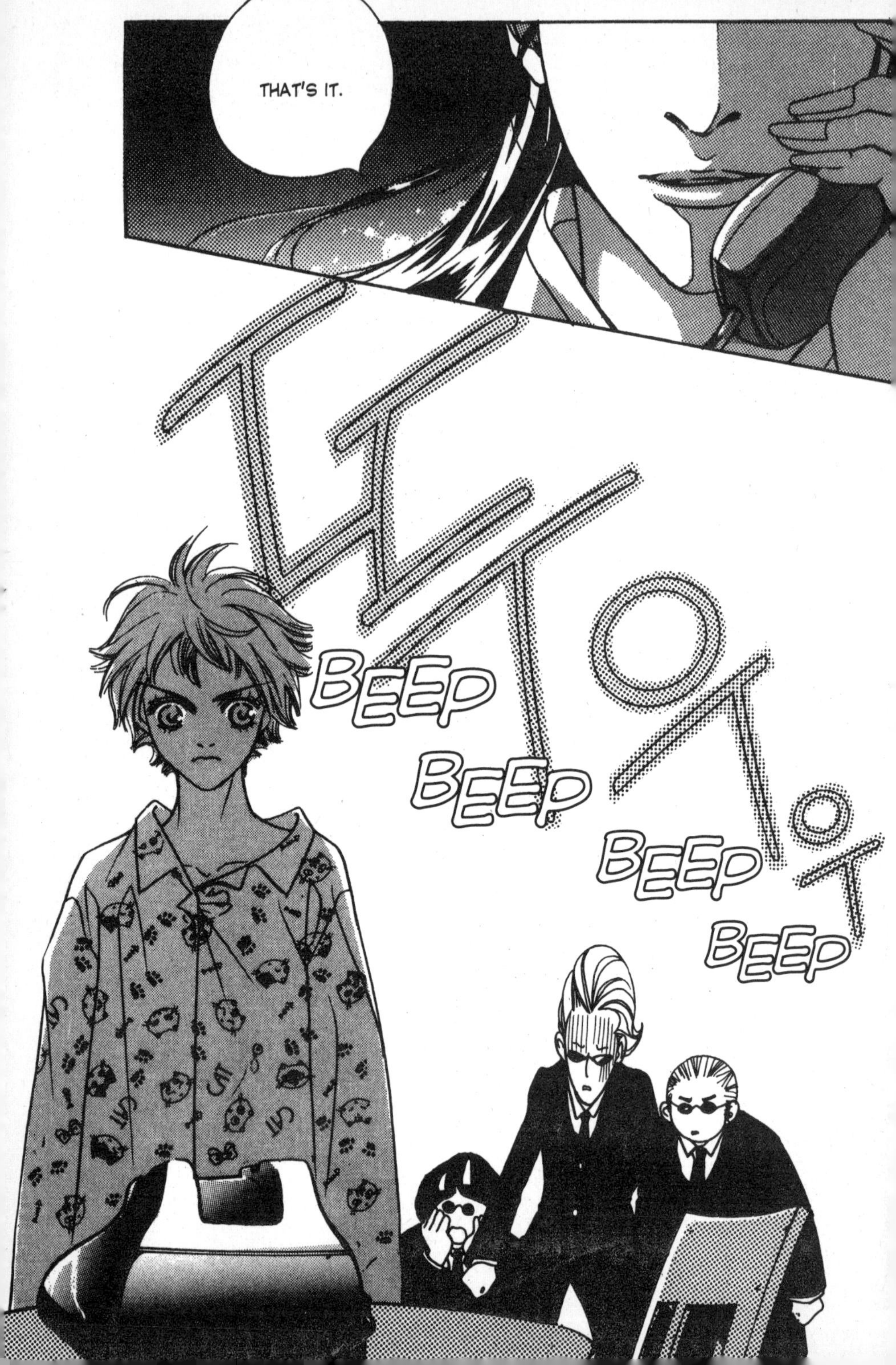
THAT'S IT.
BEEP
BEEP
BEEP
BEEP

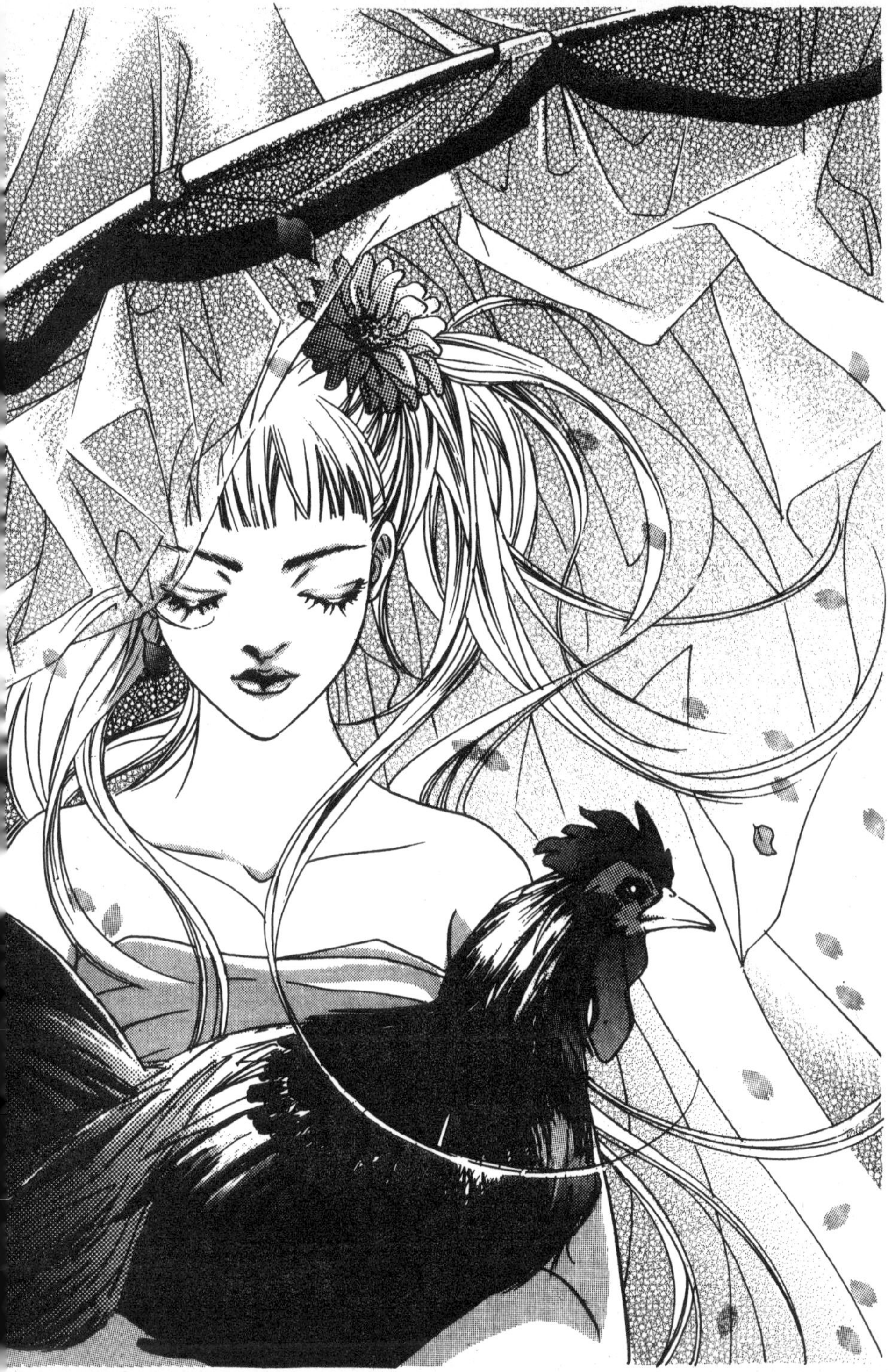

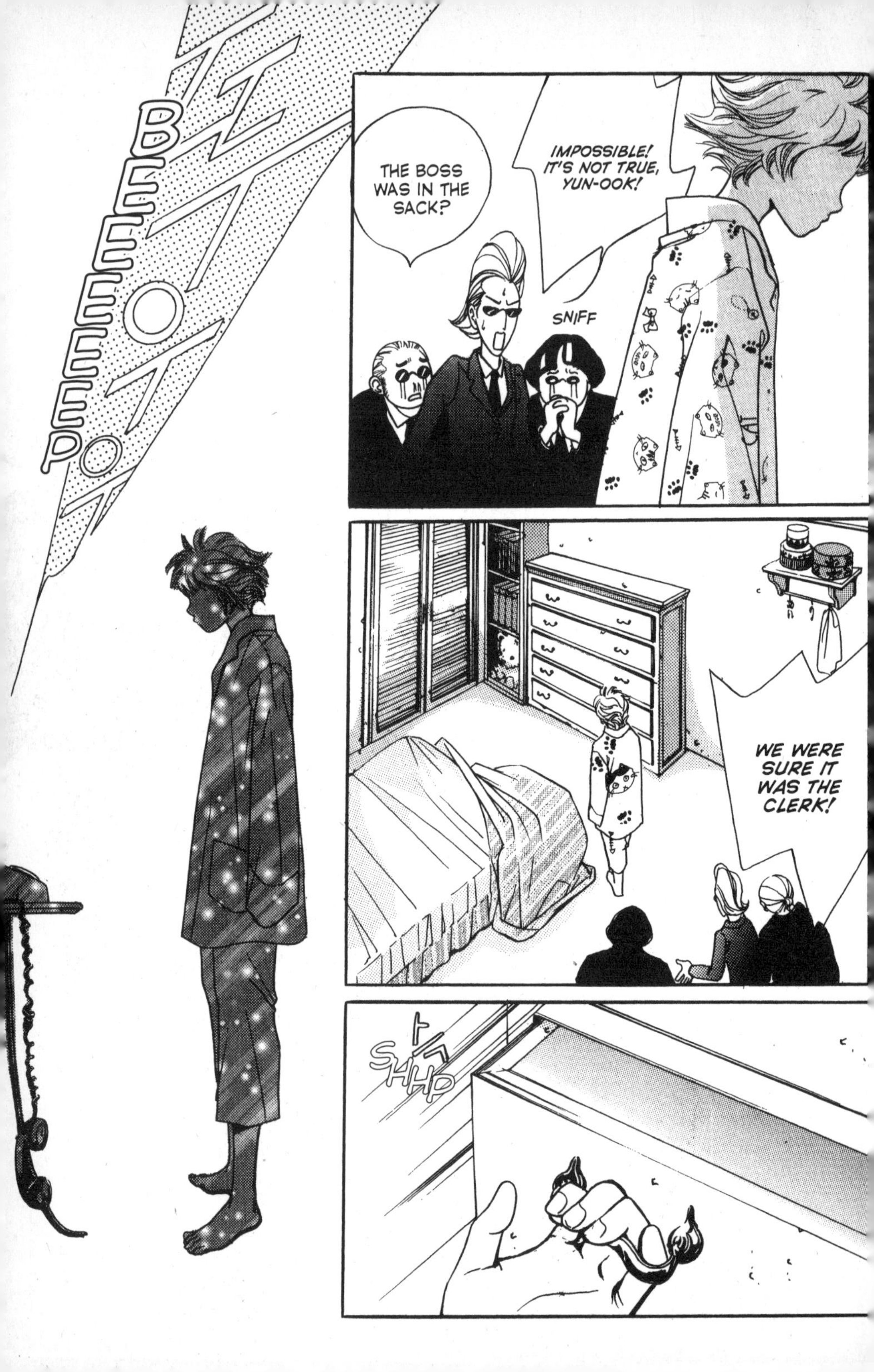
BEEEEEEP
THE BOSS WAS IN THE SACK?
IMPOSSIBLE! IT'S NOT TRUE, YUN-OOK!
SNIFF
WE WERE SURE IT WAS THE CLERK!
SHHP

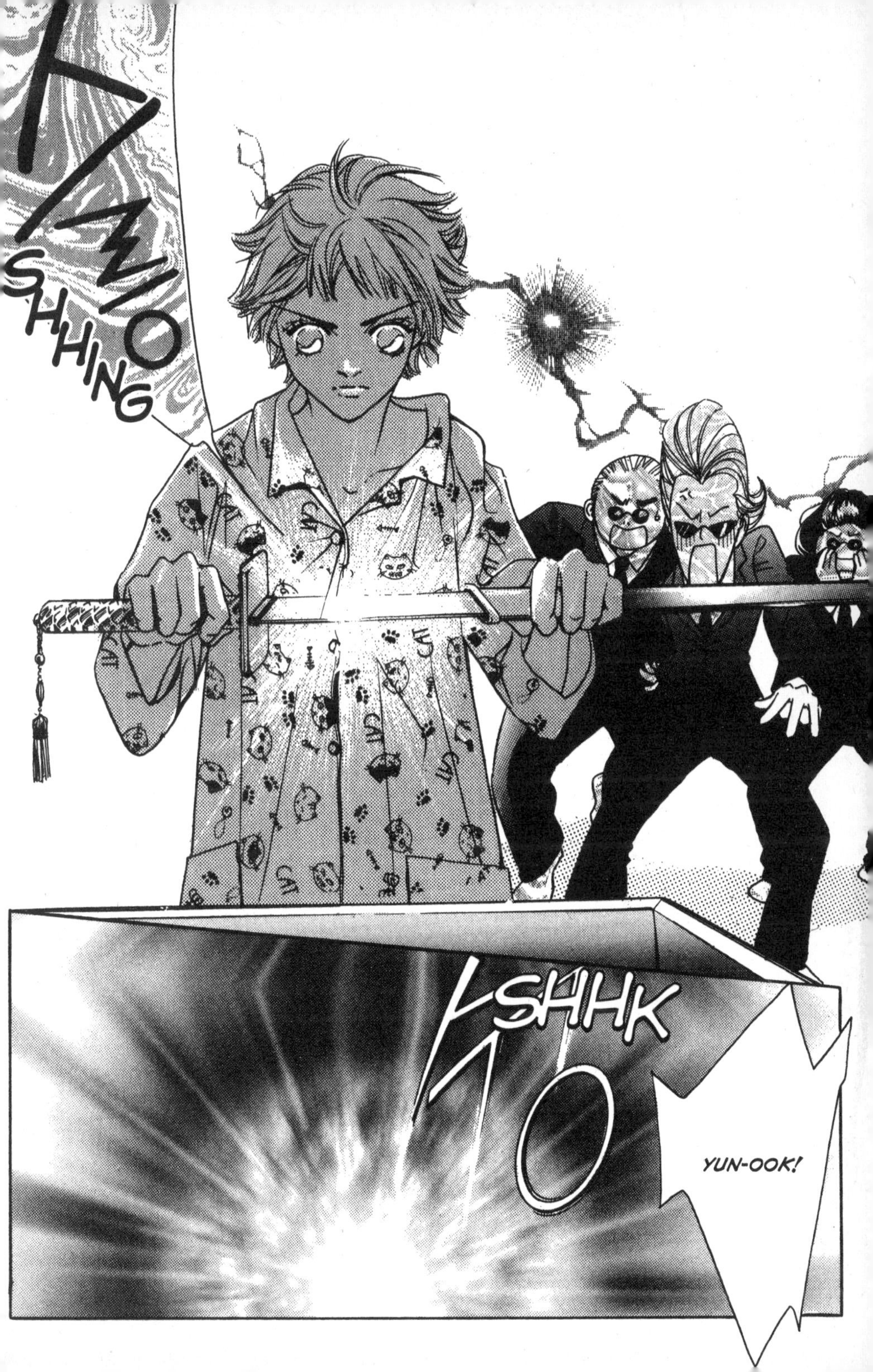
SHHING
SHHK
YUN-OOK!

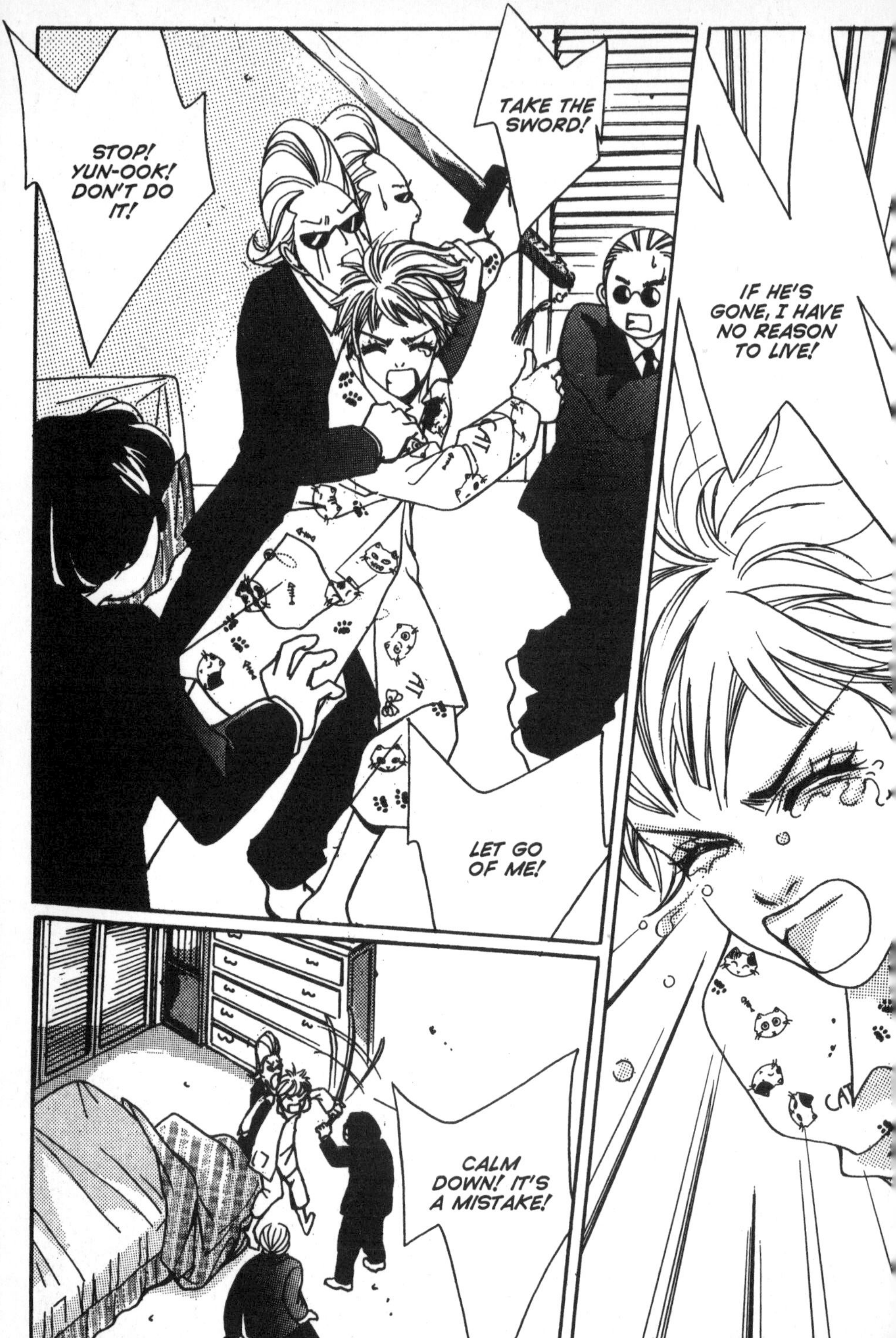
STOP! YUN-OOK! DON'T DO IT!
TAKE THE SWORD!
LET GO OF ME!
CALM DOWN! IT'S A MISTAKE!
IF HE'S GONE, I HAVE NO REASON TO LIVE!

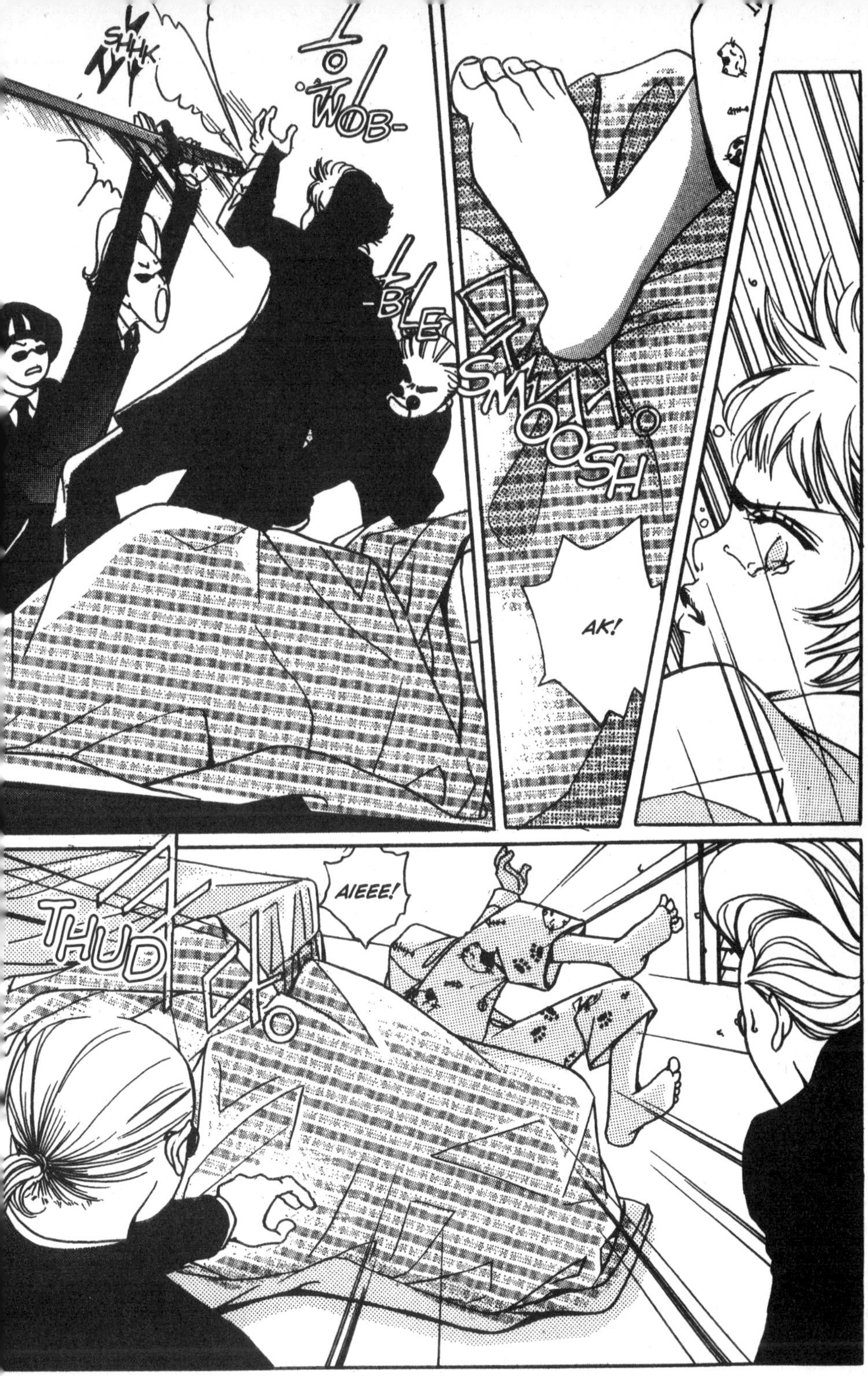
SHHK
WOB-
-BBLE
SMOOSH
AK!
THUD
AIEEE!

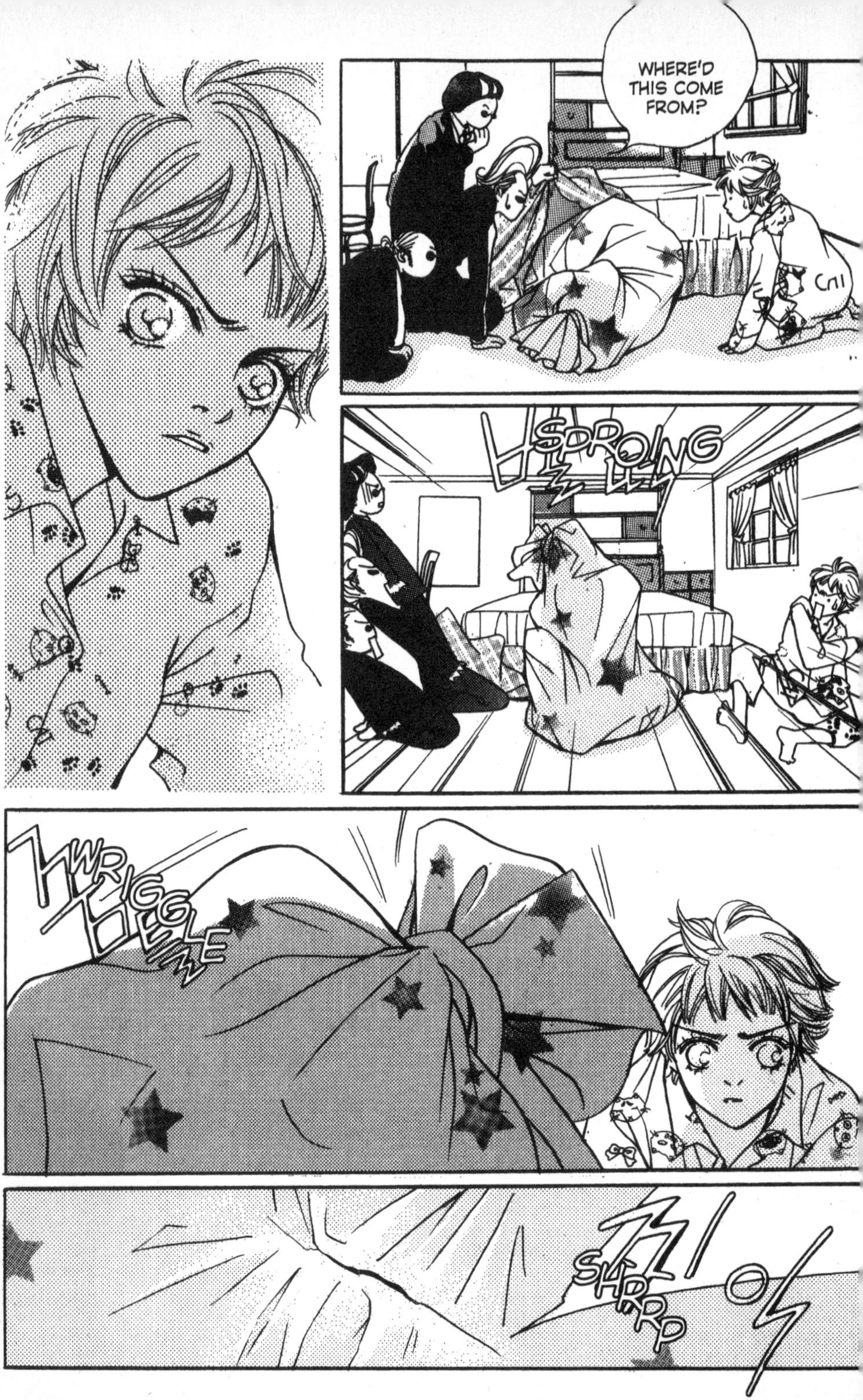
WHERE'D THIS COME FROM?
SPROING
WRIGGLE
SHRRP

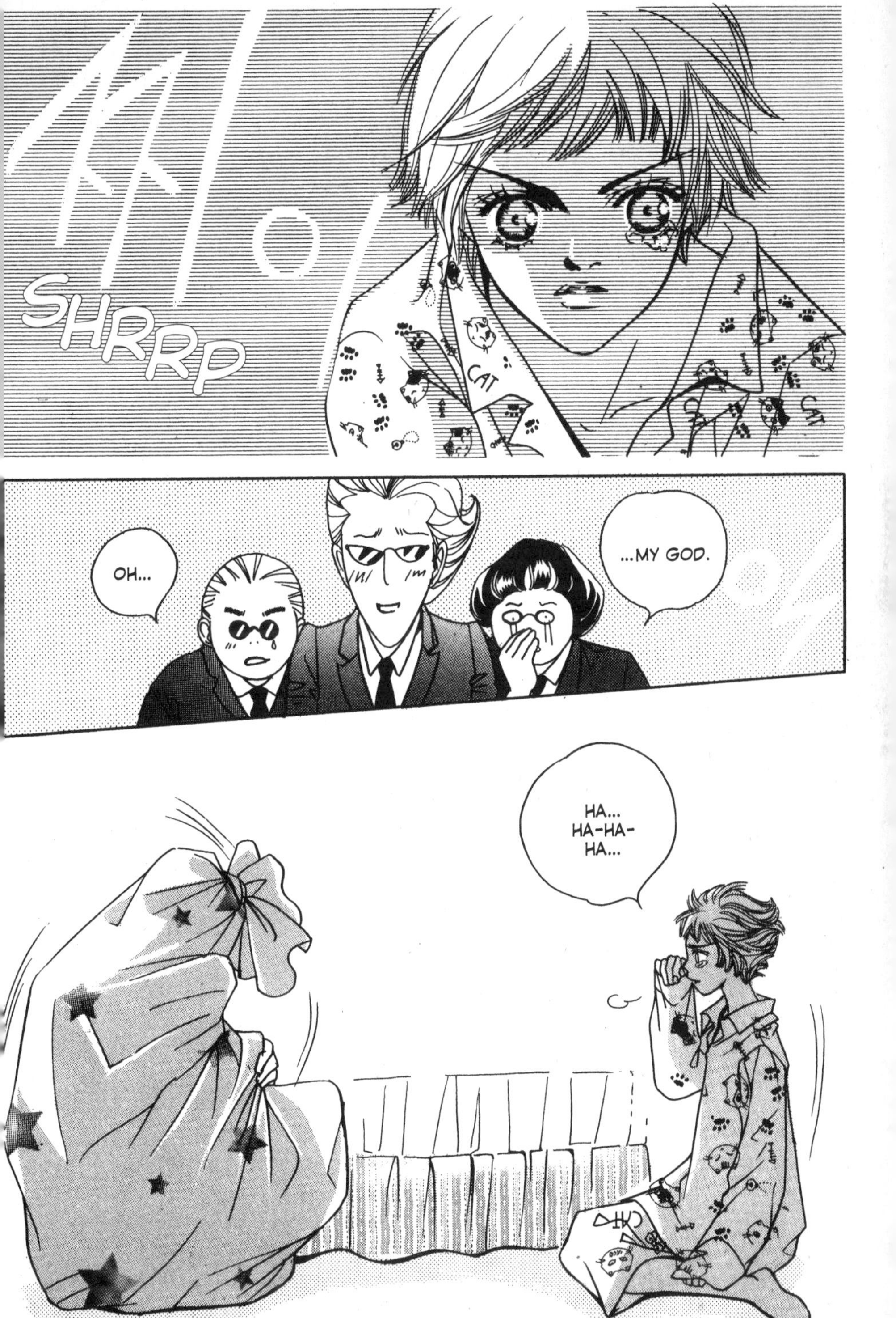
SHRRP
OH...
...MY GOD.
HA...
HA-HA-
HA...

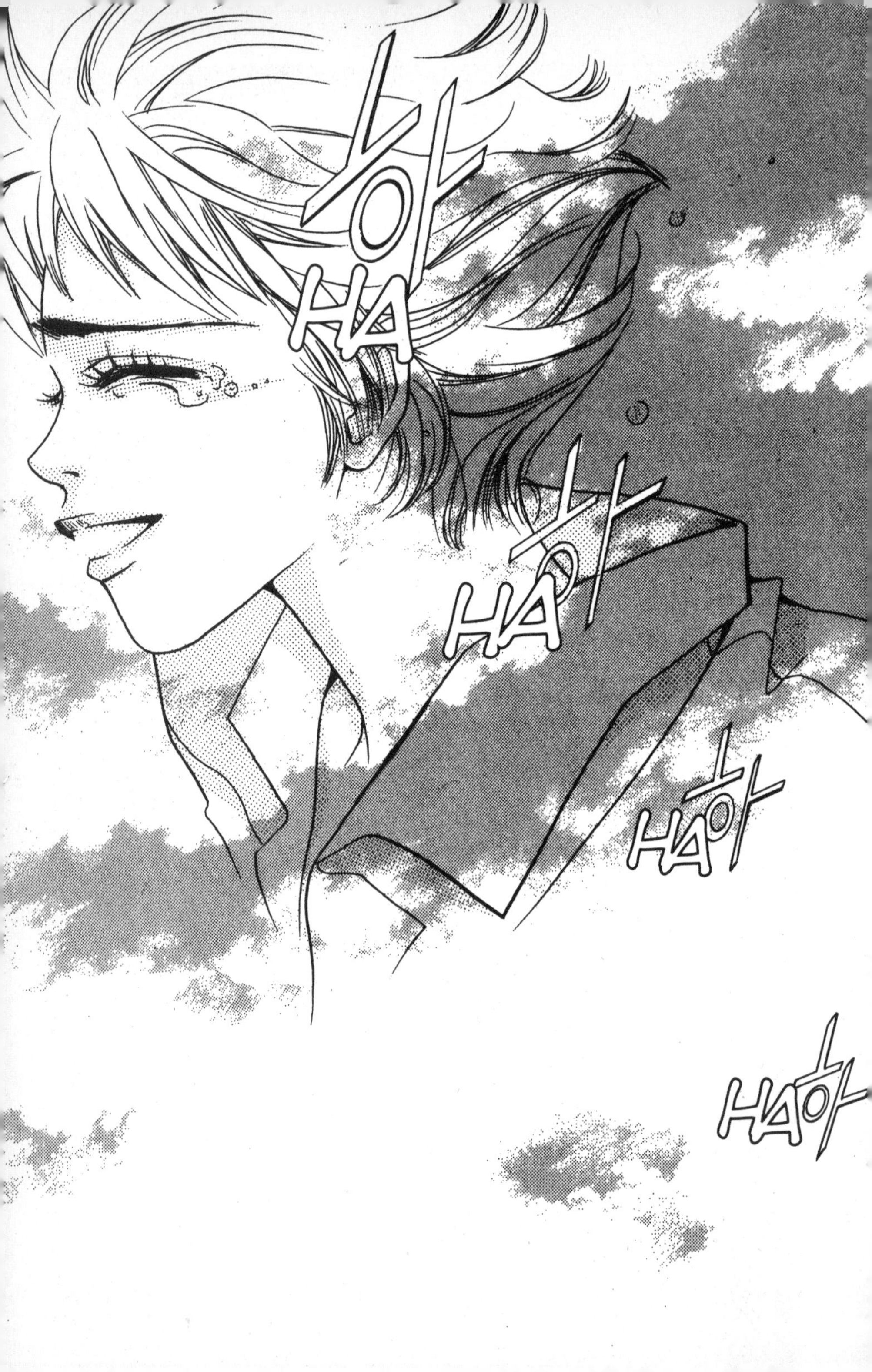

하 HA
하 HA
하 HA
하 HA

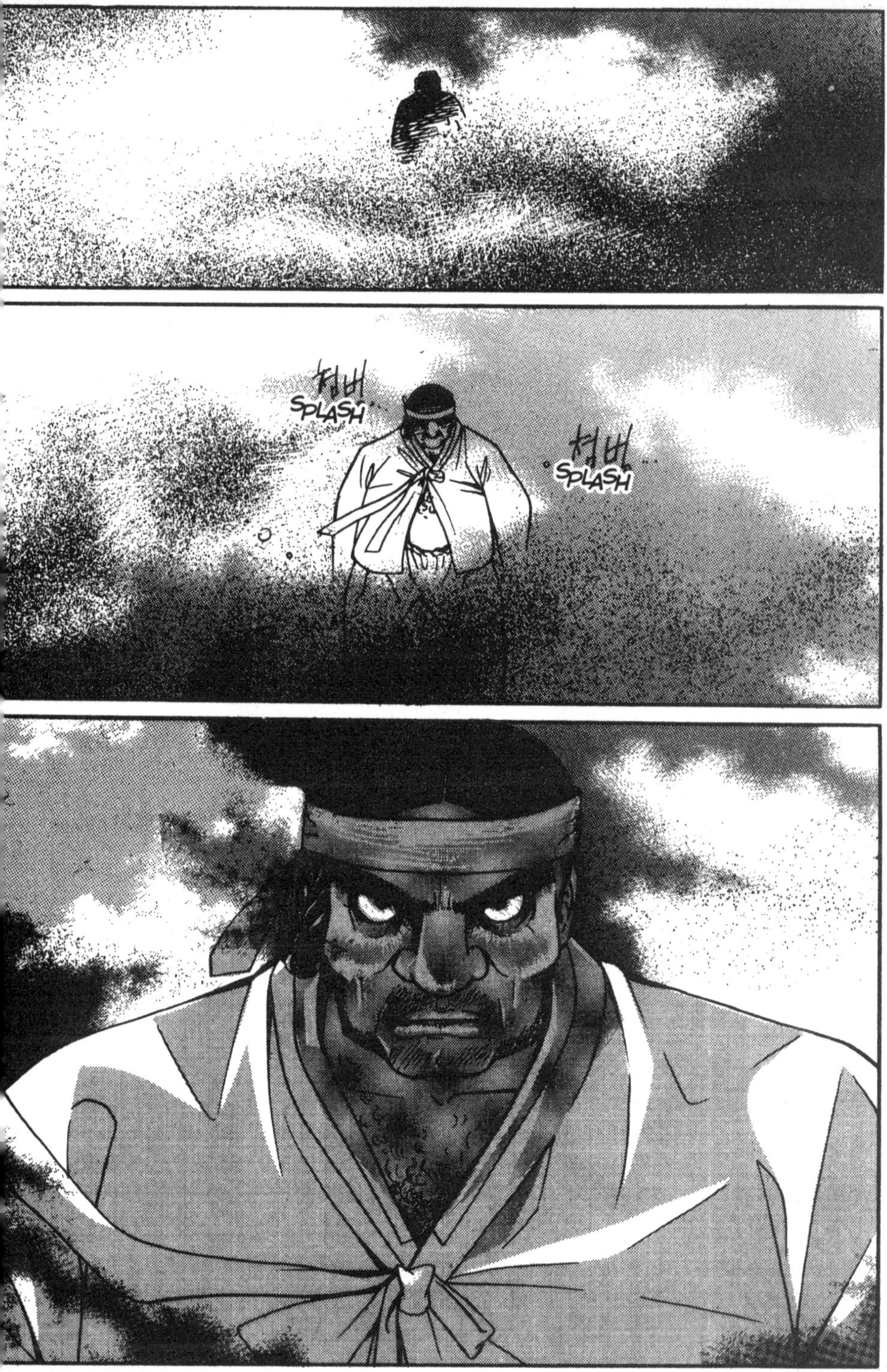
첨벙
SPLASH
첨벙
SPLASH

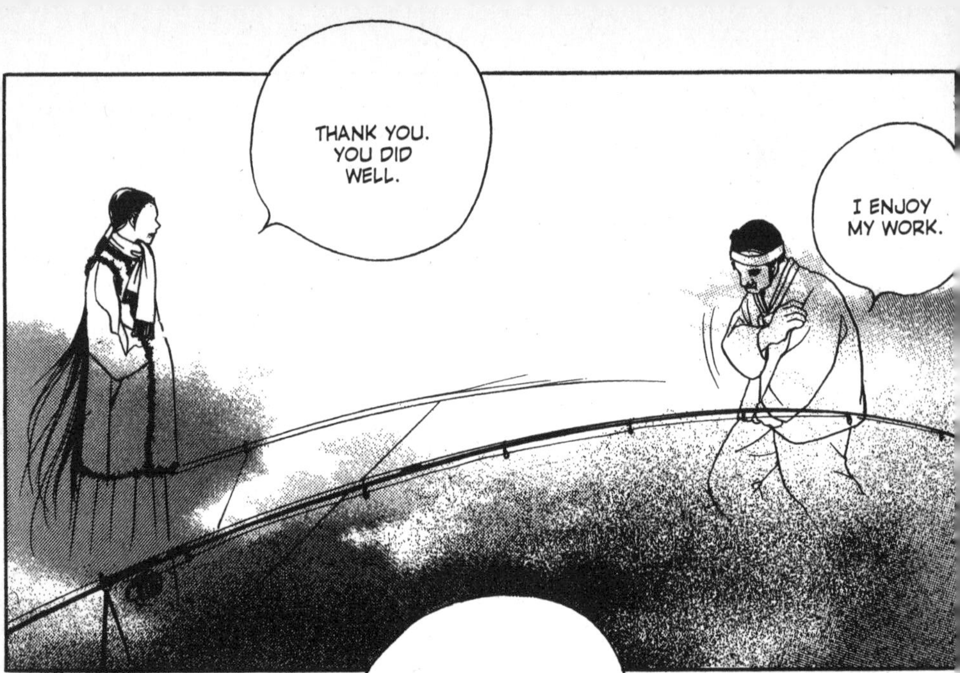
THANK YOU. YOU DID WELL.
I ENJOY MY WORK.
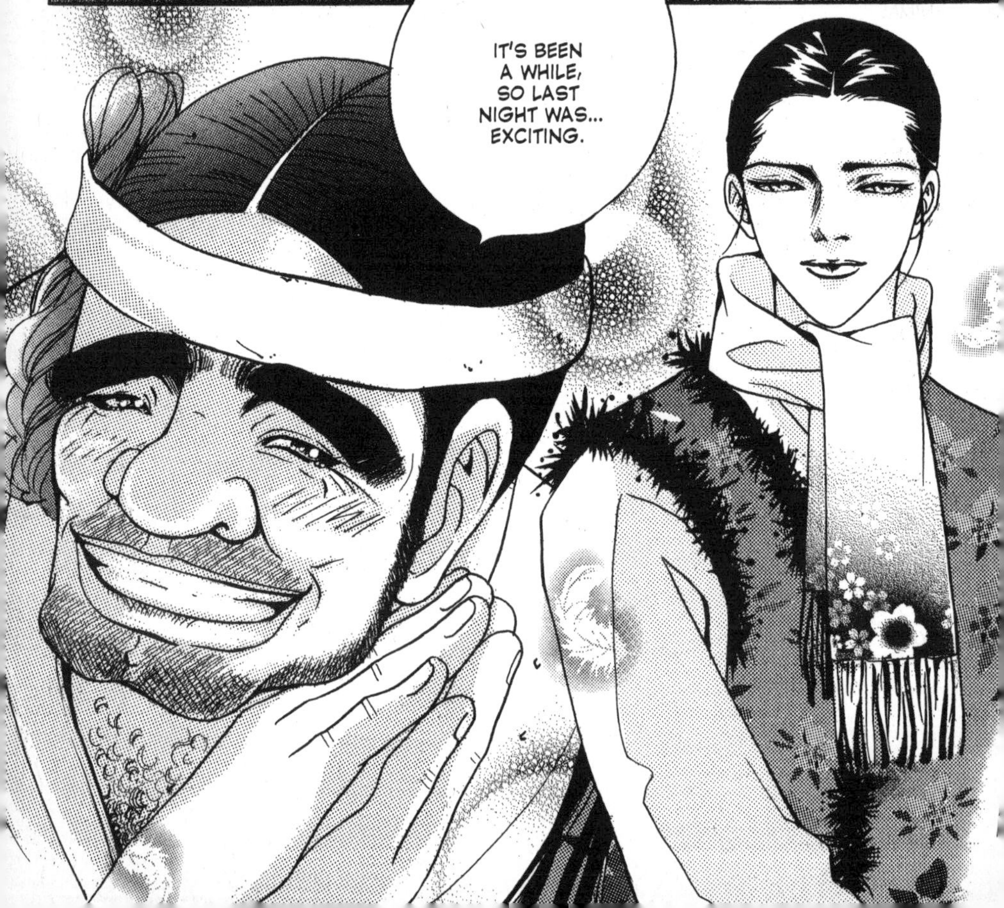
IT'S BEEN A WHILE, SO LAST NIGHT WAS... EXCITING.

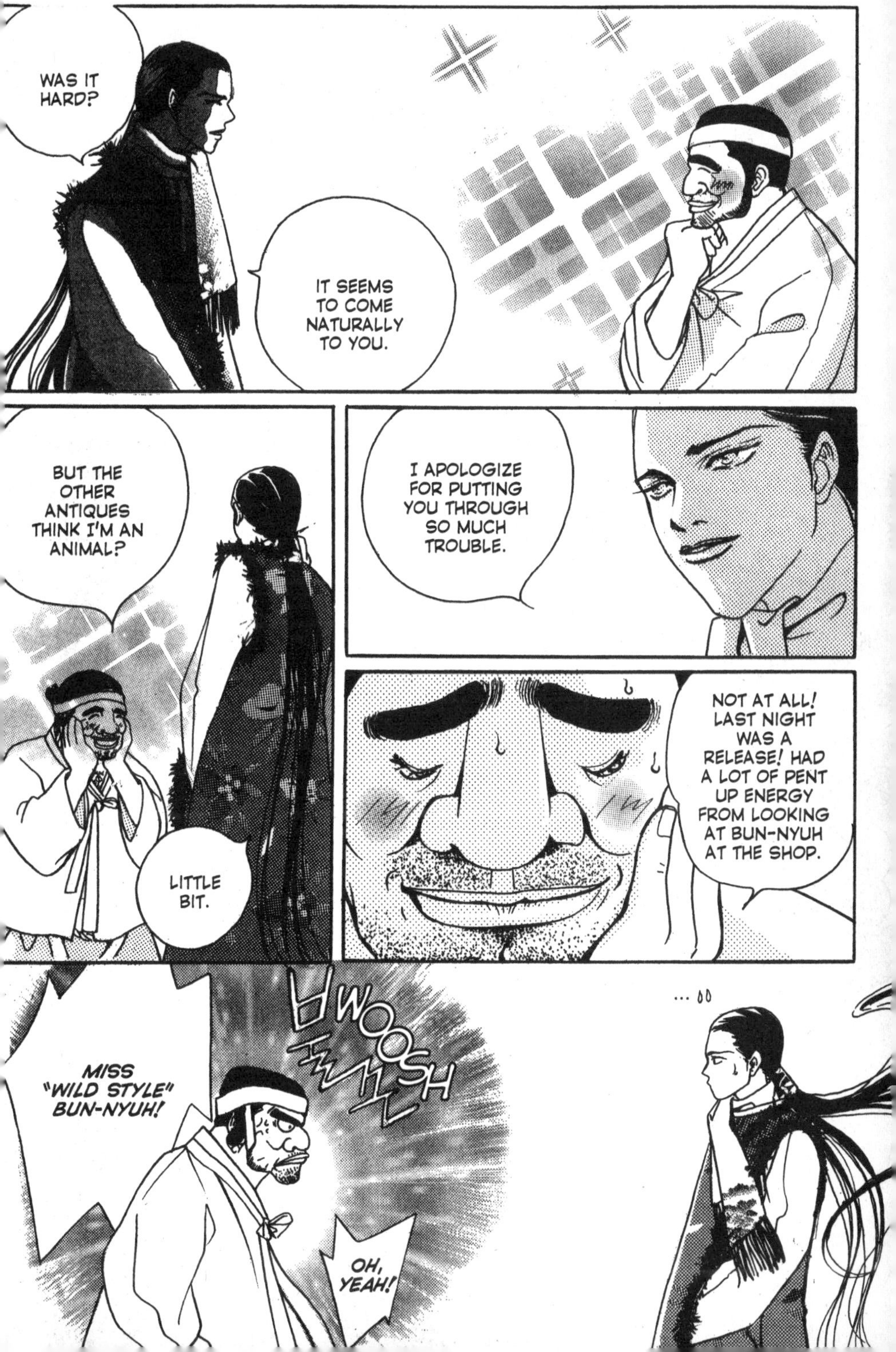
WAS IT HARD?
IT SEEMS TO COME NATURALLY TO YOU.
BUT THE OTHER ANTIQUES THINK I'M AN ANIMAL?
LITTLE BIT.
I APOLOGIZE FOR PUTTING YOU THROUGH SO MUCH TROUBLE.
NOT AT ALL! LAST NIGHT WAS A RELEASE! HAD A LOT OF PENT UP ENERGY FROM LOOKING AT BUN-NYUH AT THE SHOP.
MISS "WILD STYLE" BUN-NYUH!
WOOSH
OH, YEAH!
...

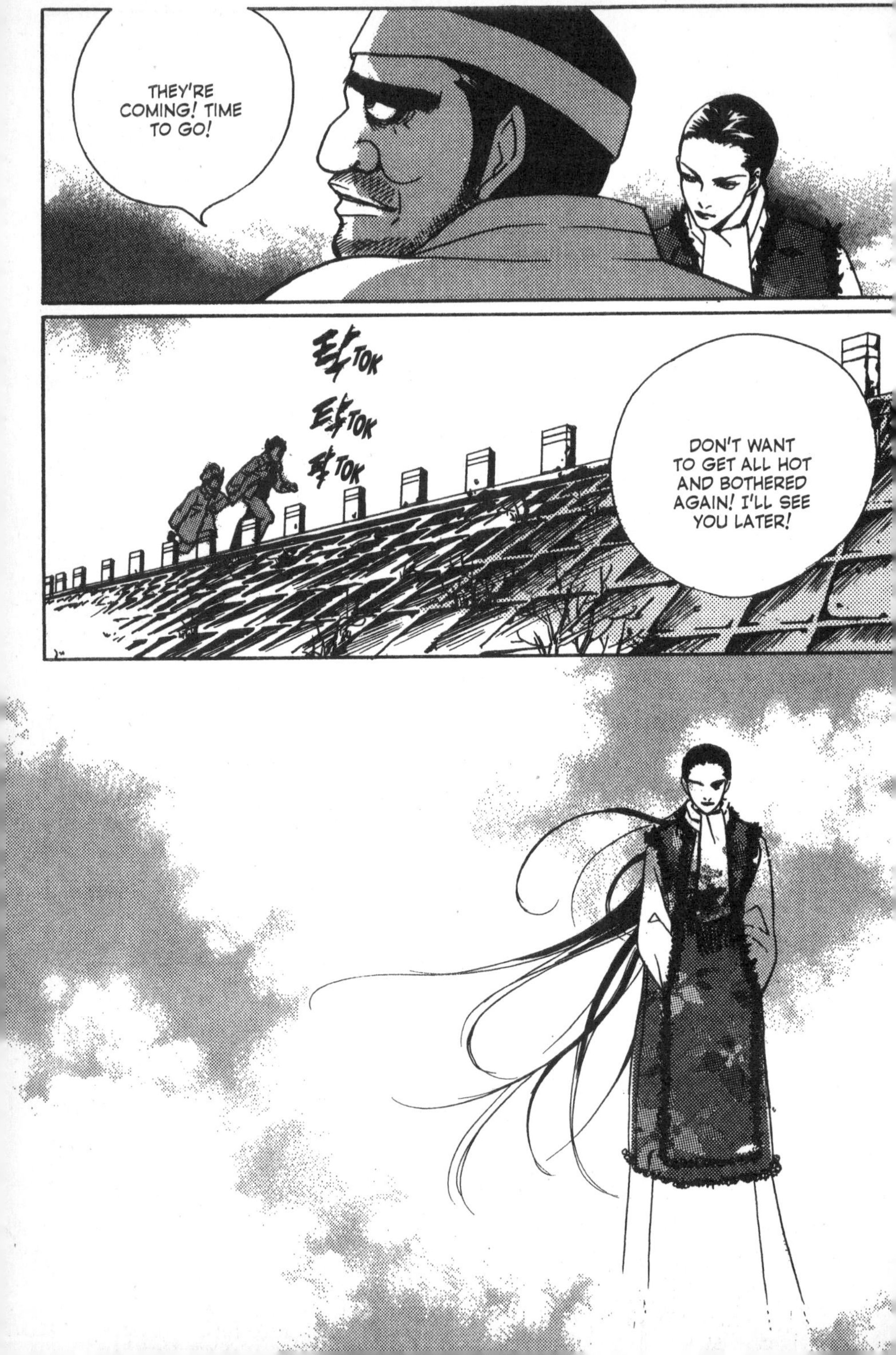
THEY'RE COMING! TIME TO GO!
TOK
TOK
TOK
DON'T WANT TO GET ALL HOT AND BOTHERED AGAIN! I'LL SEE YOU LATER!

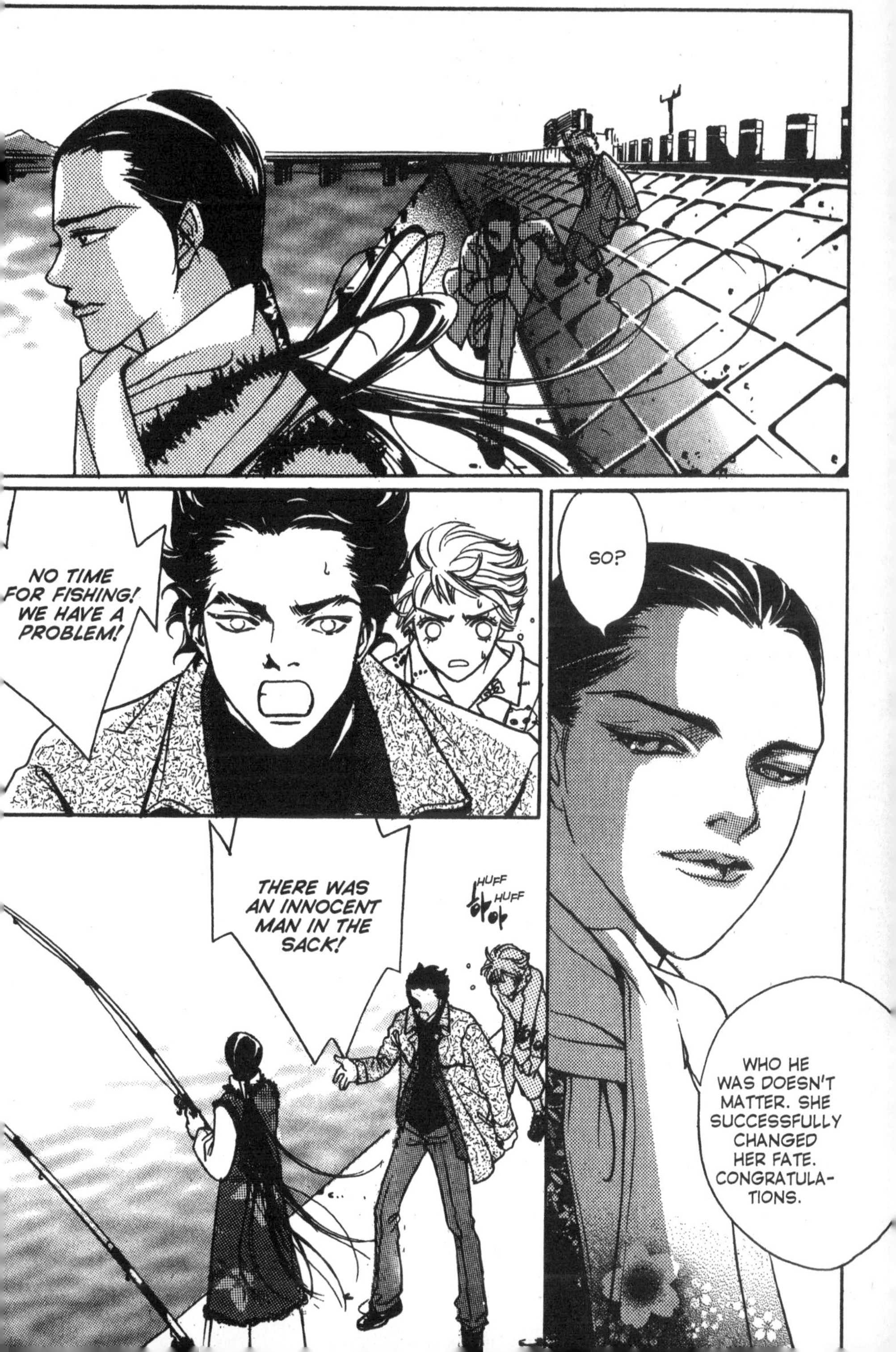
NO TIME FOR FISHING! WE HAVE A PROBLEM!
SO?
THERE WAS AN INNOCENT MAN IN THE SACK!
HUFF HUFF
WHO HE WAS DOESN'T MATTER. SHE SUCCESSFULLY CHANGED HER FATE. CONGRATULATIONS.

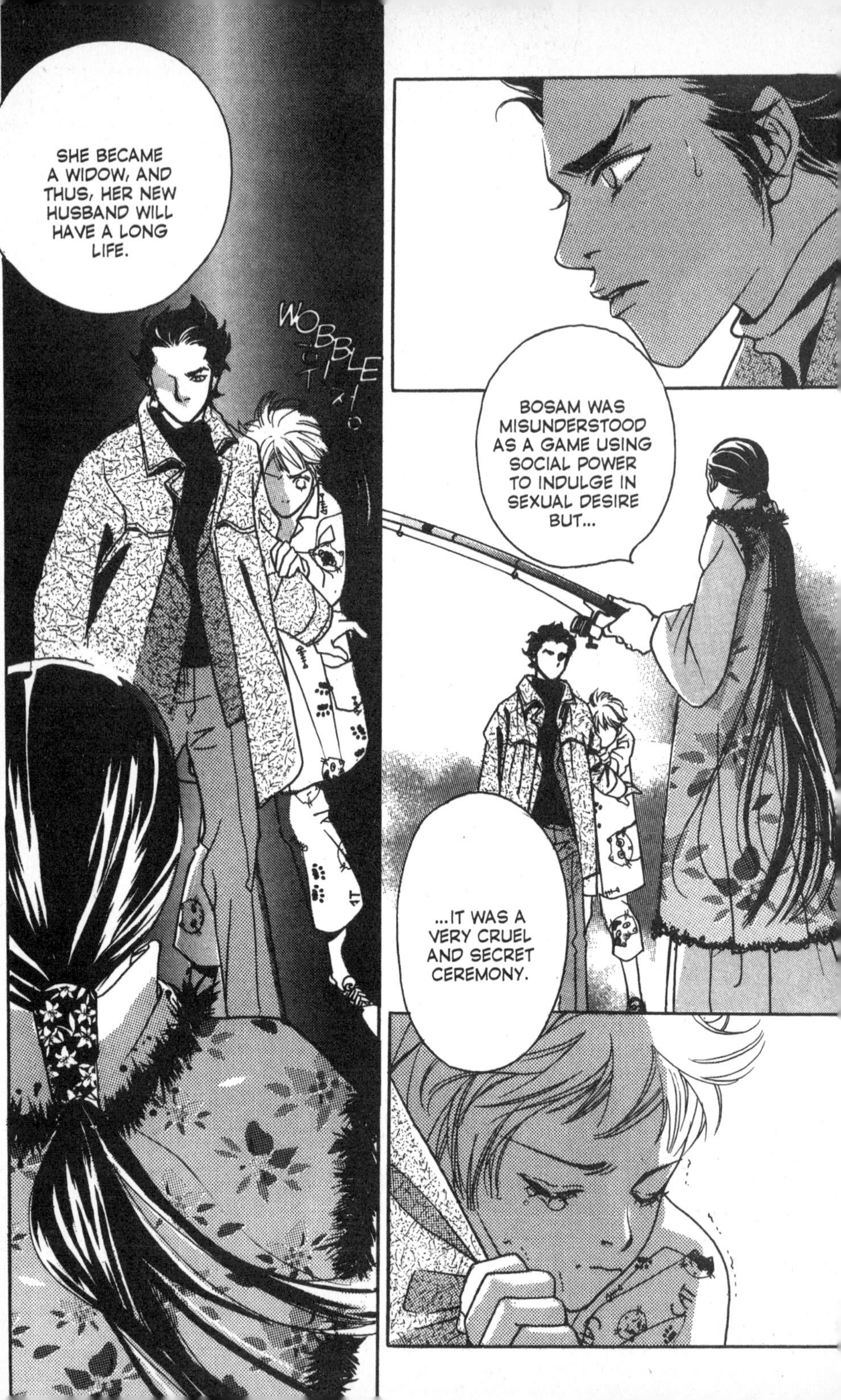
SHE BECAME A WIDOW, AND THUS, HER NEW HUSBAND WILL HAVE A LONG LIFE.
WOBBLE
BOSAM WAS MISUNDERSTOOD AS A GAME USING SOCIAL POWER TO INDULGE IN SEXUAL DESIRE BUT...
...IT WAS A VERY CRUEL AND SECRET CEREMONY.

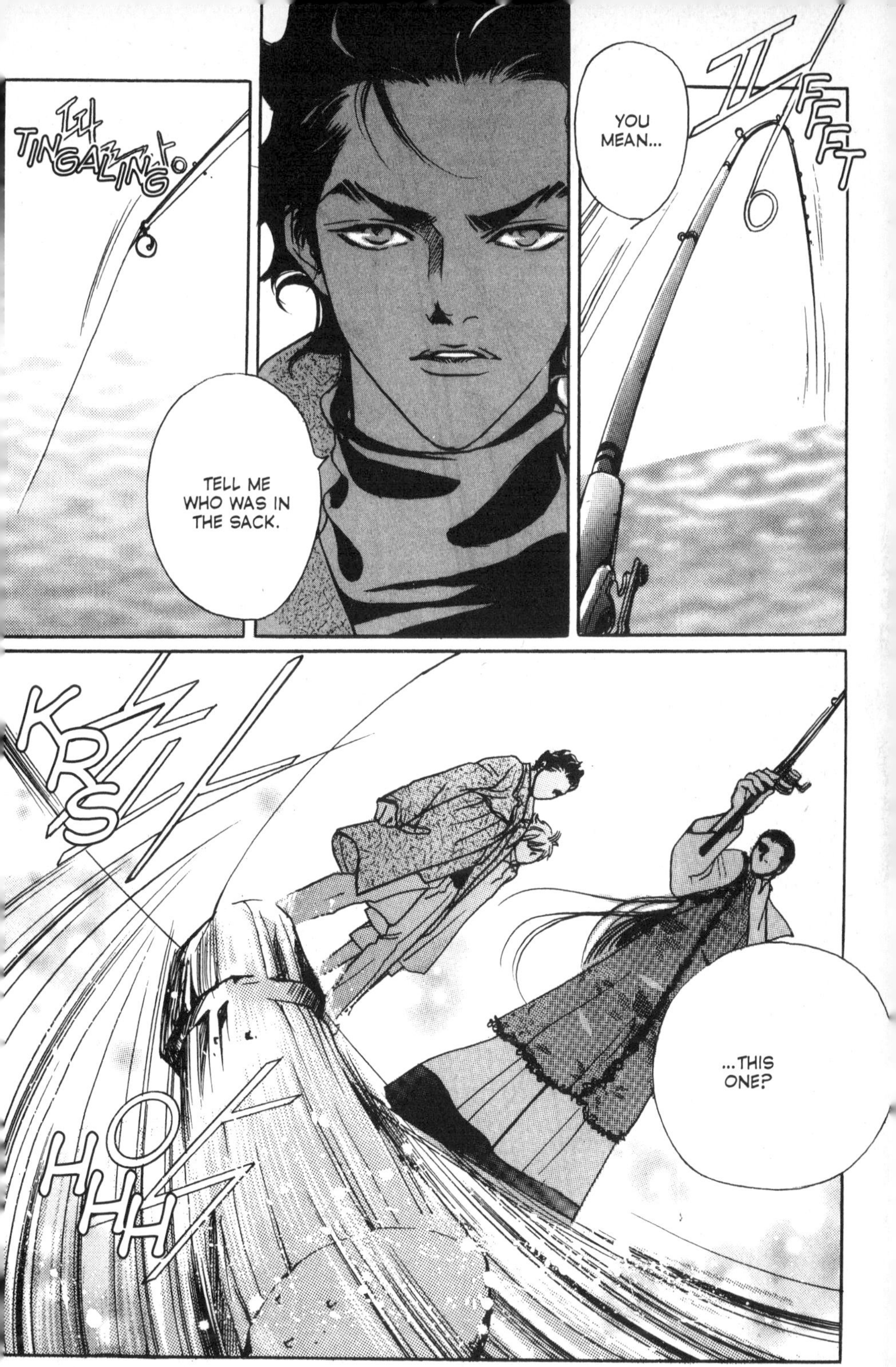
TINGALING
TELL ME WHO WAS IN THE SACK.
YOU MEAN...
FFFFT
KRS
...THIS ONE?
HHHH

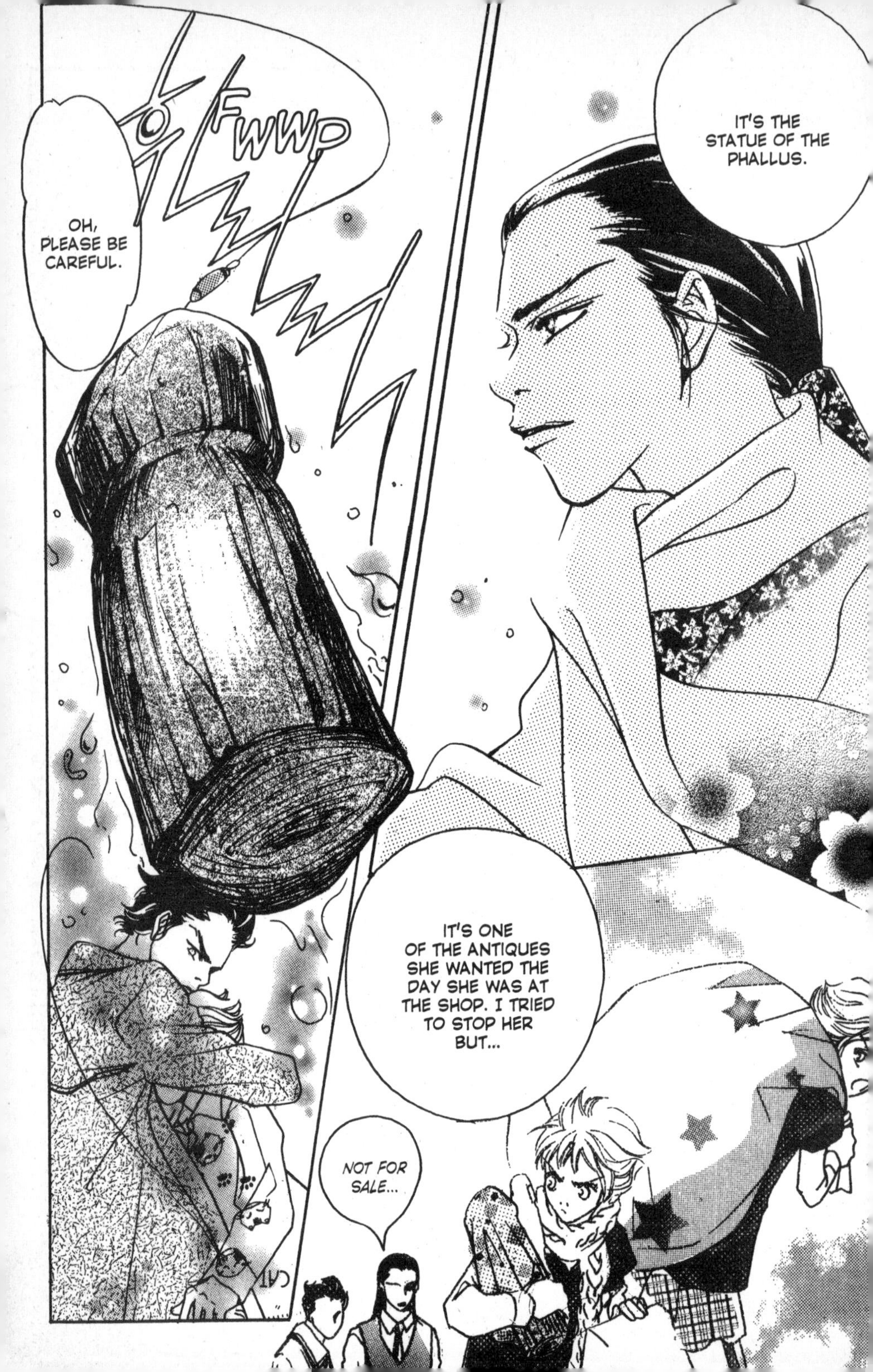
OH, PLEASE BE CAREFUL.
FWWP
IT'S THE STATUE OF THE PHALLUS.
IT'S ONE OF THE ANTIQUES SHE WANTED THE DAY SHE WAS AT THE SHOP. I TRIED TO STOP HER BUT...
NOT FOR SALE...

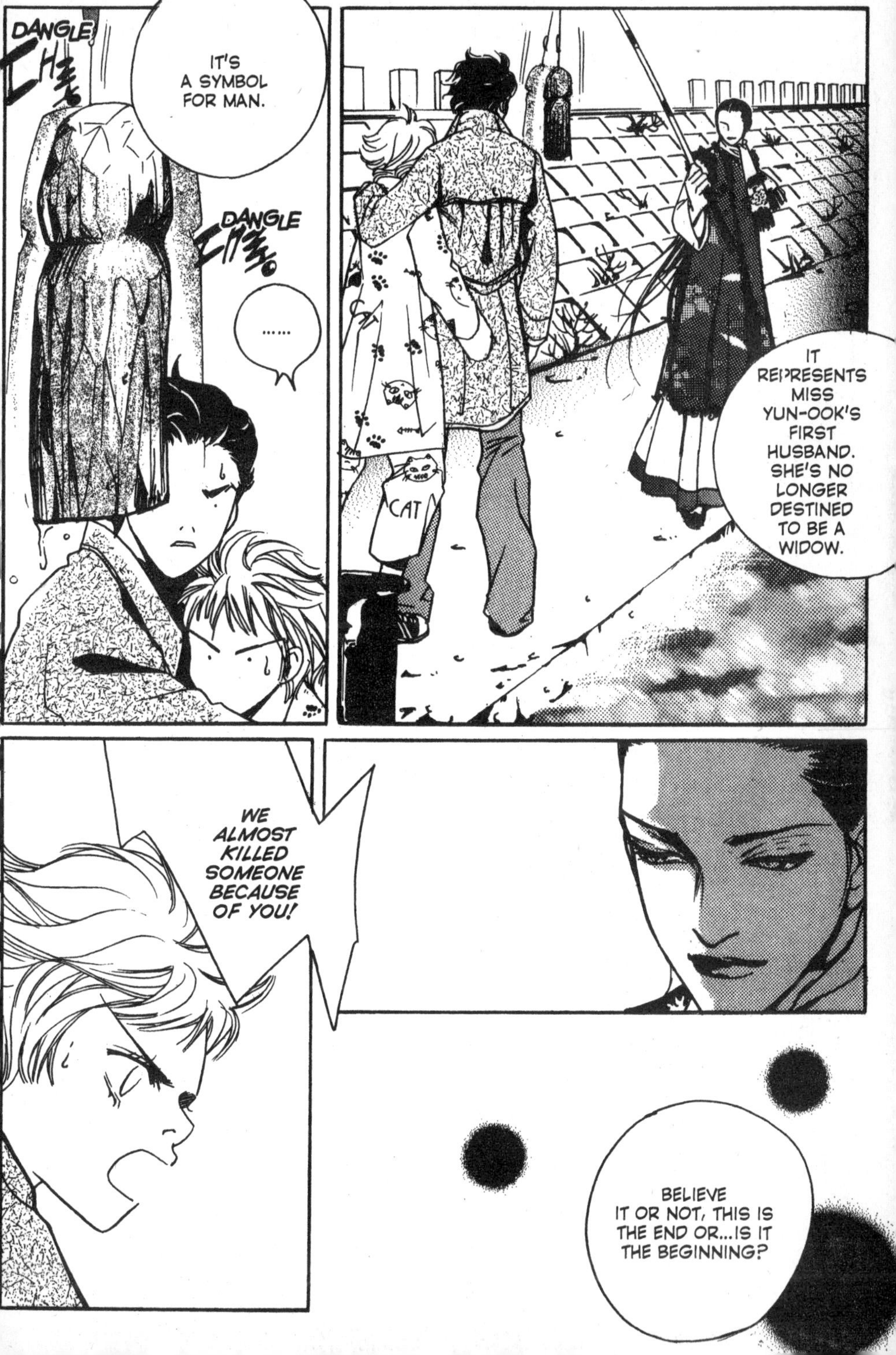
DANGLE
IT'S A SYMBOL FOR MAN.
DANGLE
......
IT REPRESENTS MISS YUN-OOK'S FIRST HUSBAND. SHE'S NO LONGER DESTINED TO BE A WIDOW.
WE ALMOST KILLED SOMEONE BECAUSE OF YOU!
BELIEVE IT OR NOT, THIS IS THE END OR...IS IT THE BEGINNING?

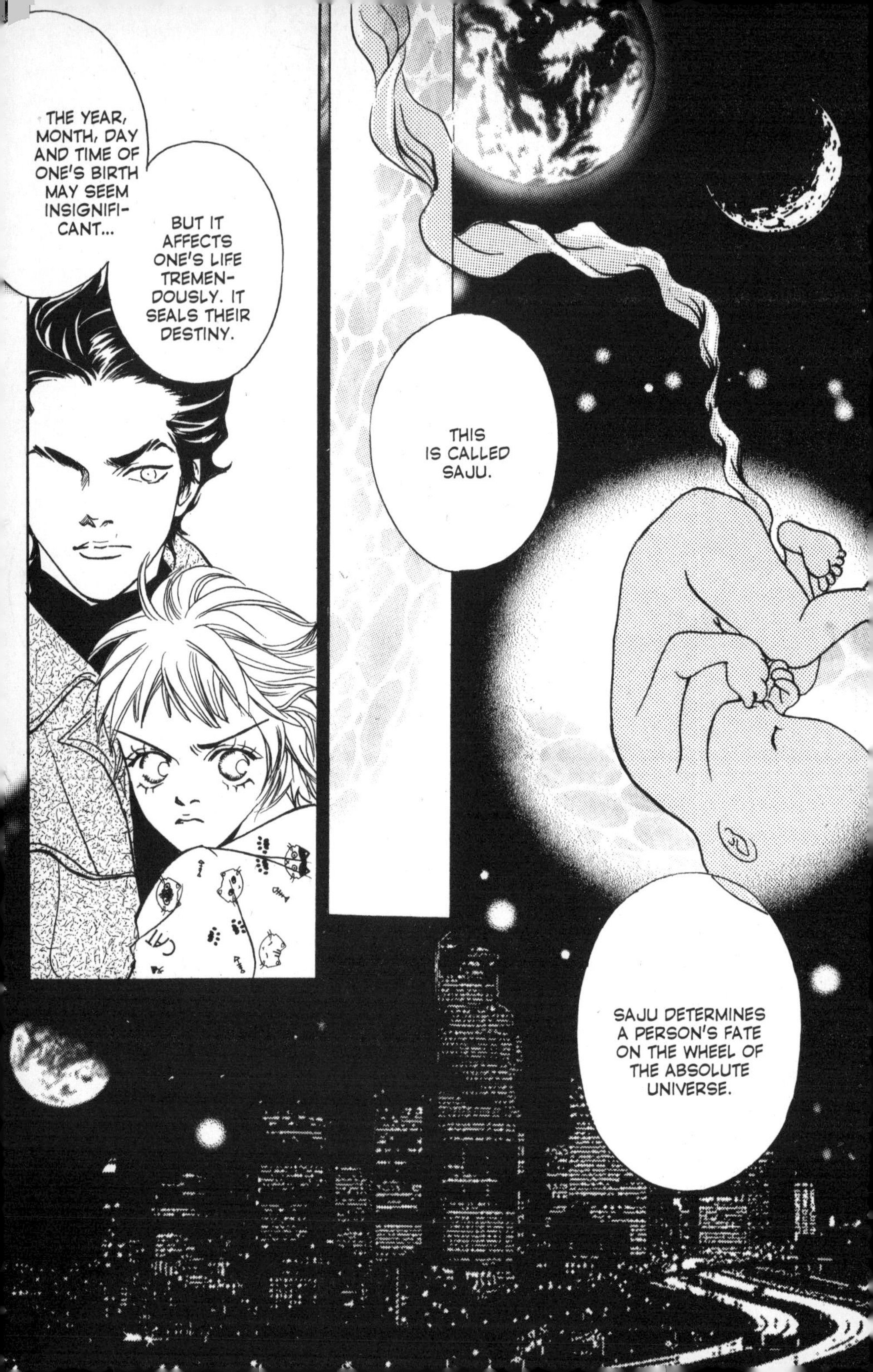
THE YEAR, MONTH, DAY AND TIME OF ONE'S BIRTH MAY SEEM INSIGNIFI-CANT...
BUT IT AFFECTS ONE'S LIFE TREMEN-DOUSLY. IT SEALS THEIR DESTINY.
THIS IS CALLED SAJU.
SAJU DETERMINES A PERSON'S FATE ON THE WHEEL OF THE ABSOLUTE UNIVERSE.

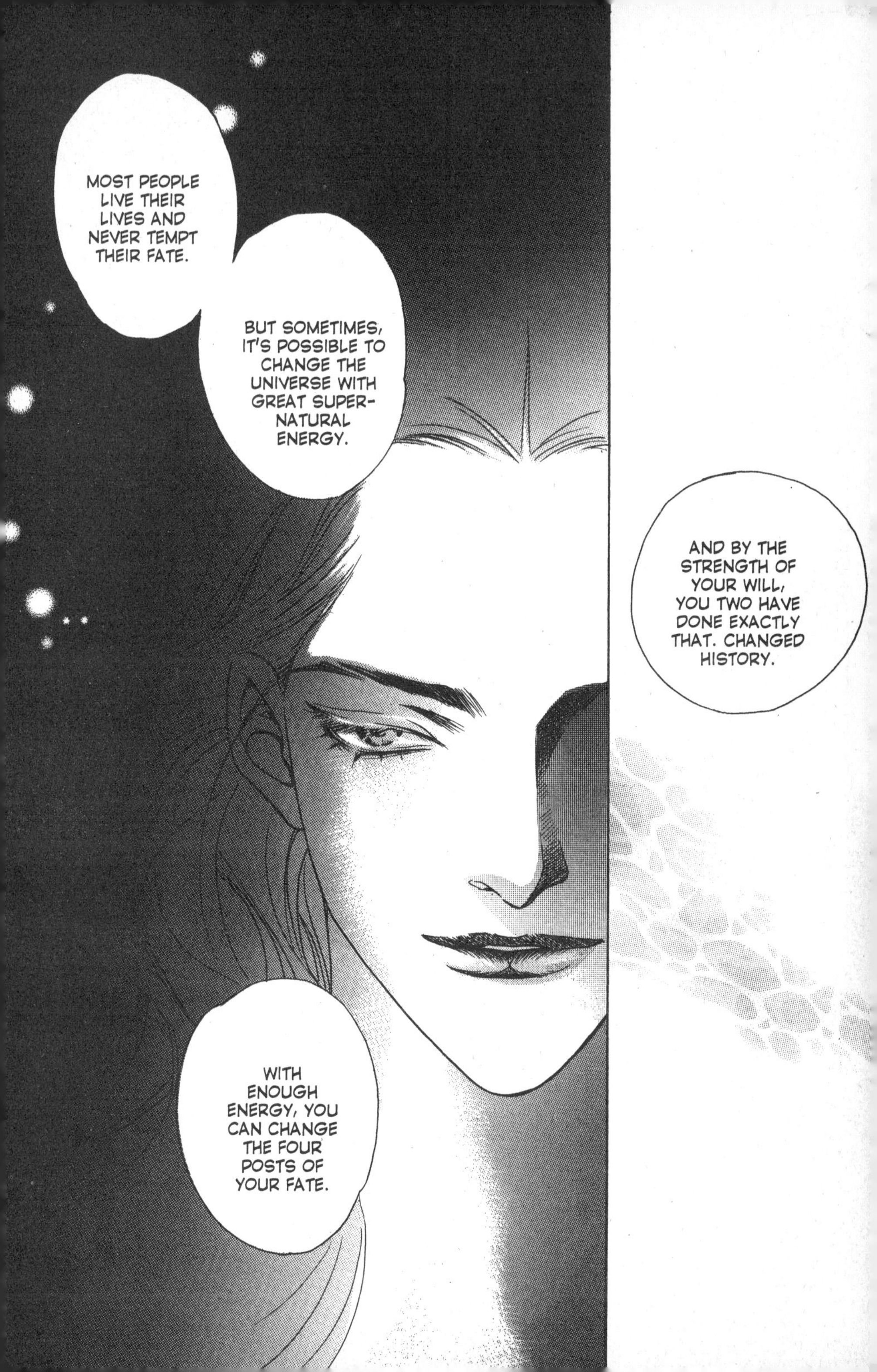
MOST PEOPLE LIVE THEIR LIVES AND NEVER TEMPT THEIR FATE.
BUT SOMETIMES, IT'S POSSIBLE TO CHANGE THE UNIVERSE WITH GREAT SUPER-NATURAL ENERGY.
WITH ENOUGH ENERGY, YOU CAN CHANGE THE FOUR POSTS OF YOUR FATE.
AND BY THE STRENGTH OF YOUR WILL, YOU TWO HAVE DONE EXACTLY THAT. CHANGED HISTORY.

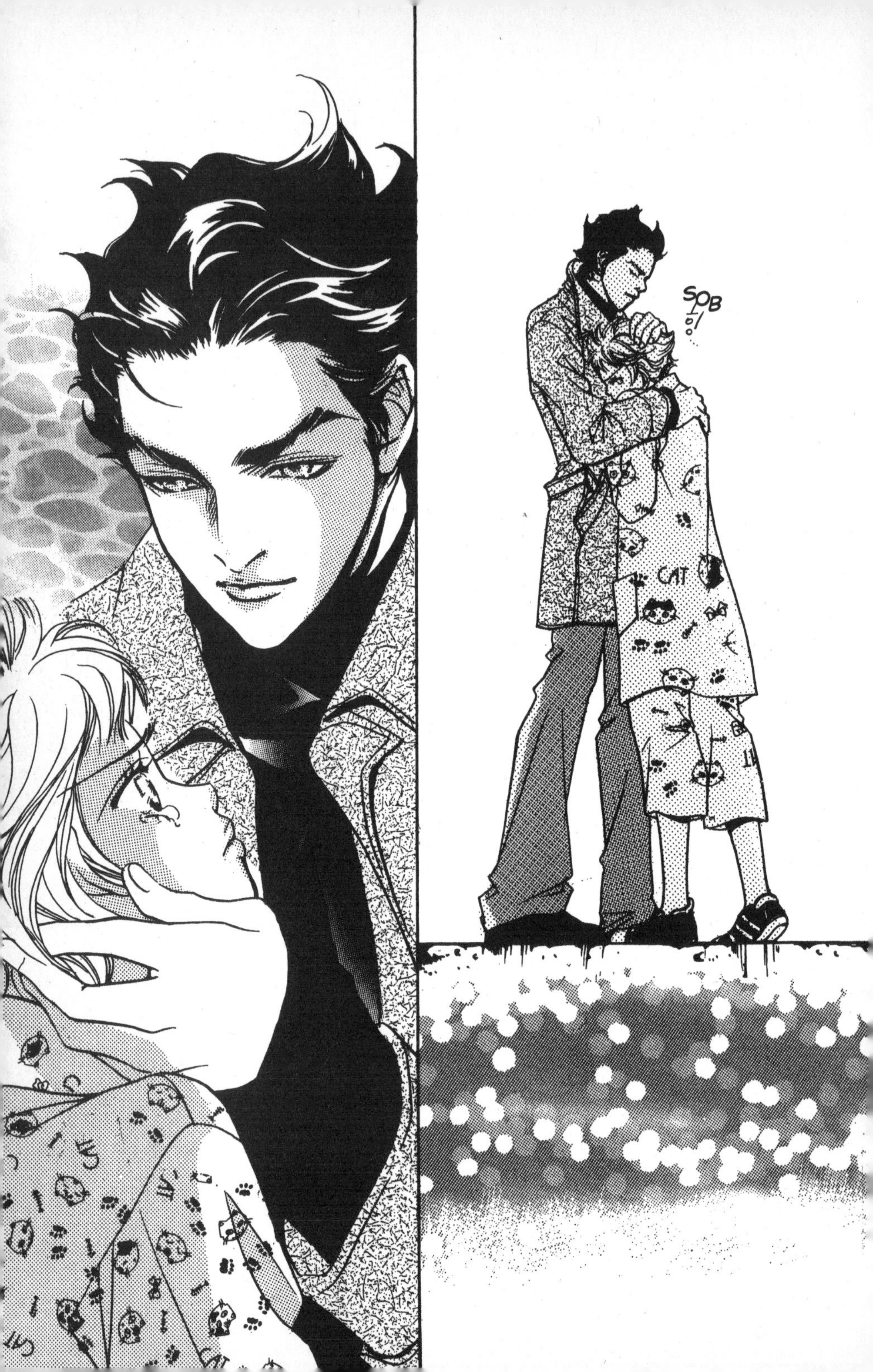
SOB

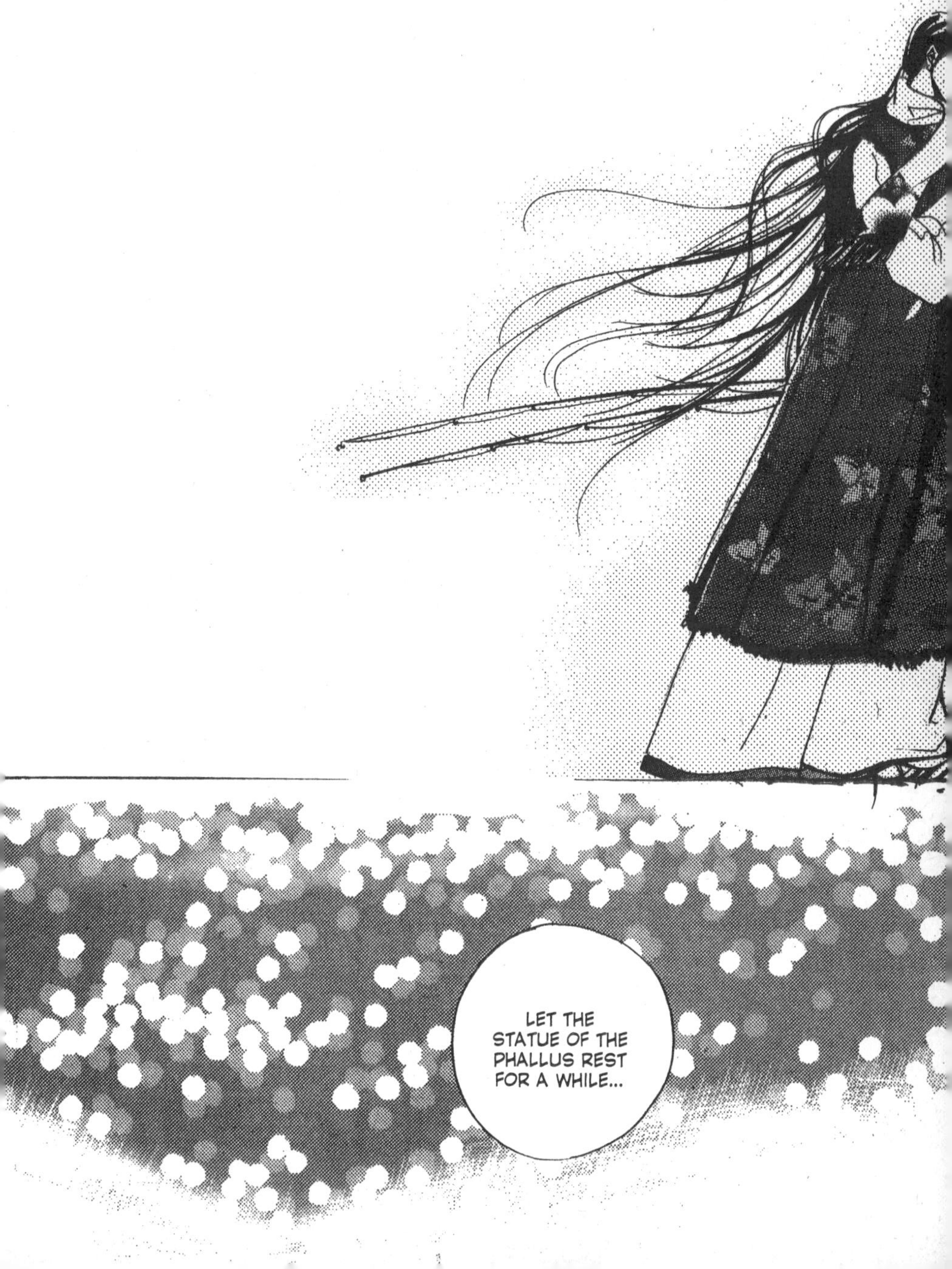
LET THE STATUE OF THE PHALLUS REST FOR A WHILE...

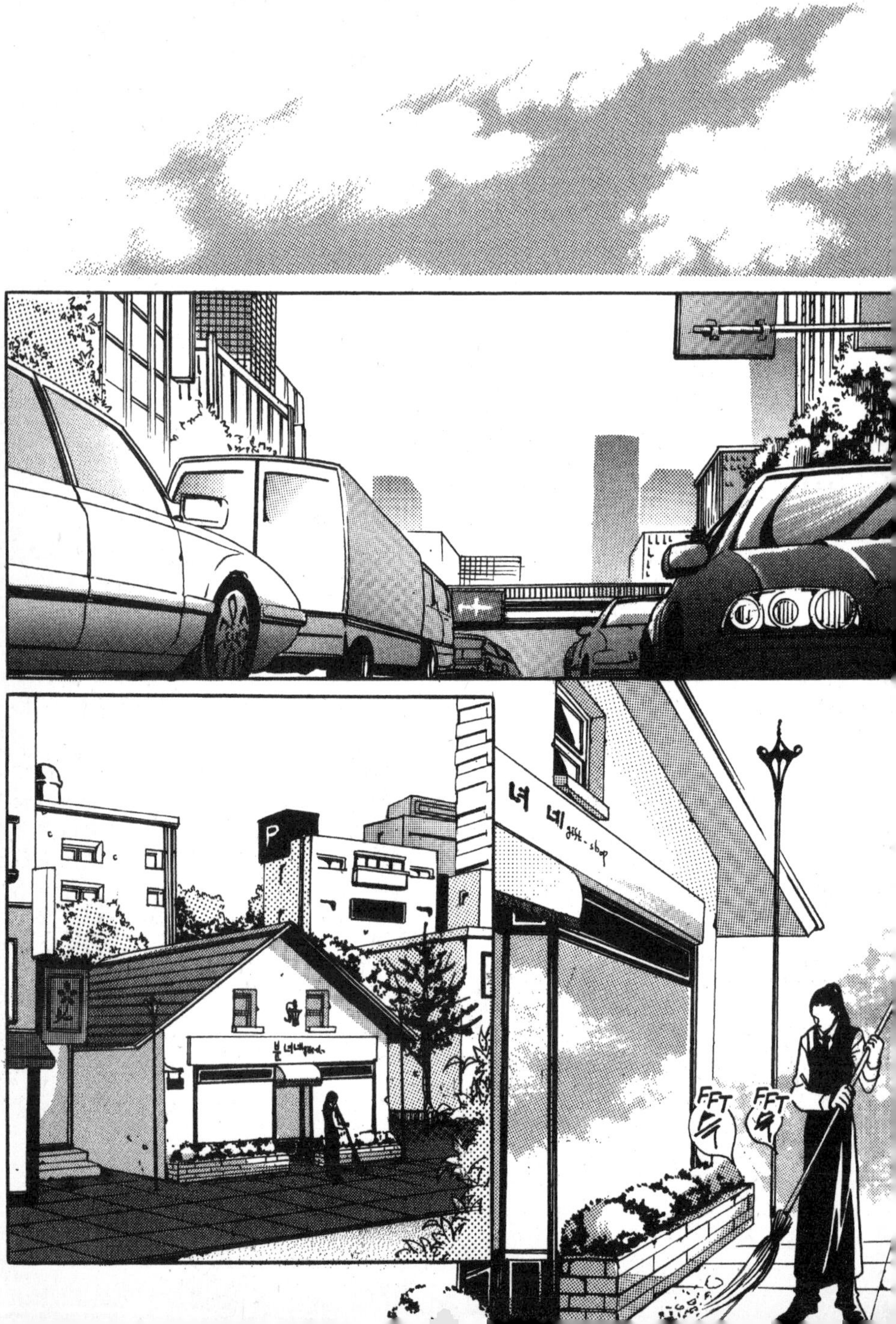
gift-shop
FFT
FFT

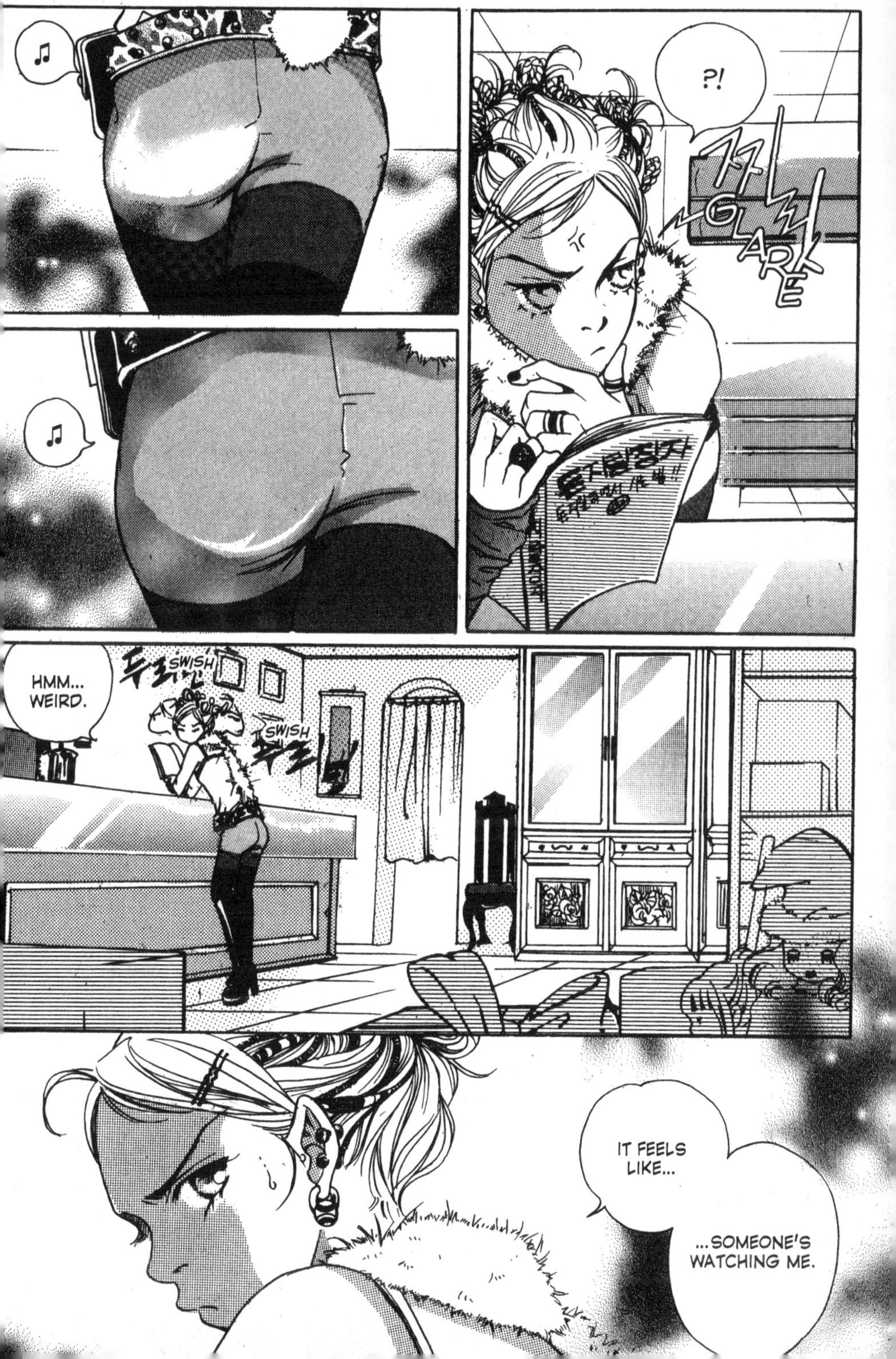
♫
♫
?!
GLARE
HMM... WEIRD.
SWISH
SWISH
IT FEELS LIKE...
...SOMEONE'S WATCHING ME.

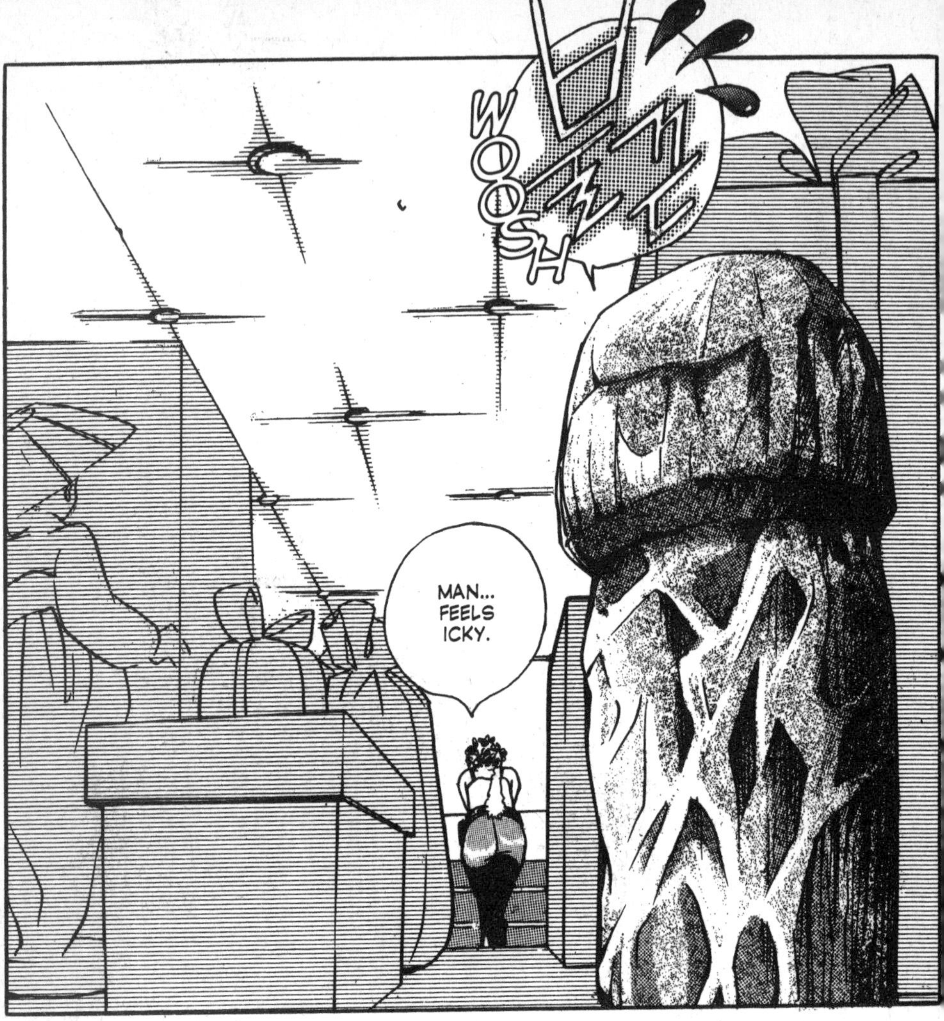
WOOSH
MAN... FEELS ICKY.

THE PHALLIC STATUE: IN THE ANCIENT RELIGIONS, THE PHALLIC STATUE WAS USED NOT ONLY AS A FERTILITY SYMBOL, OR A CHARM TO HELP HAVE A SON, BUT ALSO A MEANS OF TOTEM FOR A GOOD HARVEST. THEY WERE MADE FROM THE WOOD OF GREAT TREES FOUND HIGH UP IN THE MOUNTAINS WHERE HUMANS RARELY VENTURED. WORSHIPPERS OFFERED IT TO THE GODDESS OF THE VILLAGE IN THE HOPES OF PROSPERITY. HOWEVER, IT WAS CONSIDERED ADULTERY, IF IT WAS OFFERED TO A MARRIED GODDESS.

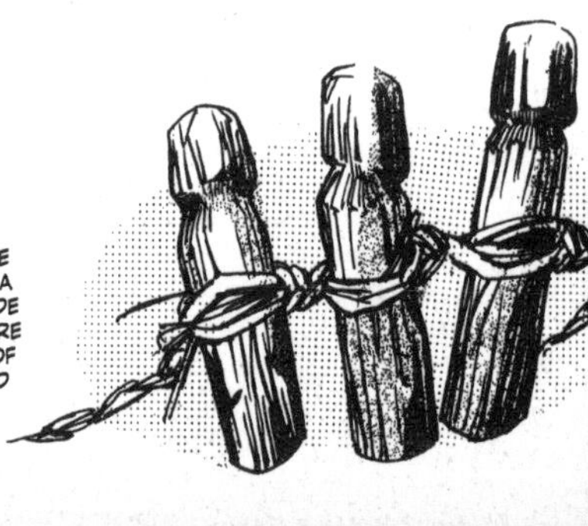

Chapter 7
Strange Family in Snow Heights

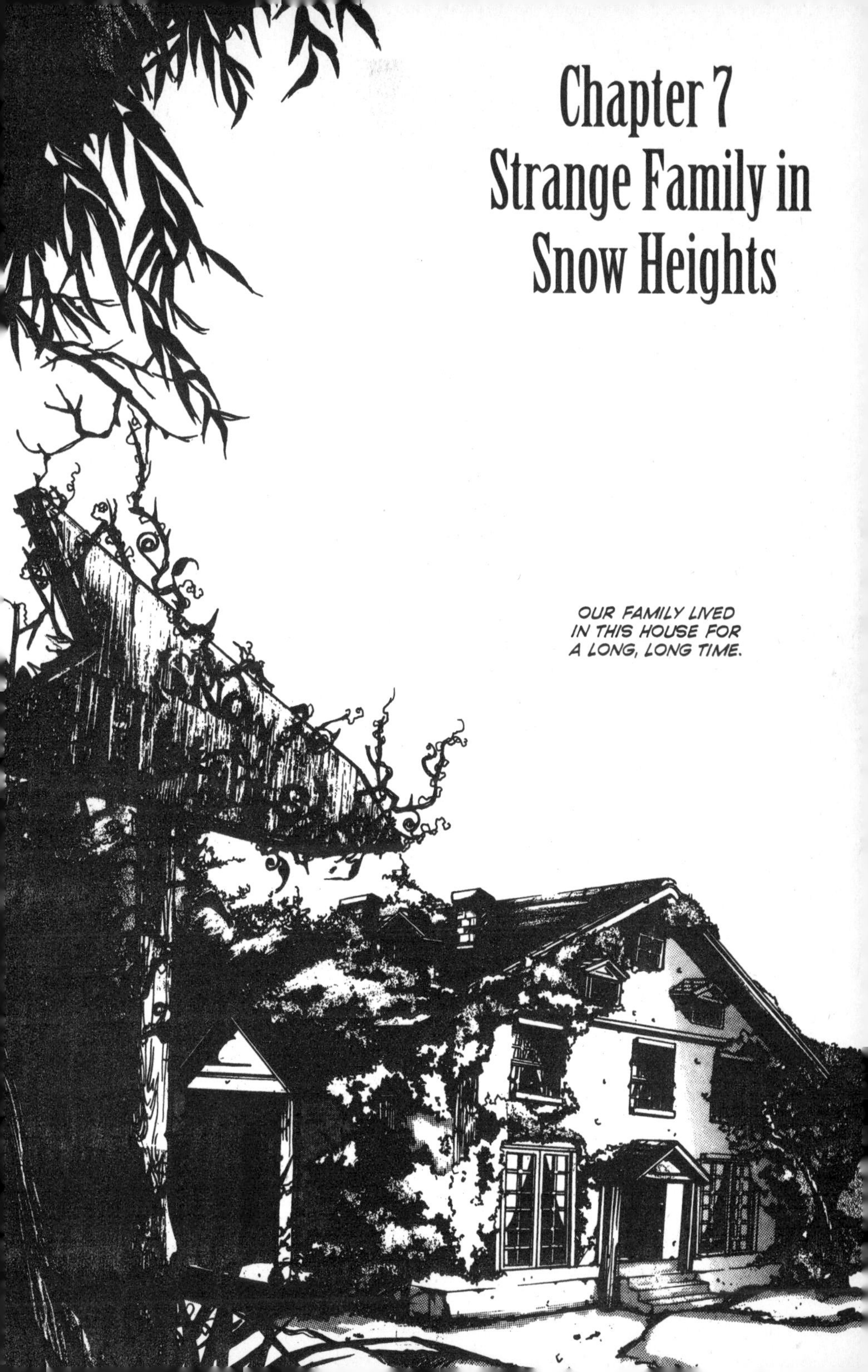
OUR FAMILY LIVED IN THIS HOUSE FOR A LONG, LONG TIME.

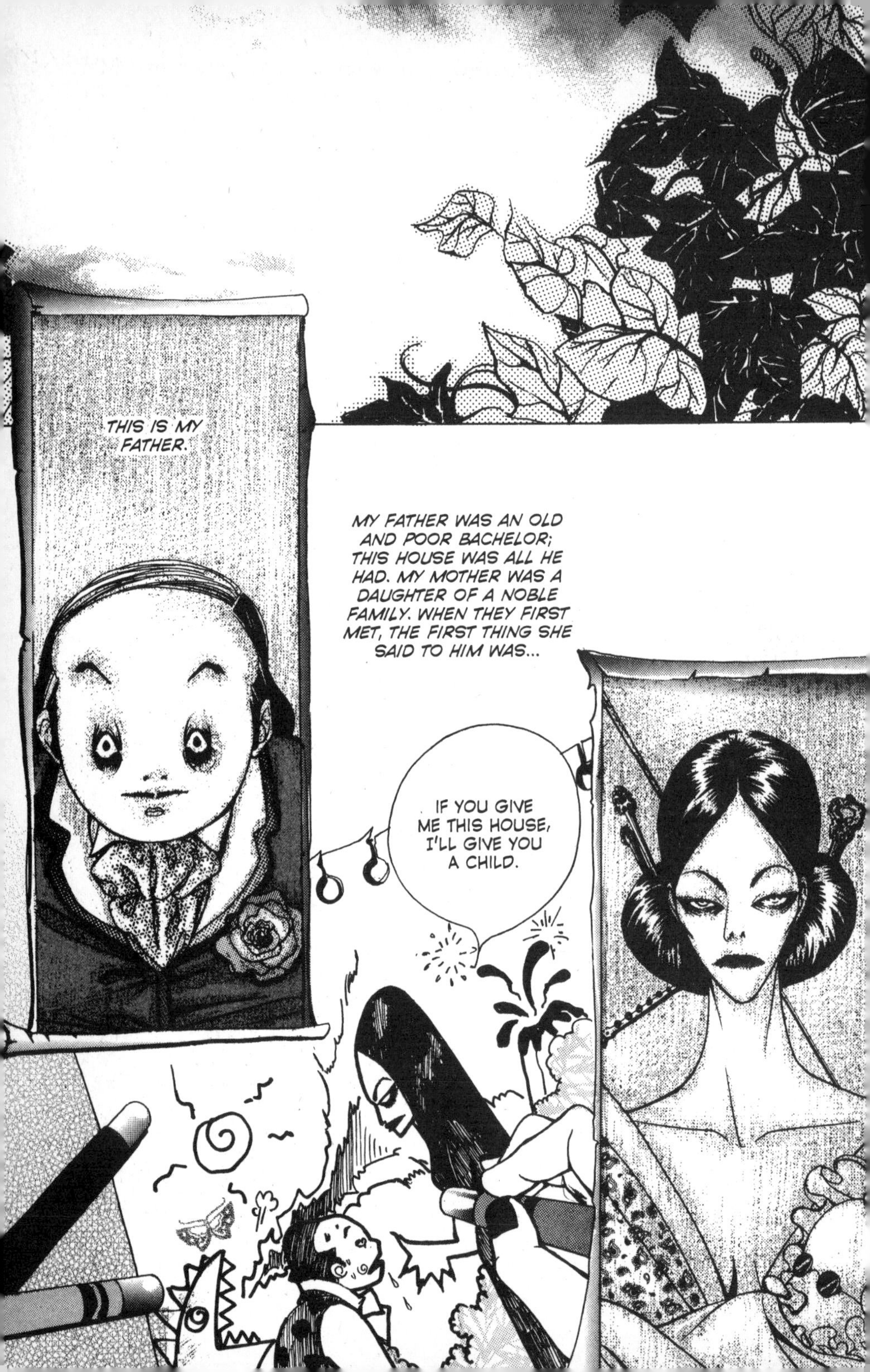
THIS IS MY FATHER.
MY FATHER WAS AN OLD AND POOR BACHELOR; THIS HOUSE WAS ALL HE HAD. MY MOTHER WAS A DAUGHTER OF A NOBLE FAMILY. WHEN THEY FIRST MET, THE FIRST THING SHE SAID TO HIM WAS...
IF YOU GIVE ME THIS HOUSE, I'LL GIVE YOU A CHILD.

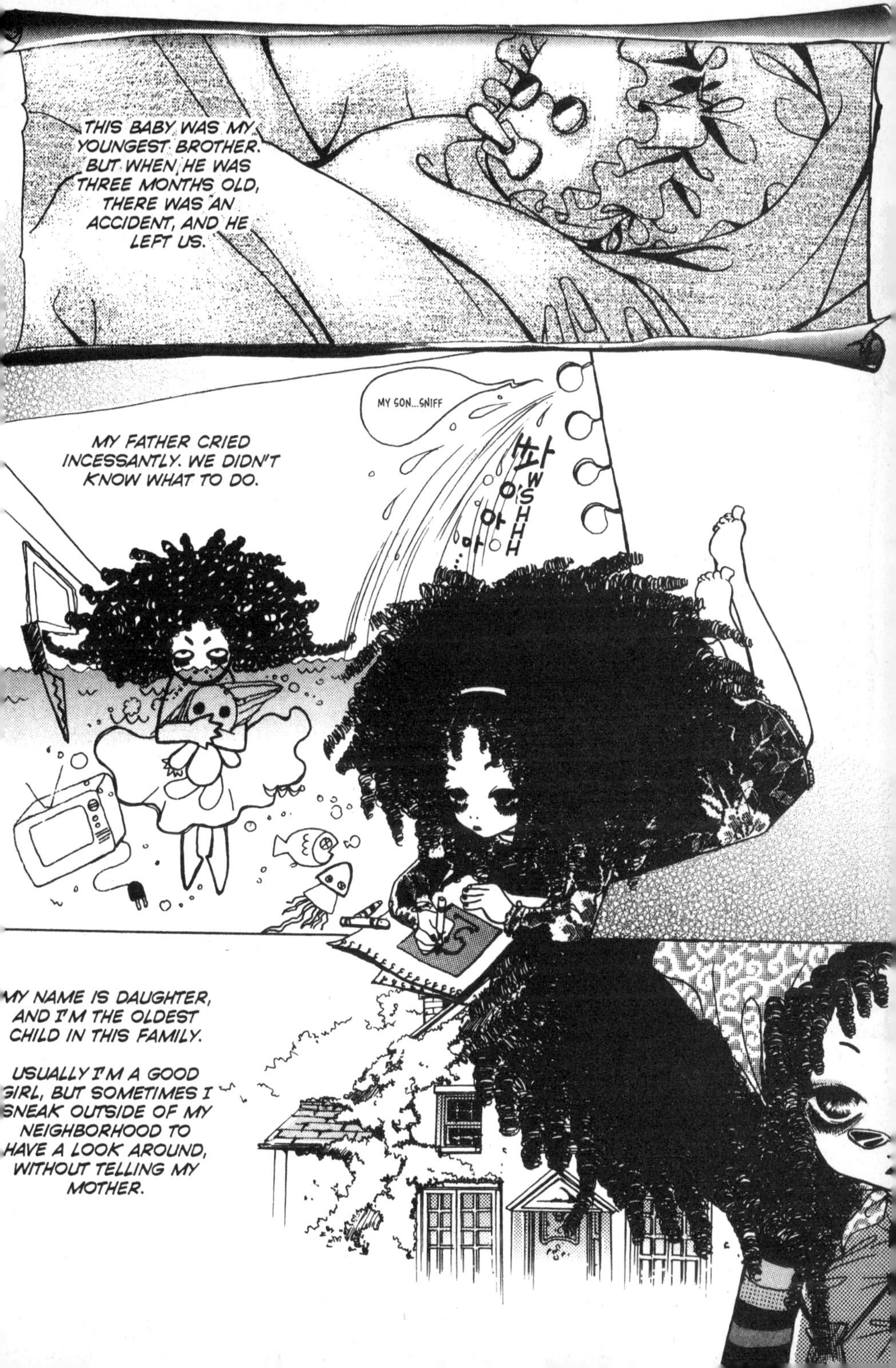
THIS BABY WAS MY YOUNGEST BROTHER. BUT WHEN HE WAS THREE MONTHS OLD, THERE WAS AN ACCIDENT, AND HE LEFT US.
MY FATHER CRIED INCESSANTLY. WE DIDN'T KNOW WHAT TO DO.
MY SON...SNIFF
쏴아아아...
WSHHH
MY NAME IS DAUGHTER, AND I'M THE OLDEST CHILD IN THIS FAMILY.
USUALLY I'M A GOOD GIRL, BUT SOMETIMES I SNEAK OUTSIDE OF MY NEIGHBORHOOD TO HAVE A LOOK AROUND, WITHOUT TELLING MY MOTHER.

AND...
...SIGH...

...THIS IS MY
YOUNGER BROTHER
"SON".

SORRY, CAN'T SHOW
YOU A PICTURE OF
HIM. SON IS
DEFORMED.

DON'T WORRY,
I'M DOING YOU
A FAVOR.

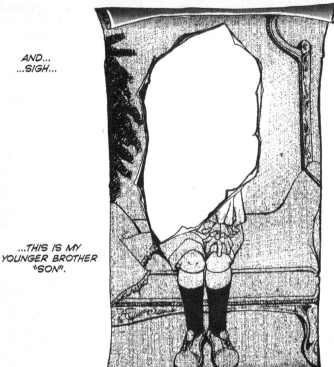

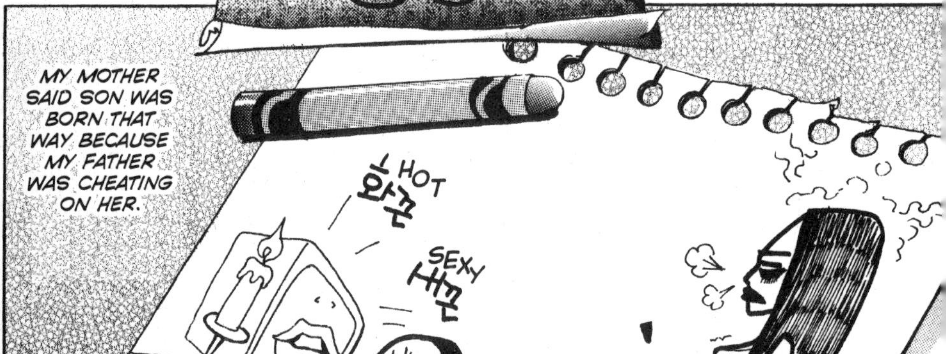

MY MOTHER SAID SON WAS BORN THAT WAY BECAUSE MY FATHER WAS CHEATING ON HER.
화끈 HOT
새끈 SEXY

ONE SNOWY
DAY...

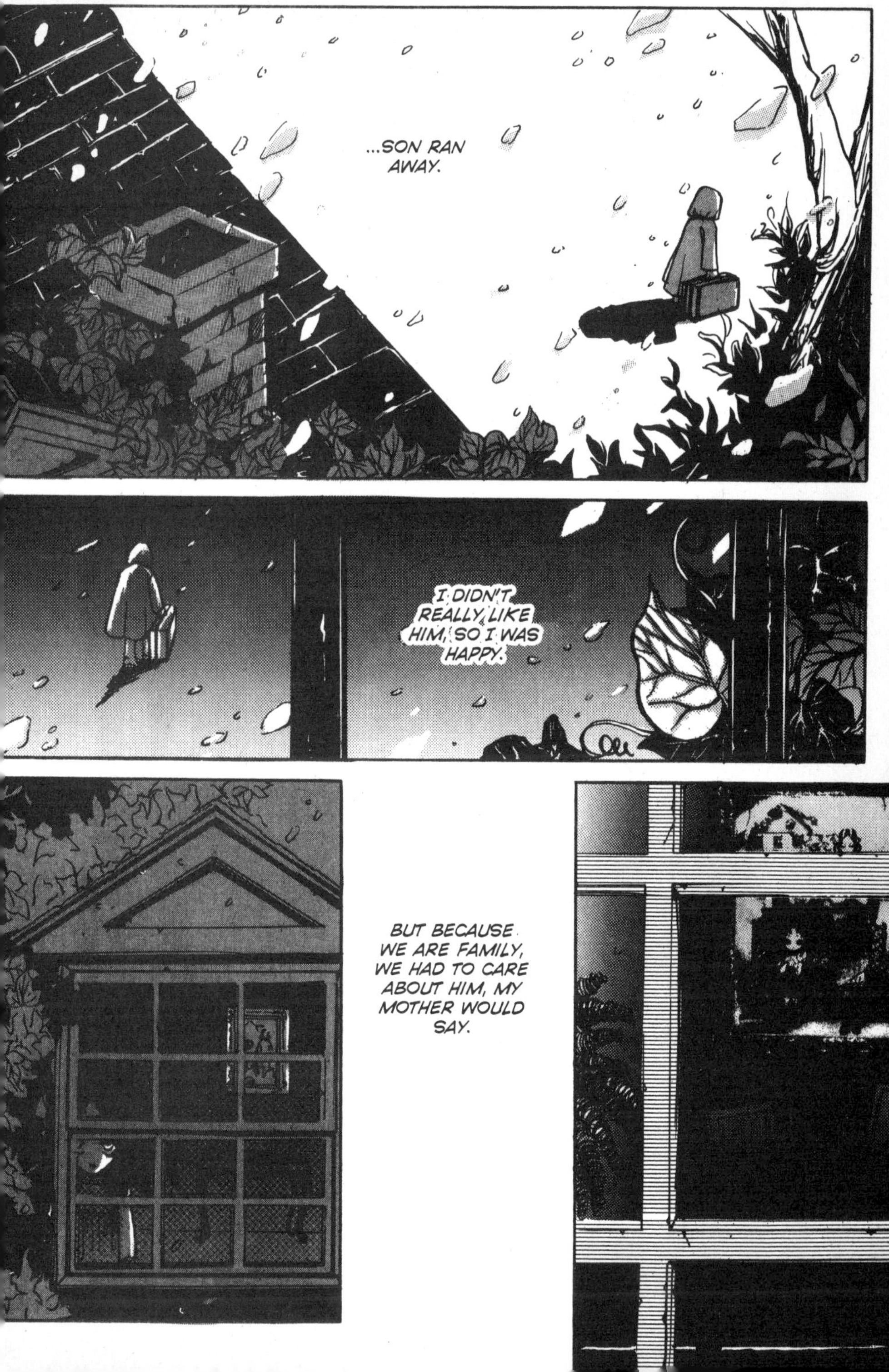
...SON RAN AWAY.
I DIDN'T REALLY LIKE HIM, SO I WAS HAPPY.
BUT BECAUSE WE ARE FAMILY, WE HAD TO CARE ABOUT HIM, MY MOTHER WOULD SAY.

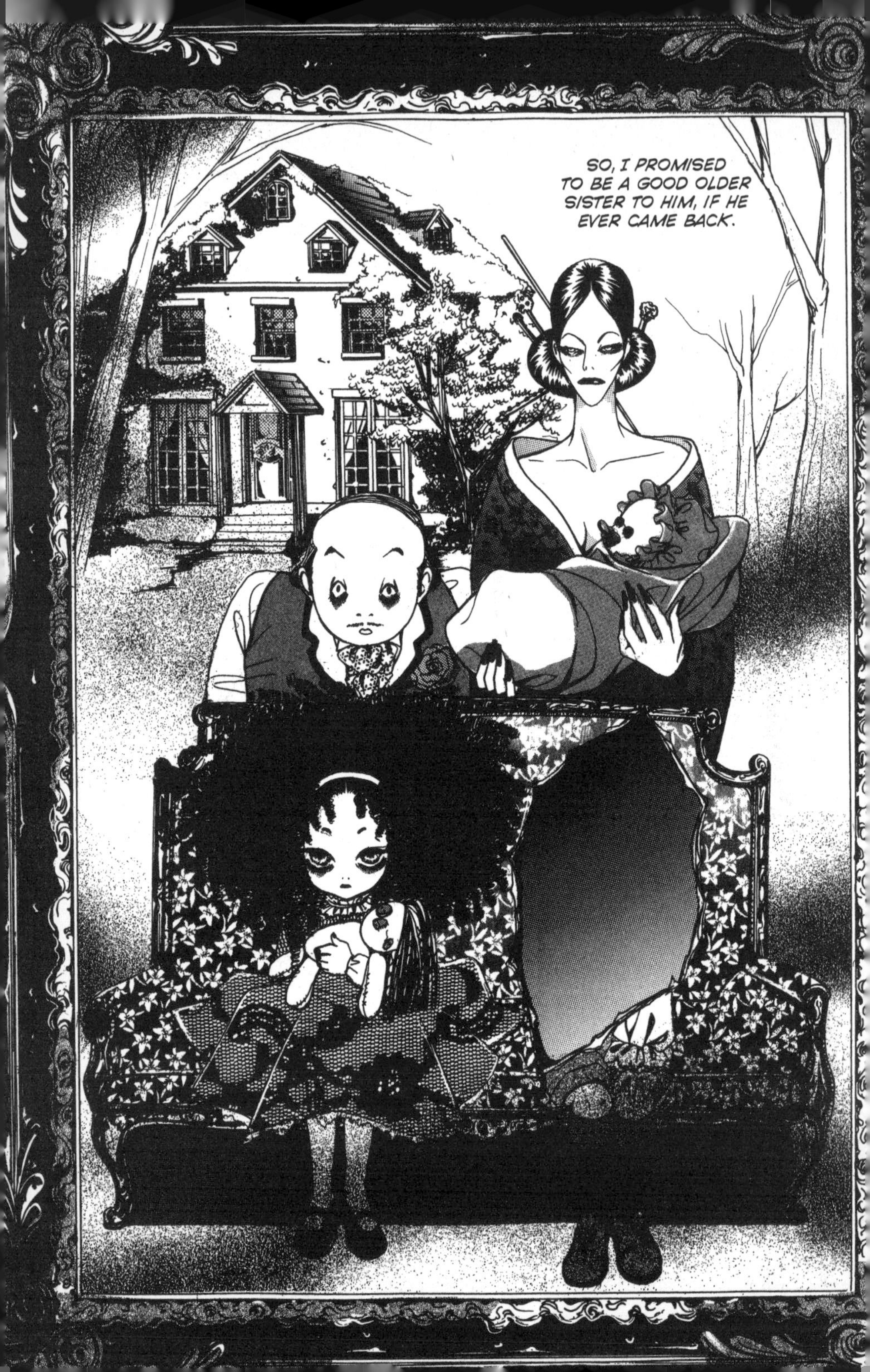
SO, I PROMISED TO BE A GOOD OLDER SISTER TO HIM, IF HE EVER CAME BACK.

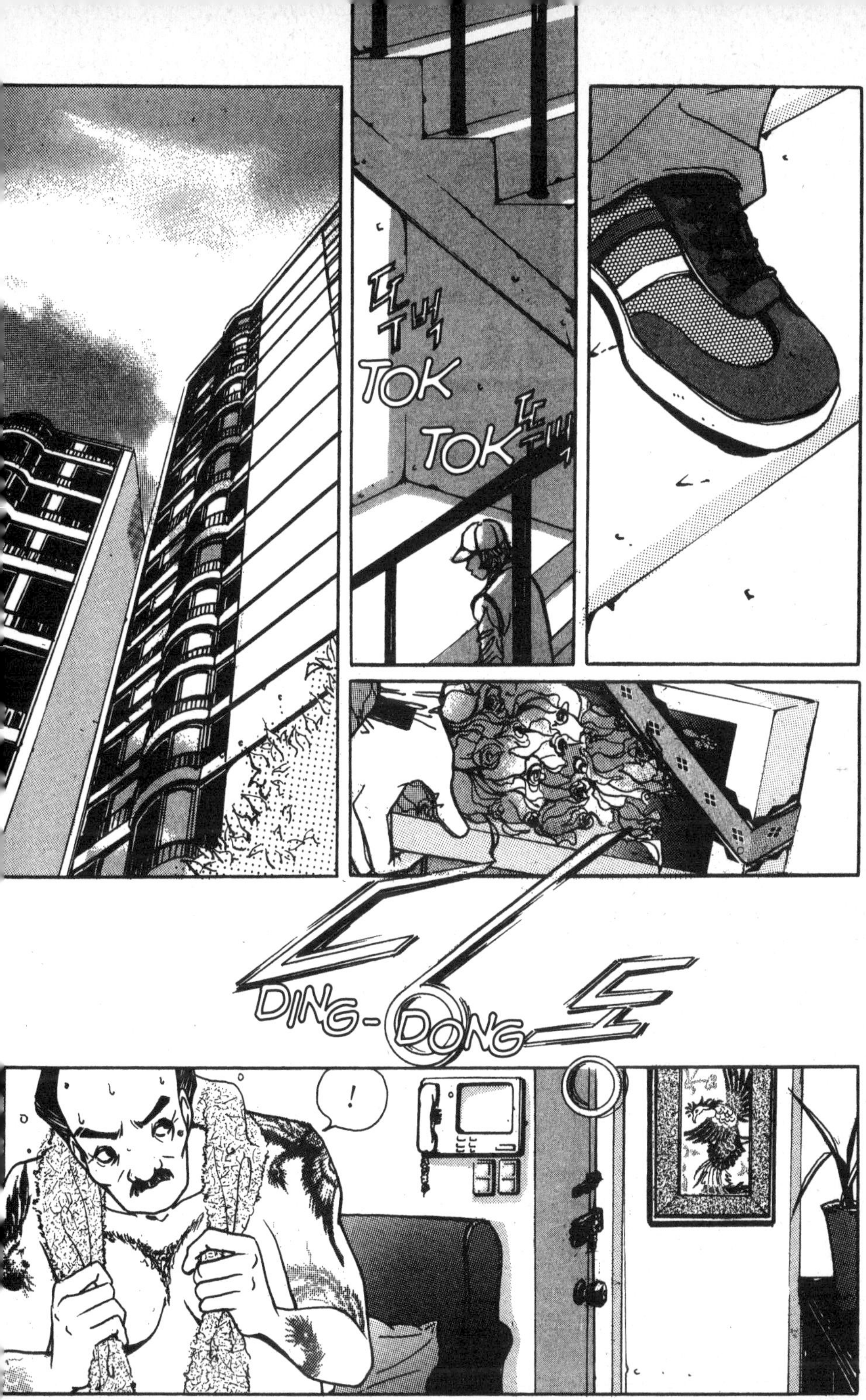
뚜벅
TOK
뚜벅
TOK
DING-DONG
!

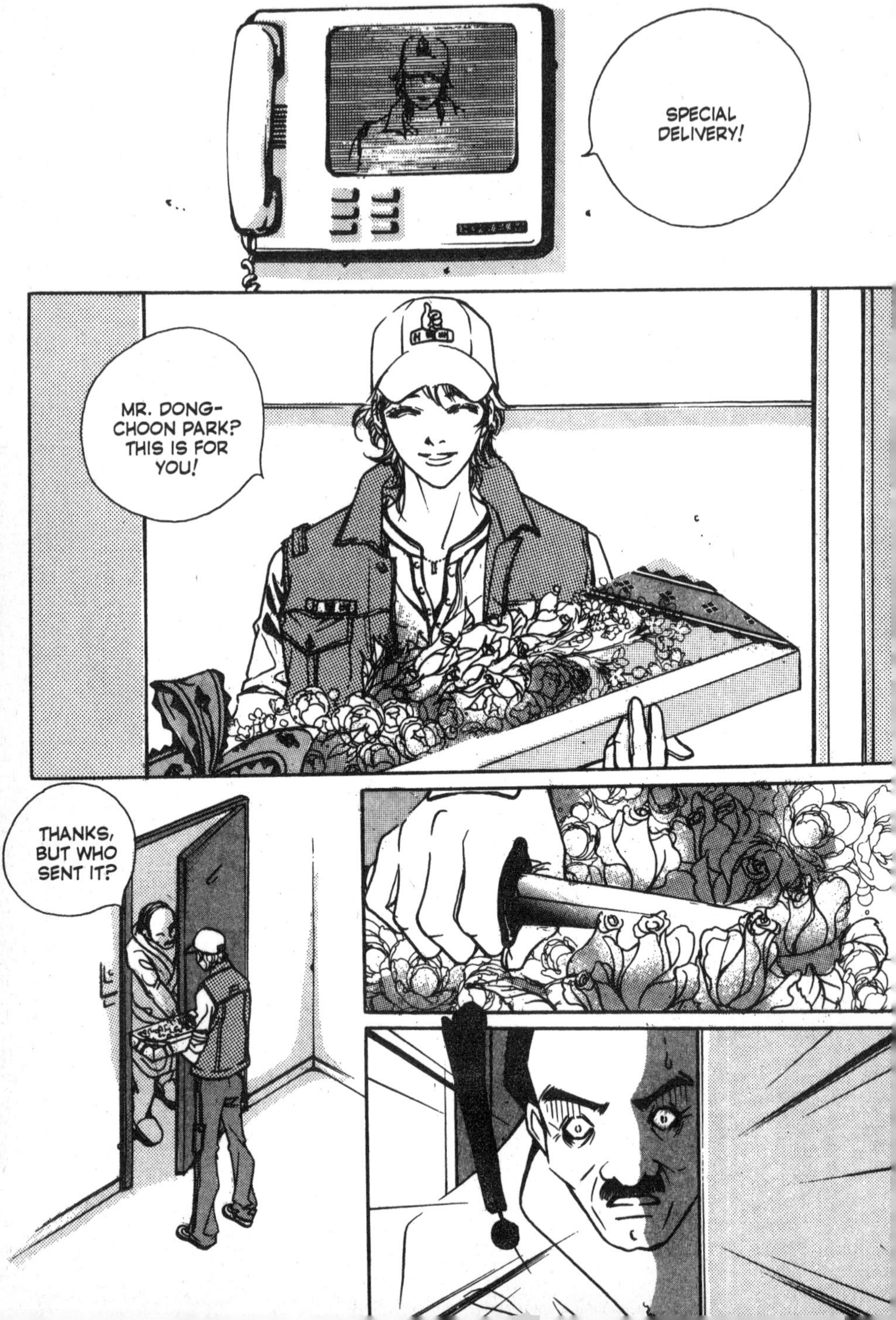
SPECIAL DELIVERY!
MR. DONG-CHOON PARK? THIS IS FOR YOU!
THANKS, BUT WHO SENT IT?

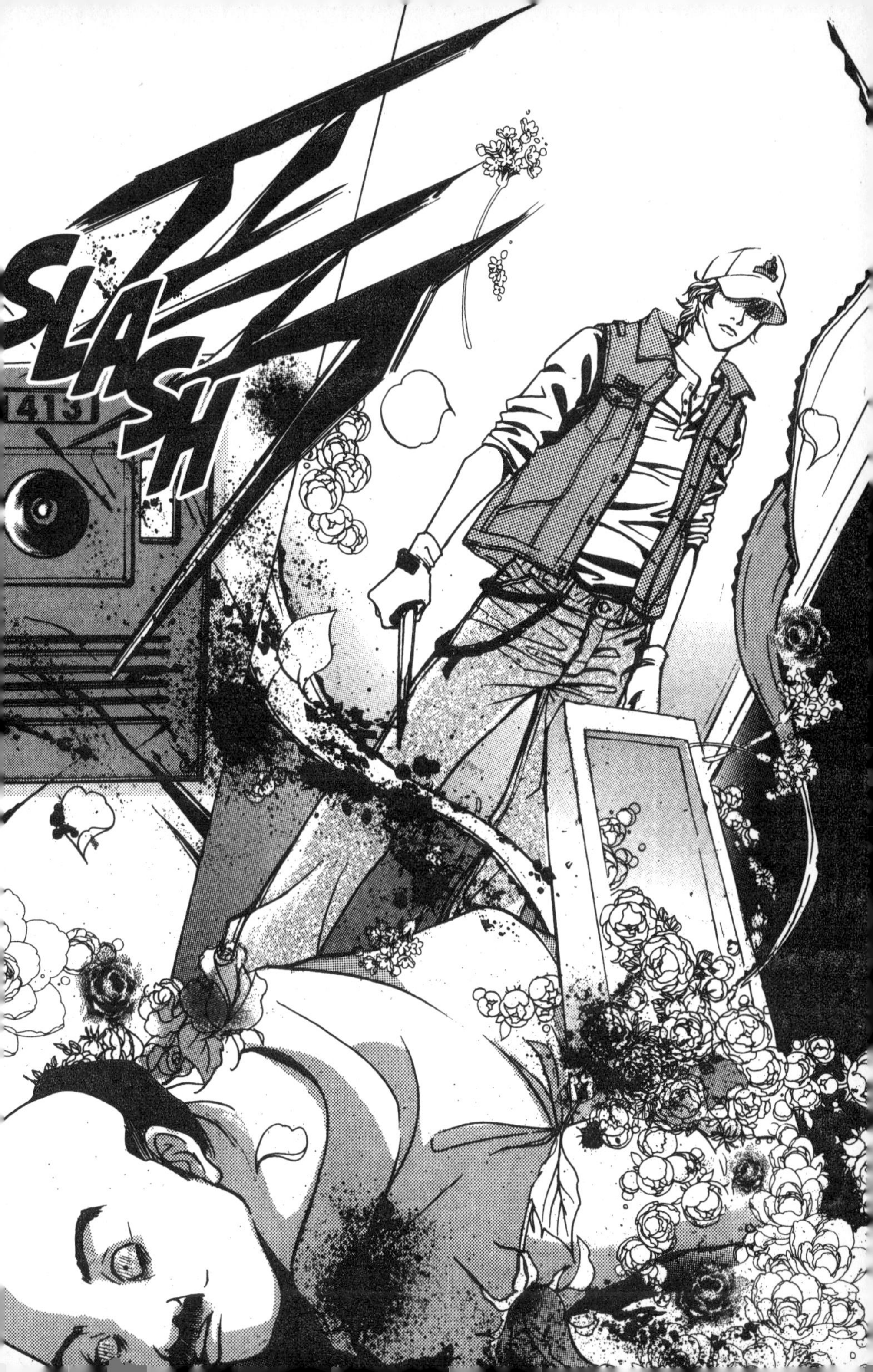
SLASH
413

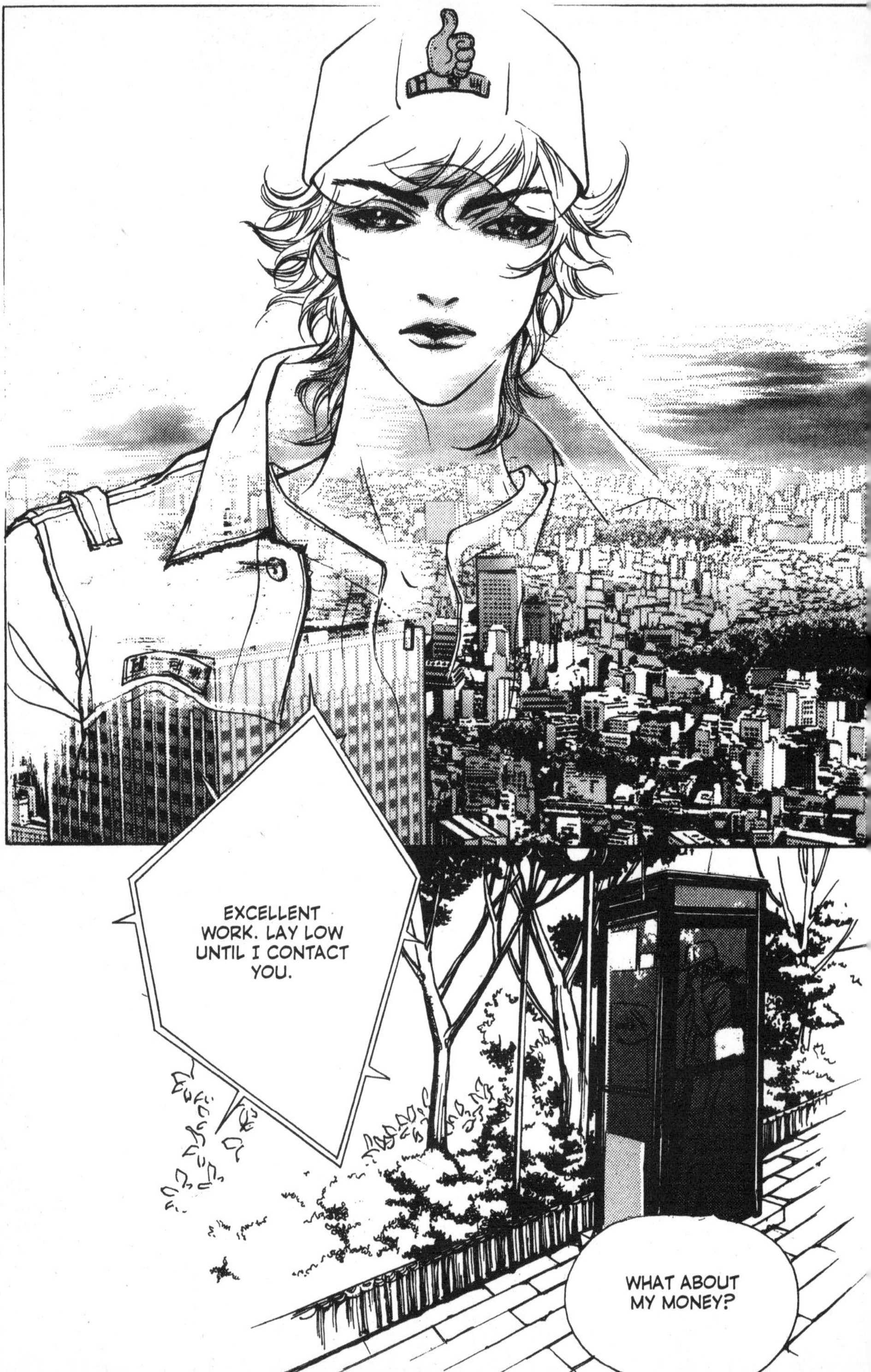
EXCELLENT WORK. LAY LOW UNTIL I CONTACT YOU.
WHAT ABOUT MY MONEY?

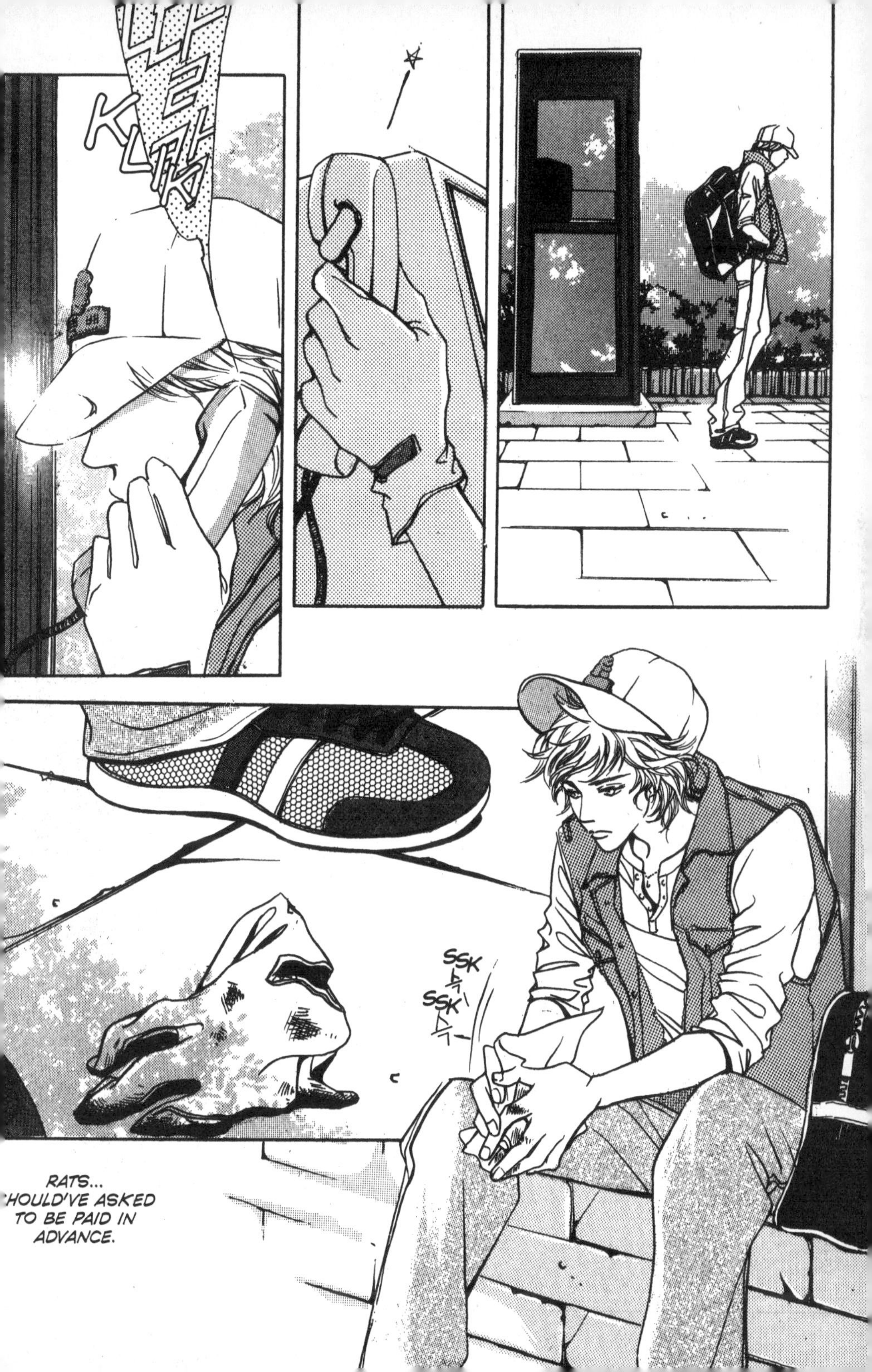
KLIK
SSK
SSK
RATS...
HOULD'VE ASKED
TO BE PAID IN
ADVANCE.

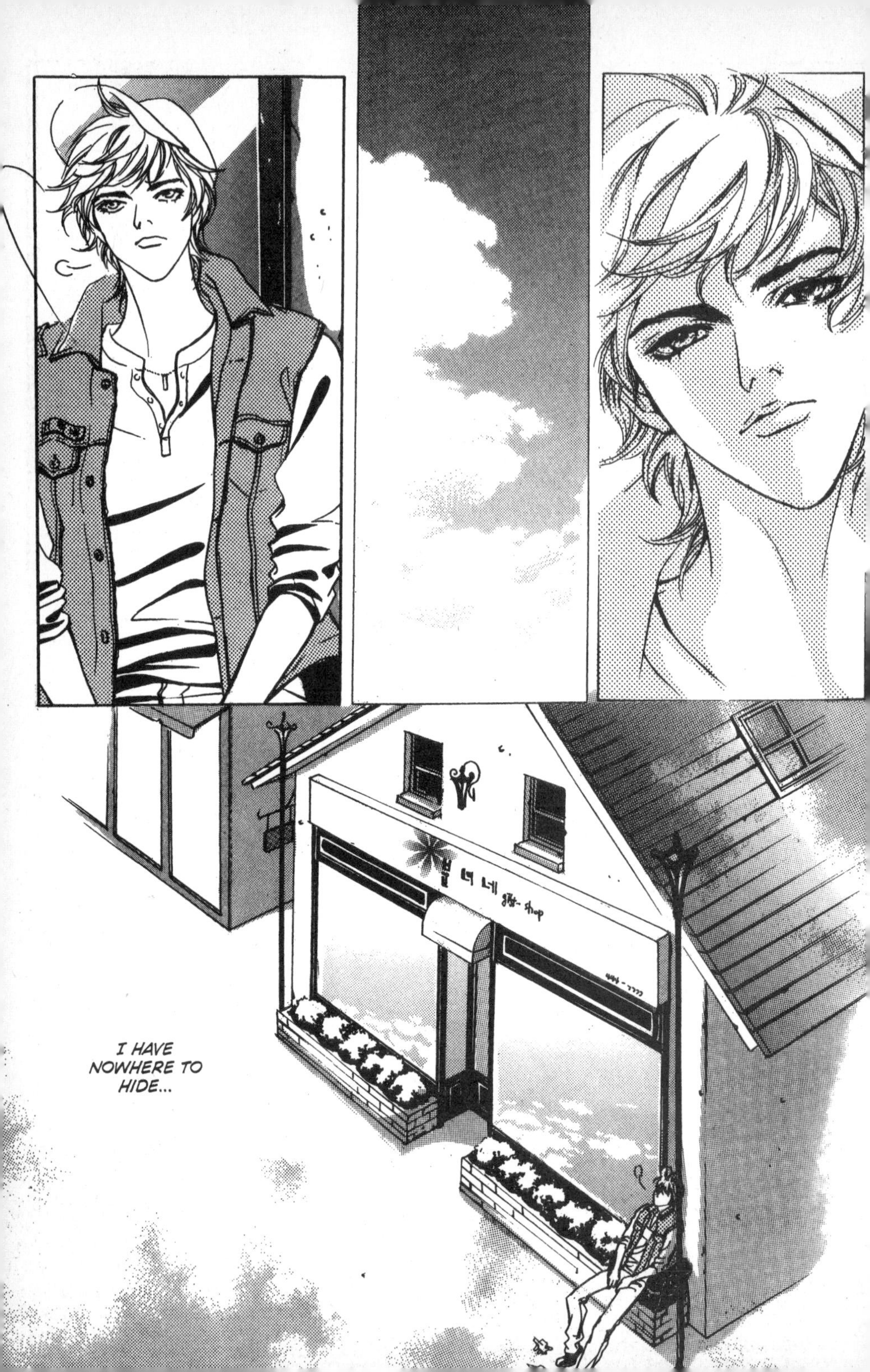
gift- shop
I HAVE NOWHERE TO HIDE...

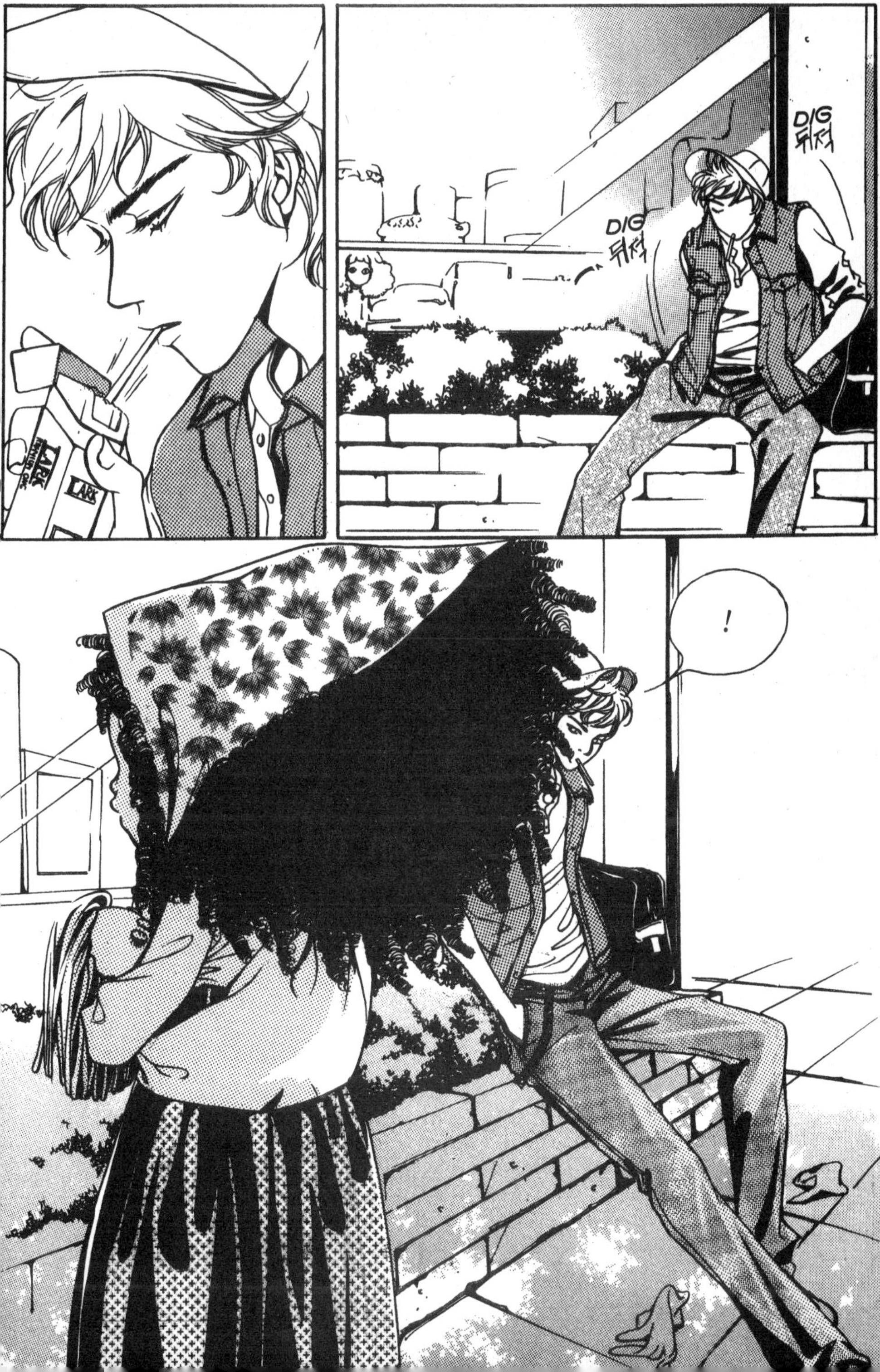
LARK
LARK
DIG 뒤적
DIG 뒤적
!

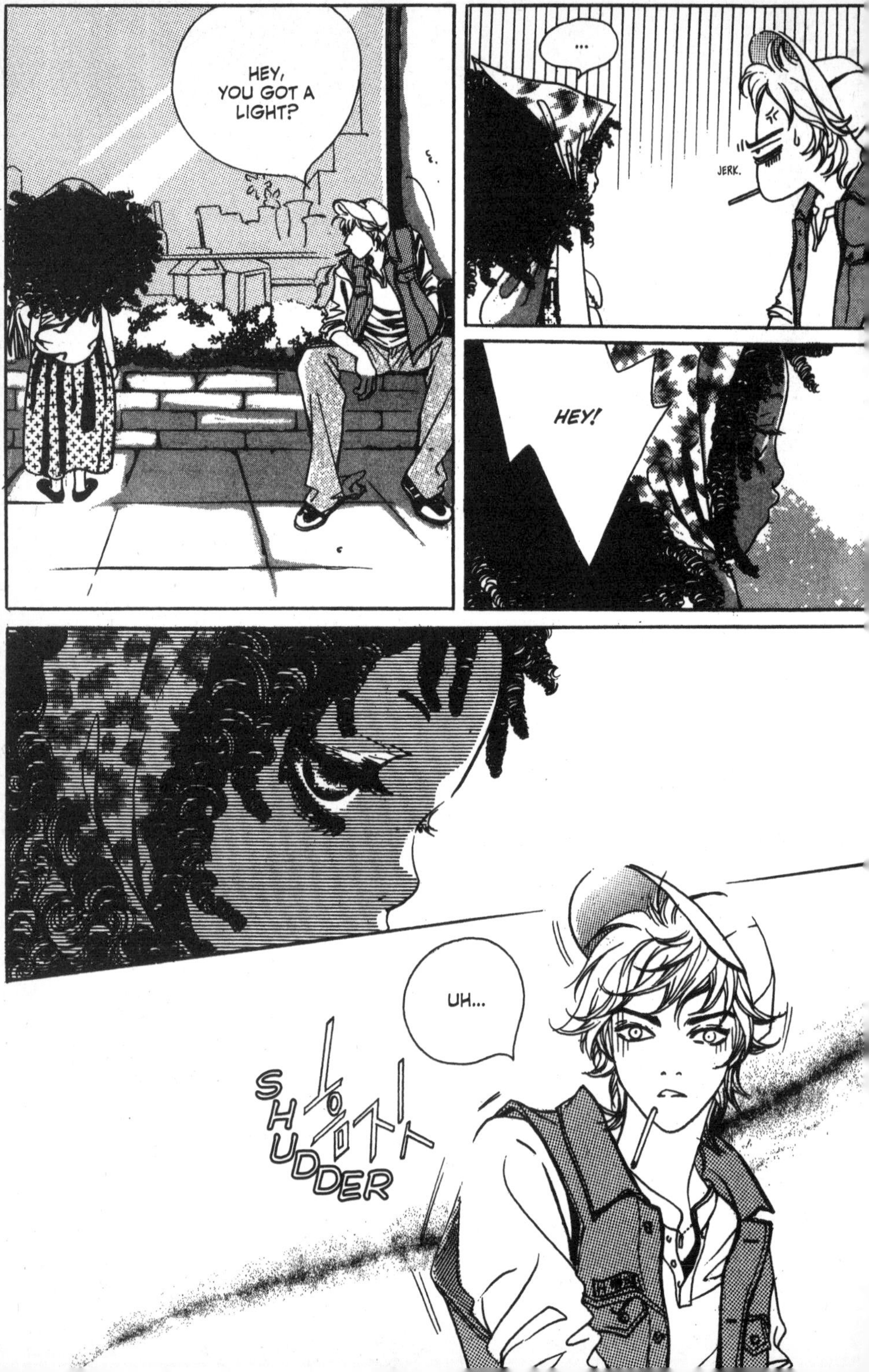
HEY, YOU GOT A LIGHT?
...
JERK.
HEY!
UH...
SHUDDER

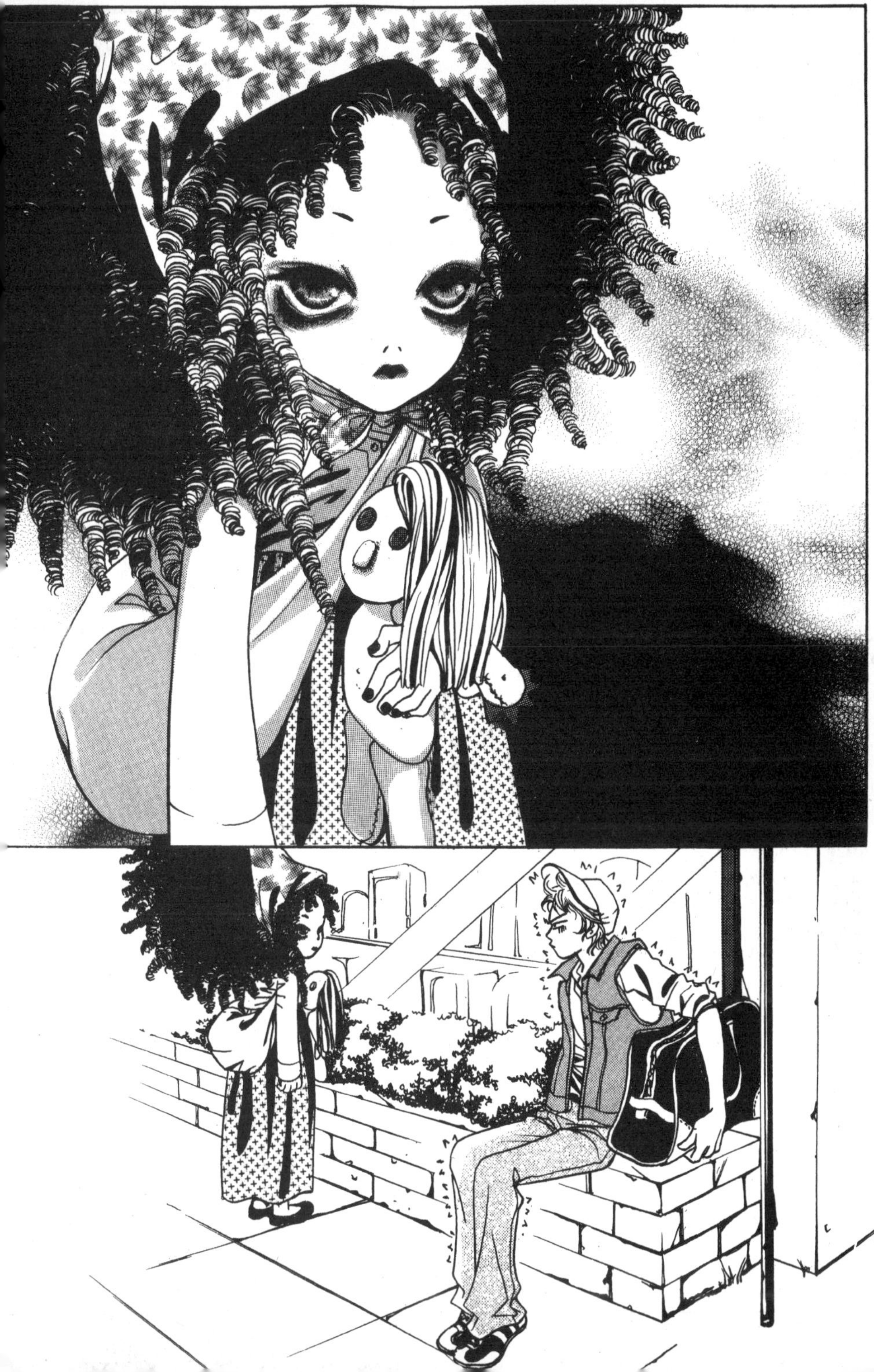

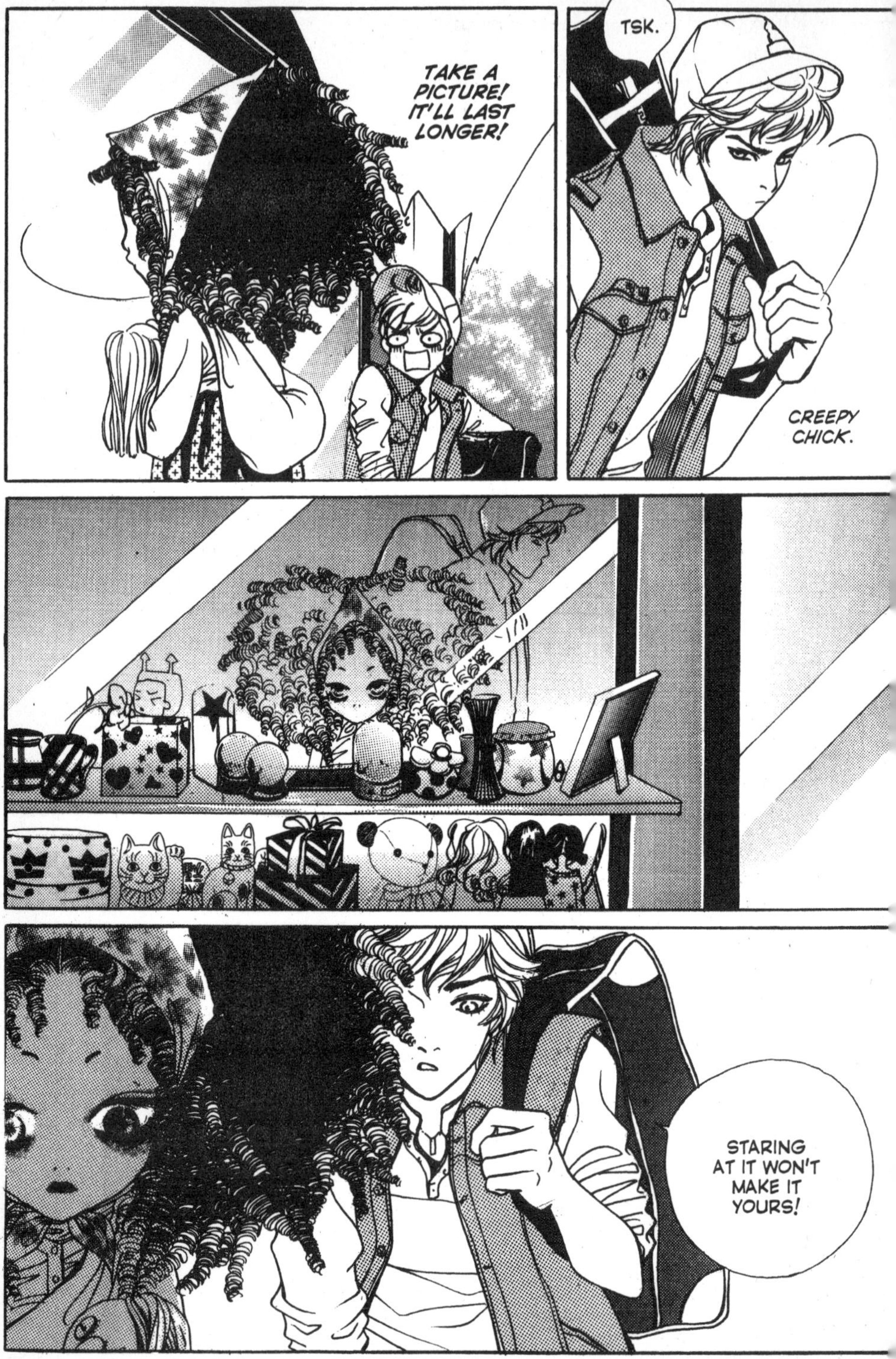
TAKE A PICTURE! IT'LL LAST LONGER!
TSK.
CREEPY CHICK.
STARING AT IT WON'T MAKE IT YOURS!

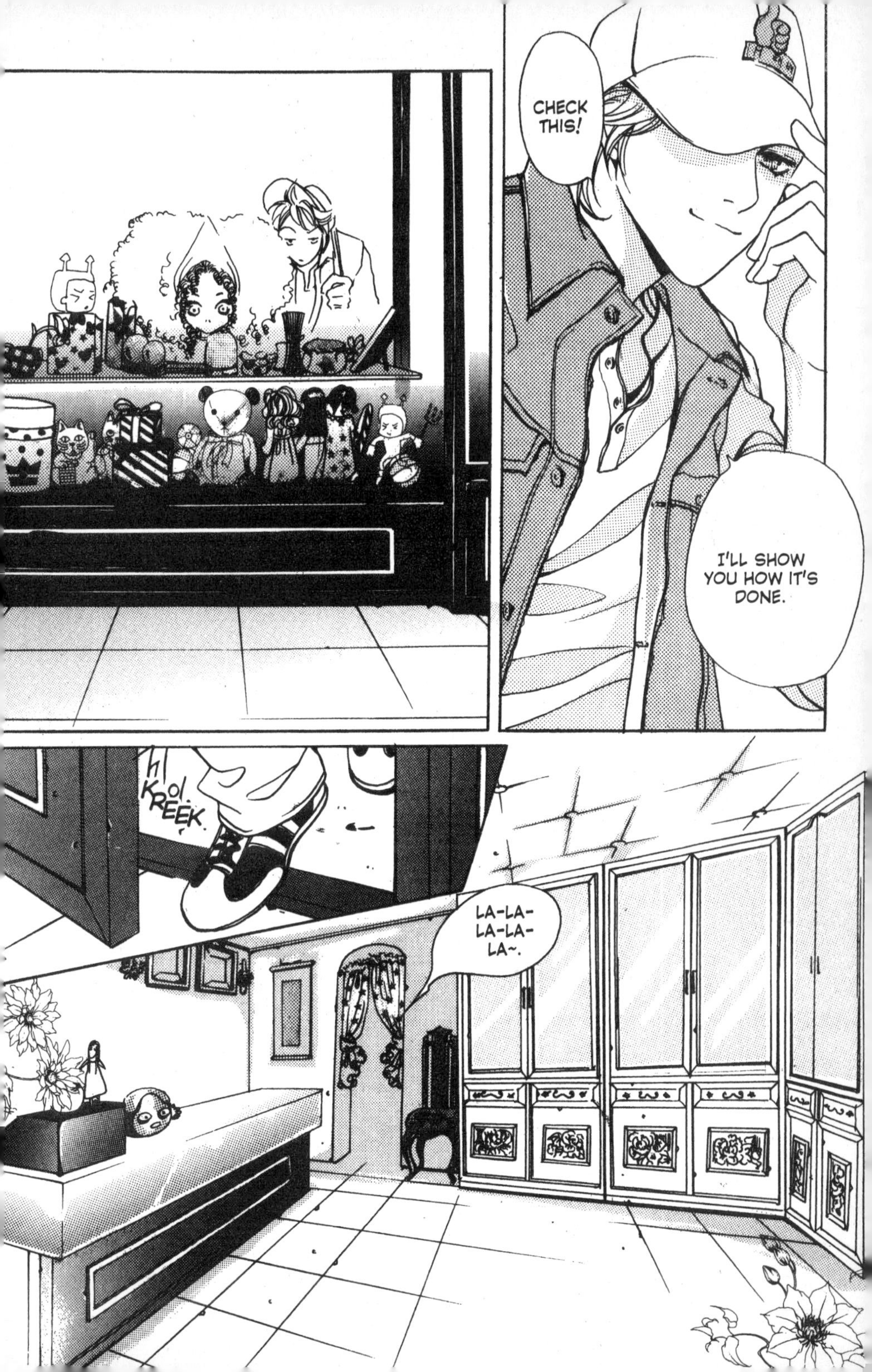
CHECK THIS!
I'LL SHOW YOU HOW IT'S DONE.
KREEK
LA-LA-LA-LA-LA~.

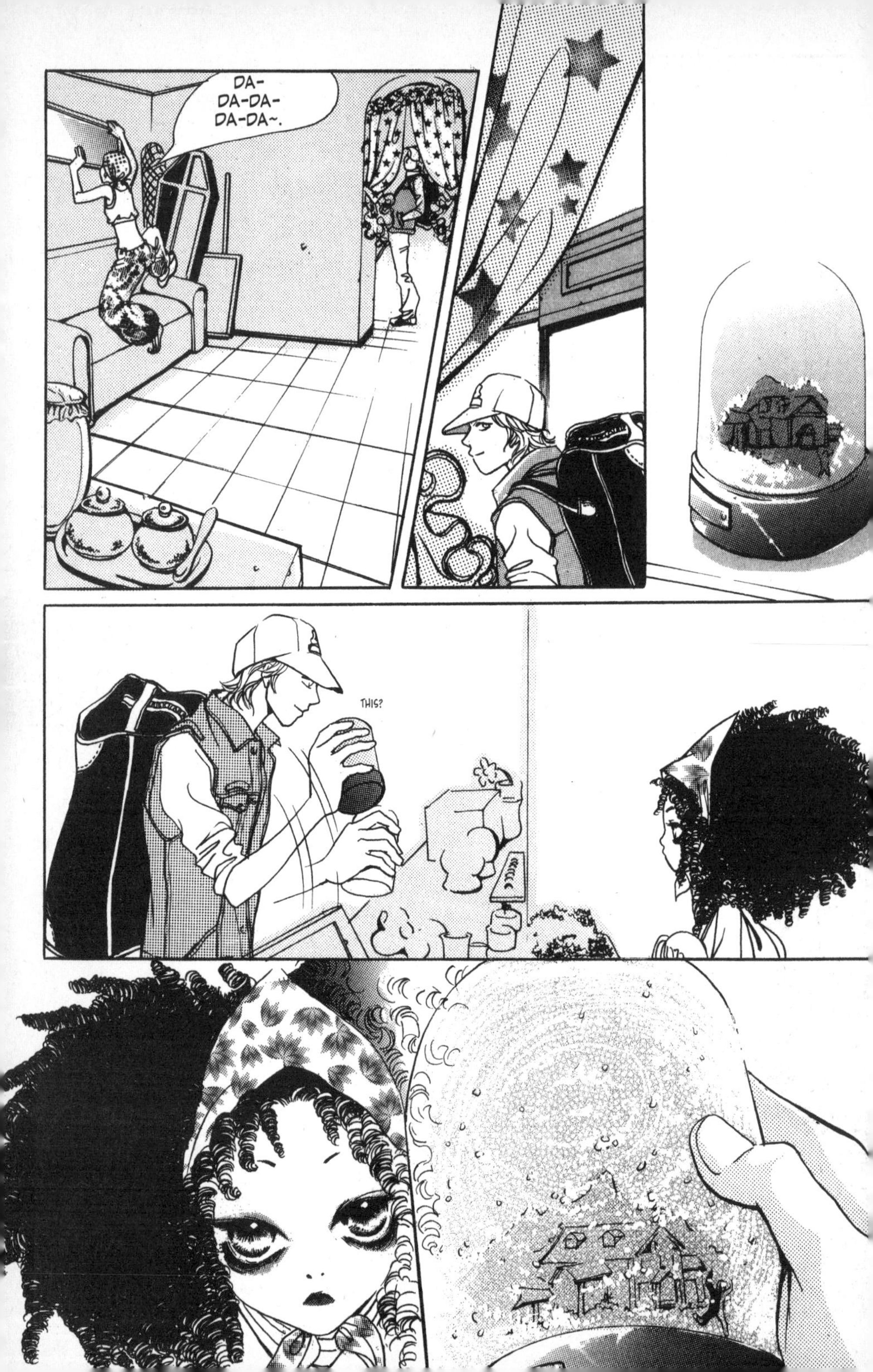
DA-
DA-DA-
DA-DA~.
THIS?

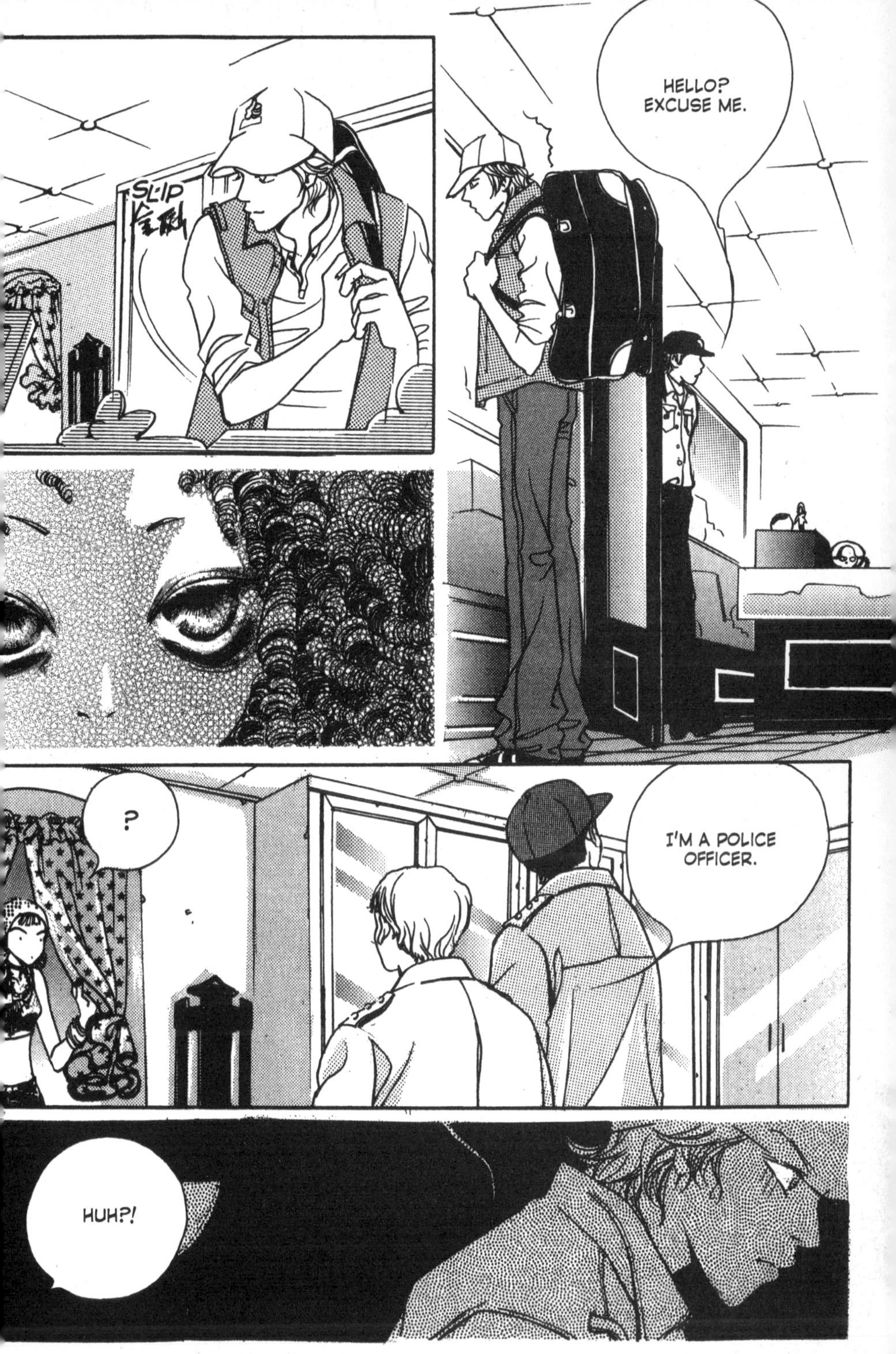
SLIP
HELLO? EXCUSE ME.
?
I'M A POLICE OFFICER.
HUH?!

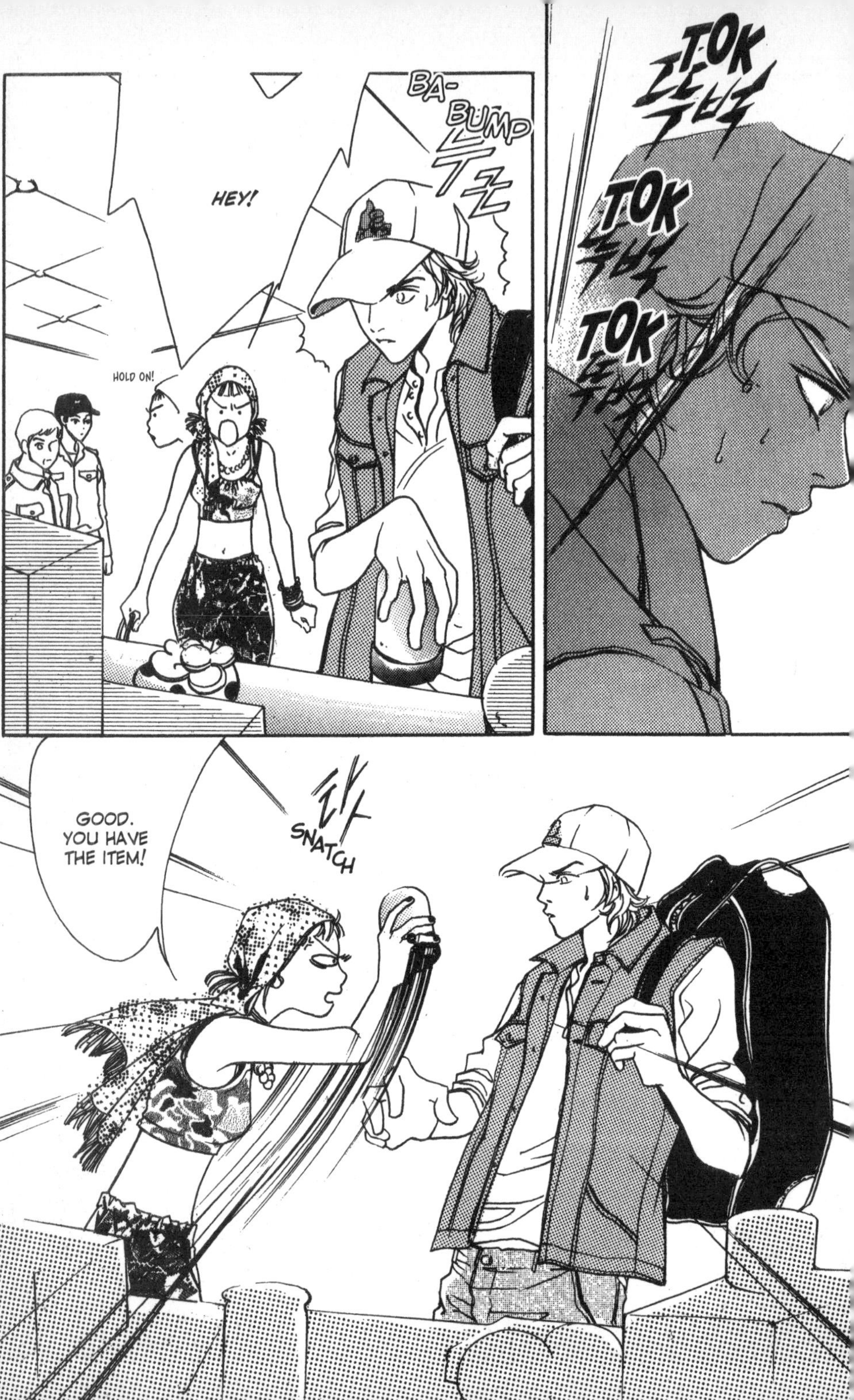
BA-BUMP
HEY!
HOLD ON!
T-TOK
TOK
TOK
GOOD. YOU HAVE THE ITEM!
SNATCH

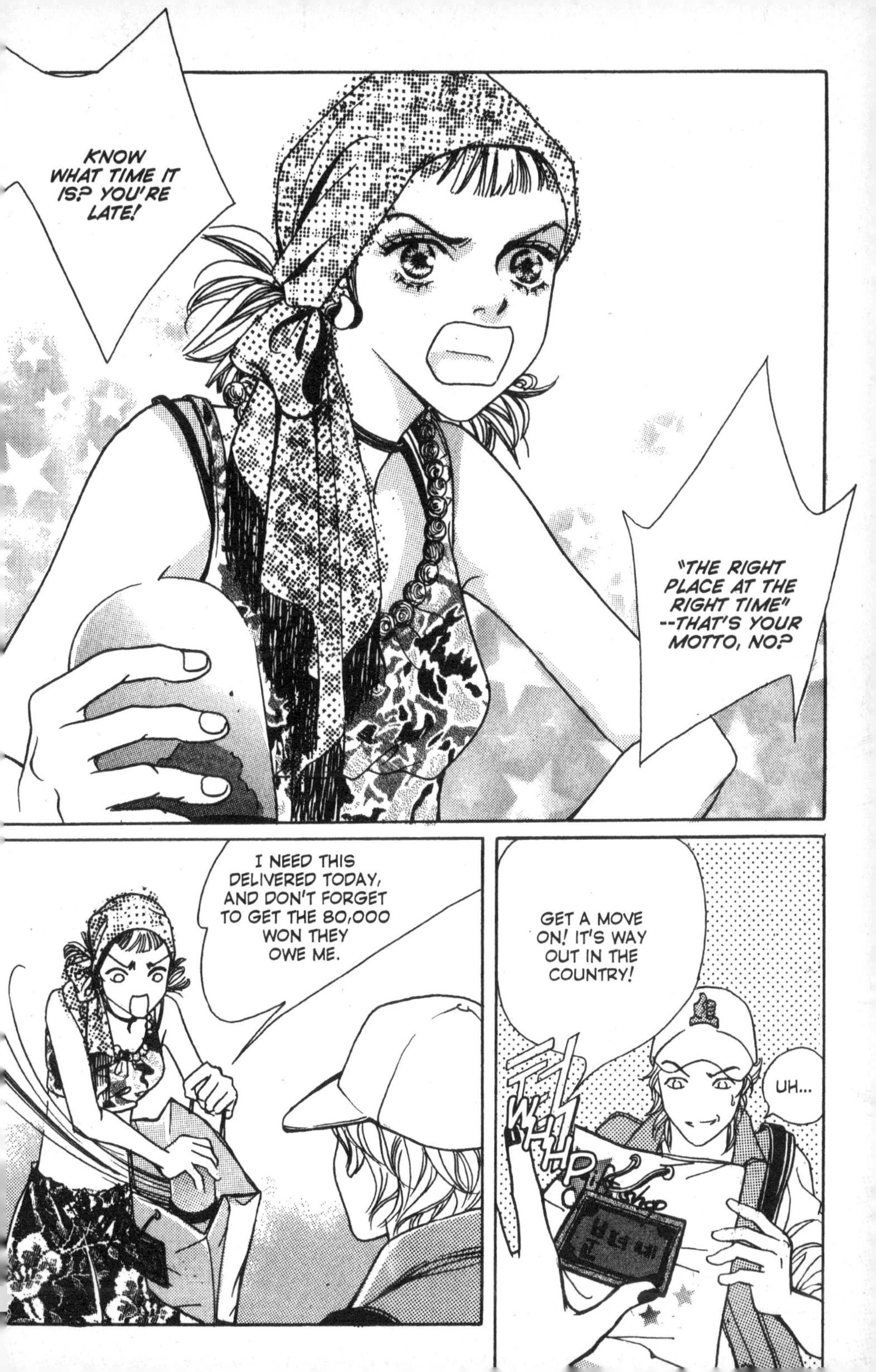
KNOW WHAT TIME IT IS? YOU'RE LATE!
"THE RIGHT PLACE AT THE RIGHT TIME" --THAT'S YOUR MOTTO, NO?
I NEED THIS DELIVERED TODAY, AND DON'T FORGET TO GET THE 80,000 WON THEY OWE ME.
GET A MOVE ON! IT'S WAY OUT IN THE COUNTRY!
WHHIP
UH...

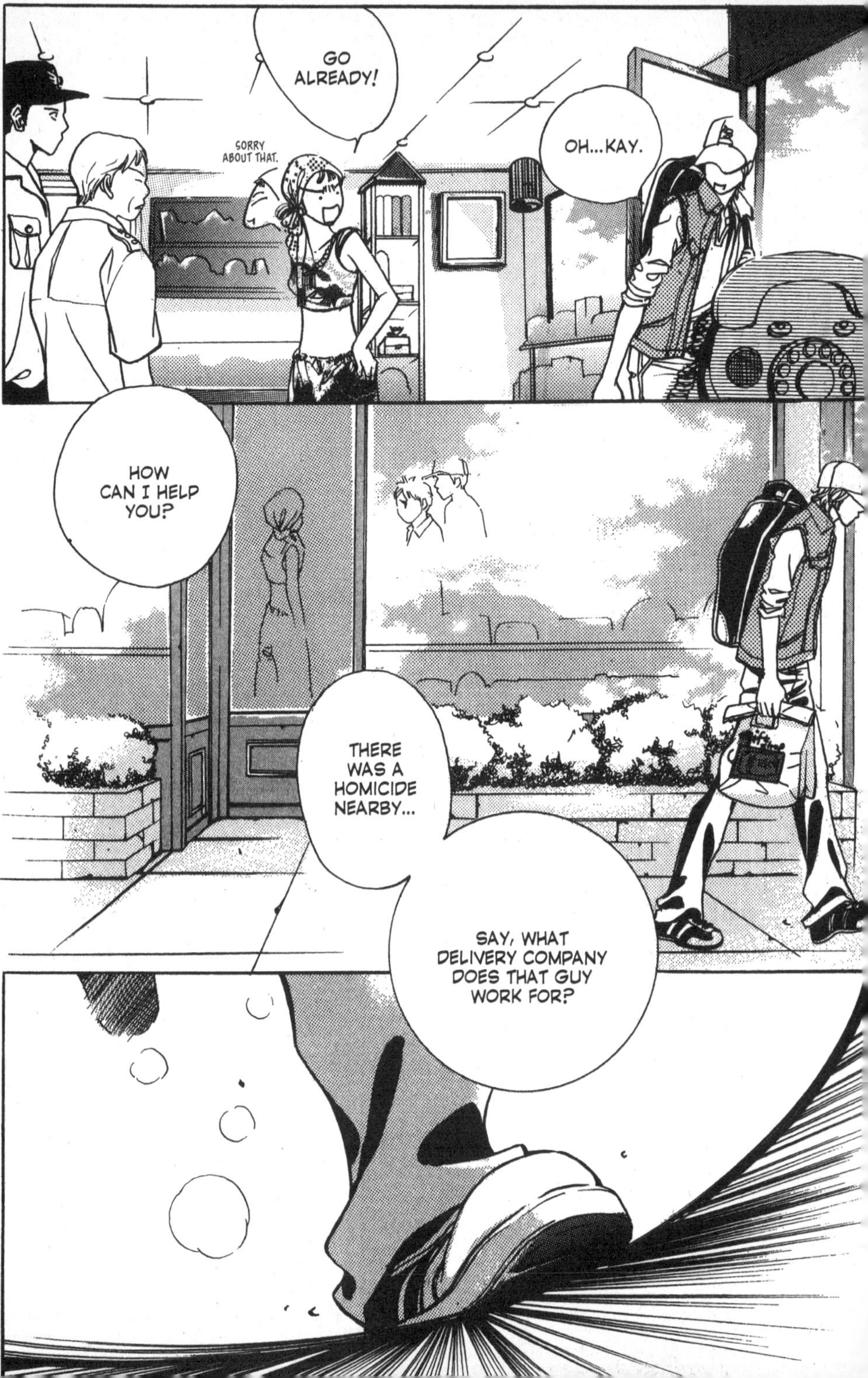
GO ALREADY!
SORRY ABOUT THAT.
OH...KAY.
HOW CAN I HELP YOU?
THERE WAS A HOMICIDE NEARBY...
SAY, WHAT DELIVERY COMPANY DOES THAT GUY WORK FOR?

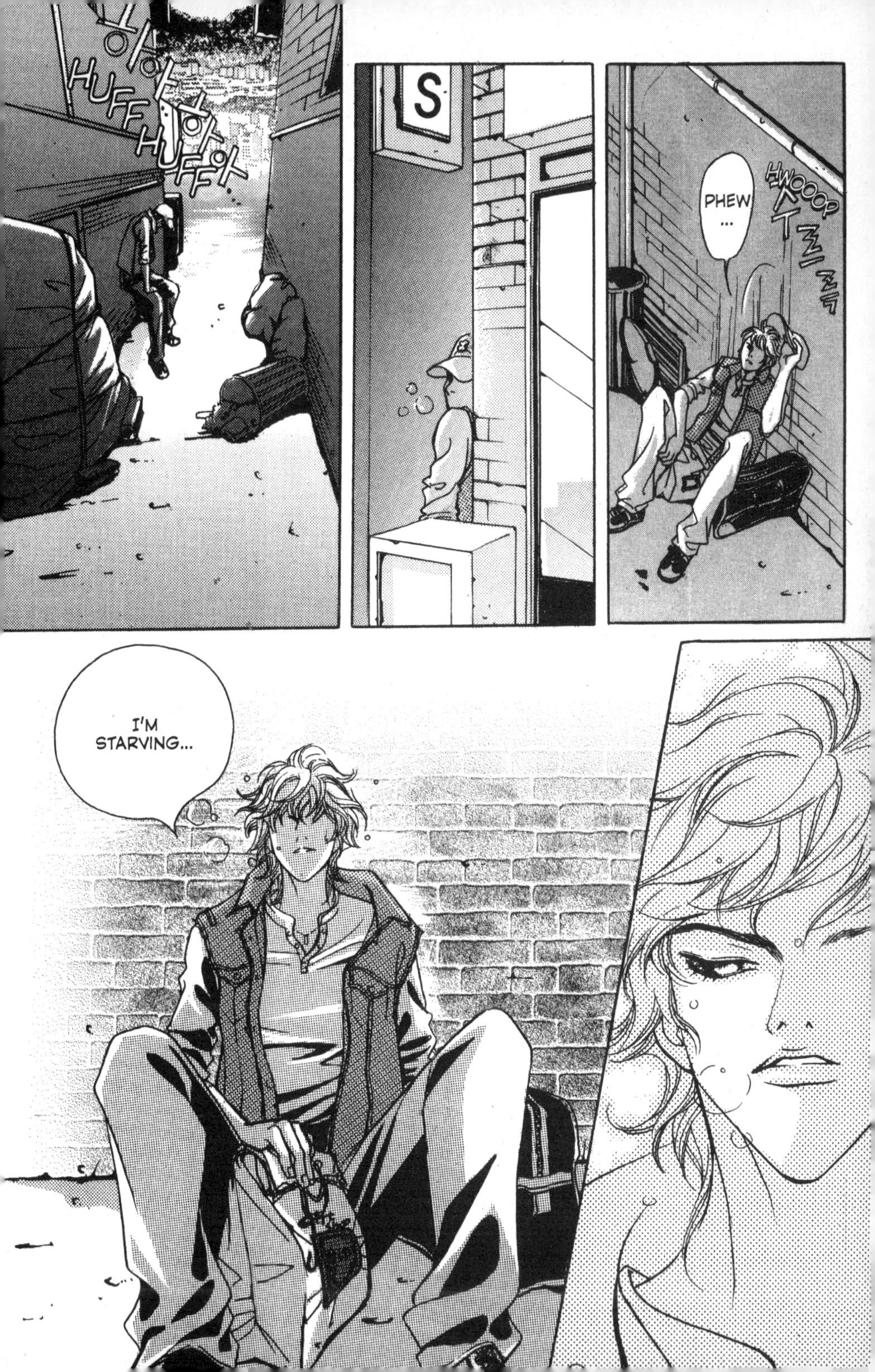
HUFF
HUFF
PHEW ...
HWOOOP
I'M STARVING...

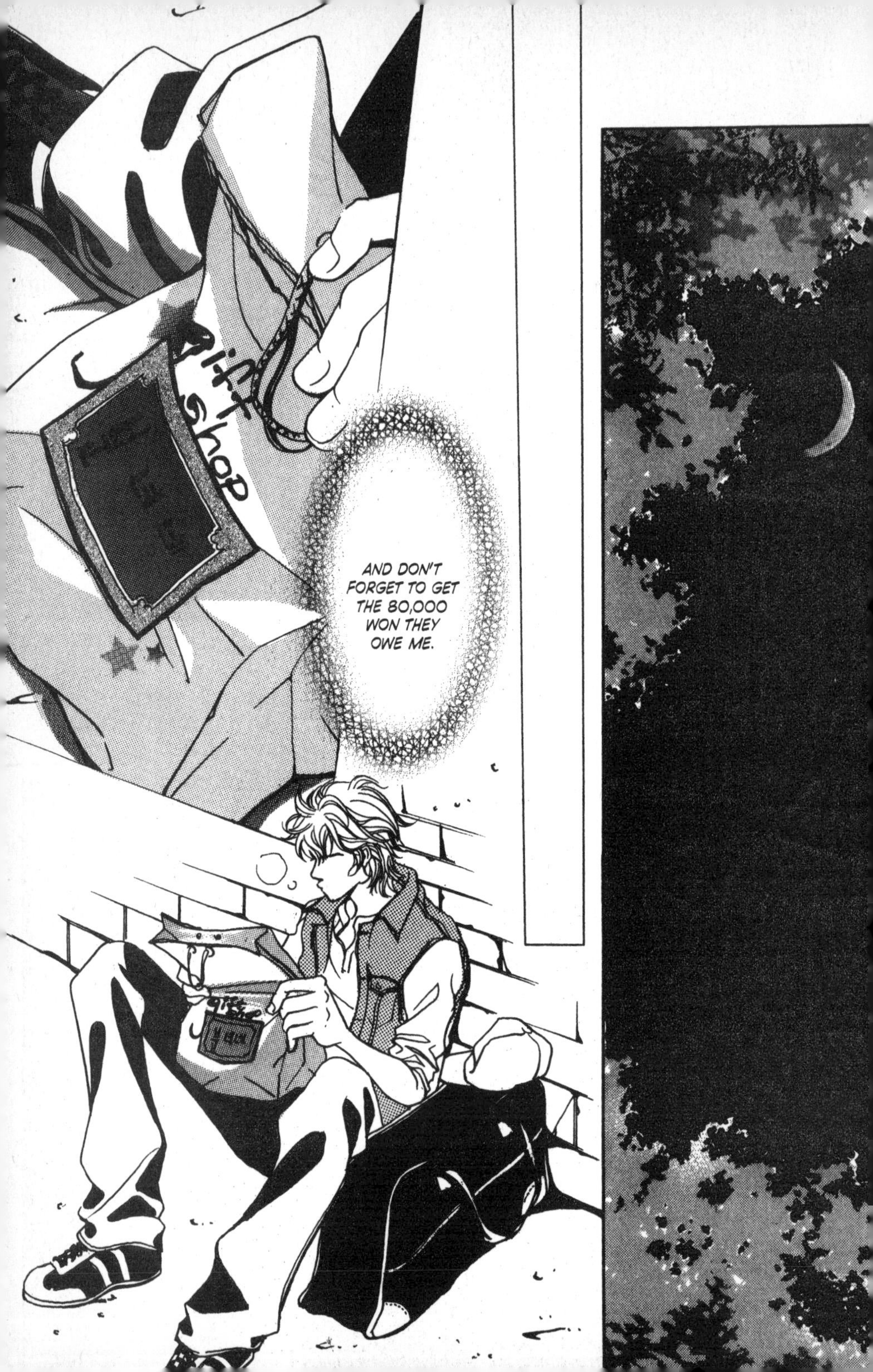
gift shop
AND DON'T FORGET TO GET THE 80,000 WON THEY OWE ME.

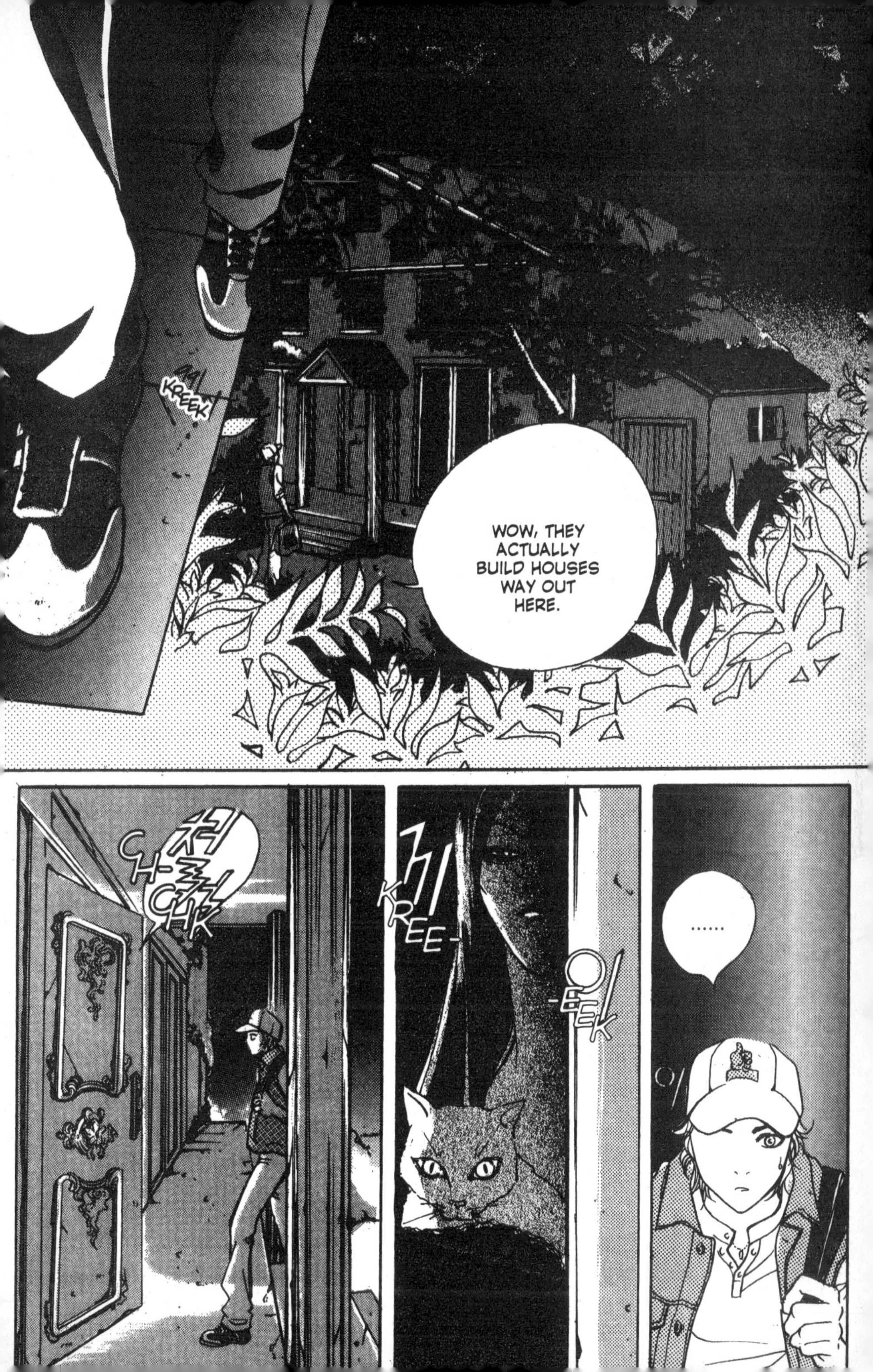
KREEK
WOW, THEY ACTUALLY BUILD HOUSES WAY OUT HERE.
CH-CHK
KREE-
-EEK
......

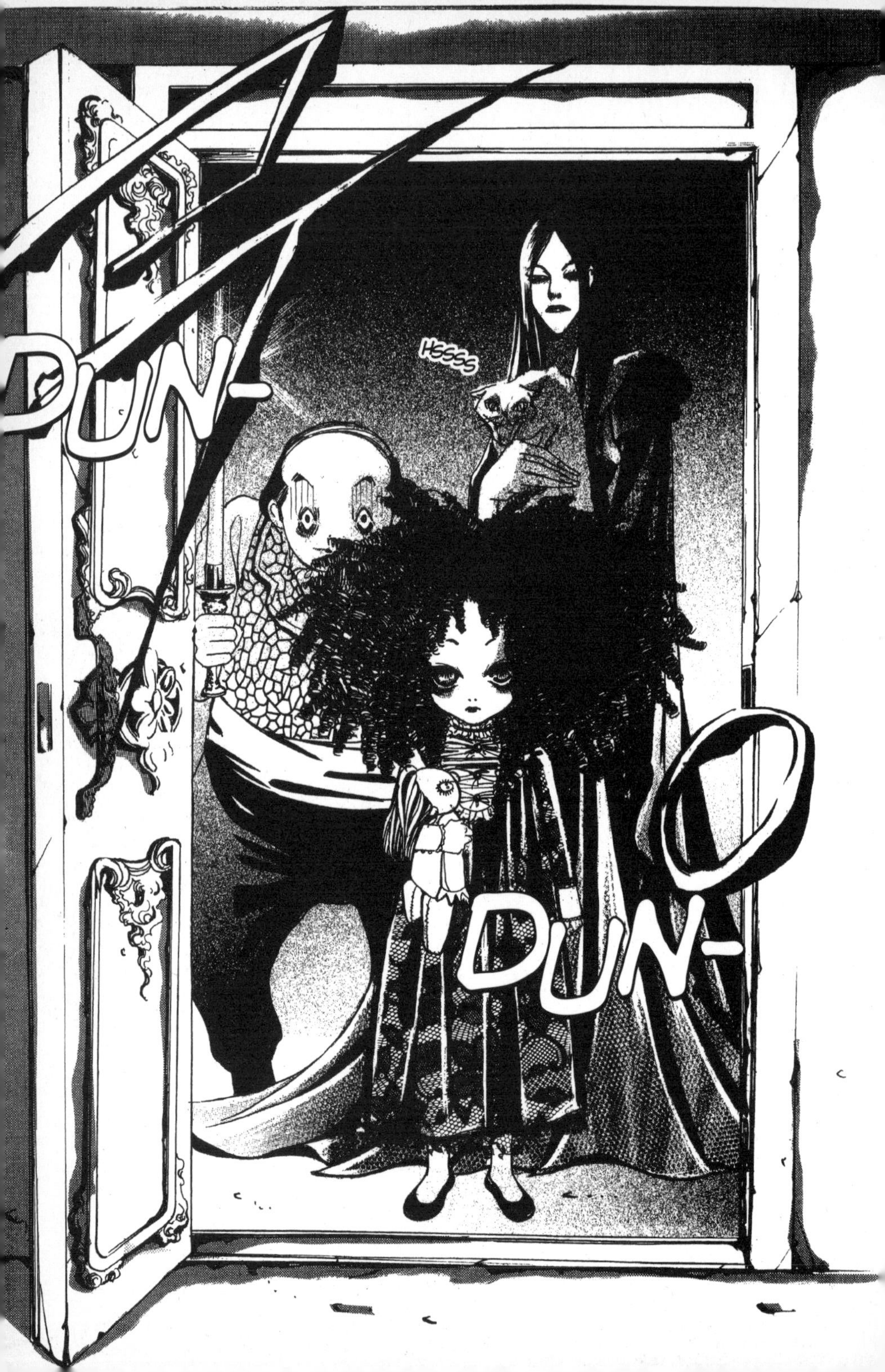

DUN-
HSSSS
DUN-

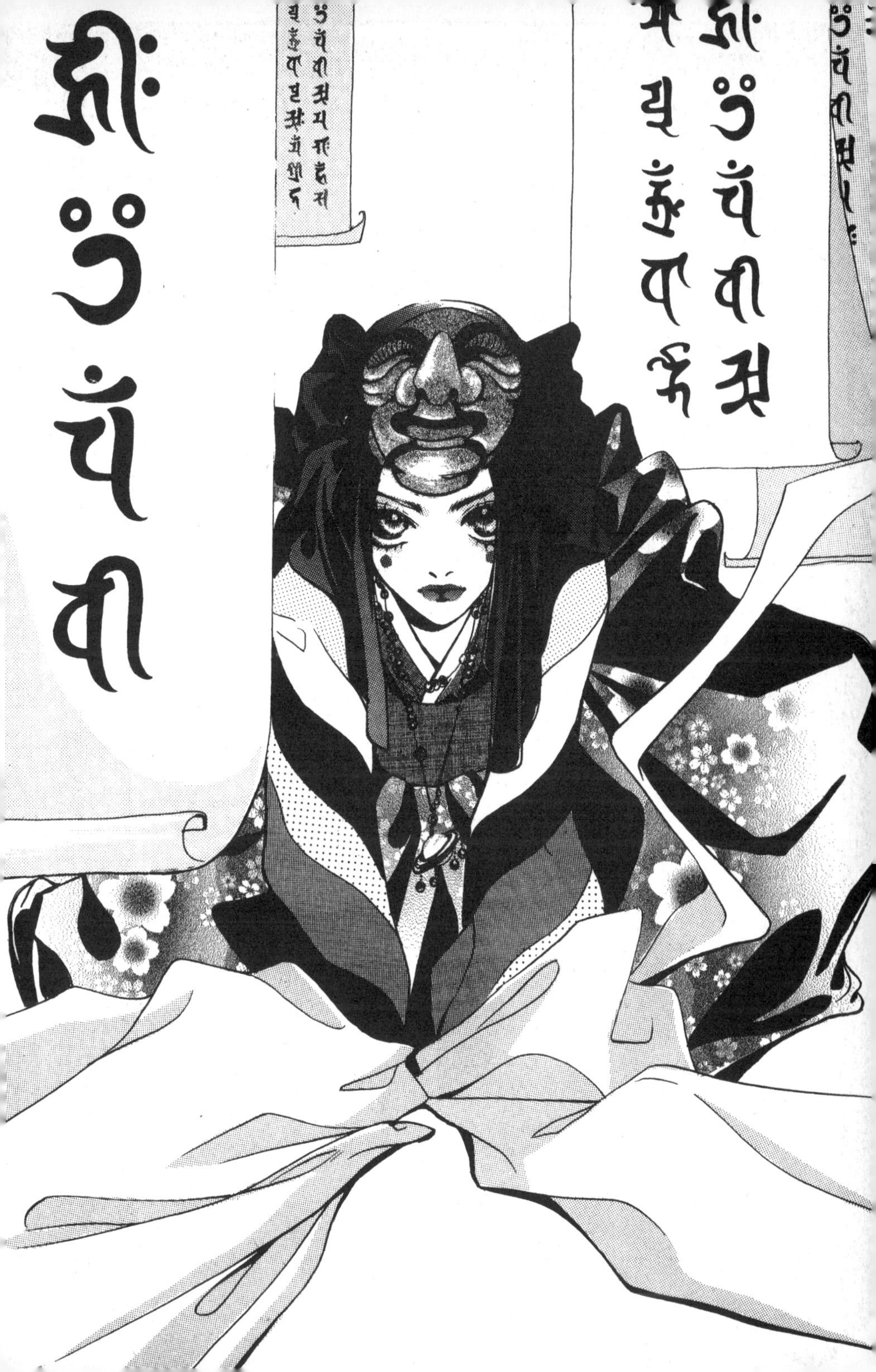

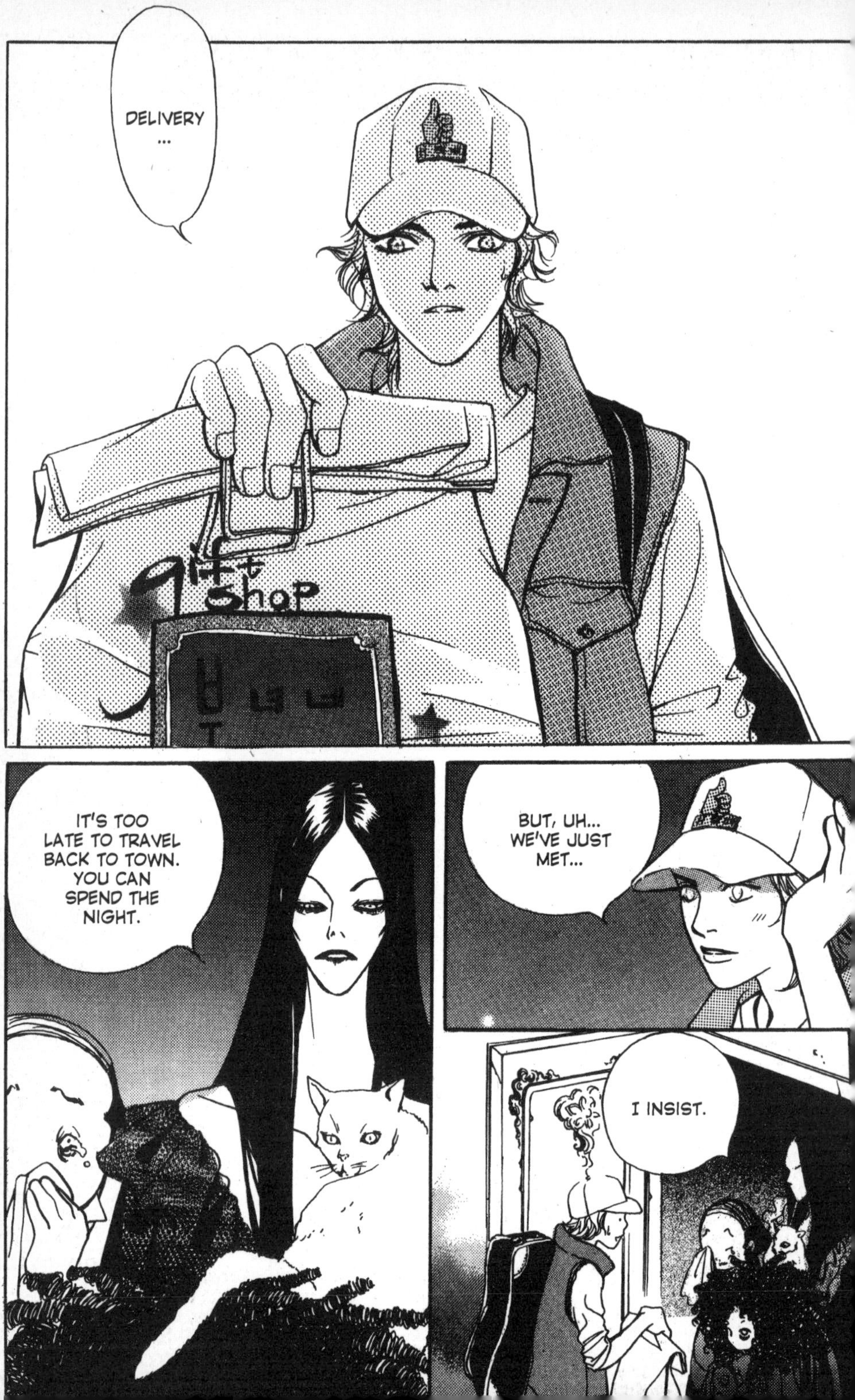
DELIVERY ...
gift shop
IT'S TOO LATE TO TRAVEL BACK TO TOWN. YOU CAN SPEND THE NIGHT.
BUT, UH... WE'VE JUST MET...
I INSIST.

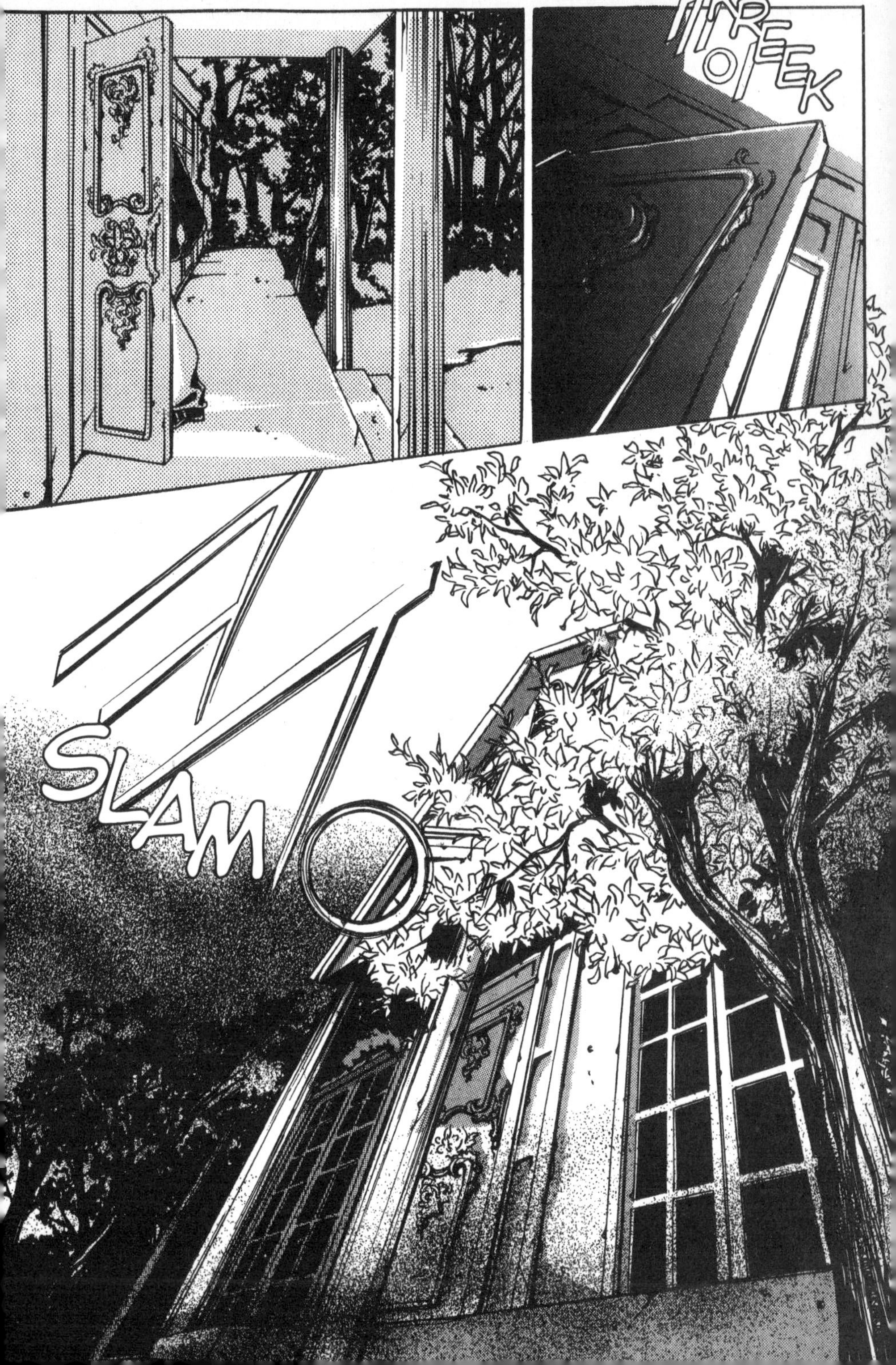
KREEEK
SLAM

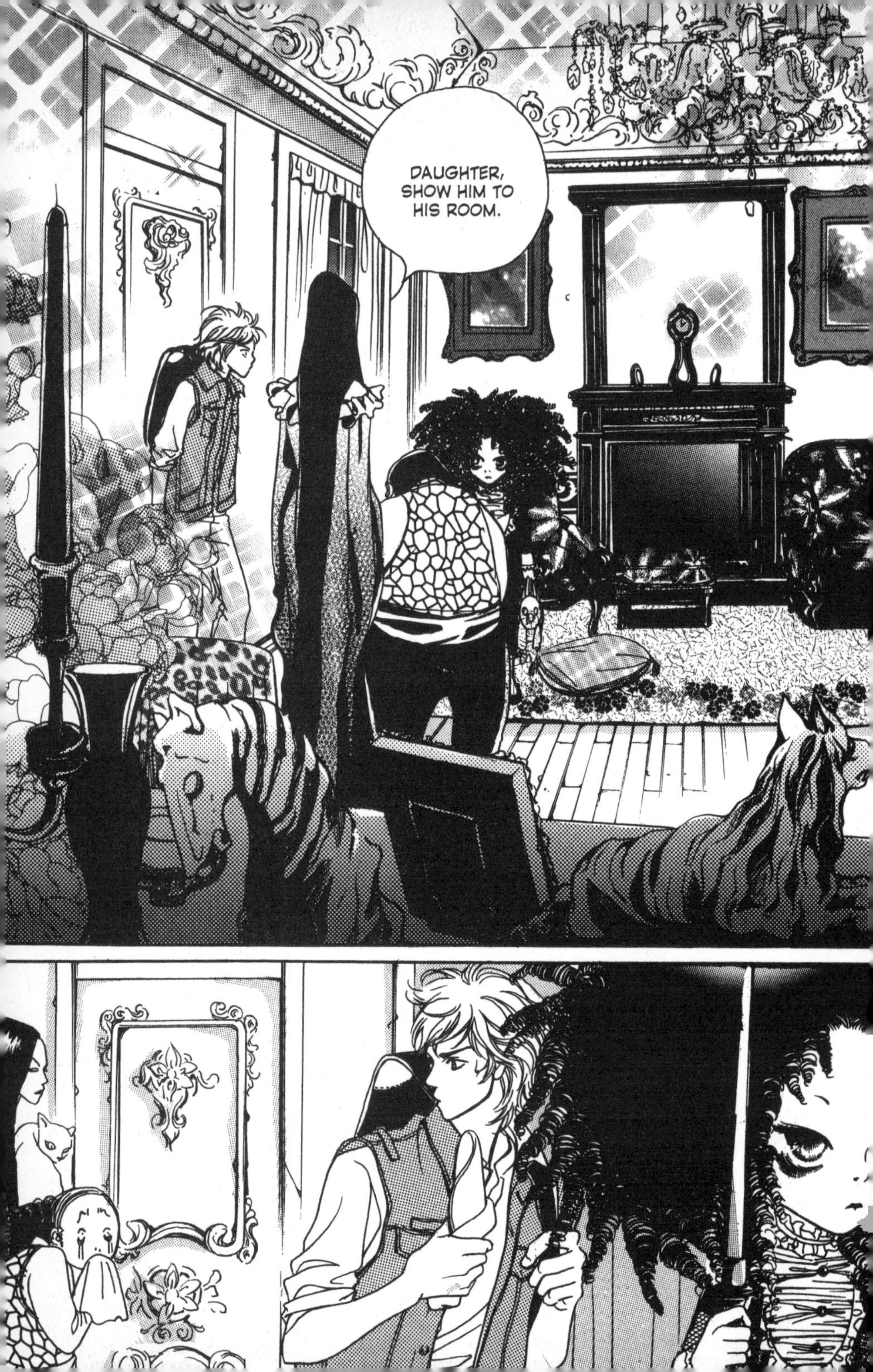
DAUGHTER, SHOW HIM TO HIS ROOM.

HEY,
DO YOU
REMEMBER
ME?

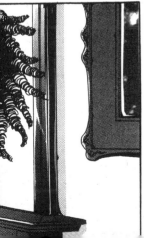

WE MET AT
THE ANTIQUE
SHOP?

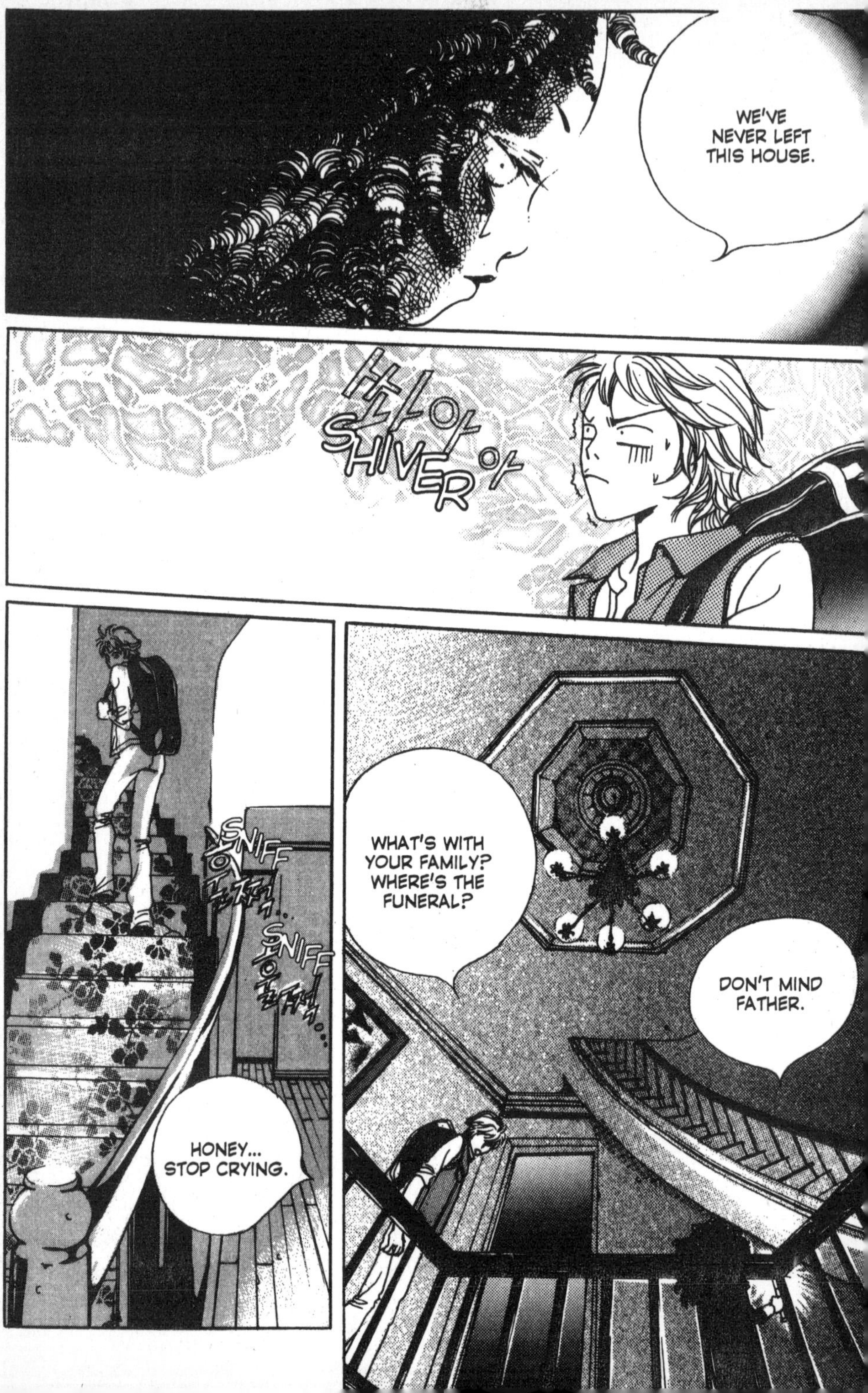
WE'VE NEVER LEFT THIS HOUSE.
SHIVER
SNIFF
SNIFF
HONEY... STOP CRYING.
WHAT'S WITH YOUR FAMILY? WHERE'S THE FUNERAL?
DON'T MIND FATHER.

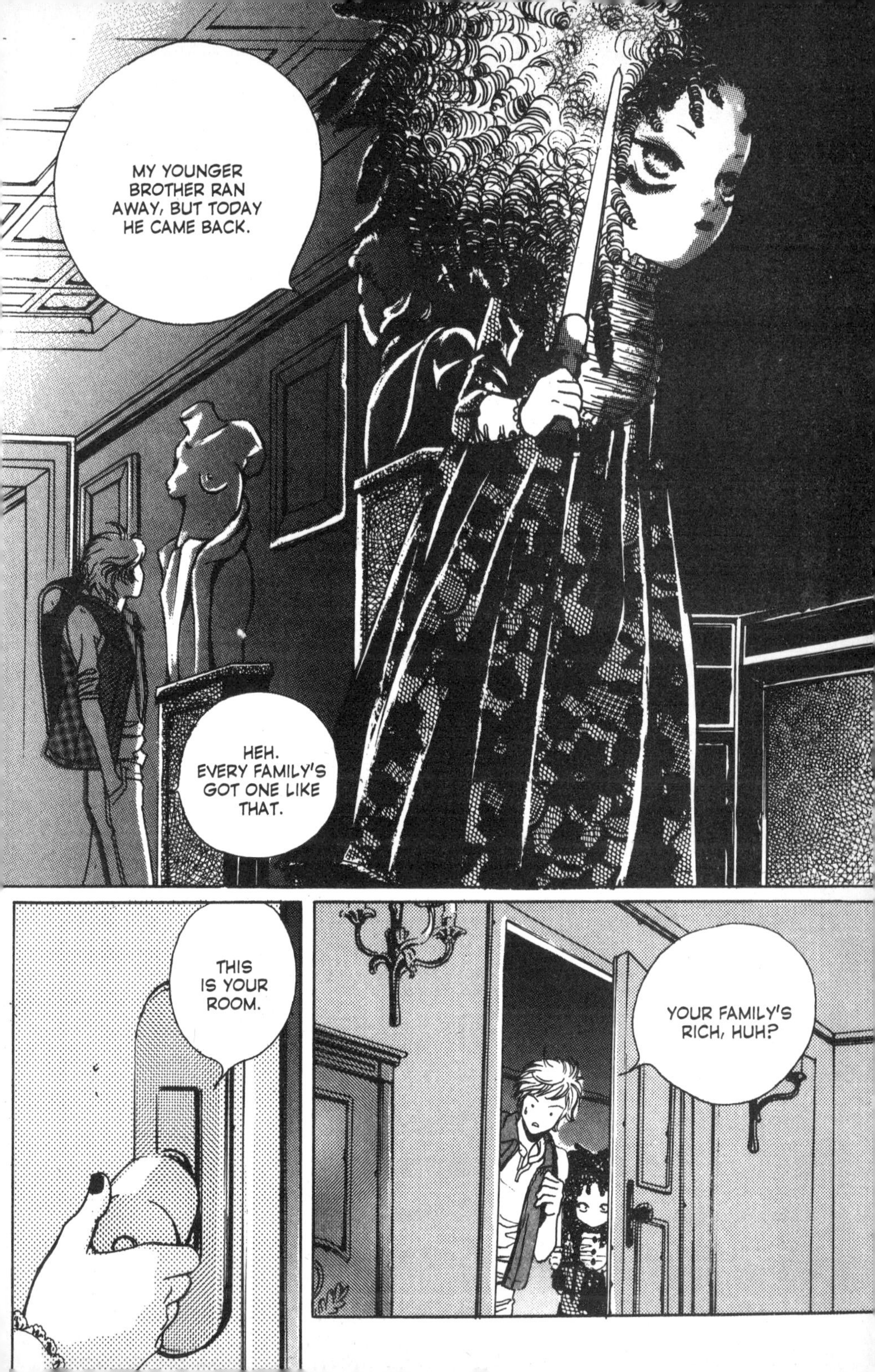
MY YOUNGER BROTHER RAN AWAY, BUT TODAY HE CAME BACK.
HEH. EVERY FAMILY'S GOT ONE LIKE THAT.
THIS IS YOUR ROOM.
YOUR FAMILY'S RICH, HUH?

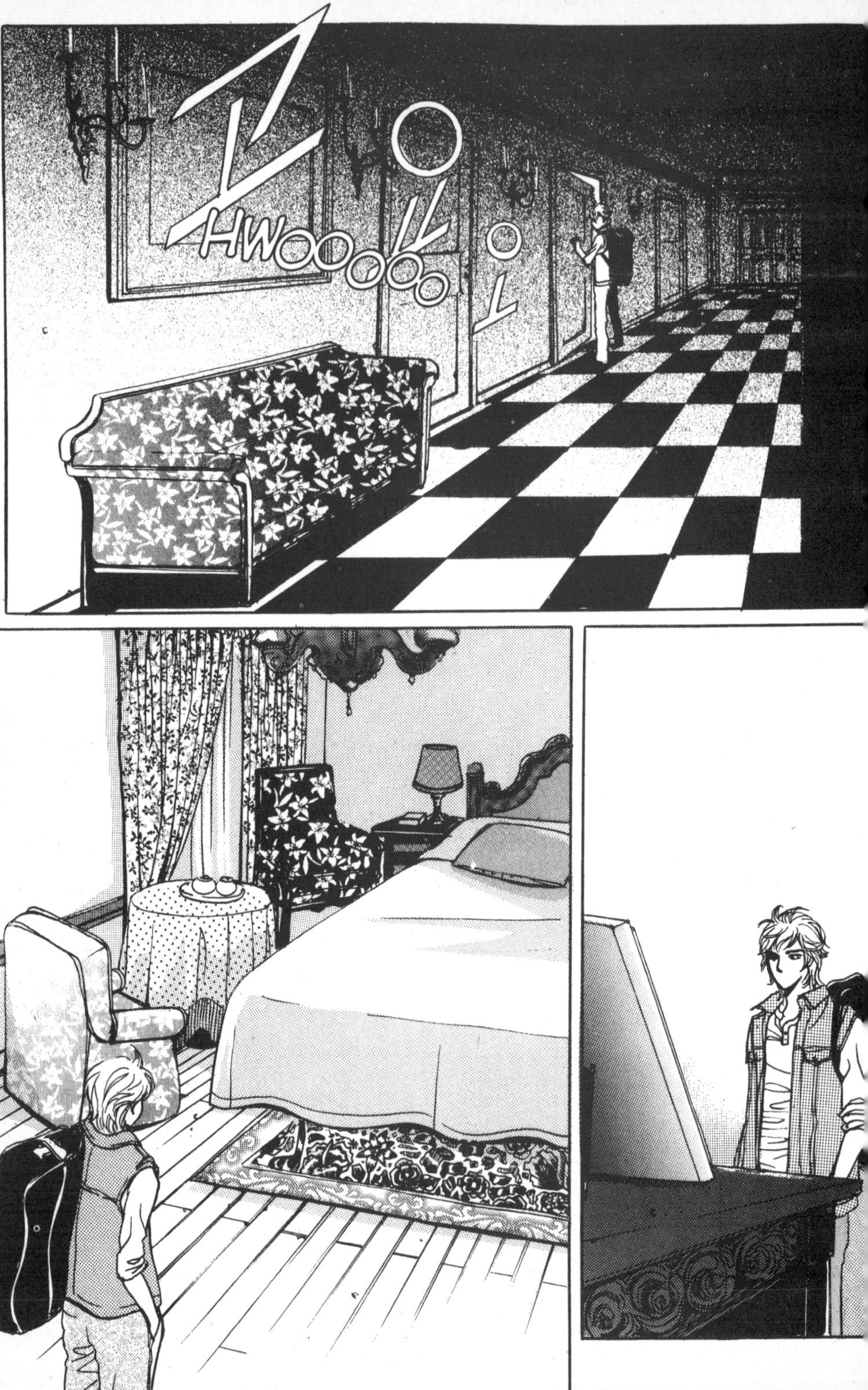
HWOOOOOO

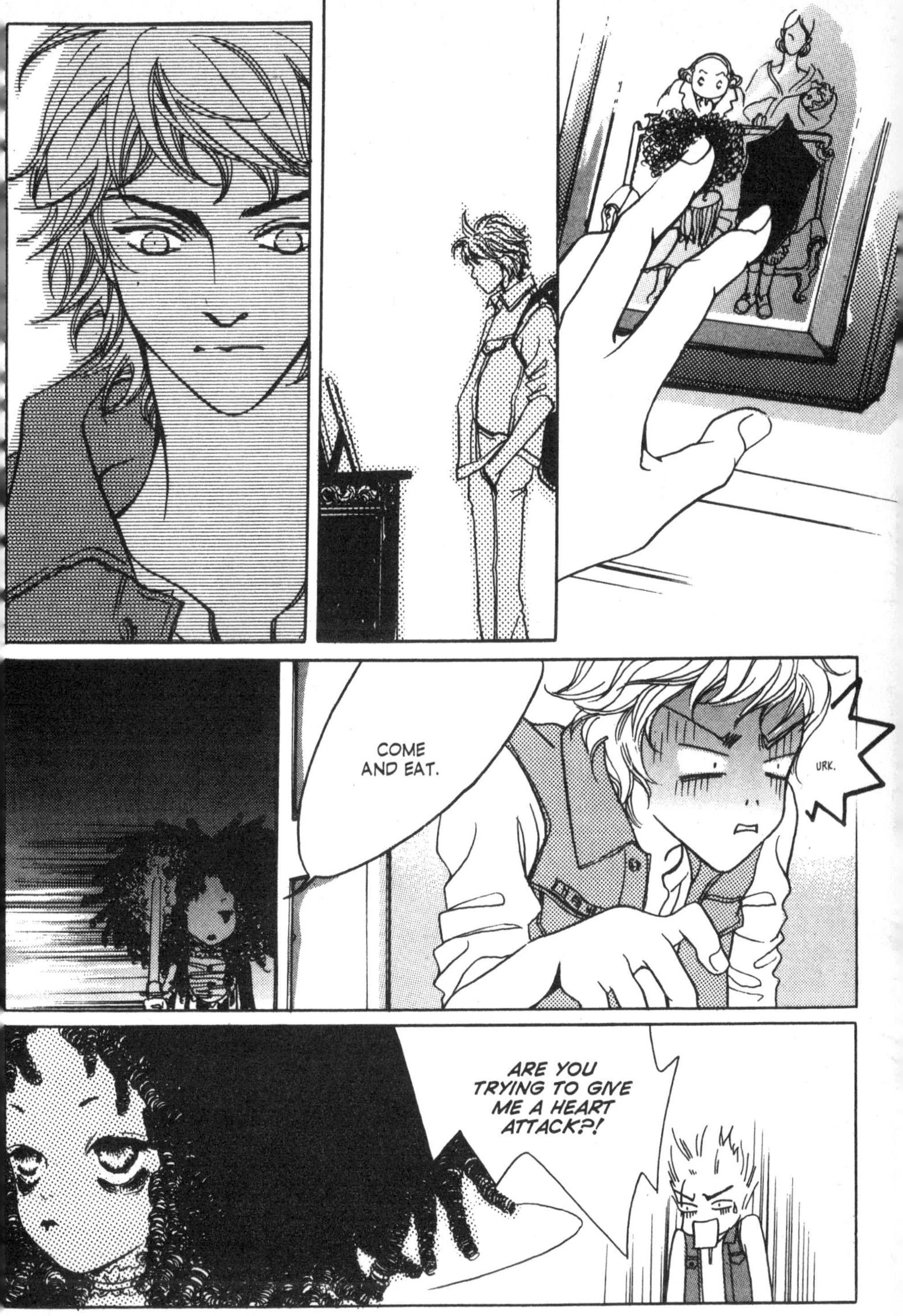
COME AND EAT.
URK.
ARE YOU TRYING TO GIVE ME A HEART ATTACK?!

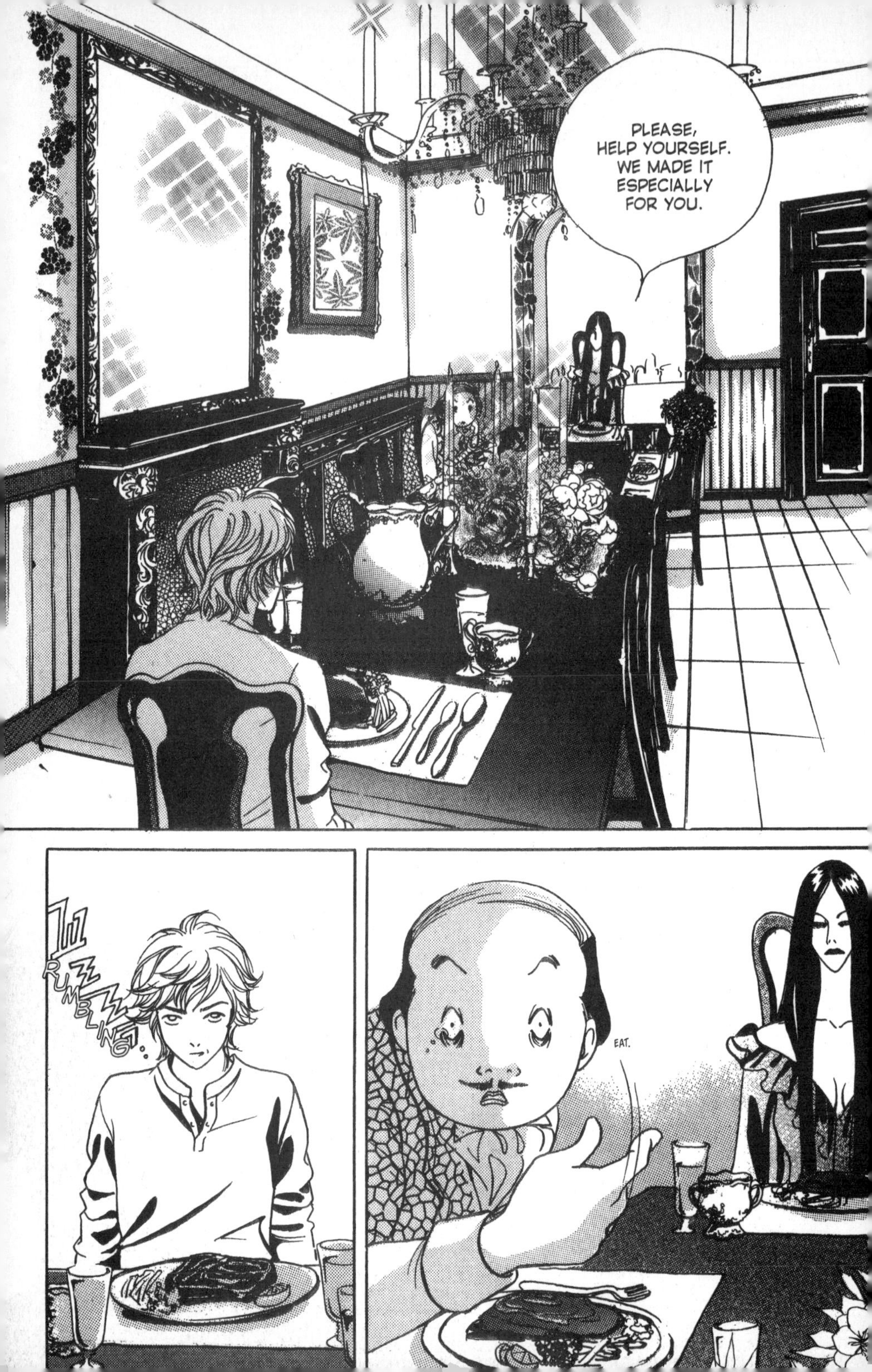
PLEASE, HELP YOURSELF. WE MADE IT ESPECIALLY FOR YOU.
RUMBLING
EAT.

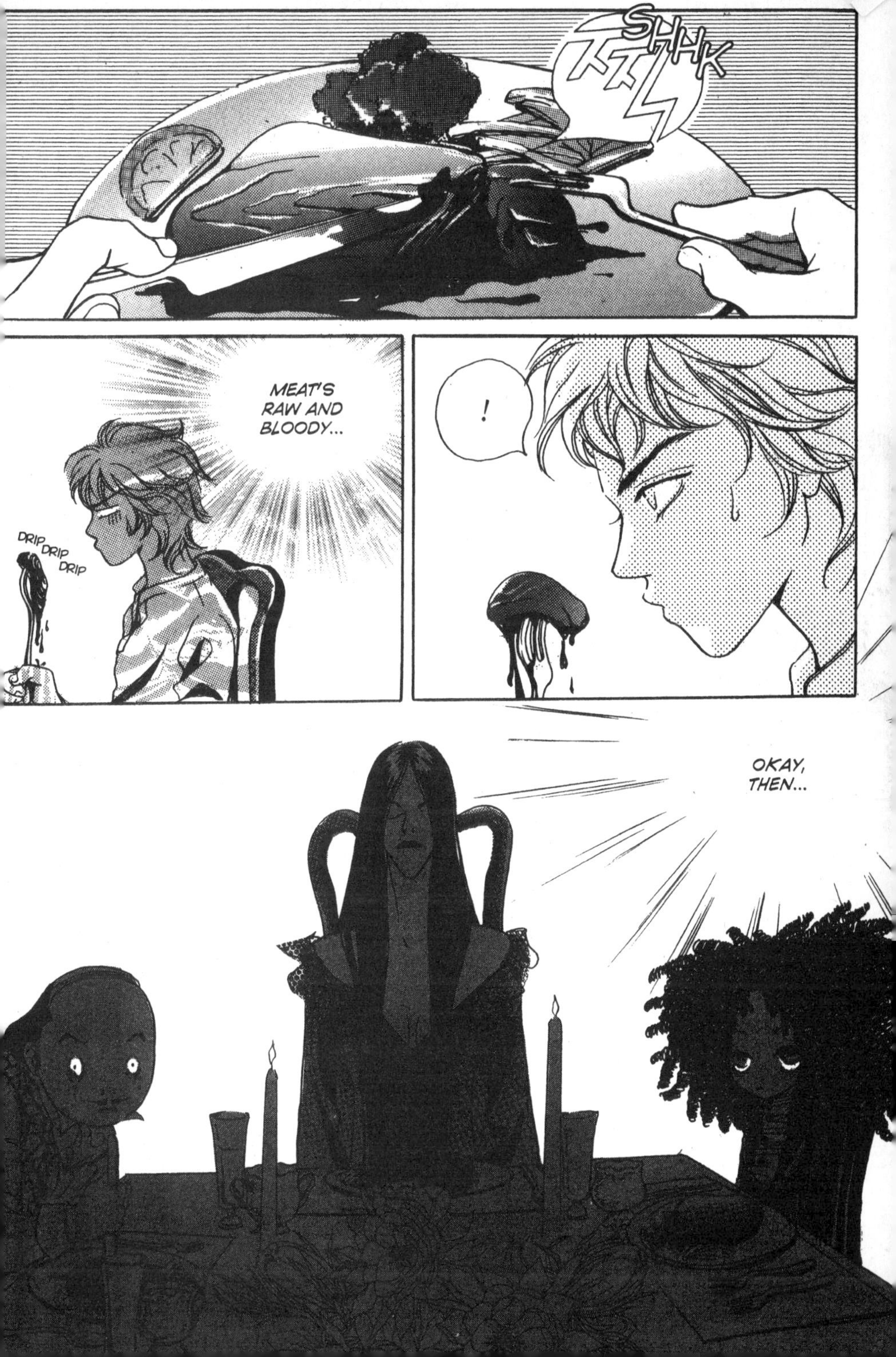
SHHHK
MEAT'S RAW AND BLOODY...
DRIP DRIP DRIP
!
OKAY, THEN...

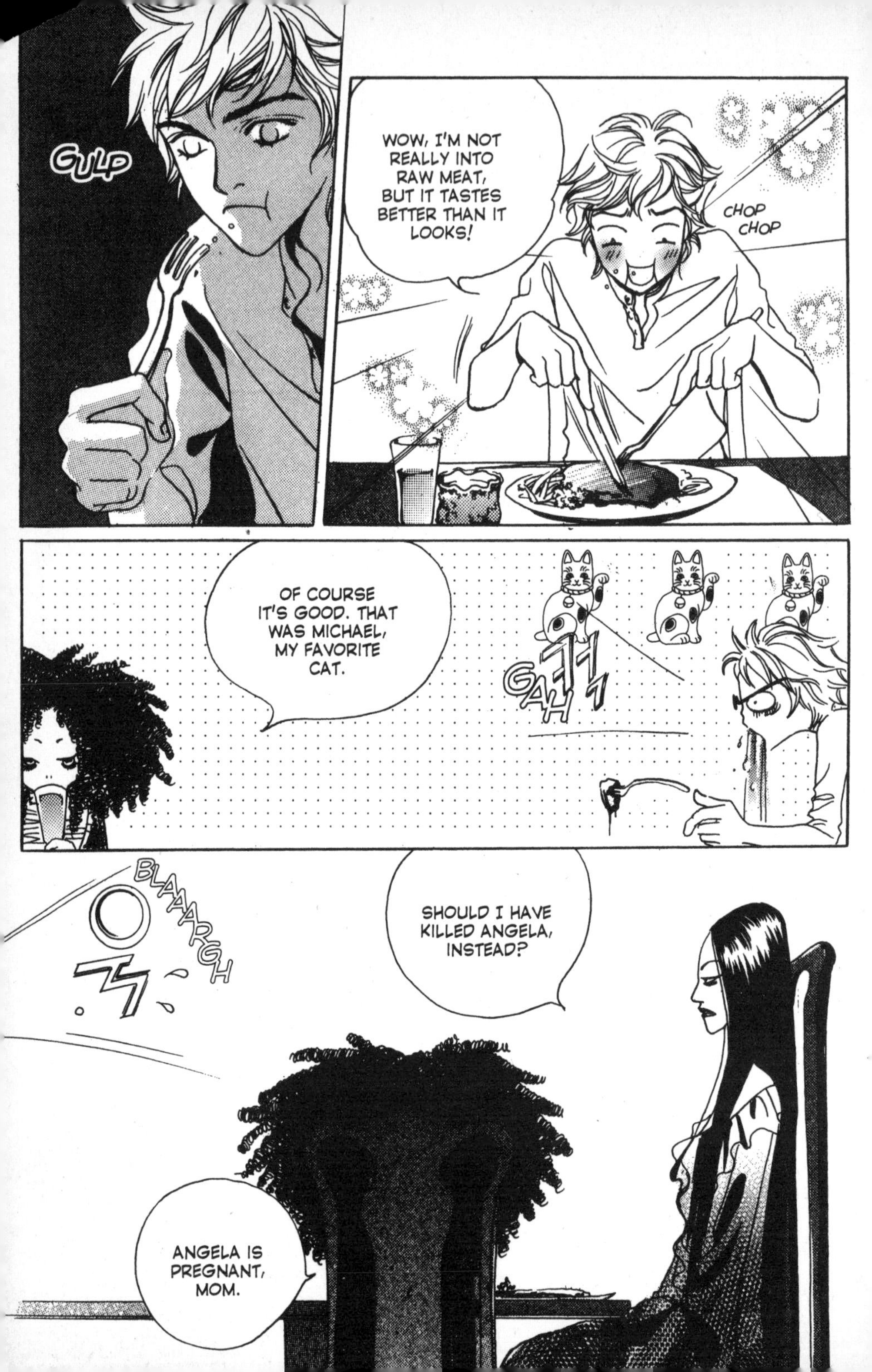
GULP
WOW, I'M NOT REALLY INTO RAW MEAT, BUT IT TASTES BETTER THAN IT LOOKS!
CHOP CHOP
OF COURSE IT'S GOOD. THAT WAS MICHAEL, MY FAVORITE CAT.
GAH
BLAAARGH
SHOULD I HAVE KILLED ANGELA, INSTEAD?
ANGELA IS PREGNANT, MOM.

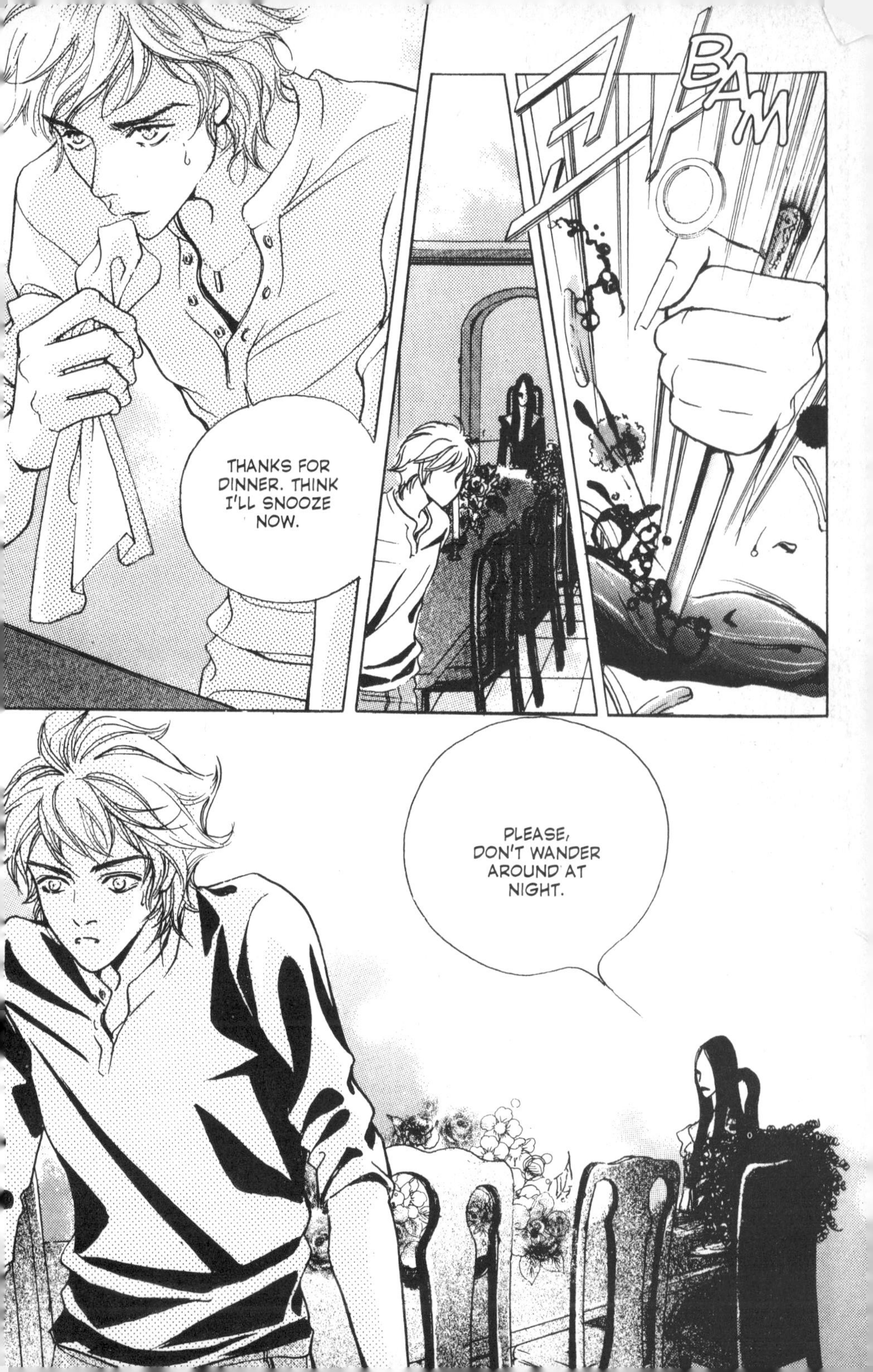
THANKS FOR DINNER. THINK I'LL SNOOZE NOW.
BAM
PLEASE, DON'T WANDER AROUND AT NIGHT.

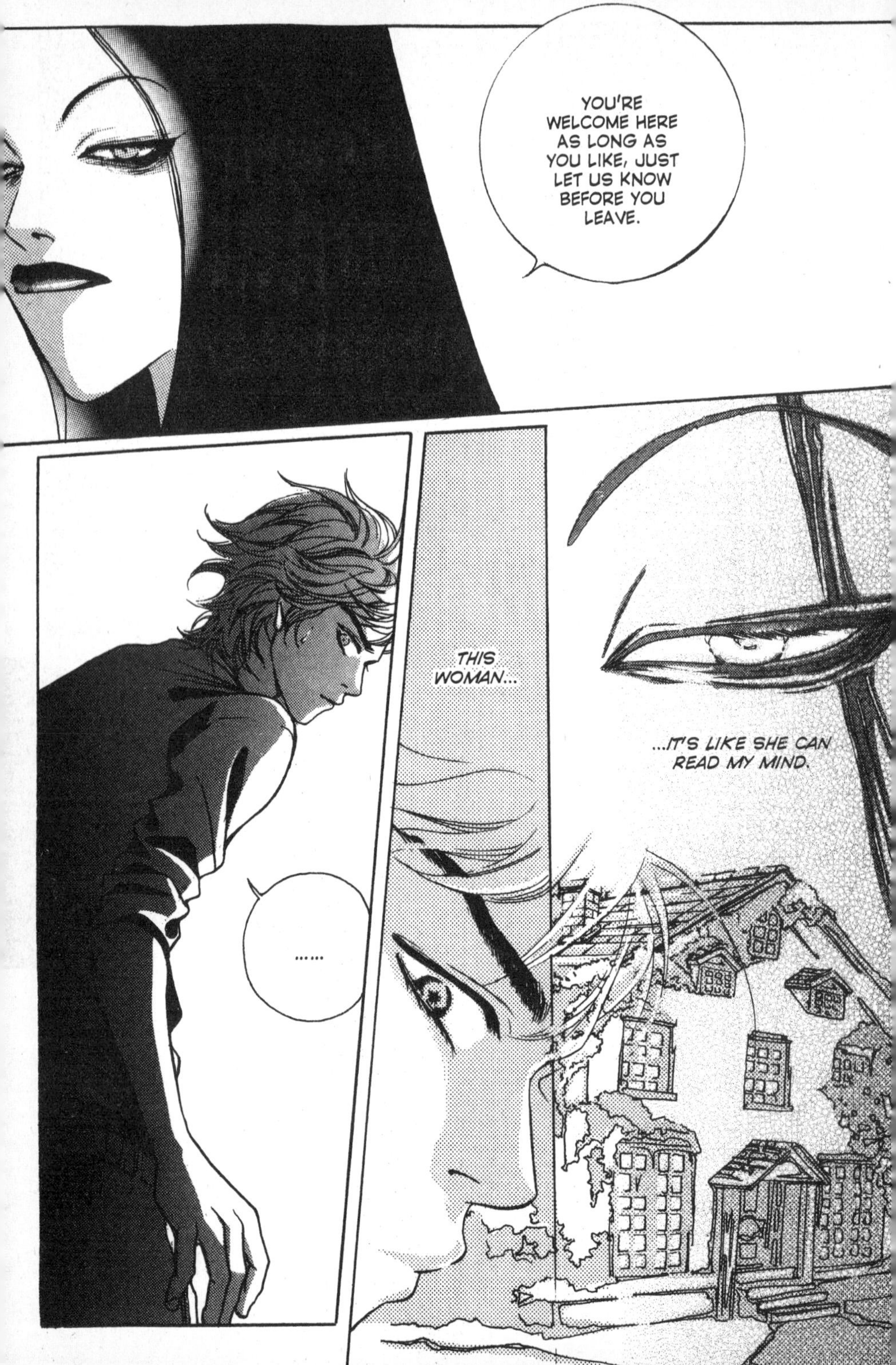
YOU'RE WELCOME HERE AS LONG AS YOU LIKE, JUST LET US KNOW BEFORE YOU LEAVE.
......
THIS WOMAN...
...IT'S LIKE SHE CAN READ MY MIND.

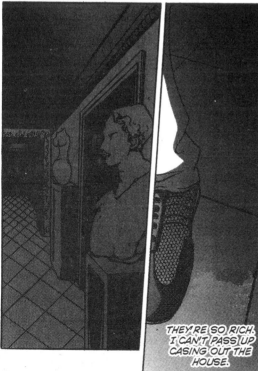

THEY'RE SO RICH.
I CAN'T PASS UP
CASING OUT THE
HOUSE.

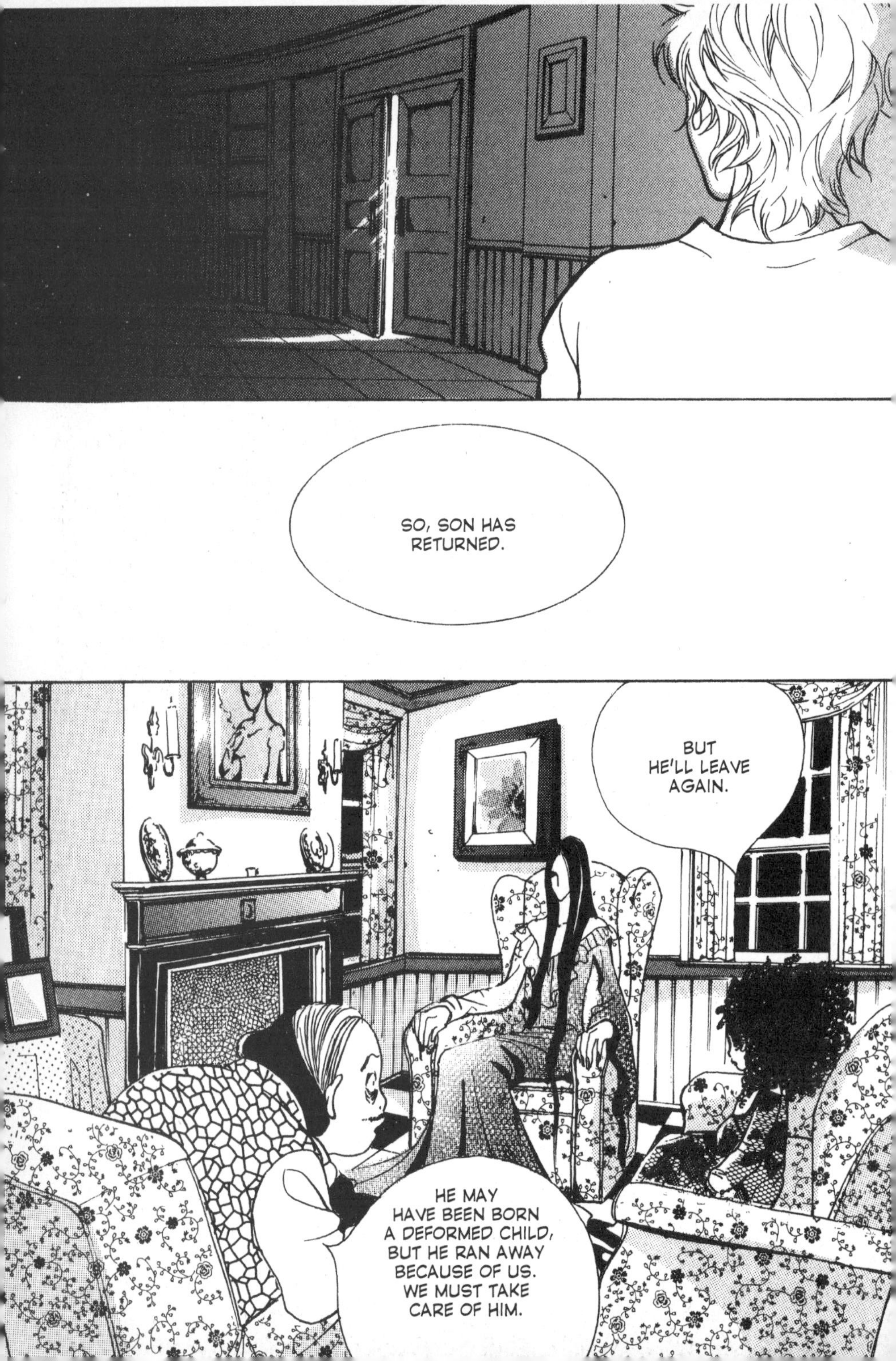
SO, SON HAS RETURNED.
BUT HE'LL LEAVE AGAIN.
HE MAY HAVE BEEN BORN A DEFORMED CHILD, BUT HE RAN AWAY BECAUSE OF US. WE MUST TAKE CARE OF HIM.

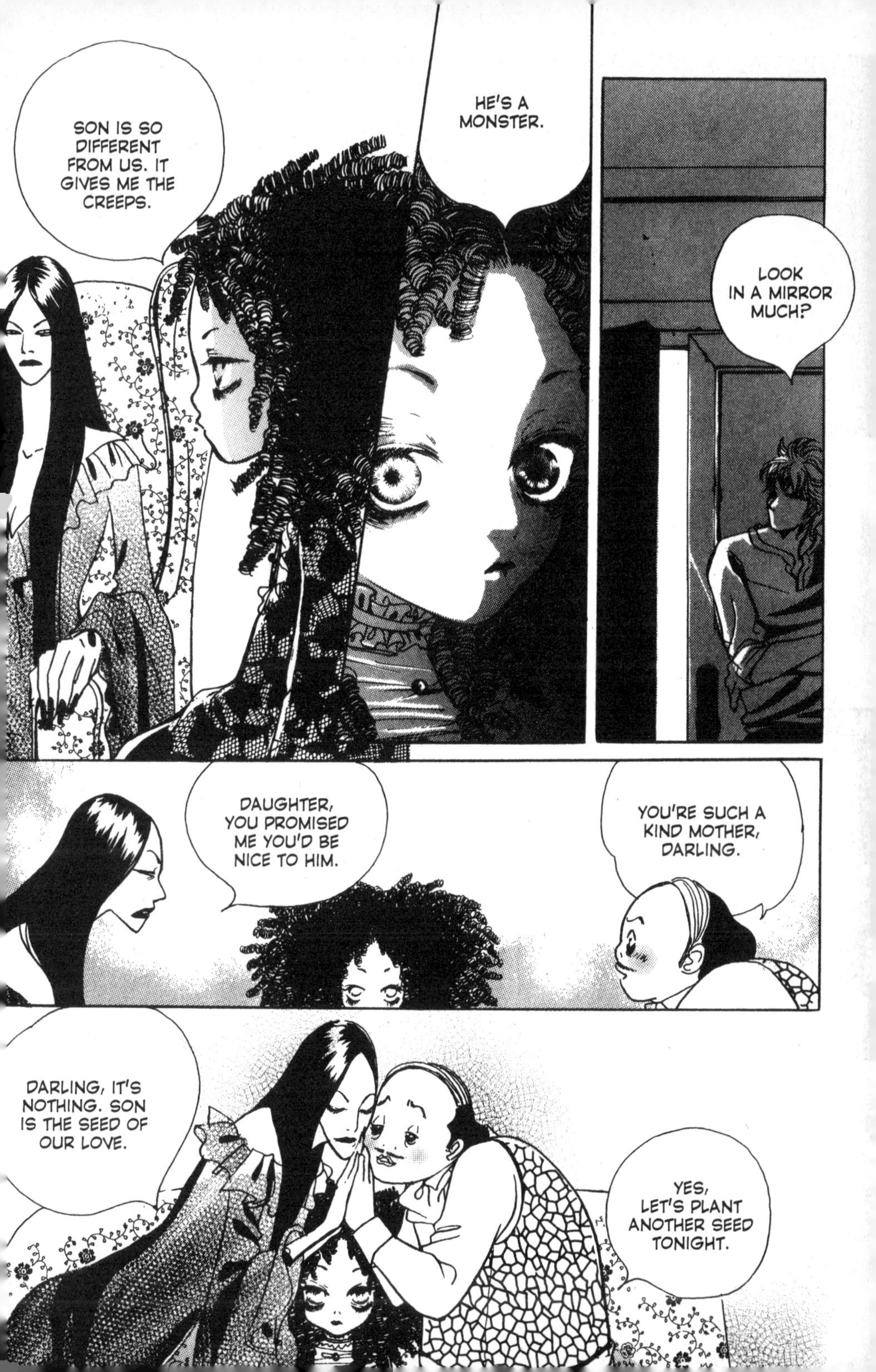
SON IS SO DIFFERENT FROM US. IT GIVES ME THE CREEPS.
HE'S A MONSTER.
LOOK IN A MIRROR MUCH?
DAUGHTER, YOU PROMISED ME YOU'D BE NICE TO HIM.
YOU'RE SUCH A KIND MOTHER, DARLING.
DARLING, IT'S NOTHING. SON IS THE SEED OF OUR LOVE.
YES, LET'S PLANT ANOTHER SEED TONIGHT.

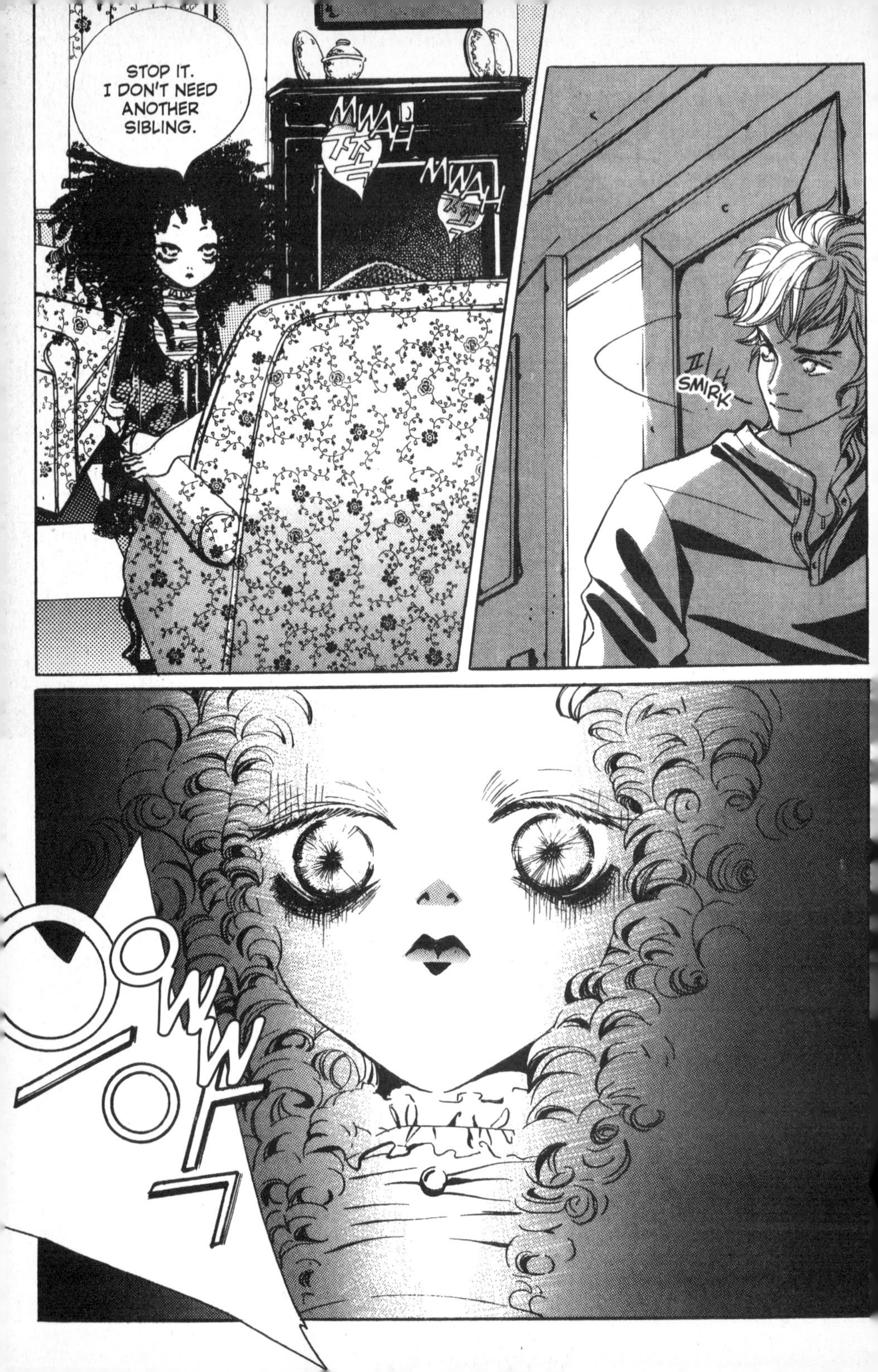
STOP IT. I DON'T NEED ANOTHER SIBLING.
MWAH
MWAH
SMIRK

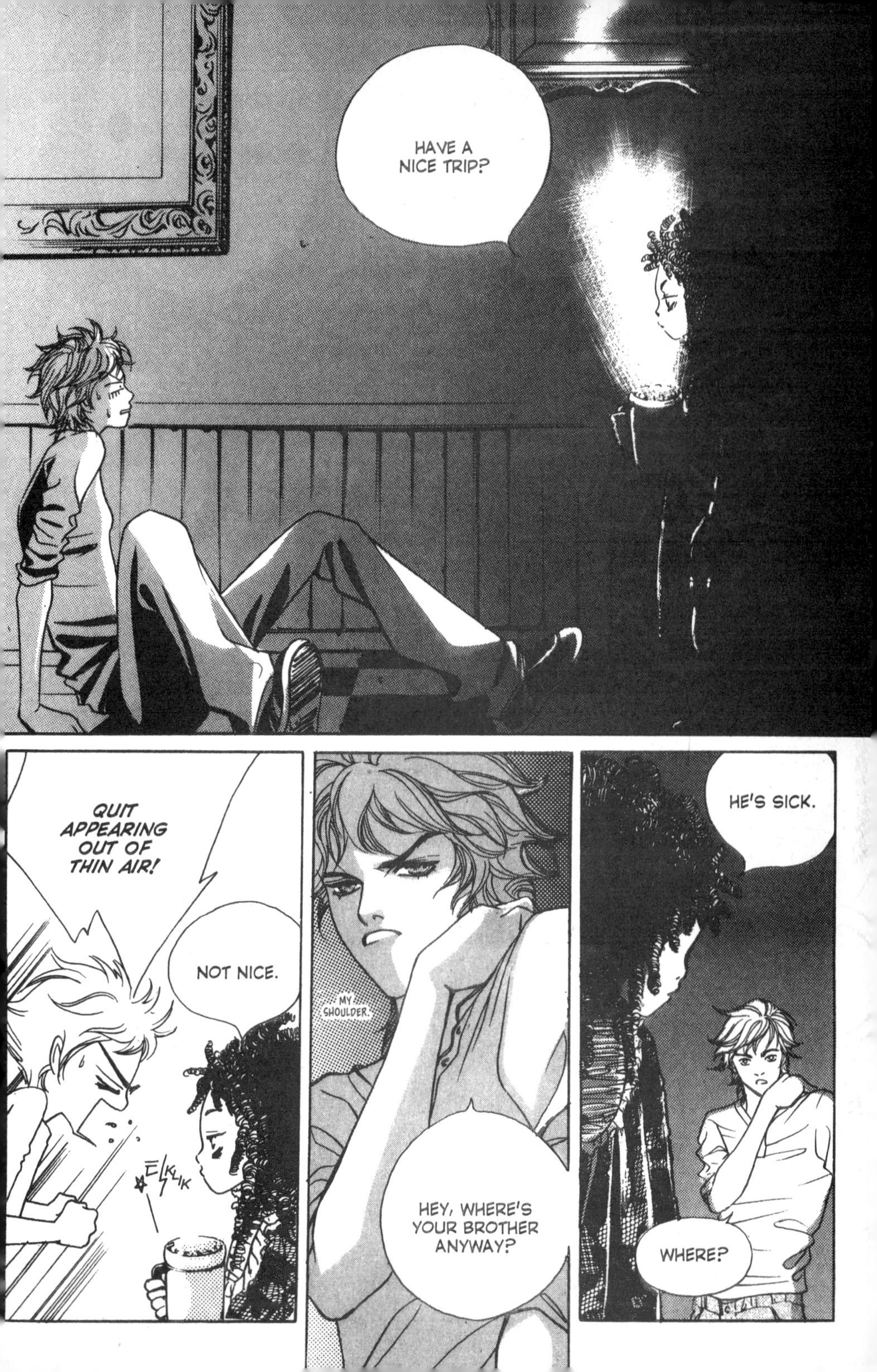
HAVE A NICE TRIP?
QUIT APPEARING OUT OF THIN AIR!
NOT NICE.
CKLIK
MY SHOULDER.
HEY, WHERE'S YOUR BROTHER ANYWAY?
HE'S SICK.
WHERE?

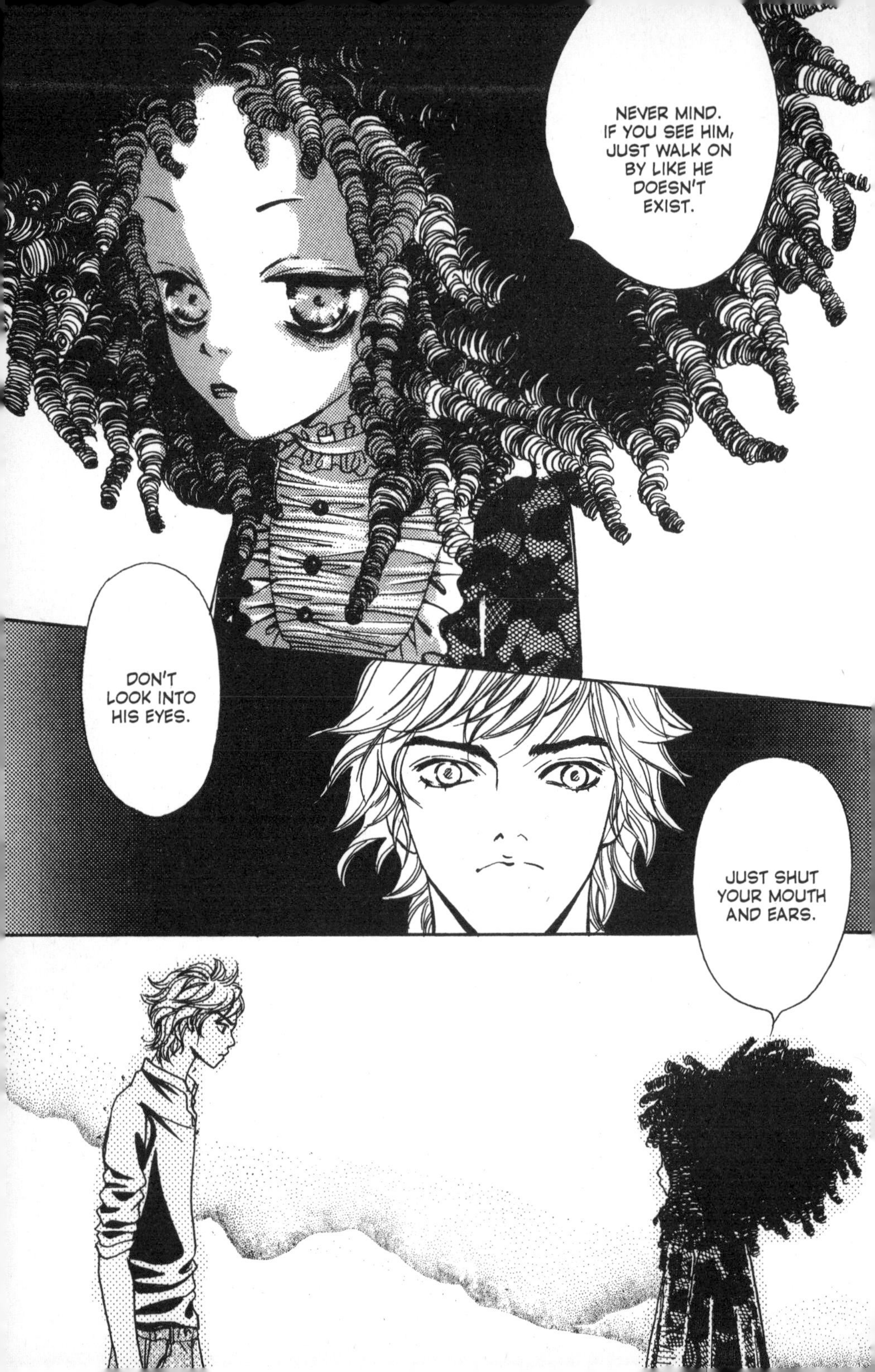
NEVER MIND. IF YOU SEE HIM, JUST WALK ON BY LIKE HE DOESN'T EXIST.
DON'T LOOK INTO HIS EYES.
JUST SHUT YOUR MOUTH AND EARS.

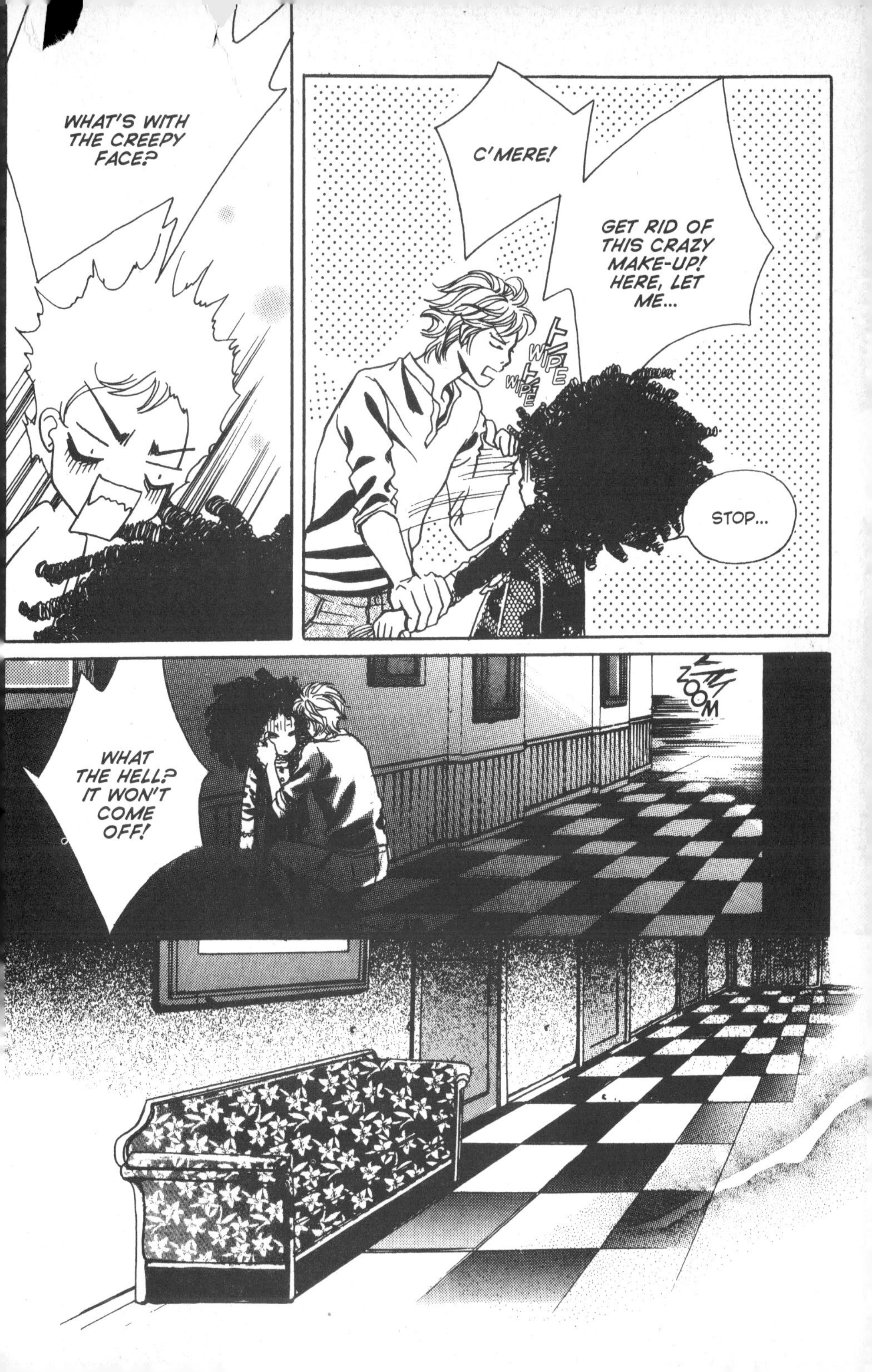
WHAT'S WITH THE CREEPY FACE?
C'MERE!
GET RID OF THIS CRAZY MAKE-UP! HERE, LET ME...
WIPE WIPE
STOP...
WHAT THE HELL? IT WON'T COME OFF!
ZOOM

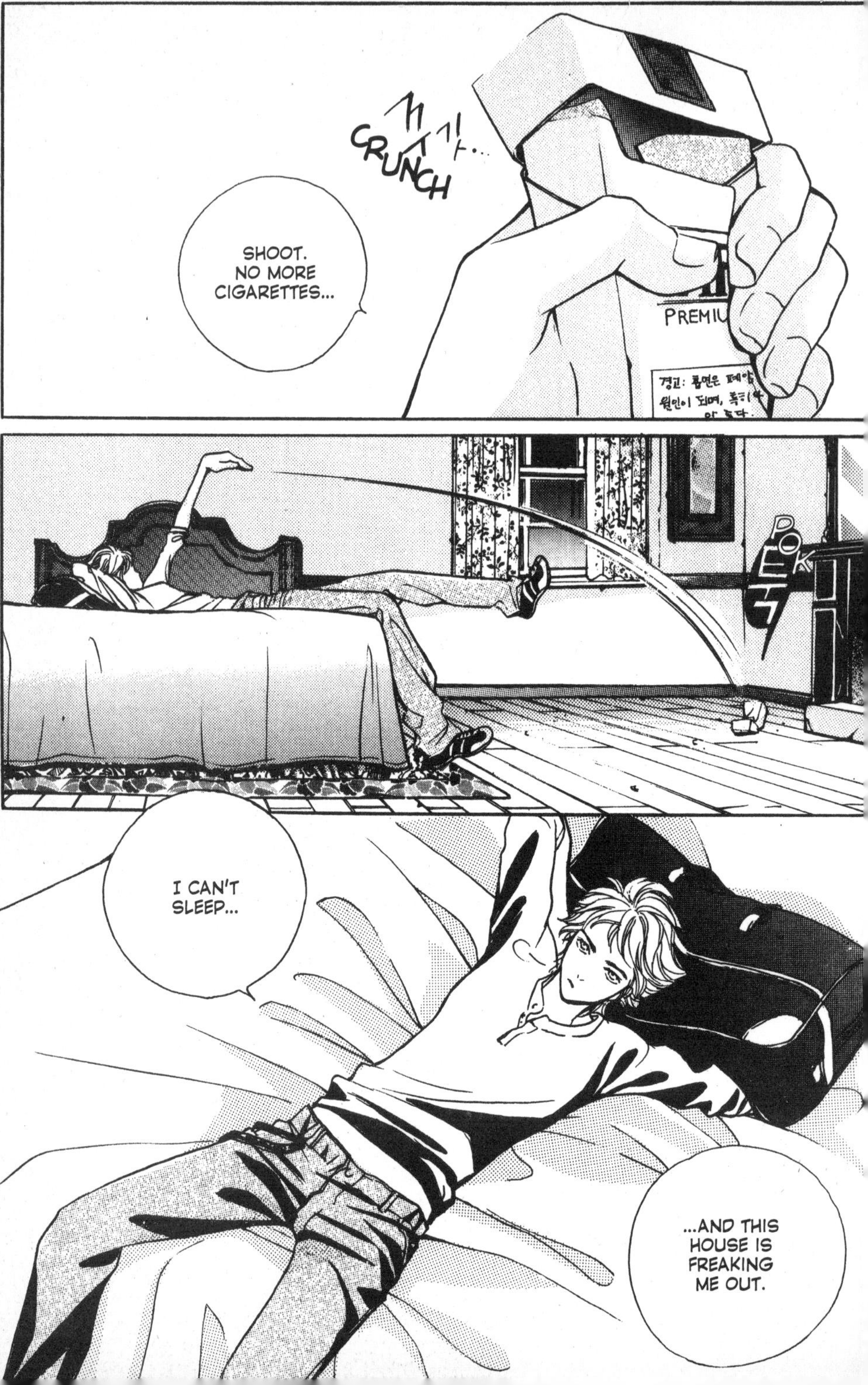
CRUNCH
SHOOT. NO MORE CIGARETTES...
PREMIU
POKE
I CAN'T SLEEP...
...AND THIS HOUSE IS FREAKING ME OUT.

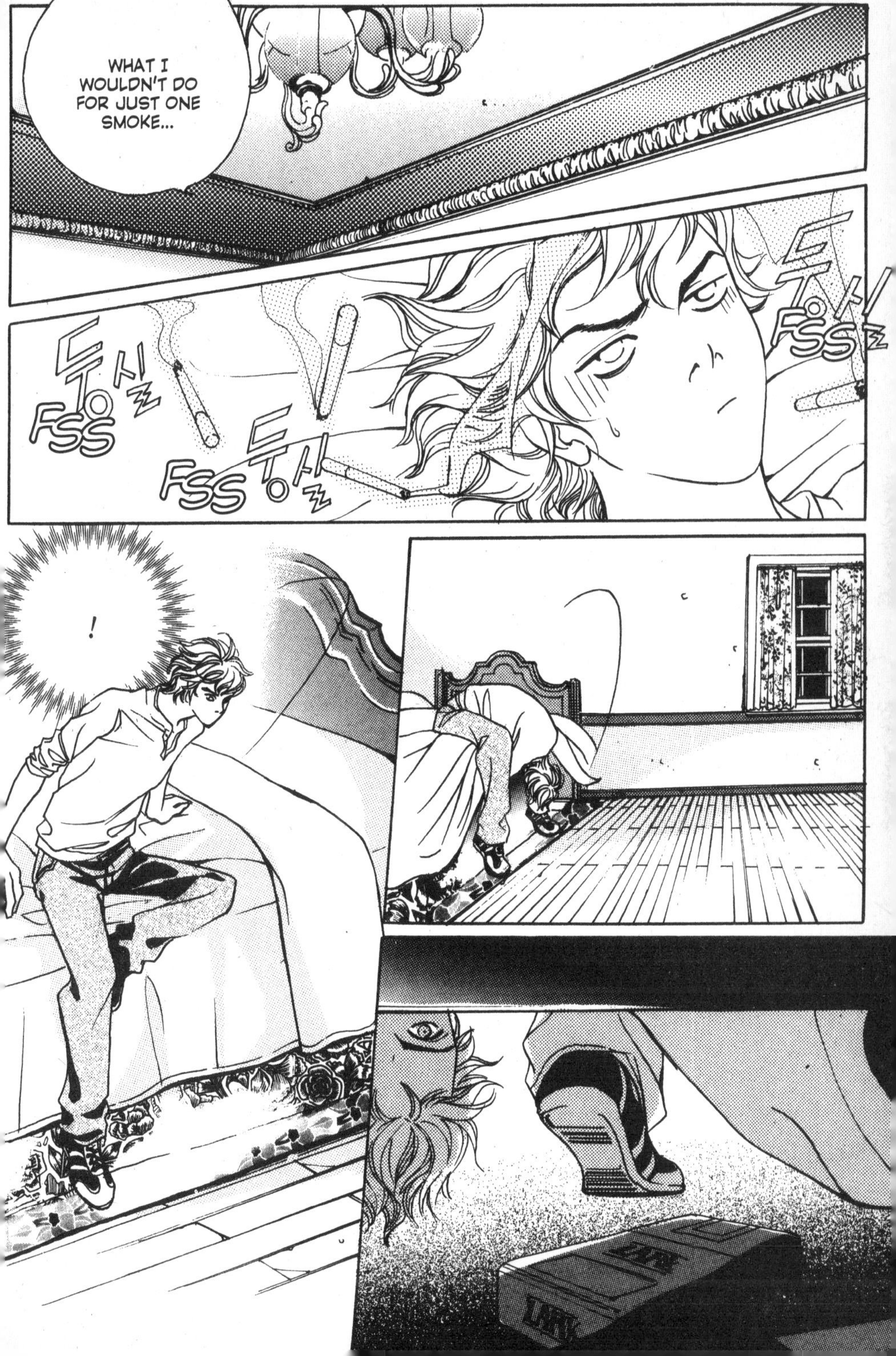
WHAT I WOULDN'T DO FOR JUST ONE SMOKE...
FSS
FSS
FSS
!

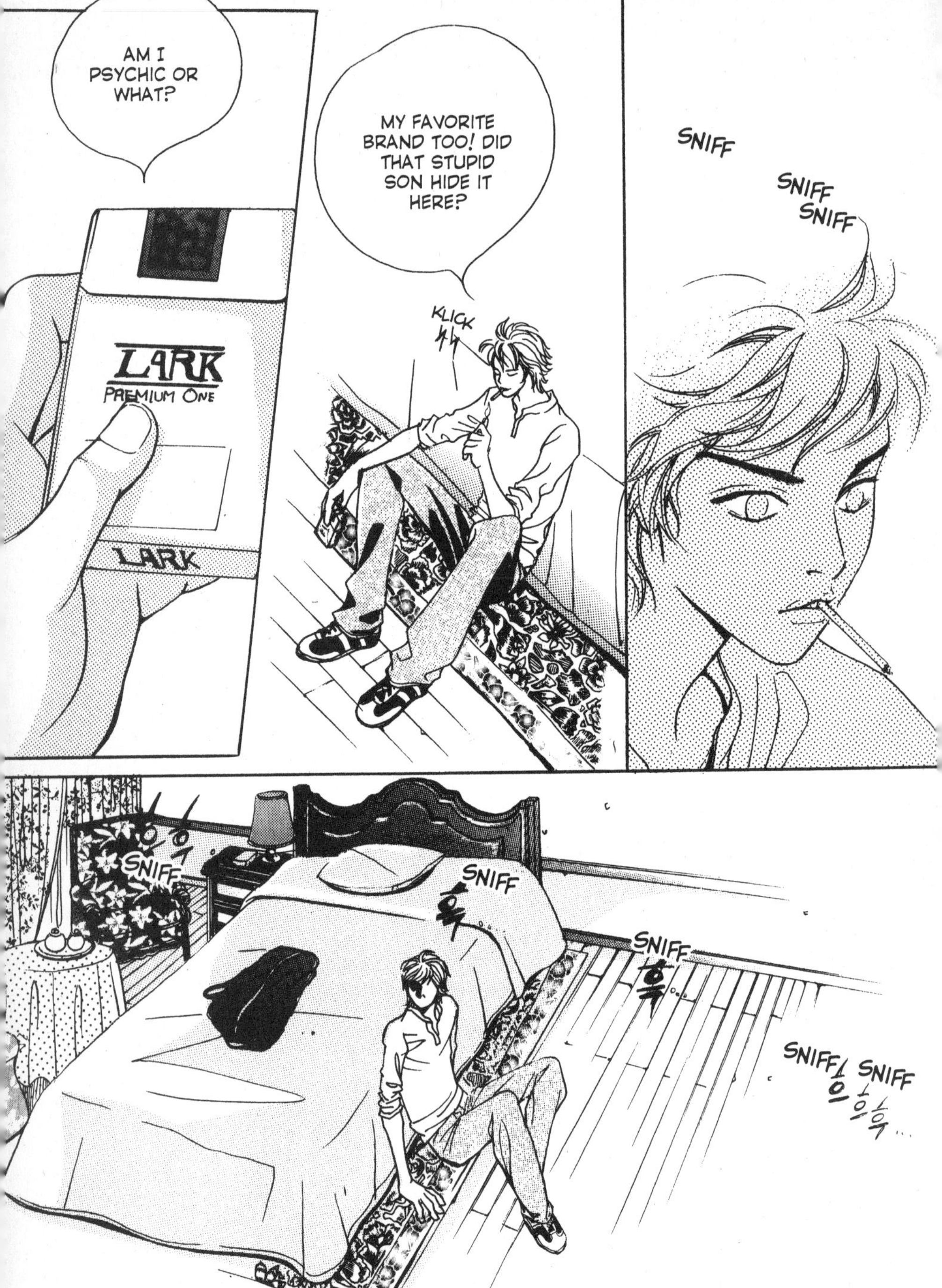

AM I PSYCHIC OR WHAT?
LARK
PREMIUM ONE
LARK
MY FAVORITE BRAND TOO! DID THAT STUPID SON HIDE IT HERE?
KLICK
SNIFF
SNIFF SNIFF
SNIFF
SNIFF
SNIFF
SNIFF SNIFF

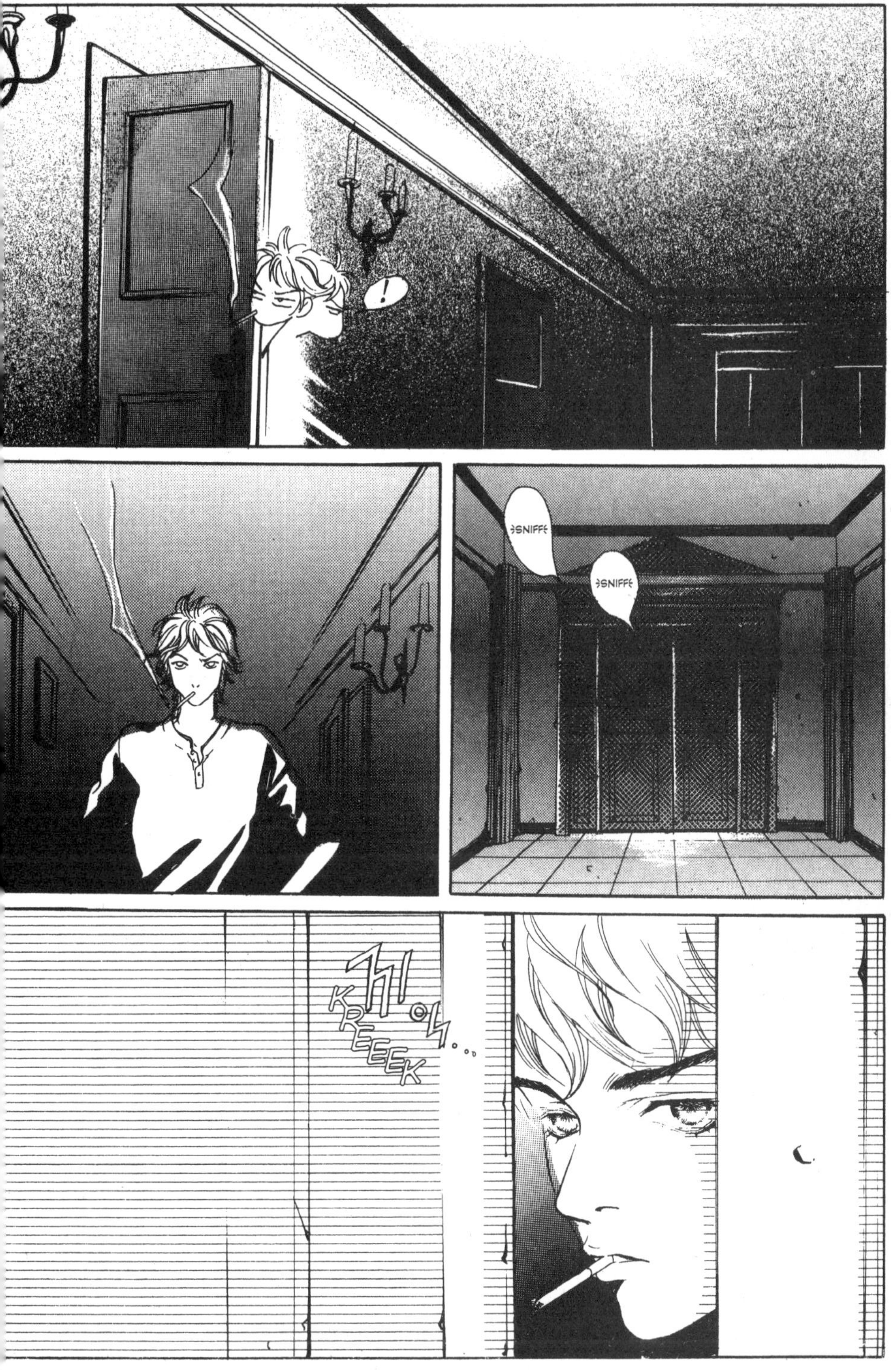
!
SNIFF
SNIFF
끼이익…
KREEEEK

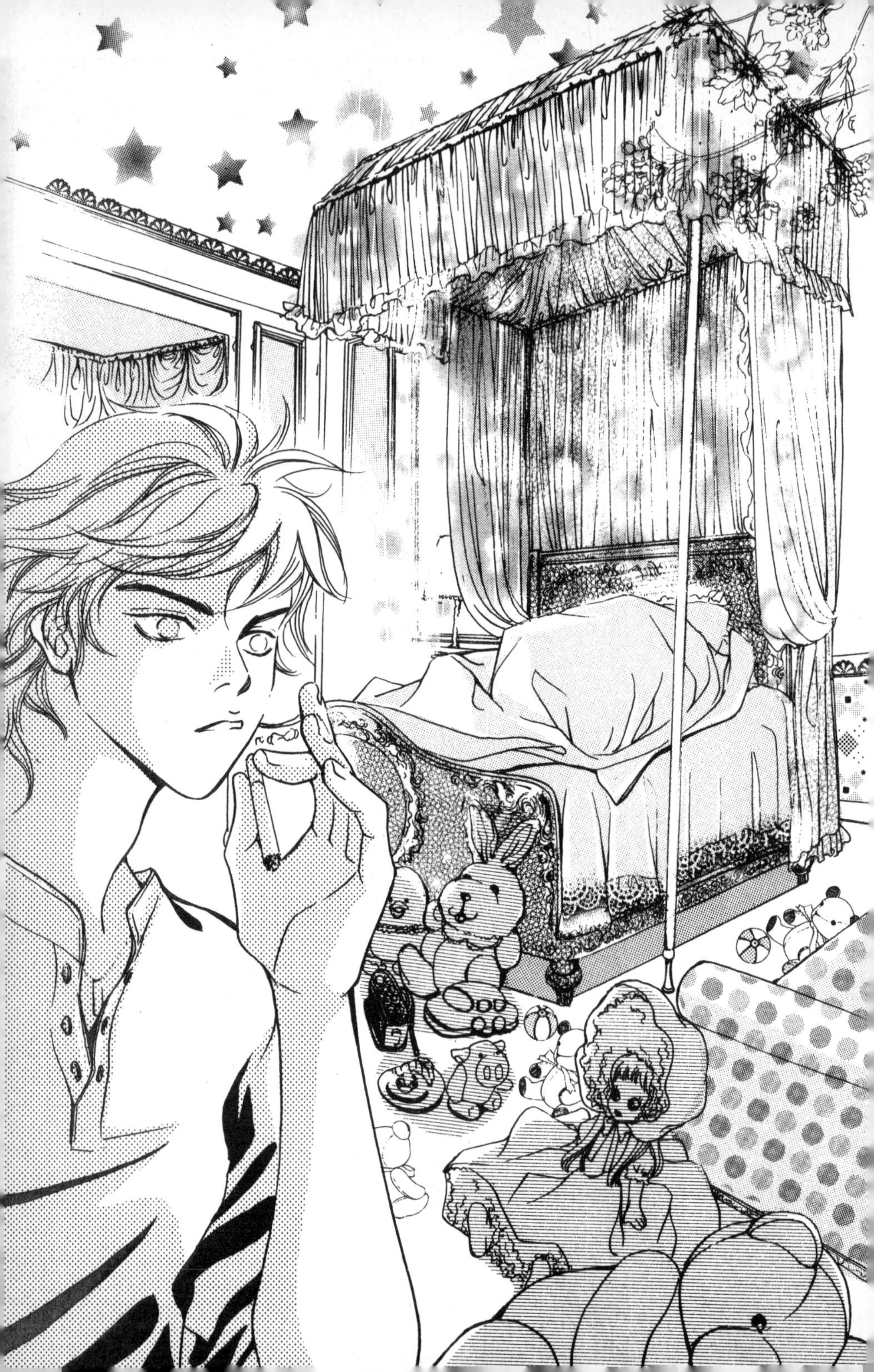

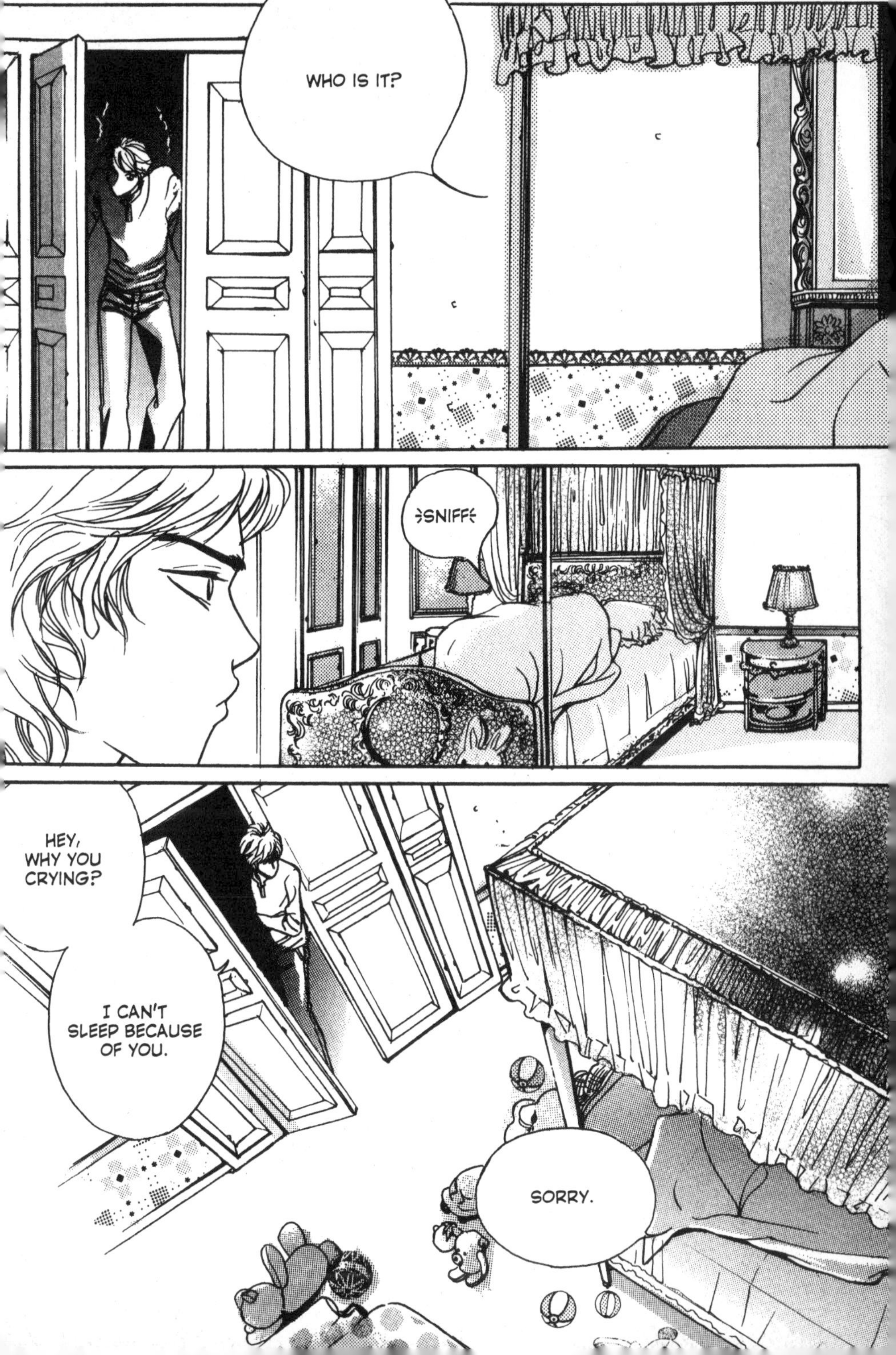
WHO IS IT?
SNIFF
HEY, WHY YOU CRYING?
I CAN'T SLEEP BECAUSE OF YOU.
SORRY.

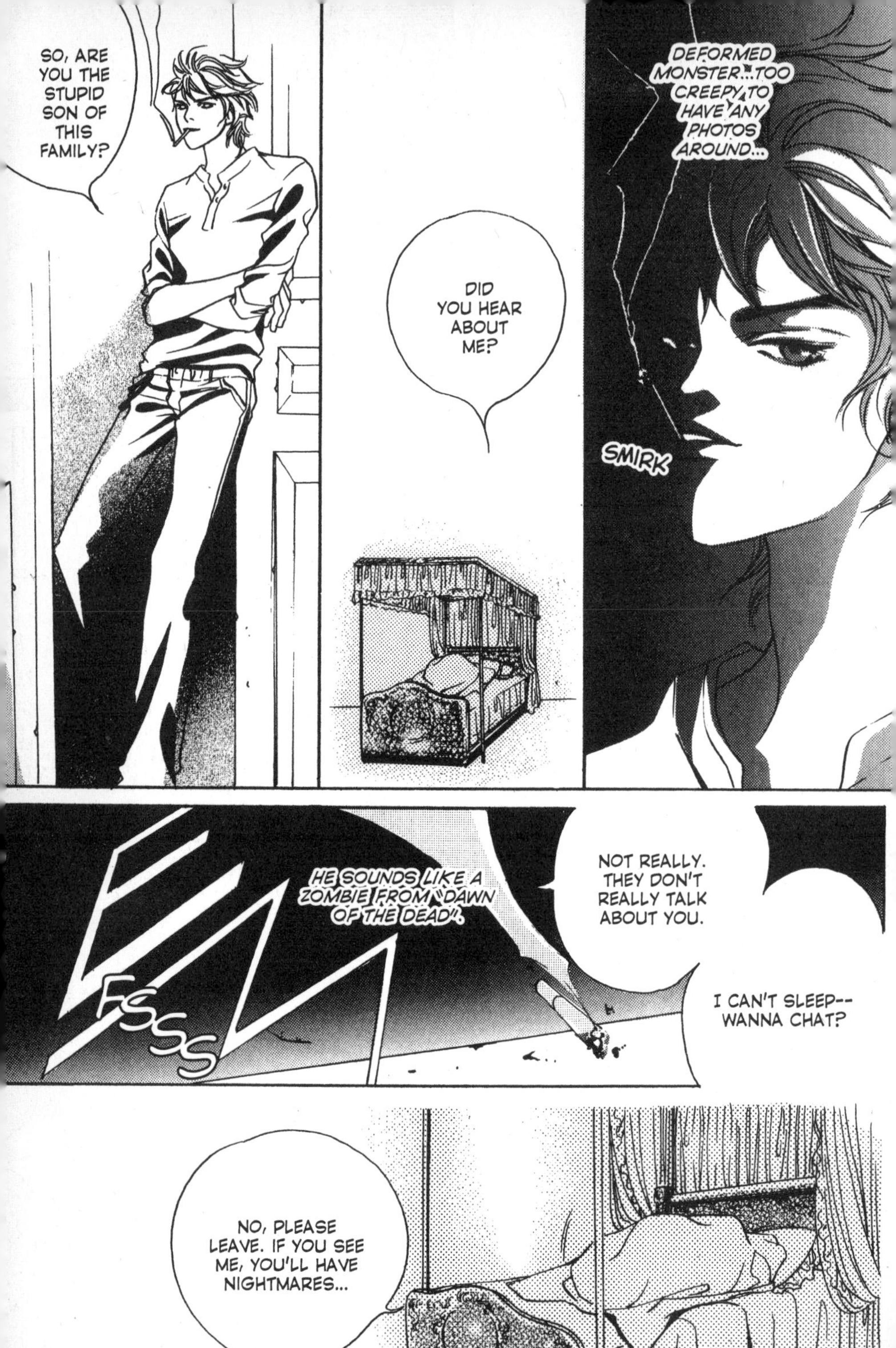
SO, ARE YOU THE STUPID SON OF THIS FAMILY?
DID YOU HEAR ABOUT ME?
DEFORMED MONSTER...TOO CREEPY TO HAVE ANY PHOTOS AROUND...
SMIRK
HE SOUNDS LIKE A ZOMBIE FROM "DAWN OF THE DEAD".
NOT REALLY. THEY DON'T REALLY TALK ABOUT YOU.
FSSS
I CAN'T SLEEP-- WANNA CHAT?
NO, PLEASE LEAVE. IF YOU SEE ME, YOU'LL HAVE NIGHTMARES...

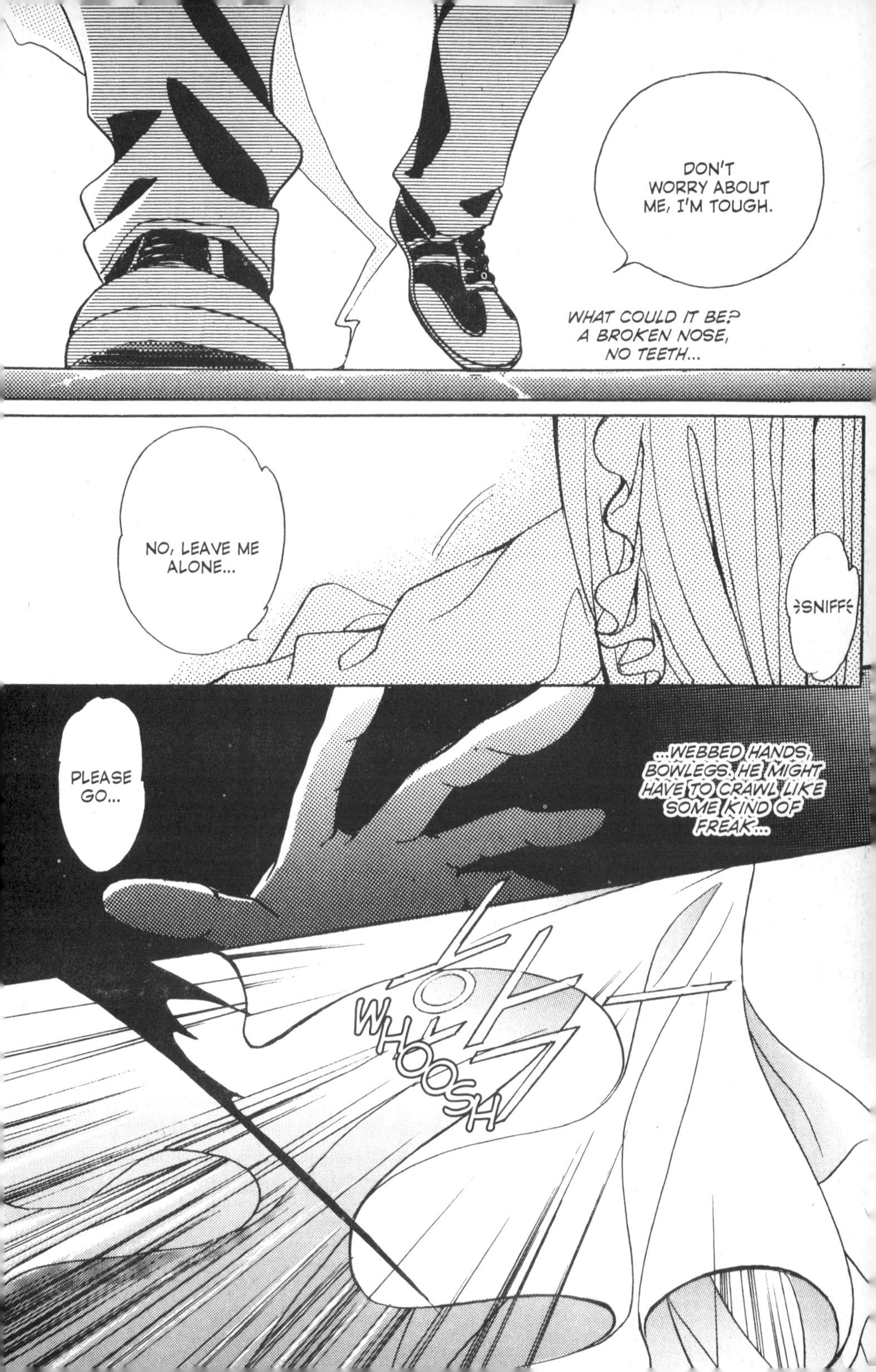
DON'T WORRY ABOUT ME, I'M TOUGH.
WHAT COULD IT BE? A BROKEN NOSE, NO TEETH...
NO, LEAVE ME ALONE...
SNIFF
PLEASE GO...
...WEBBED HANDS, BOWLEGS. HE MIGHT HAVE TO CRAWL LIKE SOME KIND OF FREAK...
WHOOSH

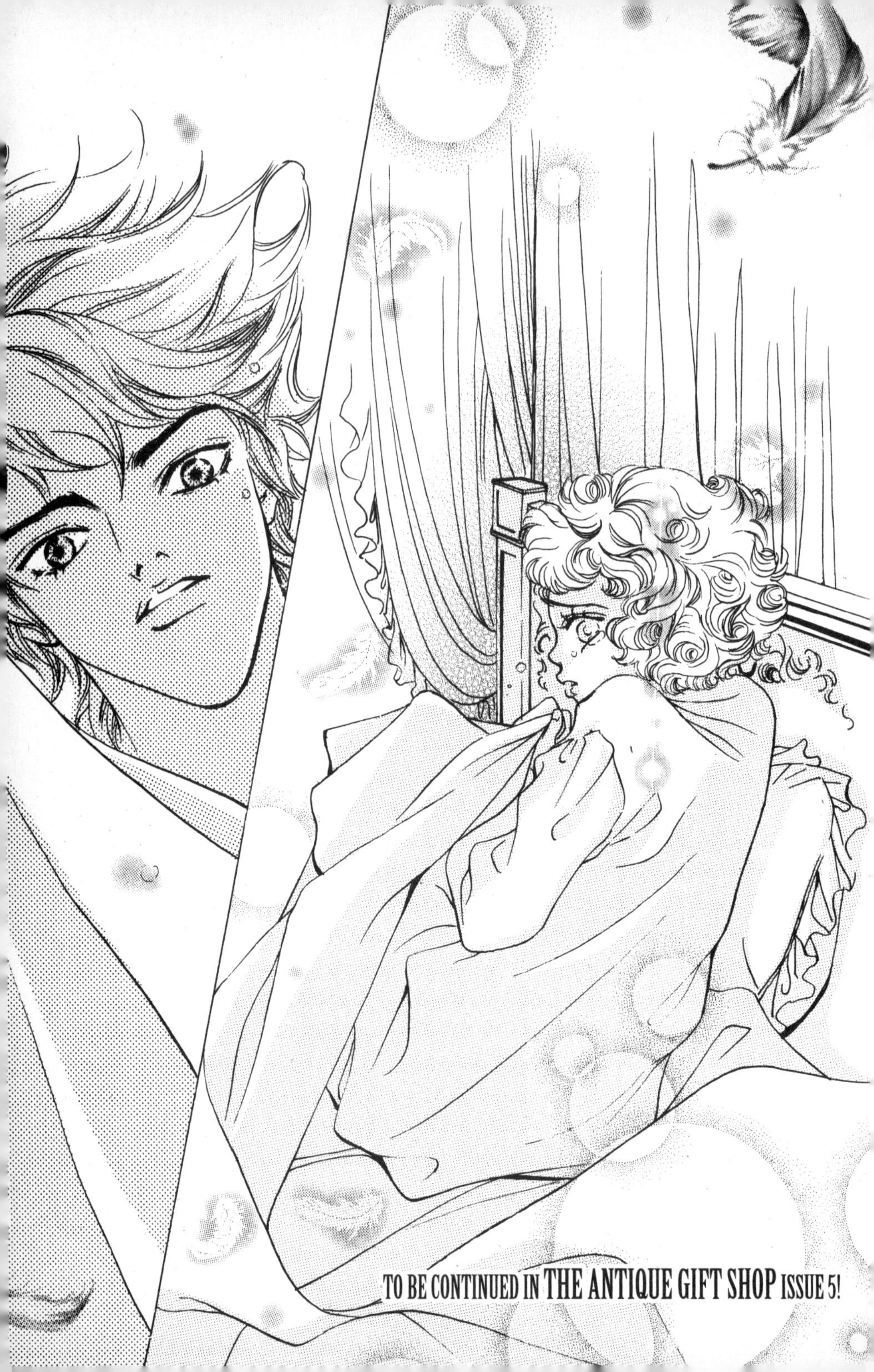
TO BE CONTINUED IN THE ANTIQUE GIFT SHOP ISSUE 5!

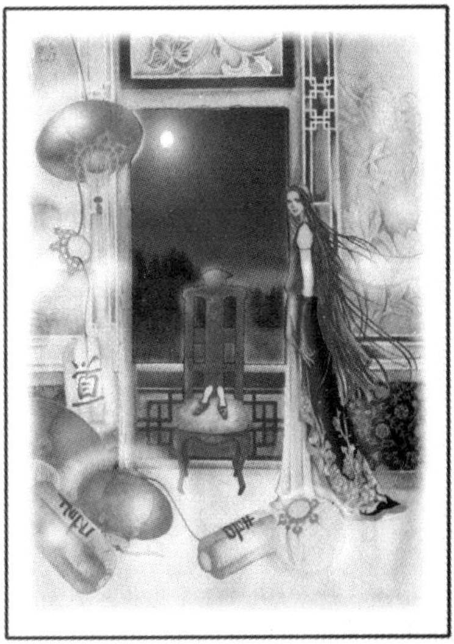
道

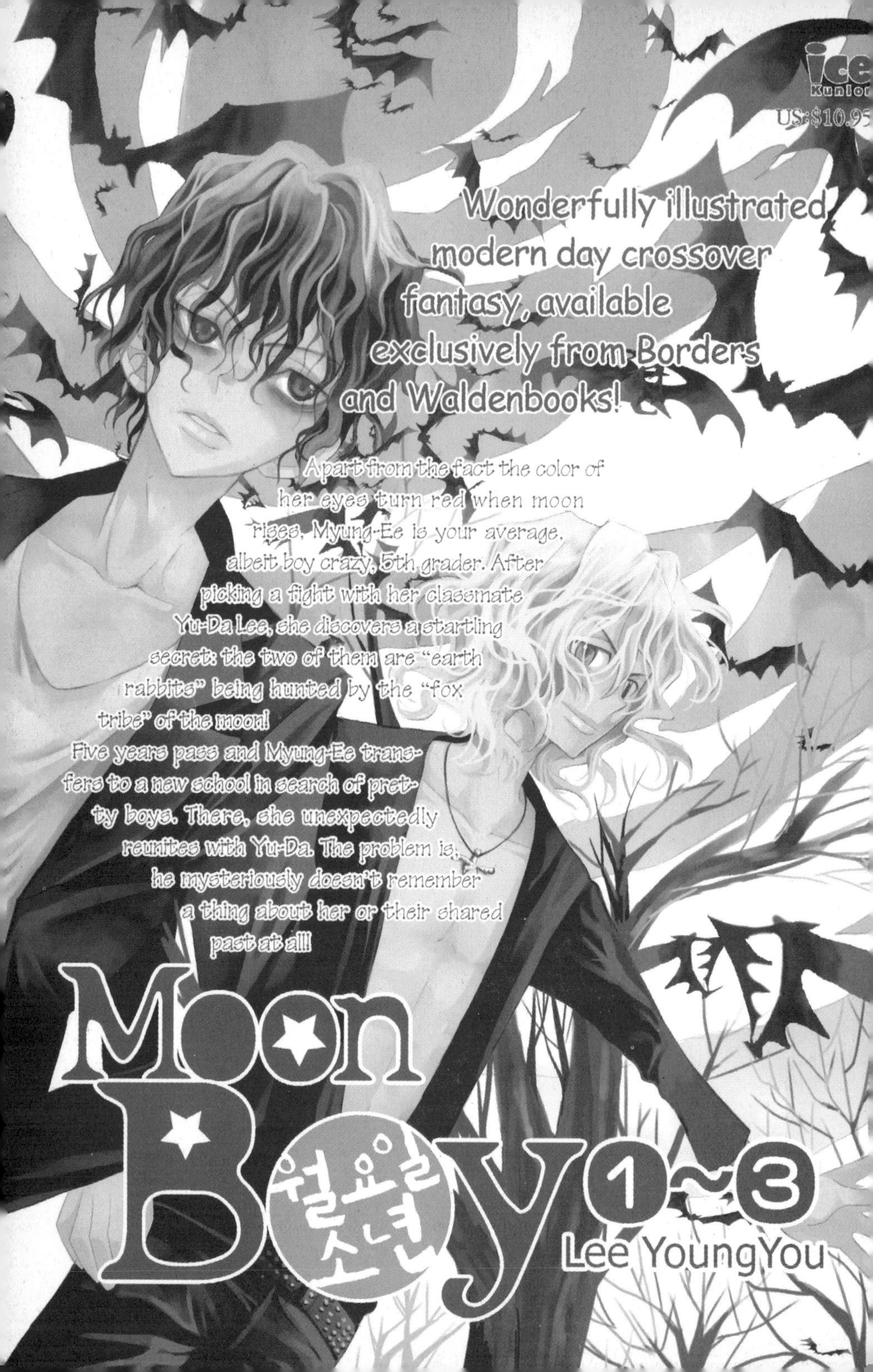
ice Kunlon
US:$10.95
Wonderfully illustrated modern day crossover fantasy, available exclusively from Borders and Waldenbooks!
Apart from the fact the color of her eyes turn red when moon rises, Myung-Ee is your average, albeit boy crazy, 5th grader. After picking a fight with her classmate Yu-Da Lee, she discovers a startling secret: the two of them are "earth rabbits" being hunted by the "fox tribe" of the moon!
Five years pass and Myung-Ee transfers to a new school in search of pretty boys. There, she unexpectedly reunites with Yu-Da. The problem is, he mysteriously doesn't remember a thing about her or their shared past at all!
Moon Boy
월요일 소년
1~3
Lee YoungYou

Totally new Arabian nights, where Shahrazad is a guy!

US: $10.95

Everyone knows the story of Shahrazad and her wonderful tales in the Arabian Nights. For one thousand and one nights, the stories that she created entertained the mad Sultan and eventually saved her life. In this version, our Shahrazad is a guy who wanted to save his sister from the mad Sultan by disguising himself as a woman. When he puts his life on the line, what kind of strange and wacky stories would he tell? This new twist on one of the greatest classical tales, Arabian Nights, might just keep you awake for another <one thousand and one nights>.

Available at bookstores near you!

One thousand and one nights 1~3

Han SeungHee · Jeon JinSeok

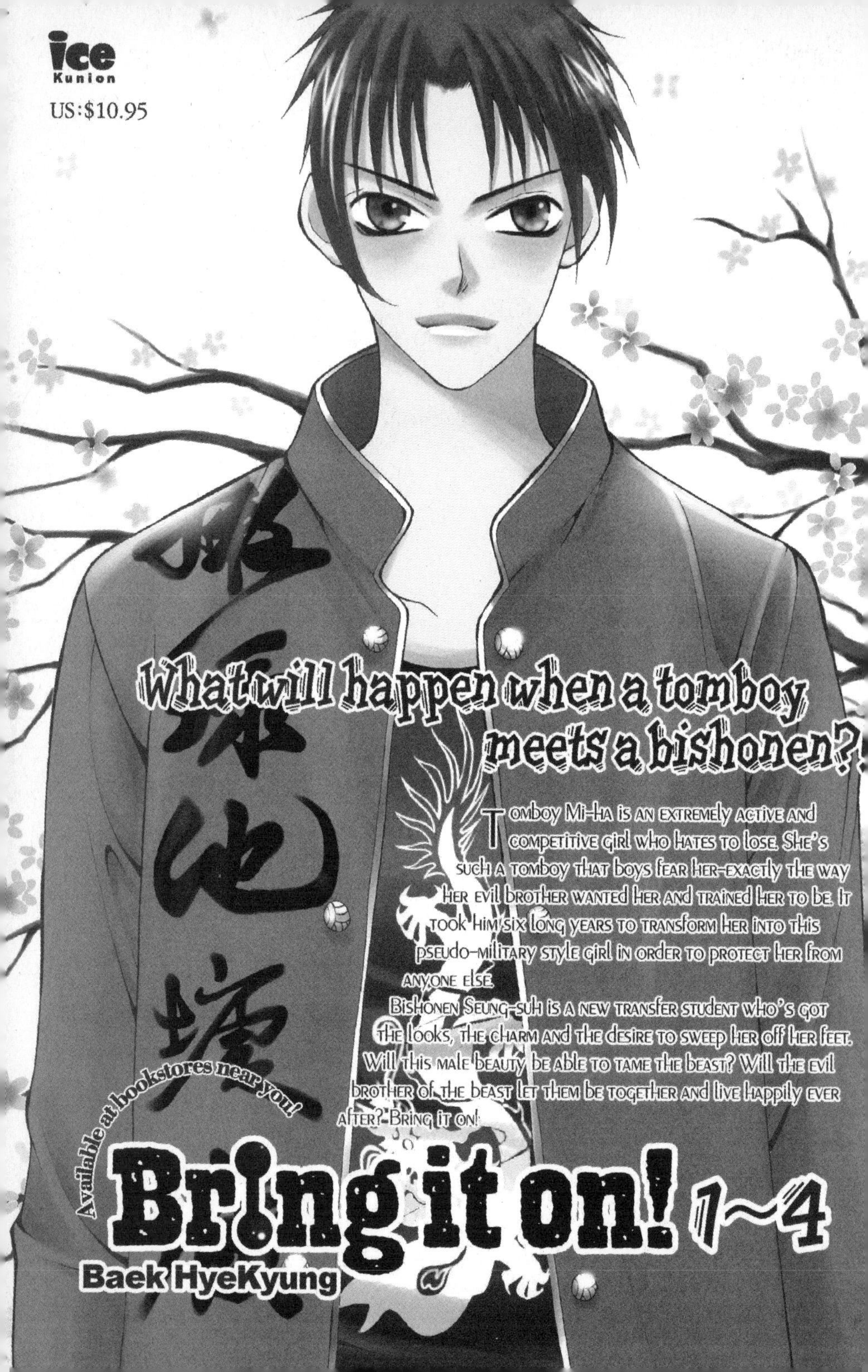
ice Kunion
US:$10.95
What will happen when a tomboy meets a bishonen?!
Tomboy Mi-Ha is an extremely active and competitive girl who hates to lose. She's such a tomboy that boys fear her-exactly the way her evil brother wanted her and trained her to be. It took him six long years to transform her into this pseudo-military style girl in order to protect her from anyone else.
Bishonen Seung-suh is a new transfer student who's got the looks, the charm and the desire to sweep her off her feet. Will this male beauty be able to tame the beast? Will the evil brother of the beast let them be together and live happily ever after? Bring it on!
Available at bookstores near you!
Bring it on! 1~4
Baek HyeKyung

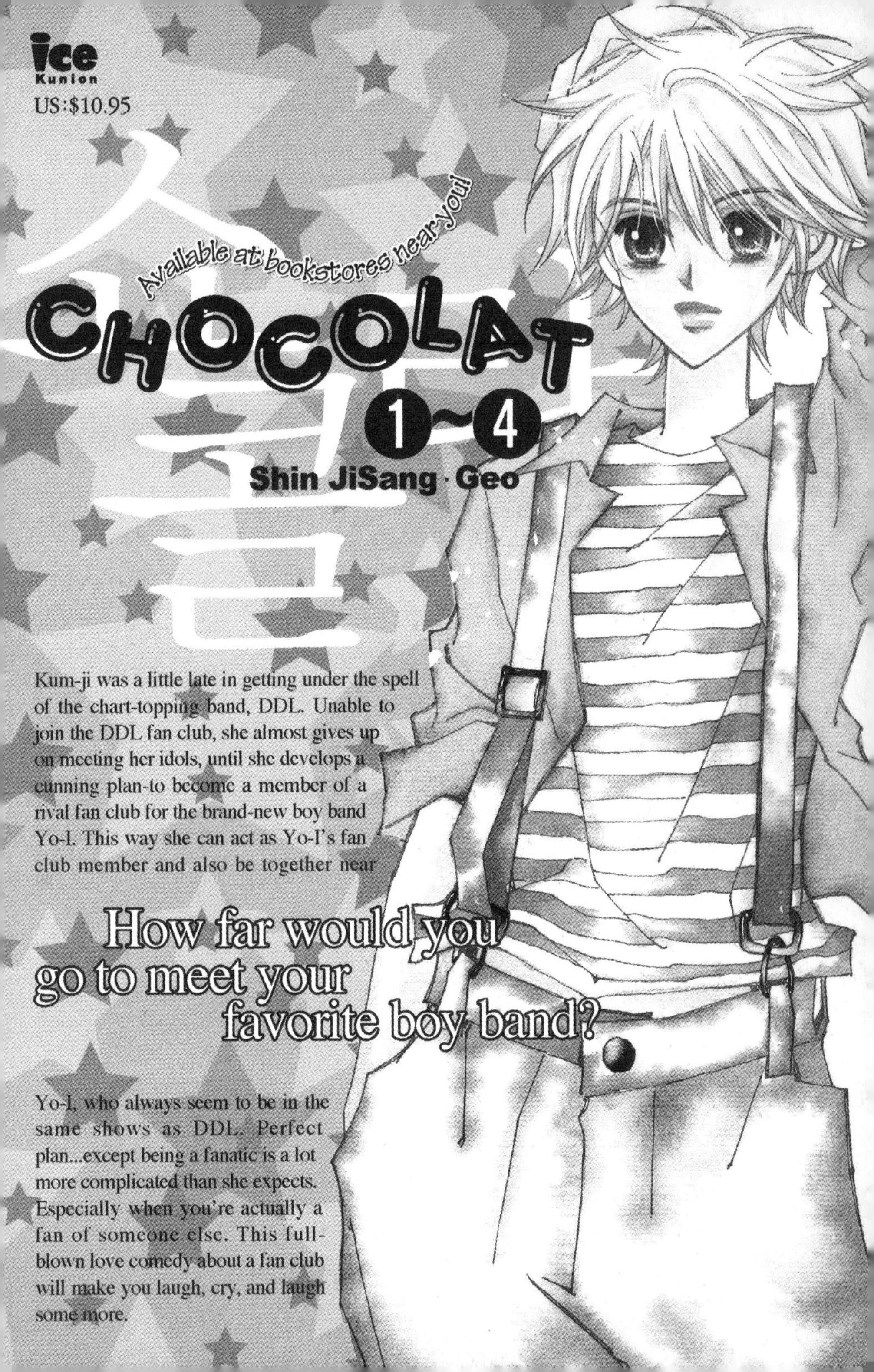

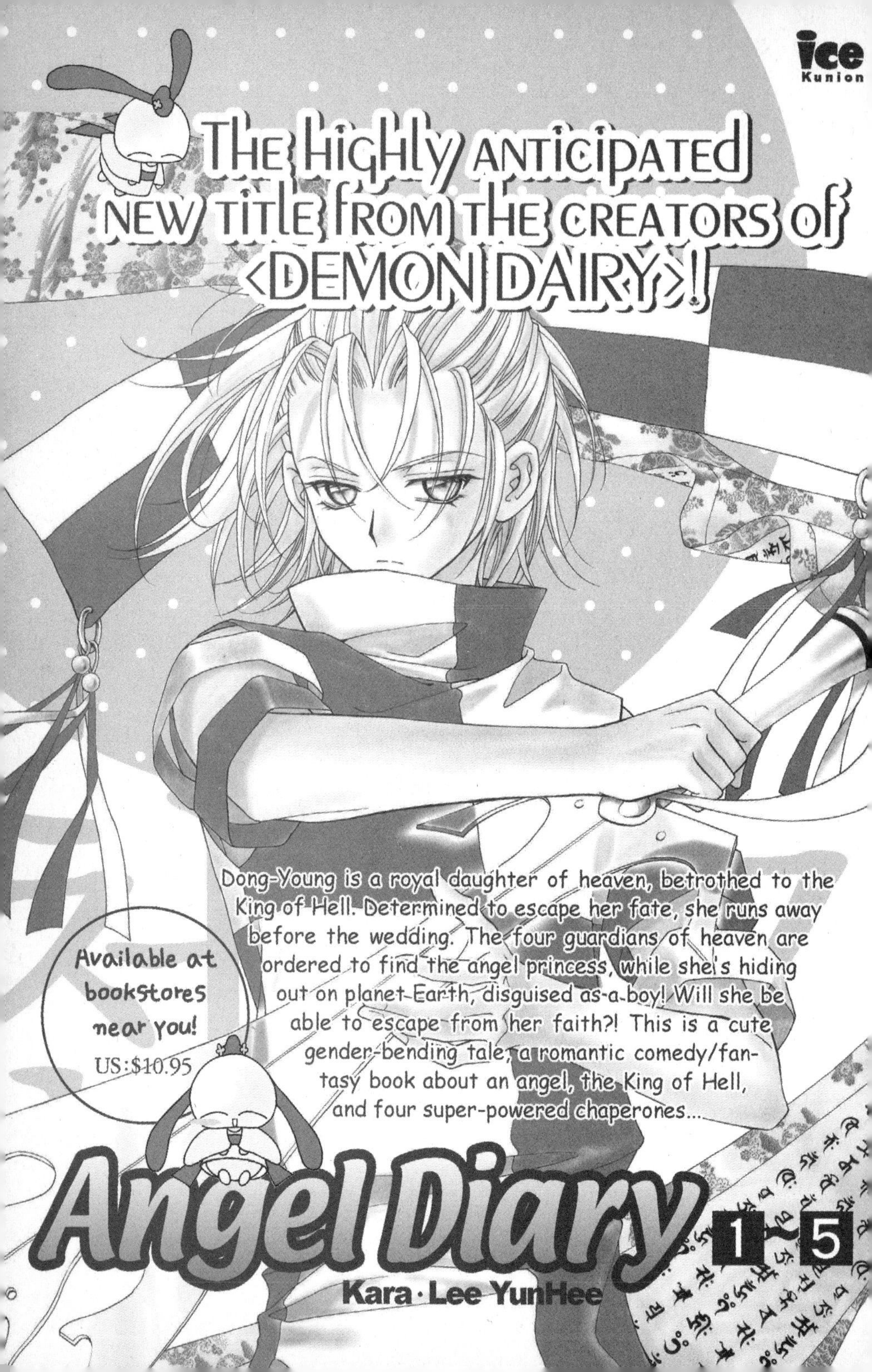
ice
Kunion
THE HIGHLY ANTICIPATED NEW TITLE FROM THE CREATORS OF <DEMON DAIRY>!
Dong-Young is a royal daughter of heaven, betrothed to the King of Hell. Determined to escape her fate, she runs away before the wedding. The four guardians of heaven are ordered to find the angel princess, while she's hiding out on planet Earth, disguised as a boy! Will she be able to escape from her faith?! This is a cute gender-bending tale, a romantic comedy/fantasy book about an angel, the King of Hell, and four super-powered chaperones...
Available at bookstores near you!
US:$10.95
Angel Diary 1~5
Kara · Lee YunHee

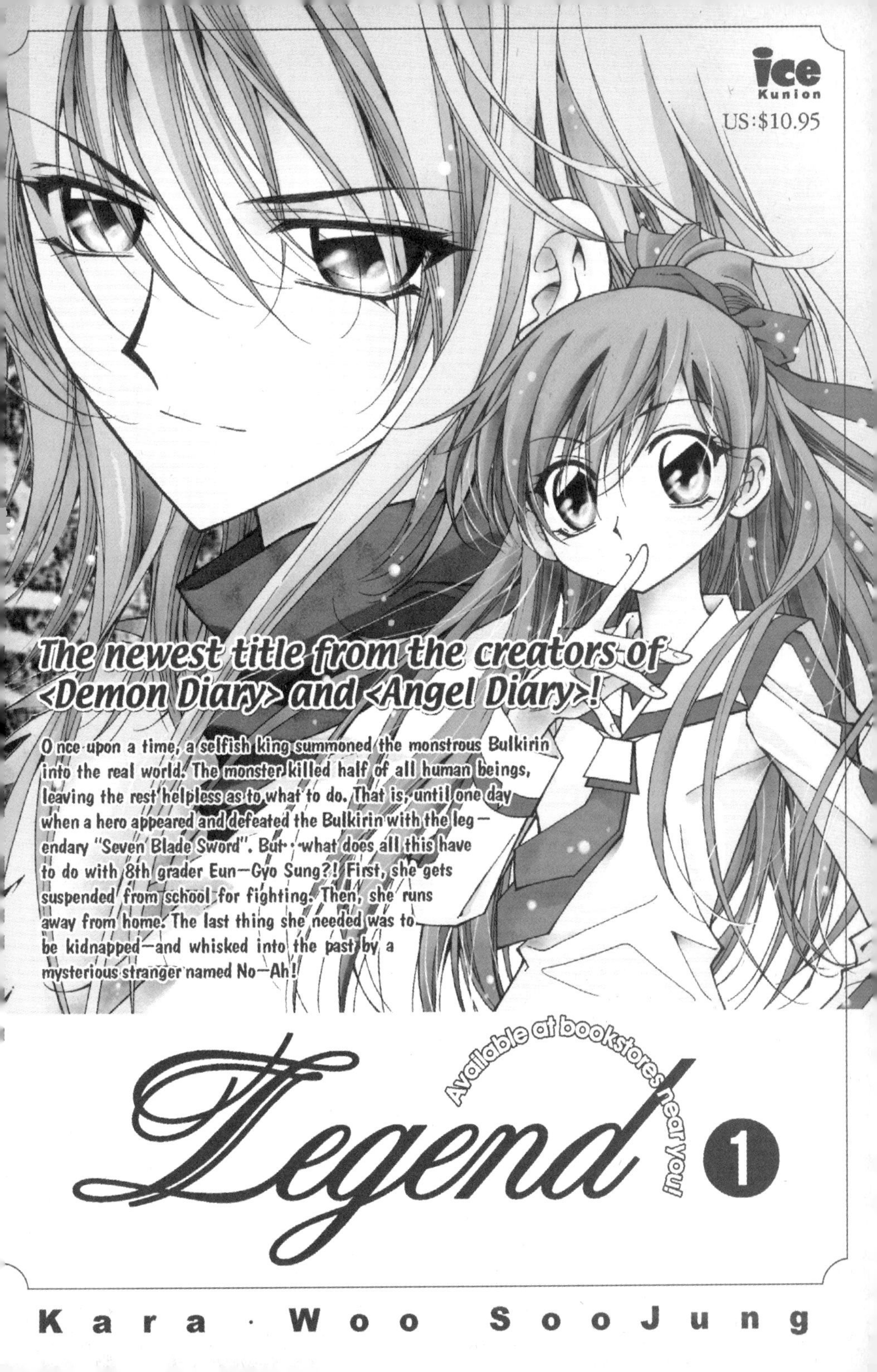
ice
Kunion
US:$10.95
The newest title from the creators of
<Demon Diary> and <Angel Diary>!
Once upon a time, a selfish king summoned the monstrous Bulkirin into the real world. The monster killed half of all human beings, leaving the rest helpless as to what to do. That is, until one day when a hero appeared and defeated the Bulkirin with the legendary "Seven Blade Sword". But··what does all this have to do with 8th grader Eun-Gyo Sung?! First, she gets suspended from school for fighting. Then, she runs away from home. The last thing she needed was to be kidnapped—and whisked into the past by a mysterious stranger named No-Ah!
Legend 1
Available at bookstores near You!
Kara · Woo SooJung

Danbi Original

The Antique Gift Shop vol.4

Story and art by Eun Lee

Translation HyeYoung Im
English Adaptation J. Torres
Touch-up and Lettering Terri Delgado · Marshall Dillon
Graphic Design EunKyung Kim

ICE Kunion

English Adaptation Editor HyeYoung Im · J. Torres
Managing Editor Marshall Dillon
Assistant Editor SoYeon Kim
Senior Editor JuYoun Lee
Editorial Director DongEun Lee
Managing Director Jackie Lee
Publisher and C.E.O. JaeKook Chun

The Antique Gift Shop © 2005 Eun Lee
First published in Korea in 2004 by SEOUL CULTURAL PUBLISHERS, Inc.
English text translation rights arranged by SEOUL CULTURAL PUBLISHERS, Inc.
English text © 2005 ICE KUNION

Published by ICE Kunion.
SIGONGSA 2F Yeil Bldg. 1619-4, Seocho-dong, Seocho-gu, Seoul, 137-878, Korea

ISBN : 978-89-527-4490-6

First printing, January 2007
10 9 8 7 6 5 4 3 2 1
Printed in Canada

www.icekunion.com/www.koreanmanhwa.com